Combining Old and New:

NATUROPATHY FOR THE 21ST CENTURY

BY

ROBERT J. THIEL, PH.D.

WHITMAN
PUBLICATIONS

The author gratefully acknowledges the permission granted to print excerpts from the following:

- Dr. Angela Burr-Madsen's unpublished lecture notes in Modules One and Two of the Naturopathic Practioner Certification Program, Gateways College of Naturopathy & Natural Therapeutics, Shingle Springs, California. Reprinted by permission of Dr. Angela Burr-Madsen, N.D., HHP

- *Naturae Medicina and Naturopathic Dispensatory* by William von Peters. Reprinted by permission of the author.

- *Transform Your Emotional DNA* by Theresa Dale. Reprinted by permission of the author.

Printed in 2000, 2011, 2017, 2018, 2019, 2021 and 2022 by:
Whitman Publications
220 Parker Street, Warsaw, IN 46580

ISBN 1-885653-08-5

Printed in the United States of America.

Table of Contents

About the Author

Dr. Robert J. Thiel is a nationally recognized researcher, scientist, and naturopath. He is not a medical doctor, but is registered as a naturopath by the Federal District of Columbia, licensed as a naturopath by the State of North Carolina, and was licensed as a naturopathic physician by Bingham County, Idaho. He believes that clinical science demonstrates that through natural interventions, the body can heal itself of both chronic and acute ailments.

Dr. Thiel began studying health in the early seventies because of his then frequent illnesses. In the mid-seventies, he moved to California where he initially studied accounting. After a close relative was told she had a 90% chance of dying within five years (she is still alive today), he began his formal studies into the areas of natural health, nutrition, and other aspects of naturopathy. These studies have included both traditional and non-traditional approaches to improving health. He has both studied and taught naturopathy at the International College of Naturopathy. He also has a regionally accredited Ph.D. in nutrition science from the Union Institute and a regionally accredited M.S. from the University of Southern California. Now in his fifties, Dr. Thiel has not taken any medication (including aspirin) since he was a teen.

Dr. Thiel's research captured the attention of the National Institute of Health, National Cancer Institute, and National Institute for Allergy and Infectious Disease, all of which have reviewed Dr. Thiel's research on nutritional supplementation on serum levels of immune system lymphocytes. In 1998, he was named *Research Scientist of the Year* by the American Naturopathic Medical Association. For years he was president of the California State Naturopathic Medical Association.

In addition to performing research, Dr. Thiel conducts private naturopathic nutritional counseling in Arroyo Grande, California. This counseling is oriented towards health improvement, health strengthening, nutrition education, and the prevention of health problems. This counseling often involves the use and role of diet, herbs, glandulars, light, clay, homeopathics, vitamins, minerals, and other naturopathic modalities in human health. Dr. Thiel is a frequent public speaker. He has lectured to various groups, has made many radio and television appearances and has taught at various California colleges. He currently teaches health professionals and was science editor for the *American Naturopathic Medical Association Monitor*.

Dr. Thiel has found that through naturopathic approaches, people can make a tremendous difference in their own health, longevity, and well being.

*This book is dedicated
to my beautiful wife, Joyce.*

Read
This
First

This book is an eclectic mix of new and old and is intended to be used by licensed health professionals who appreciate and understand the role of naturopathy as a complement to other therapies. For non-licensed readers of this guide, it is intended that information herein be discussed with a licensed health professional to determine whether or not naturopathic approaches are possibly applicable or if they may be somehow contraindicated. The opinions expressed are simply that, opinions. The author has included some public domain writings of earlier naturopaths (which are sometimes edited) to more precisely convey the intent and sense of naturopathy in days gone by as well as to show the eclectic nature of this field. They are not intended treatments or prescriptions for any disease or medical condition (nor are any writings in this book) even if the authors may have originally intended them to be; nor are they intended as replacements for standard therapies, nor should they be used to delay seeking standard treatment(s). They are hoped to be of interest to help people understand naturopathy; they are not suggestions of treatment or cure. Nor does the author of this book necessarily agree with them.

The information contained in this guide is presented for general naturopathic/nutritional educational purposes only. Thus, it is not a substitute for specific medical advice. Neither the author nor the publisher assume responsibility or liability for any consequence for the failure of any reader to obtain specific medical advice from a qualified, licensed doctor, nor for any consequences of any readers attempting to treat their own (or anyone else's) health problems by using any or all of the information contained in this guide.

Some of the information in this guide is based on solid, scientific evidence. Other information is based on preliminary research, observation, personal interpretation, older and other writings (which may not have been scientifically validated or which even may have scientifically disproved), extrapolation, clinical experience, and personal beliefs. Professionals, can and do, often disagree on the application of health information. The author, in many cases, has reached different conclusions than many researchers, scientists, and other health professionals have (including those he has cited). It is important to note that all cautions are not mentioned in this guide (it is assumed that licensed practitioners have been trained in, or have access to, information concerning cautions associated with supplement ingredients as well as medical and health interactions as well as more detailed instructions about naturopathic modalities). In all situations, the author strongly believes in the adage of "first do no harm." He believes that all health professionals should "first do no harm" which includes the concept of not delaying useful standard therapies or treatments and to not employ any technique that the health professional has insufficient knowledge and training to implement safely.

Although many of the approaches in this book have been proven to the author to help people who suffer from various forms of ill health, none of the statements in this book have been evaluated by the U.S. Food and Drug Administration or other authorities.

This book is divided into several sections with writings from different authors. It is not intended to have the same type of story flow as a novel, but is intended to be a collection of principles and practices of naturopathy. All the chapters could be extended into complete books. Many of the chapters are condensed versions of actual books. Although this book has a beginning, naturopathy really has no end, as no book can contain everything about natural healing (and this one is expected to be added to).

Additional Note: The presented research material is intended for current/historical interest for professional internal use only. No claims as to the usage is intended for the diagnosis, treatment, or cure of any disease or condition. This publication is not intended as labeling for any product or to be employed by anyone as labeling. Certain experts may agree or disagree with these opinions, but the opinions are deemed to be of interest. All opinions are issued in accordance with the author's rights to freedom of speech, religion, and the press under the First Amendment to the U.S. Constitution.

The author wishes to thank Norma Helbling and Joyce Thiel for their assistance with this book. Also, thanks go to the Halcyon Library for allowing access to many out-of-print books written by many early naturopathic pioneers.

1

A Brief History of Naturopathy

Naturopathy was the earliest known healing system. Before surgery and synthetic isolation of chemical substances, foods, water, and whole herbs were used by many cultures for a wide range of problems. The Chinese, for example, used kelp 3,000 years ago for thyroid health [1]. The ancient Egyptians used liver for night blindness [2]. Native American (as well as most other) cultures used various herbs to promote healing. Various forms of hydrotherapy have been used by many cultures (Egyptians, Chinese, Hebrews, Greeks, Assyrians, Persians, Hindus, etc.) for thousands of years [3,4].

"Excavations of ancient ruins, especially after the work carried on in Egypt, disclose the fact that disease was treated by fasting, purging, emetics, sweats—all with the very evident aim of assisting Nature to unload encumbering waste that was plainly causing the disorder...It seems that the accepted teachings in the manner of the care of the ill were very similar to our present methods of naturopathy, being in line with Nature's indicated efforts during illness" [3]. "Chakara, the illustrious founder of the Ayurvedic Medical system and the oldest of Naturopathic Physicians known" advocated air and water therapies [5].

In the Western sense, Hippocrates (circa 400 B.C.), who studied in Egypt, was possibly the best known of the older naturopathic scientists (the Ayurvedic herbalists, and others, preceded him). "Throughout his professional life he exhibited the greatest respect and reverence for Nature, and taught his followers, students and initiates that the healing of all diseases was 'up to' Nature...He stated that only nature could cure, and that the province of the Physician was merely to assist, to make the healing more pleasant or less painful" [3]. Probably his best contribution to naturopathy was the principle of "first do no harm" (**premum no nocere**). In medieval times the Catholic Church fostered and was in charge of the healing arts, among which Natural Healing Methods were outstanding [6].

Perhaps the most historically relevant legal view of what became known as naturopathy was the Herbalist Charter (34 & 35 Hen VIII, C.8; 1542-1543). It was granted by King Henry the VIII in 1512 [7]. This codified English statute became part of what is still known as "common-law" (which has not been repealed by any of the States). As can be seen below, the Herbalist Charter allowed non-medical doctors to recommend herbs, roots, and water for health concerns:

WHERE in the Parliament holden at Westminster in the third Year of the King's most gracious Reign, amongst other Things, for the avoiding of Sorceries, Witchcrafts, and other Inconveniences, it was enacted, that no Person within the City of London, nor within Seven Miles of the same, should take upon him to exercise and occupy as Physician or Surgeon, except he be first examined, approved, and admitted by the Bishop of London and other, under and upon certain Pains and Penalties in the same Act mentioned: Sithence and making of which said Act, the Company and Fellowship of Surgeons of London, minding only their own Lucres, and nothing the Profit or ease of the Diseased or Patient, have sued, troubled, and vexed divers honest Persons, as well Men and Women, whom God hath endued with the Knowledge of the Nature, Kind and

1

Operation of certain Herbs, Roots, and Waters, and the using and ministering of them to such as been pained with customable Diseases, as Women's Breast's being sore, Pin and the Web in the Eye, Uncomes of Hands, Burnings, Scaldings, Sore Mouths, the Stone, Strangury, Saucelim, and Morphew, and such other like Diseases: and yet the said Persons have not taken anything for their Pains or Cunning, but have ministered the same to poor People only for Neighbourhood and God's sake, and of Pity and Charity: and it is well known that the Surgeons admitted will do no Cure to any Person but where they shall be rewarded with a greater Sum or Reward than the Cure extendeth unto; for in case they would minister their Cunning into sore People unrewarded, there should not so many rot and perish to death for Lack or Help of Surgery as daily do; but the greatest part of Surgeons admitted been much more to be blamed than those Persons that they troubled, for although the most Part of the Persons of the said Craft of Surgeons have small Cunning yet they will take great sums of Money, and do little therefore, and by Reason thereof they do oftentimes impair and hurt their Patients, rather than do them good. In consideration whereof, and for the Ease, Comfort, Succour, Help, Relief, and Health of the King's poor Subjects, Inhabitants of this Realm, now pained or diseased: Be it ordained, established and enacted, by authority of this present Parliament, That at all Time from henceforth, it shall be lawful to every Person being the King's subject having Knowledge and Experience of the Nature of Herbs, Roots, and Waters, or of the Operation of the same, by Speculation or Practice, within any part of the Realm of England, or within any other the King's Dominions, to practice, use, and minister in and to any outward Sore, Uncome Wound, Aposternations, outward Swelling or Disease, any Herb or Herbs, Ointments, Baths, Pultess, and Emplaisters, according to their Cunning, Experience, and Knowledge in any of the Diseases, Sores, and Maladies beforesaid, and all other like to the same, or Drinks for the Stone, Strangury, or Agues, without suit, vexation, trouble, penalty, or loss of their goods; the foresaid Statute in the foresaid Third Year of the King's most gracious Reign, or any other Act, Ordinance, or Statutes to the contrary heretofore made in anywise, notwithstanding. [6,8]

Please re-read the above charter. Isn't it interesting that the King felt that the medical profession should not bother those involved in natural health, that natural health practitioners should be allowed to practice, and that he felt that natural health practitioners were often more effective than the "mainstream" of his day?

In 1924 it was written,

What is now known as osteopathy was really practiced two hundred years before the name osteopathy was known, in parts of Scandinavia; what are now called chiropractic and naprapathy were practiced a hundred and fifty years before these names were heard of, in Bohemia; and what is known as mechano-therapy today has been practiced in China, Japan, Egypt, the South Sea Islands and other parts of the earth since long before the dawn of the Christian era. It is true, of course, that these various systems have undergone much development and modification at the hands of rather recent therapeutics, but the basic principle underlying each system was not new when such "system" appeared under the names we are now familiar with. Those old-time natural healers were in reality Naturopaths, regardless of what they called themselves, and those men of more recent times who have developed these "branches" were really making developments in the mechanical sphere of Naturopathy. [9]

The modern nature-cure movement seems to have started...when Priessnitz (1799-1851)...established a hydrotherapy institute... Rickli (1823-1926) born in Austria, was the father of the sunlight and air cures... Berg made extensive contributions in Vegetarian Diet, and Finsen in ultra-violet treatment; Schroth (1798-1856) is the originator of the theory of warm moisture and the idea of dry diet and fasting cure. Christian was a food scientist... Kuhne, who died in 1907, practiced in Leipzig, Sasconia. He formulated the theory of 'Unity of Disease', claimed 'disease is the presence of foreign matter in the body'. Just died in 1939...Among the truths he expounded are: 'Nature does not err'. He was first to advance the theory that 'acute diseases are favorable healing crises and should be greeted with joy'...Lahn is the author of the first book on Iridology ever published in this country... Lindlahr...became the founder of the first Naturopathic College in Chicago... Schulte...became the pioneer practitioner of Naturopathy in California. [8]

In the 1800s in Germany this form of healing was termed "natur-heilkinde" [10]. Also in Germany, a Catholic Priest named Sebastian Kneipp founded the famous "Water Cure" in Woerschofen. Dr. Benedict Lust, who after being given up to die from tuberculosis, sought and received help from Sebastian Kneipp (Dr. Lust lived until 1945). In 1892, Dr. Lust came to the U.S. Dr. Lust is considered to be "the father of naturopathy in the U.S.A." Further south, the Mayas and Incas actually developed natural therapeutics to a fairly high degree when the Europeans were greatly far behind [7,8].

In the U.S., the term "naturopathy" was apparently first coined by Dr. John Schell in 1895 to describe his approach to health (details regarding this and Dr. Lust do involve historical controversy). In 1896, Dr. Lust established a school (Kneipp Water Cure Institute [6]) which called its graduates 'hydropaths' [4]. Also in 1896, Dr. Lust opened the Kneipp Sanitarium in New York with Dr. William Steffens [6]. Dr. Lust felt there was more to naturopathy than hydrotherapy as he wrote, "The Kneipp-Cure was largely prescriptive—Naturopathy is first instructive, then inspiration, and ultimately growth...Naturopathy, with all its various methods of treatment, has always one end in view and one end only: to increase the vital force." Dr. Lust was the originator of "health food stores" and received the Eclectic M.D. degree from the Homeopathic Medical College in 1914 [7].

In 1897, Sebastian Kneipp died and Dr. Hugo Wendell began to study water with Dr. Lust and utilized the modalities water, food, herbs, clay, and electricity. Dr. Wendell, who was referred to as a Naturarzt, Magnetopath, and Osteopath, opened clinics in New York and New Jersey [11]. Dr. Lust purchased the rights to the term "naturopathy" in 1900 from Dr. Schell [7]. In 1901, a Kneipp convention adopted the name "naturopathy" and declared "that all methods of drugless healing should be taught" [7]. They also declared that drugless modalities included psychotherapy, pyscho-analysis, mental-therapy, new thought, higher thought, magnet-therapy, suggestive-therapy, mesmeric-therapy, hypnotherapy, herbal-therapy, homeopathy, biotherapy, bio-chemistry, pneumatotherapy, massage, bonesetting, mechanotherapy, osteopathy, chiropractic, hydrotherapy, dietetics, electrotherapy, heliotherapy, chromotherapy, phototherapy, Kneipp methods, Bilz methods, Kuhne methods, Schroth methods, Just methods, and divine healing [7] (all naturopaths do not believe in or practice all of those modalities). In 1904, Otto Carque started teaching iris diagnosis (Iridiagnosis) from the eye which also became a naturopathic modality [11]. It is of historical interest to note that some have referred to naturopaths as quacks since the 1800s (please see the chapter 2 on Naturopathic Philosophy) [10].

Dr. Angela Burr-Madsen has written the following information about the history of naturopathy in California:

> "The Naturopathic Institute Sanitarium and College was opened in Los Angeles by Dr. Carl Schultz as president. In 1907, in the State of California legislation was passed that allowed three forms of certificates to practice in the healing arts. 1) Medicine and Surgery, 2) Osteopathy, and 3) 'Any other system or mode of treating the sick or afflicted not referred to in legislation.' Eight persons practicing naturopathy were granted certificates under this legislation.
>
> In 1909, also in California, a six month period was established during which the board of medical examiners would endorse a properly validated certificate issued by the 'Association of Naturopaths of California' incorporated August 8, 1904.

The applicant for this validation had to be in practice prior to the passage of this act. This is the only time official recognition of the practice of naturopathy has been made in California legislation. The Association of Naturopaths of California examined each applicant for membership and upon passing the examination was 'issued a diploma conferring the degree of Doctor of Naturopathy'. *This was not a license.* 103 certificates were endorsed under this legislation. In 1957 about 8 were still practicing" [6].

The U.S. House of Representatives discussed naturopathy in the 1929 Act of Congress dated February 27, 1929 (Chap. 352@ 1326, S. 3936, Public No. 831) and its clarifying amendment (H.R. 12169 of May 1930 and January 28, 1931). This seems to have established the "congressional intent" that naturopathy is a separate branch of the healing arts and should be on the same level as other forms including medicine, chiropractic, and osteopathic. The Act of Congress dated February 7, 1931 makes that fairly clear (see Image 1).

In addition, the *Congressional Record* also dated February 7, 1931 contained the following comments on naturopathy by Katherine G. Langely who was a Congressional representative from Kentucky (see Images 2 and 2B).

What is interesting about Representative Langley's comments is that even in 1931 there was debate on whether or not naturopaths should administer medications or perform surgeries. Her conclusions are that essentially by definition, such interventions are not "naturopathic." Since Dr. Lust purchased rights to the term "naturopathy", if he actually wanted the field of naturopathy to include the prescribing of drugs or the performance of surgeries, he probably would have had that added to either the *Act of Congress* or the *Congressional Record*. Instead, they declare the opposite view, "Naturopathy does not contemplate drugs and surgical operations, nor is it within the scope of the science of their practice" (Congresswoman Langley, 1931).

During the depression as well as during World War II, there seems to have been a decreased interest in the practice of naturopathy. Dr. Lust died on September 4, 1945. After WWII interest in naturopathy began to increase. A Golden Jubi-

lee for naturopathy was celebrated in 1947 which adopted standards for the profession (they are listed in Chapter 2). A "pseudo-group" opposed this jubilee and did not adopt these standards [12]. It was reported that this "pseudo-group" proposed a hospitalization plan and tried to take over the profession [12]. Also "it continues its vicious propaganda to mislead physicians everywhere, while at the same time its officers plead they want harmony and unification. What they want is Domination" [12]. These types of battles are still continuing within the profession.

In the early 1950s, naturopathy began to flourish mainly on the East Coast. It then began to regain some of its popularity out West [11]. Now it is becoming more popular almost everywhere (although the practice of naturopathy has been considered by some authorities to be illegal in South Carolina).

Originally most naturopaths were medical doctors (including "Eclectic M.D.s") who were dissatisfied with medical options, while some were straight naturopaths (those who used only natural modalities and/or who were not medical doctors). In the U.S. when the homeopathic medical schools closed down, few medical doctors became naturopaths. Around that time, naturopathy seemed to become a domain of some chiropractors (this is not surprising as chiropractic was considered a naturopathic modality). Actually some older chiropractors have degrees in chiropractic-naturopathy. As the chiropractic profession has grown, there has been a movement within that profession to concentrate more on 'straight chiropractic' (defined essentially as providing alignments to address subluxations) and less on non-standard chiropractic (which sometimes has included naturopathy) [13]. Also, even though they employ naturopathic manipulations (including massage), modern naturopaths generally do not practice chiropractic or osteopathy (although some chiropractors and osteopaths do practice naturopathy).

The Present and Future

In recent decades there have developed at least two major views of naturopathy within the naturopathic profession. One view is essentially that naturopaths should be licensed as physicians and are a type of medical doctor who uses herbs,

An Act of Congress

Passed February 7, 1931

THE FOLLOWING DEFINITION OF NATUROPATHY was passed by the United States Congress on February 7, 1931, without a dissenting vote. There was very great opposition by 35 medical doctors present, by the Board of Commissioners of the Healing Act (allopathic), and by special representatives and attorneys of the American Medical Association and other allopathic forces.

"Section 2. It is further enacted that 'NATUROPATHY,' as used in the aforesaid Act, approved February 27, 1929, hereafter shall comprehend, embrace, and be composed of the following acts, practices, and usages, ---

"DIAGNOSIS and PRACTICE of physiological and material sciences of healing as follows, ---

"The physiological and mechanical sciences such as mechanotherapy, articular manipulation, corrective orthopedic gymnastics, neurotherapy, PSYCHOTHERAPY, hydrotherapy, and MINERAL BATHS, electrotherapy, thermotherapy, phototherapy, chromotherapy, vibrotherapy, thalmotherapy, and DIETETICS WHICH SHALL INCLUDE THE USE OF FOODS OF SUCH BIOCHEMICAL TISSUE-BUILDING PRODUCTS AND CELL SALTS AS ARE FOUND IN THE NORMAL BODY; and the use of vegetal oils and dehydrated and pulverized fruits, flowers, seeds, barks, herbs, roots, and vegetables uncompounded and in their natural state.

"Passed the House of Representatives February 7, 1931.   Attest: Wm. Tyler Page, Clerk."

Thus all mineral baths of any and all natural elemental, and tissue and cell chemicals and salts required for the health of the body organism, and for all its functions of health and wellbeing, - are authorized in usage as the legitimate right of each and every person in NATUROPATHIC PRACTICE, by a definite and specific Act of the United States Congress.

And as any Act of Congress is a SUPREME RULING above any contrary laws of the individual States, - this Act at once exempts any and all NATUROPATHIC PRACTITIONERS from the medical and legislative rerestrictions in the various States; giving Naturopaths freedom to practice Naturopathy in any and all its departments according to their professional schooling and training.

Therefore now and hereafter any graduate of any department of Naturopathy who according to his or her skill and training diagnoses sickness, disease and human ailments, and who treats the sick, diseased and suffering, and all and varied human ailments and afflictions according to the methods and processes here defined; and who restores health and wellbeing by the processes and methods outlined in this Act of the United States Congress, - ARE NOT PRACTISING MEDICINE OR SURGERY WITHOUT A LICENSE, as formerly asserted by the allopathic trust, and as specified by their various legislative enactments. They are rightfully and legitimately practicing NATUROPATHY.

And thus this Act nullifies all such legislative enactments; for the Federal Laws -- the Laws of the United States Government at Washington -- ARE THE SUPREME LAWS OF THE LAND.

For so it is written in the Constitution, - "This Constitution, AND THE LAWS OF THE UNITED STATES WHICH SHALL BE MADE IN PURSUANCE THEREOF, (this includes all Acts of Congress) . . . SHALL BE THE SUPREME LAW OF THE LAND; and the judges in every State shall be bound thereby, - ANYTHING IN THE CONSTITUTION OR LAWS OF ANY STATE TO THE CONTRARY NOTWITHSTANDING." - Article Six, Clause Two.

Image 1

homeopathy, manipulation, nutrition, isolates, counseling, prescription medications, injections, and sometimes minor surgery [11]. This view (when it employs modalities other than counseling and homeopathy) tends to make prescriptions (including herbs) based mainly on the basis of diagnostics as opposed to individual characteristics [e.g.14]. The other view is essentially that naturopathy is in the public domain, and that naturopathic practitioners are not medical doctors, should employ only those modalities that are natural, and should not perform surgery or write prescriptions [10,11]. This view (when properly employed) tends to make recommendations mainly on the of basis of individual characteristics, tries to stay away from synthetics or isolates, and uses data such as a diagnosis as supplemental (not the primary) information for those recommendations. The latter major view is more closely related to my own. There are of course also other views and combinations of views held by many naturopaths.

Even though the medical view of naturopathy would seem to be a contradiction, several states have ignored the traditional naturopathy, and have licensed certain medically-oriented "naturopathic doctors" and allowed them to prescribe medications and do other non-traditionally naturopathic treatments. As most of those who espouse the drugless approach to naturopathy feel that naturopathy is in the "public domain", they tend not to introduce bills which would restrict naturopathy or change it into a form of medicine. If surgeries

(Not printed at Government expense)

UNITED STATES   OF AMERICA

Congressional Record

PROCEEDINGS AND DEBATES OF THE 76ᵗʰ CONGRESS, THIRD SESSION

NATUROPATHY

EXTENSION OF REMARKS
OF
HON. KATHERINE G. LANGLEY
OF KENTUCKY
IN THE HOUSE OF REPRESENTATIVES
Saturday, February 7, 1931

Mrs. LANGLEY. Mr. Speaker and Members of the House, as author of H. R. 12169, a bill to amend the meaning and intention of an act of Congress, entitled "An act to regulate the practice of the healing art; to protect the public health of the District of Columbia," approved February 27, 1929, I wish to point out the error in the action of the Commissioners of the District of Columbia in denying the full definition of naturopathy as embodied in the original bill H. R. 12169.

I wish also to call attention to the misleading statement as issued to the public through the medium of the press that naturopathy desires the authority to use drugs and to perform surgical operations, as follows:

COMMISSIONERS HIT DRUGLESS HEALERS—CAPITAL HEADS RECOMMEND ADVERSE ACTION ON BILL OF NATUROPATHISTS

Efforts of the naturopathists to extend the legal scope of their healing activities struck a snag yesterday when the District Commissioners asked Congress not to enact the pending bill authorizing naturopathists to administer drugs. Definition of "naturopathy" was one of the difficult tasks confronting the Commission on Licensure of the Healing Arts. The definition proposed by the naturopathists was so broad as to include every branch of healing. The definition finally adopted provided for the licensing of naturopathists, but the definition restricted them from administering drugs or performing operations on the person. Apparently the naturopathists wanted broader fields of activity and had introduced a bill upon which the Commissioners commented so adversely yesterday.

Naturopathy has always been known as a system of drugless healing and it would seem, therefore, that internal medication could have no part whatever in their method of healing. For these reasons the Commissioners recommended an adverse action on the bill.

Naturopathy does not contemplate drugs and surgical operations, nor is it within the scope of their science of practice. To the contrary, they do not use or prescribe drugs as a part of their treatment, nor do they advocate or perform surgical operations upon their patients. I herewith submit as part of these remarks, under leave granted me, the report of the House Committee on the District of Columbia, House Report No. 2432, Seventy-first Congress, third session, to clarify the meaning and intention of act to regulate the practice of the healing art.

278774—19819

The Committee on the District of Columbia, to whom was referred the bill (H. R. 12169) to amend the meaning and intention of an act of Congress entitled "An act to regulate the practice of the healing art; to protect the public health of the District of Columbia," approved February 27, 1929, having considered the same, report back to the House with the recommendation that the legislation be passed.

The purpose of this bill is to clarify the definition of naturopathy. The Commissioners of the District, in defining the type of work that might be performed by the naturopaths under the act of February 27, 1929, excluded from their definition the right of naturopaths to diagnose the case or to administer drugs, medicines, or perform surgical operations. The naturopaths are not concerned with the use of drugs, and do not desire to perform surgical operations, because naturopathy does not contemplate drugs or surgical operations, nor is it within the scope of their science or practice. They have advised the committee that never, as any part of any such treatment, have they ever used drugs or ever performed or attempted to perform any surgical operation.

Naturopaths practice and teach that the living body is a vital machine, and that the retention of waste products in the body and the nonelimination of drugs are considered the most underlying causes of disease, so that they could not consistently prescribe them.

Naturopathy, they aver, is a system of natural methods comprising the use of air, earth, sunshine, water, heat and cold, harmonized food, the use of dehydrated vegetables, herbs, fruits, and any natural modalities and it is their belief, and the belief of this committee, that they should not be excluded from the use of vegetable oils and herbs, fruits, and any other natural modalities in their practice.

The committee, therefore, recommends the early passage of this measure so that the type of service to be performed by those in the naturopathy profession may be clearly defined.

A naturopath claims when waste matter, ptomaines, or poisonous alkaloids and acids produced in the body, as a result of wrong diet and other violations of Nature's laws, have brought about destruction and corrosion in vital parts of organs, when dislocations and subluxations of bony structures or new growths and accumulations in the forms of tumors, stones, or gravel obstruct the blood vessels and nerve currents, shut off the supply of the vital fluids, and thus cause malnutrition and gradual decay of the tissues. When in addition to this the organism has been poisoned or mutilated by drugs and surgical operations, then not only must the mechanism of the body be cleaned and freed from ob-

Image 2

 CONGRESSIONAL RECORD

structive and destructive material, but the injured parts must be repaired, morbid growths and abnormal formations dissolved and eliminated, and lesions in the bony structures corrected by manipulated treatment.

In organic diseases the vitality is usually so low and destruction so great that the organism cannot arouse itself to self-help. Even the cessation of suppressive treatment and the stimulating influence of mental and metaphysical therapeutics are not sufficient to bring about the reconstructed healing process, and this can only be accomplished by the combined influence of all the natural methods of living and of treatment. The Ling System of Swedish movement cures, founded in 1805, has always been part of the naturopathic treatment.

Dietetics also plays a most important part in the treatment and the use of foods of such biochemical tissue-building products as cell salts as are found in the normal body, and the use of vegetal oils and dehydrated and pulverized fruits, flowers, seeds, barks, herbs, roots, and vegetables uncompounded and used in their natural state. And the use of herbs, fruits, and plants dates back to the earliest practitioners. In the year 1512 King Henry VIII granted what is known as the herbalist charter, which became a part of the law of the Thirteen Original States and continues in force as a part of the common law of today.

Naturopathy has kept pace with the advance of modern natural sciences and methods of healing, and in the future will be adopted to new discoveries in the healing art in the natural sciences.

Naturopathy is not the invention of any human mind; it does not place its origin at any given date but is the accumulation of knowledge pertaining to natural methods of living and healing throughout the centuries. Naturopathy is more than a system of curing aches and pains; it is a complete revolutionizing of the art of living.

Naturopathy is the philosophy of healing basing its treatment of all physiological functions and abnormal conditions of the body on the natural laws governing the body. The success of naturopathy is due to the fact that they do not rely on one method of treatment but must include in their work all that is good in the different systems of natural healing. Naturopathy as approved in aforesaid act, February 27, 1929, hereafter shall comprehend and embrace and be composed of the following acts and practices and usages of the physiological and mechanical and material sciences of healing, as follows: Iridology, diagnosis, and the practice of physiological, mechanical, and material sciences of healing; the physiological and mechanical sciences, such as the mechano-therapy, articular manipulation, corrective and orthopedic gymnastics, neurotherapy, psychotherapy, hydrotherapy and mineral baths, electrotherapy, thermotherapy, radiotherapy, phototherapy, chromotherapy, viobrotherapy, thalamotherapy, and orificial dilatation and other stimulation of the sympathetic nervous system through the orifices, and dietetics, which shall include the use of foods of such biochemical tissue-building products and cell salts as are found in the normal body; and the use of vegetal oils and dehydrated and pulverized fruits, flowers, seeds, barks, herbs, roots, and vegetables uncompounded and used in their natural state.

In conclusion, I feel that this great group of Nature's healers are performing a wonderful service to humanity, and it can be truthfully said of them—

> Lives of great men all remind us
> We can make our lives sublime,
> And, departing, leave behind us
> Footprints on the sands of time.

278774—19819

are ever to be done, they should be performed by surgeons—not naturopaths. Dr. Lust himself wrote, "Naturopathy is not the practice of medicine or surgery…All the methods of a Naturopath are natural methods, the agents of life such as food, air, sun, exercise, relaxation, sleep, the use of herbs" [7].

Dr. Lust also thought the mainstream would embrace naturopathy, which it has not (even when they use herbs, the medical model considers them medically, not nutritionally nor naturopathically). The materia medicas (both natural and synthetic) were much smaller in Dr. Lust's day—Dr. Lust himself had an N.D., D.C., D.O., and an Eclectic M.D. (essentially an unconventional medical doctor who used homeopathy and other methods)—and could be somewhat mastered then [7]—the totality of these fields cannot possibly be mastered today in a four-year school (let alone trying to master drugs and surgery at the same time).

In today's knowledge explosion, it is impossible for even medical doctors to properly know what they need in order to serve their patients. It is even less possible for a naturopath to master all the naturopathic modalities, keep up with naturopathic research and to keep up with everything that one would need to know to be a true expert in medical interventions. Naturopaths should spend more time studying naturopathy and less time trying to be some sort of medical doctors—this is what suffering humanity (the public) really needs. As air, water, and food become more adulterated, and as behavioral standards in society continue to lower, the need for naturopathy in the 21st century will only increase.

Regarding the future for professional naturopaths, Dr. Sara Whitherton writes,

> If naturopathic doctors believe what they say, and that is that 'two out of three people seek natural health care', then why not be a true naturopathic doctor and use natural health care and stop trying to use surgical procedures and synthetic drugs? Since this country already has allopaths and osteopaths practicing traditional medicine, does it make sense to have individuals with only a naturopathic degree attempting to practice medicine?...Many involved in this debacle should admit the truth and apologize so the past can be put behind us and the future for Naturopathy can be ensured [11].

References

[1] Ensminger, A.H., et al. Food & Nutrition Encyclopedia, 2nd ed. CRC Press, New York, 1993.

[2] Ross, A.C. Vitamin A and Retinoids. In Modern Nutrition in Health and Disease, 9th ed. William & Wilkins, Balt. 1999:305-327.

[3] Wendell, P. Naturopathic Farmocopeia - Naturopathic Physician's Guide. Paul Wendell, New York, 1950.

[4] Kellogg, J. Rational Hydrotherapy, 2nd ed. F.A. Davis, Phil., 1902.

[5] Kulkarni, V.M. Healing Through Naturopathy. Reprint by B. Jain Publishers, New Delhi (India), written circa 1925.

[6] Burr-Madsen, A. Natural Therapies, Module 1. Gateways College, Shingle Springs (CA), 1996.

[7] Wendell, P. Standardized Naturopathy: The Science and Art of Natural Healing. American Society of Medical Missionaries, Priest River (ID), 1951.

[8] Spitler, H.R. Basic Naturopathy: A Textbook. American Naturopathic Association. Washington (D.C.), circa 1950.

[9] Cordingley, E. W. Principles and Practice of Naturopathy. Reprint from Health Research, Mokelumne (CA), written 1924.

[10] Zvenia, B. Historic overview of the profession of naturopathy. ANMA Monitor, 1997;1(1):12-13.

[11] Whitherton, S. Naturopathy a Half Century. ANMA Monitor, 1998;2(3):14-15.

[12] Gehman, J. M. Official Bulletin of the American Naturopathic Association, Inc. ANA, Washington D.C., January 25, 1948.

[13] Ehmann, L. C. The Changing Face of Chiropractic. Alternative Healthcare Med, 1999; 2(3):22-24.

[14] Murray, M. and Pizzorno, J. Encyclopedia of Natural Medicine. Prima Publishing, Rocklin (CA), 1991:9.

2

Naturopathic Philosophy

What is naturopathy? "Naturopathy," to quote Benedict Lust, "is a distinct school of healing, employing the beneficent agency of Nature's forces, of water, air, sunlight, earthpower, electricity, magnetism, exercise, rest, proper diet, various kinds of mechanical treatment, and mental and moral science. As none of these agents of rejuvenation can cure every disease (alone), the Naturopath rightly employs the combination that is best adapted to each individual case. The result of such ministrations is wholly beneficent. The prophylactic power of Nature's finer forces, mechanical and occult, removes foreign or poisonous matter from the system, restores nerve and blood vitality, invigorates organs and tissues, and regenerates the entire organism" [1]. Note, as used by Dr. Lust, the term occult meant beyond present understanding (as opposed to the spirit world as it is commonly considered to mean now).

Although naturopathy is based on several principles as mentioned above, the foundational one should be "first do no harm" (**premum no nocere**) [2]. Natural does not always mean safe. Several poisons are natural. Dust and pollens are natural, yet can be harmful for those who are allergic to them. Therefore, naturopaths try not to recommend interventions that can cause harm. However, this does not always mean without side effects. For example, if a naturopath recommends that someone avoid caffeine, it is possible that individual may have an unpleasant caffeine withdrawal reaction. Although this is still consistent with the concept of "first do no harm", it would also be appropriate for the naturopath to inform the individual about this somewhat probable reaction. It should be added that it is not practical or even possible for the naturopath to inform someone of every possible negative reaction that something can cause as many are rare or unknown.

Naturopaths practice and believe in the healing power of nature (**vis medicatrix naturae**) [2,3]. This belief includes the concept that the body can heal itself of just about anything (short of amputations, etc.) if clear of toxins and if given proper nutrition, rest, mental outlook, and natural stimulation. It also acknowledges that no health practitioner can know everything there is to know about human health (including side effects and individual reactions), thus when in doubt, the naturopath recommends the most natural approach possible—the naturopath trusts that the natural processes within the body want it to heal. This is one of the reasons why naturopaths tend to recommend whole herbs (as opposed to synthesized isolates), natural vitamins in foods (as opposed to synthetic isolates), water (for therapy and for drinking), breathing (clean air), avoidance of toxins, and rest (nightly and weekly).

Naturopaths deal and work with the cause (**tolle causam**) [2]. Symptoms give an indication of the cause. Identify the cause and support its healing and everything else will improve. Naturopaths work with the whole person and understand that there is a multifactorial nature of health and disease. However, no naturopath (or other health professional) can possibly know everything about health, individual reactions to recommendations, and individual differences (including physical, mental, and spiritual).

Naturopaths believe in prevention. Prevention is the best "cure" [2]. Regarding "cure", modern naturopaths rarely use that term. Naturopaths, and the modalities that we employ, do not cure. The body "cures" itself. Naturopaths are facilitators. We try to identify the cause of problems, eliminate toxins, recommend substances to deal with deficiencies, and stimulate the body's own natural healing abilities.

Everyone is different. Biochemically, genetically, mentally, environmentally, and spiritually. Naturopaths do not believe that everyone with the same problem will benefit with the same solution. E.W. Cordingley, Ph.D., N.D. wrote, "As cases vary, remedies must vary. What will help Nature to cure one disease will only aggravate another. For this reason, a system that is truly eclectic or selective must be the ultimate healing art, and the one, and the only one that can permanently endure" [1]. For example, although some people with mild depression benefit from St. John's Wort, not everyone with mild depression notices improvement with that particular herb. The highest success rates in helping the chronically fatigued are achieved precisely because the recommended interventions are varied for people with this problem (see Appendix A). Naturopaths must vary interventions by the person, not just the "diagnosis."

Dr. Samuel Hahnemann (the founder of homeopathy) and Dr. Lust (considered by many to be the founder of modern naturopathy) advised avoidance of toxins and/or toxic environments. Dr. Hahnemann even wrote that the positive benefits of homeopathic remedies could be eliminated by being exposed to a toxic environment [4]. It is important to remember that toxin plus antidote does not equal no toxin. For example, if caffeine contributes to someone's headache, it is not enough to simply recommend white willow bark, feverfew, and/or some other herb. It is also necessary to avoid caffeine (if that is the suspected offending substance). If someone is regularly exposed to chemicals that bother, then the exposure needs to be reduced—simply consuming some herb is not enough from a naturopathic view.

Dr. V.M. Kulkarni was one of the Indian naturopathic pioneers (and a natural hygienist); he wrote,

Since 1889 [Kulkarni has] been... treating patients...on Naturopathic principles... The principles of Naturopathy are:

1. A healthy human body does not contain any poisons in it.

2. Human beings do not get ill if they lead a natural life and take no poisons in their system.

3. They need no poisons to get cured when they get ill.

4. If blood is kept pure and vitality preserved, they continue to be healthy; even if they inhale millions of microbes, the disease germs will perish as they cannot thrive in pure blood.

5. But if the blood gets impure even a single microbe will propagate millions of its species in the human bodies; nay even if they do not inhale a single disease germ they will get some disease, with innumerable microbes peculiar to that disease, as microbes are the scavengers of wise Nature.

In such cases:

Fresh air, pure water and bright light
With proper food will set us right.
And in fact there is not a need
Of any poisonous drugs indeed.

All diseases even so called incurable ones can be treated successfully with fresh air, pure water, bright light and Nature's food supply. No drugs, no poisons, no injections, nor any unnatural drastic measures are needed in the treatment of diseases according to Naturopathy." [5].

E. W. Cordingley, a Ph.D. naturopath, wrote,

After having studied practically all systems of healing, and graduating in many of them, [it can be said] with some authority that Naturopathy is the greatest healing system the world has ever known. It is the most comprehensive of all, and the members of the Naturopathic profession… have [been] found to be the most intelligent and broad-minded of any in the healing art. [It is hoped] it will ever be thus, and that as time goes on, the Naturopath will in even a greater measure be capable to rendering the greatest possible assistance to the sick and afflicted.

As we review the history of the healing art, we find that mankind has constantly delved into methods of eradicating human disorders that lead away from unnatural drugging, and tend toward Nature.

The theories that have been advanced regarding the cause of disease are legion. Wrong chemical combinations, germs, impingement of nerves, wrong habits of eating, faulty mental states, and a host of others have each been held responsible as the sole cause of disease by a host of enthusiastic disciples.

However, after all is said and done, it must be admitted by any fair investigator that each single system has its shortcomings. Each method will accomplish some good, but no single method is infallible. For this reason the more intelligent among those who are devoting their attention to the prevention and cure of disease have come to realize that a perfect system must include all natural, non-drug methods in so far as each one is adapted to an individual case.

As cases vary, remedies must vary. What will help Nature to cure one disease will only aggravate another. For this reason, a system that is truly eclectic or selective must be the ultimate in the healing arts, and the one, and the only one, that can permanently endure.

[It is not] necessary to discuss the system that depends upon the administration of drugs. Learned medical authorities are practically all agreed that drugging is an unnatural practice, and that drugs possess no power to heal or cure. Some of them may seem to be of some value temporarily in relieving symptoms, or "killing pain," until Nature is enabled to effect a cure, but doubt[ful] if it is hardly ever desirable to administer such poisons that are so much at variance with Nature. For that reason, this treatise deals only with natural, drugless methods of healing,

and those natural systems, whatever they may be called by "single branch" practitioners, are, after all, simply a part of the complete and composite system known as Naturopathy [1].

Not all modern "learned medical authorities" would agree with Dr. Cordingley. Furthermore, Dr. Cordingley wrote,

…the definition of Naturopathy as given by Dr. J. E. Cummins is the best brief definition ever given. It is as follows: "Naturopathy is the science, art and philosophy of adjusting the framework, correcting the mental influences, and supplying the body with its needed elements. Osteopathy, chiropractic, mechano-therapy, dietetics, Christian Science and other 'single branch' systems all have their day. They all do some good and gain many adherents, but it cannot be denied that **all** such 'branches' have their limitations, and for that reason they will all eventually have to make room for a system that includes the best of the underlying principles of all of them—and that system is Naturopathy.

This introduction would be incomplete if [it] did not add the beautiful idealistic definition of Edward Earle Purinton… "Naturopathy is the perfected Science of Human Wholeness, and it includes all agencies, methods, systems, regimes, practices and ideals of natural origin and divine sanction whereby human health may be restored, enhanced, maintained." [1]

Dr. Lust wrote,

"Naturopathy is the mother, all-inclusive, of natural therapy. It is the basic platform for all healing; without it any healing art will be a failure…Naturopathy is the only healing system that is not a cult, nor a fanatical narrow creed, nor a system controlled by one man, one or one group; it is the science of nature, the biological way of living right, the natural way to cure… All the other systems, if they are biologically correct, must belong to naturopathy or nature cure; and if contrary to nature, superstitious, dangerous, criminal in their practices and results, they are sure to belong to regular medicine—regular licensed quackery" (1925).

At the Golden Jubilee meeting of 1947, the following standards were drawn up for the practice of naturopathy:

Naturopathy

We believe that…

1. the body under normal natural conditions is a self sustaining organism.

2. the theory of health and disease is based on Nature itself.

3. the body is governed by definite natural laws with regard to the physical, chemical, biological and physiological basis.

4. ill-health is, therefore, as a result of a departure, from healthful living out of harmony with Nature's laws.

5. to the degree that man adheres to and applies Nature's beneficial laws, to that degree will the body, through its natural inherent powers restore itself to normal.

6. Naturopathy is a philosophy, art and science and recognizes the body's inherent processes of healing, and acts in no way to suppress, antagonize or hinder these vital life forces, but, rather to arouse, assist and cooperate with the body to a restoration to normal.

7. to this end Naturopathy proceeds as follows; it makes use of the healing properties of such natural agencies as air, sunshine, water, light, heat, electricity, manipulations, rest, natural vital foods, organic vitamins, organic minerals, herbs in conjunction with cleansing and eliminating processes of other physical and mental cultures.

8. Naturopathy does not make use of synthetic or inorganic vitamins or minerals or of drugs, narcotics, surgery, serums, vaccines, anti-toxins, toxoid, injections and inoculations.

9. Naturopathy also provides for the prevention of disease and the preservation of health by teaching the basic fundamental laws of natural living and the application in daily life. [3]

These standards should be adopted by all naturopaths. This does not mean naturopaths must always be against all surgery, medications, etc., but that naturopaths should not employ those modalities. Dr. Burr-Madsen had a practical observation on this subject when she wrote, "Even if Naturopathy was the accepted form of medicine in this country, we would still need allopathic medicine both for emergencies, surgical procedures and for the pharmaceutical industry, simply because the demand for instant, lazy ways outs is so enormous. Even though naturopaths do not believe in drugs, if the patient has lived a life that has been so abusive to his body, then invasive intervention may be necessary to save the person's life, with the hopes that they will then learn to respect the human body and stop the abuses" [3].

Also, most naturopaths believe that each individual is responsible for making decisions about his/her own health. Naturopathic doctors do not prescribe treatments for disease. They educate (the word doctor means teacher) and inform their clients about natural health and some of the options of which they know. However, the reality is that not all individuals are willing to shoulder responsibilities for their own health and thus not all individuals are ready for naturopathy.

Different Views of Health

Dr. Cordingley has written,

We would furthermore like to have it distinctly understood that we do not consider that we have adopted any technic and applied the name "Naturopathy" to it from any present day "system." We feel that the original research that we have done has enabled us to go back before the time of osteopathy, chiropractic, etc., to select the technic that we are here describing, and which we have "woven into the wool and woof" of Naturopathy. For that reason a Naturopath who is using this technic in his practice cannot be rightly charged with practicing any other system under the name of Naturopathy. We desire to stress this point because some osteopathic, chiropractic and other State Licensing Boards may attempt to obtain jurisdiction over Naturopathic practitioners, and we feel that that would be as unjust as if the case were reversed. Naturopathy is truly a distinct school of practice. It is in reality the oldest drugless school of healing in existence. It is no part of the practice of medicine, osteopathy, chiropractic or any other method [1].

Furthermore he added,

"We do not demand that medical doctors, osteopaths, chiropractors, lawyers, ministers, civil engineers, pharmacists, embalmers or members of any other profession submit their credentials to us to determine their right to practice, and we consider our profession so separate and distinct from all of theirs that we request the same rights that we concede to them." [1].

Naturopathy (like this book) is an eclectic mixture of modalities intended to encourage the body to heal itself. The medical model tends to view the body as a chemical mix, thus medicines (chemicals) are often prescribed. As mentioned previously, the naturopathic model believes that the body can heal itself, thus modalities to encourage the body are what are preferred.

Even though it is claimed that everything is made up of chemicals, this is not completely true. If chemicals are strictly defined as that which is composed of elements and combinations of elements (molecules), then many things are not chemical. Obvious examples would include life, light, sound, motion, heat, wind, magnetism, gravity, thoughts, and attitudes. A recently dead body contains all the same chemicals as a living one. Every compass points to magnetic north, but this never changes the chemical composition of the compass. If one throws (or drops) an object, the object moves, but its chemical composition does not change. Even though homeopathic remedies with potencies of greater than 12c should be "chemically identical" (since they are beyond Avogadro's number [6]. The author has noted that different remedies can have different effects on people's health. Even though some *cis* and *trans* fatty acids are chemically identical, their structures often are not (*cis* tend to be liquids, with *trans* normally solid) and there appear to be major differences on their effects on human health [7]. Interestingly, even "mainstream nutritionists" understand that particle size is an important factor in nutrient absorption even though it is not detected by chemical assessment [8]. Thus nature is not just chemistry. In naturopathy, we try to utilize all that is part of nature. We try to work with life and the forces of life to encourage the healing process.

Naturopaths have been criticized by some because it is claimed that our herbs, etc. are simply chemicals, thus there really is no difference between certain naturopathic and medical interventions. However, there are major differences. An example may help explain the differences.

Medical Example

Suppose someone has the symptoms of mild hypothyroidism and has low thyroxine concentrations confirmed by a blood test. The medical model tends to conclude that since the thyroxine levels are low, then the thyroid is not capable to produce enough thyroxine itself. The medical doctor then prescribes a synthetic (or sometimes natural) version of thyroxine. This chemical will raise serum thyroxine levels, and in many cases, improve some of the symptoms associated with hypothyroidism. Now all this seems to be good, but this may not have addressed the true cause of the problem. By taking the thyroid hormone (whether or not "natural"), the anterior pituitary will sense that serum thyroxine levels are higher. It will then secrete less of the thyroid-stimulating hormone. The thyroid will receive less stimulation to produce thyroid on its own. This can lead to thyroid atrophy [9]. This is one of the reasons that many who take thyroid medications have to remain on them for their entire life—the hormone never "fixes" the thyroid, it only replaces some of its functions (this is one of the reasons that most medical doctors do not prescribe thyroxine on the basis of symptoms alone). Furthermore, since the thyroid produces other hormones (such as calcitonin) it is possible that its other functions may reduce over time as well (there is a major medical debate currently on whether or not taking thyroxine increases osteoporosis).

Naturopathic Example

Suppose the same person sees a naturopath instead. The naturopath assumes that the thyroid can heal itself if it has what it needs (which could include minerals, peptides, enzymes, phytonutrients, reduced caffeine intake, etc.). There are many possible naturopathic interventions, but let us assume that in this situation the naturopath recommends that the person consume kelp (the Chinese have been recommending kelp for low thyroid function for at least 3,000 years [10]). Kelp is an herbal food, and as such is composed of a variety of "chemicals" including the mineral iodine. The purpose for iodine in the body is to be part of thyroxine (chemically identified as "tetraiodothyronine"). By feeding the body, the thyroid can thus produce thyroxine on its own. This strengthens the thyroid and does not result in the atrophy of any of its functions. Consuming kelp does not lead to dependency (any natural iodine containing food can be consumed instead as part of the diet). For this reason, naturopaths may recommend kelp for thyroid concerns even when not confirmed by a blood test.

In both examples, "chemicals" were used. But they were used in different ways. The naturopathic model is preferable, but it should be noted that not everyone who has thyroid problems needs kelp or iodine—it can even be contraindicated in hyperthyroidism. Also, if you look at the studies shown in the exhibits, you will see that many with apparent thyroid concerns have responded to naturopathic interventions for the thyroid. There has been success in helping people rebuild their thyroids who had been taking thyroid medications, but such situations are quite individualized and will not be discussed in this book.

Naturopaths Have Been Called Quacks

Naturopaths have been called quacks for a long time. Around 100 years ago, Dr. Schweninger, one of the most celebrated allopathic doctors of his day said,

The medical profession is losing its prestige and any thinking person must know why. We ourselves are mostly at fault. But the driver curses the bad road if he upsets his cart when drunk; the child beats the table against which it has bumped its head and the doctor blames the 'quack' who robs him of the esteem of men.

We read daily articles of anger and warning as to the ways of wise women; constant accounts appear of the evils wrought by incorrect diagnosis; yet patients consult the 'quacks' and men like Kuhne and Gossel have the most important practices in the Kingdom.

How is this? Are people really so foolish that they think the quack cleverer than the doctor? Surely not; where there is a choice between sour cheap wine and damaged champagne we choose the former and in the same way the person whom the doctor has deceived goes to the quack.

The mockery of prescriptions is so obvious the chemist alone believes in them now, for his faith is in his income; patients know that there is quackery in the "profession" and that they would rather trust themselves to the quack who follows the dictates of Nature and to Homeopathy rather than to the apothecary's (poisonous) mixtures prescribed by Diplomaed Doctors.

When Muller senior dies, Dr. Crow says that he was wrongly treated by Dr. Smith; but then the latter can tell how Dr. Crow used cold water frictions for Mrs. Werner who was consumptive. So long as medical men put into practice the old saying of the pot calling the kettle black, it is natural that patients will go to quacks and that the latter will write them all down as—fools. And it is we who thus drive the public to quacks.

Who now is the quack? What right have we to persecute any other medical practitioner as if he were a murderer ? Who instituted the water treatment? Priessnitz, a quack; who originated hygienic gymnastics? Ling, a quack; how about these and all the other quacks who, caused the lame to walk, cured women's diseases which were considered incurable by us and taught us all about massage and muscular exercise? Priessnitz, Hessing, Ling, Wolf, Brand, Kneipp and Thomas will leave their mark indelible in the history of the art of healing even long, after our most celebrated names have been forgotten.

Despised Homoeopathists have proved that patients need not swallow the contents of a chemist's shop (poisonous drugs) to get well. Yet, we still despise natural means of healing but these will drive allopathic medical science to the wall and the day will come when its teachers will no longer be looked upon with scorn [5].

In more recent times, it has been written

Quacks contend that most health problems are caused by poor nutrition and therefore can be corrected with proper nutrition...Quacks claim that 'natural' vitamins are better than synthetic ones...Quacks use hair analysis and other unproven diagnostic tests to detect 'alleged' deficiencies [11].

Similarly under "Thirty tips to help spot vitamin pushers and food quacks" the 1999 edition of *Modern Nutrition in Health and Disease*, includes such relevant 'tips' as

They claim most Americans are poorly nourished" (but a peer-reviewed paper says, "Most of the U.S. population does not routinely adhere to a health-promoting diet. Less than 10% consume the appropriate amount of fruits and vegetables [12]),

They say that most diseases are due to faulty diet and can be treated with 'nutritional' methods" (there is much peer-reviewed proof that nutritional problems do respond to nutritional interventions [13]),

They allege that modern processing methods and storage remove all nutritive value from our food" (no responsible naturopath ever said it removes all nutritive value, but even *Modern Nutrition in Health and Disease* admits that all essential vitamins can be reduced through modern processing and storage methods [14]),

They claim that diet is a major factor in behavior" (please see the study in Appendix A, on *Nutrition-Based Interventions for Attention-Deficit Disorder and Attention-Deficit Hyperactive Disorder*),

They claim that fluoridation is dangerous" (there is a higher incidence of fluorosis in areas that fluoridate the water supply [15]),

They claim that soil depletion and the use of pesticides and 'chemical' fertilizers result in food that is less safe and less nourishing" ("Soils in many areas of the world are deficient in certain minerals; this can result in low concentration of major or trace minerals in drinking water, plant crops, and even in tissues of farm animals, thus contributing to marginal or deficiency dietary intakes in humans" [16]),

They claim that you are in danger of being 'poisoned' by ordinary food additives and preservatives" (various additives have been removed because they have been considered dangerous [17], also to refer to these substances as 'ordinary' seems a bit misleading),

They charge that the recommended daily allowances (RDAs) are set too low (even mainstream researchers suggest that the RDA for vitamin C should be 200mg per day instead of 60mg [18]),

They recommend a wide variety of substances similar to those found in your body" (would they prefer that we recommend artificial chemical additives that are not similar?),

They claim that 'natural' vitamins are better than synthetic ones" (naturopaths have claimed this for over 50 years [5], please also see chapter 22),

They routinely sell vitamins and other 'dietary supplements' as part of their practice" (where else would people get unusual homeopathic remedies, herbs, and other specialized natural products that are not in all health-food stores?),

They use anecdotes and testimonials to support their claims" (so does the legal system; it should be noted that thousands of studies on nutritional approaches as published in scientific publications each year [13]),

They display credentials not recognized by responsible scientists or educators" (this of no surprise since naturopathy is not 'mainstream' and in this same chapter they list the credential N.D. as one of those questionable credentials [19]),

They claim they are being persecuted by orthodox medicine" (what else would one call this list of tips but a basis for persecution?),

They sue to intimidate their critics" (according to the Herbalist Charter [3] as shown in Chapter 1, the mainstream physicians and surgeons are who started with this; also for the record, the courts are welcome to throw out cases that are baseless), and finally,

They encourage patients to lend political support to their treatment methods" (by this last definition medical doctors must be highly suspect since the American Medical Association spends more money on lobbyists than all the alternative practitioners do combined) [19].

This list also included several 'tips' that would not apply to most naturopaths.

What is a "Quack"?

Quack is actually defined as "an untrained person who practices medicine fraudulently" (naturopaths are not untrained and do not practice medicine), "any person who pretends to have knowledge or skill that he does not have in a particular field; charlatan" (legitimate naturopaths do not pretend), and finally "quack is almost always used of a fraudulent or incompetent practitioner of medicine" (naturopaths are not fraudulent nor incompetent nor are they practitioners of medicine) [20]. Thus, if naturopathy is analyzed according to the mainstream dictionary, its beliefs and practices are not quackery—why are we still subject to this type of persecution? Some simply do not like the ideals for which we stand. It was actually written that, "The best strategy to avoid entanglement with an unqualified nutritionist is to avoid all prac-

titioners who sell supplements in their offices or espouse the statements listed" under the '30 tips'. Thus, all naturopaths, people who have different opinions (such as the common-sense belief that natural vitamins are better than synthetic ones) or wish to exercise their constitutional rights are unqualified nutritionists according to this line of thinking. [ed.note: Many naturopaths consider themselves as clinical nutritionists; the author happens to have a regionally accredited Ph.D. in nutrition science—it is the author's understanding that those who wrote the '30 tips' do not.]

What is striking is how most 'tips' to spot quacks are often contradicted by others in the mainstream, yet self-appointed guardians of the status quo feel justified in teaching people to improperly label others (both of the books cited are used to train various health professionals about nutrition). Be that as it may, naturopaths should understand that we have been and probably will continue to be criticized just for being who and what we are and what we believe.

Sometimes We Win

It is sometimes frustrating to be improperly labeled when naturopaths help people and often stand for clinically-valid interventions. But sometimes we win.

Back in December 2000, I had a paper published in a major scientific/medical journal that started off with the following:

> Several frequently used nutrition books are leading to a distortion of scientific fact. Some, when discussing the how to spot quacks, include this comment from authors Barrett and Herbert, "They claim that 'natural vitamins' are better than 'synthetic' ones." [21]

I took issue with the authors of the "Thirty tips to help spot vitamin pushers and food quacks." I also cited other authors in the same book (*Modern Nutrition and Health Disease*) who effectively proved that natural vitamins were better than synthetic ones.

Well, it took 14 years, but the 11th edition of *Modern Nutrition and Health Disease* eliminated its chapter titled "Fads, Frauds, and Quackery" as well as the "Thirty tips to help spot vitamin pushers and food quacks."

While it would have been nice if *Modern Nutrition and Health Disease* would have cited my paper and boldly stated that natural vitamins were superior to synthetic ones (which the conclusion of my paper states—the mainstream changed my title to say "may" which is NOT how I originally submitted it), at least it stopped a lot of its improper name-calling.

It is nice when the scientific community backtracks against us, yet do not expect the mainstream to necessarily embrace much of what we do. But it is nice when we win.

References

[1] Cordingley, E. W. Principles and Practice of Naturopathy. Reprint by Health Research, Mokelumne Hill (CA), written 1924.

[2] American Naturopathic Medical Association Code of Ethics. ANMA, Las Vegas, 1996.

[3] Burr-Madsen, A. Natural Therapics, Module 1. Gateways College, Shingle Springs (CA), 1996.

[4] Hahnemann, S. Organon of Medicine. Reprint by B. Jain Publishers, New Delhi (India), originally written 1833 and translated into English by R. Dudgeon, 1893.

[5] Kulkarni, V. M. Healing Through Naturopathy. Reprint by B. Jain Publishers, New Delhi (India), written circa 1930.

[6] Vithoukas, G. The Science of Homeopathy. Grove Press, New York, 1980.

[7] Asherio, A, and Willett W.C. Health effects of *trans* fatty acids. Am J Clin Nutr, 1997;66:1006S-1010S.

[8] Jenkins, D. and Wolever, T. Diet factors affecting nutrient absorption and metabolism. In Modern Nutrition in Health and Disease, 8th ed. Lea & Febiger, Phil.,1994:583-602.

[9] Physician's Desk Reference, 53rd ed. Medical Economics, Montvale (NJ), 1999.

[10] Ensminger, A. H., et al. Food & Nutrition Encyclopedia, 2nd ed. CRC Press, New York, 1993.

[11] Whitney, E. N. and Rolfes, S. R. Understanding Nutrition, 7th ed. West Publishing, St. Paul, 1996.

[12] Halbert, S. C. Diet and nutrition in primary care from antioxidants to zinc. Primary Care, 1997; 24(2):825-843.

[13] Hamilton, K. Clinical Pearls in Nutrition and Preventive Medicine. ITServices, 1998.

[14] Williams, A. W. and Erdman, J. W. Food Processing: Nutrition, Safety, and Quality Balance. In Modern Nutrition in Health and Disease, 9th ed. Williams & Wilkins, 1999:1813-1821.

[15] Depaola, D. P. and Faine M.P., Palmer C.A. Nutrition in Relation to Dental Medicine. Modern Nutrition in Health and Disease, 9th ed. Williams & Wilkins, 1999:1099-1124.

[16] Bauerenfeind, J. C. Nutrification of foods. In Modern Nutrition in Health and Disease, 8th ed. Lea & Febiger, Phil., 1994:1579-1592.

[17] Hatchcock, J.N. and Rader, J. I. Food Additives, Contaminants, and Natural Toxins. In Modern Nutrition in Health and Disease, 9th ed. Williams & Wilkins, 1999:1835-1860.

[18] Levine, M., et al. Vitamin C. In Present Knowledge in Nutrition, 7th ed. ILSI Press, Washington, 1996:146-159.

[19] Barrett, S. and Herbert, V. Fads, Frauds, and Quackery. In Modern Nutrition in Health and Disease, 9th ed. Williams & Wilkins, 1999:1793-1810.

[20] Guralnik, D. B. Webster's New World Dictionary. 2nd College Edition. William Collins+World Publishing, New York, 1974.

[21] Thiel R.J., Natural Vitamins May Be Superior to Synthetic Ones. Medical Hypotheses, 2000; 55(6):461-469

3

Toxemia as a Cause of Disease

Naturopathic philosophy includes the concept that disease is due to an accumulation of toxins. This chapter will primarily include the writings of Dr. Cordingley, Dr. Henry Lahn (M.D.), Sebastian Kneipp, and Dr. John H. Tilden (M.D.) on this subject. Although most "authorities" will not agree with them, these are essentially the causes of disease from a naturopathic prospective.

Dr. Cordingley and the cause of disease:

"Naturopathy is a system of disease-eradication based on the theory that, as Dr. Cummins says, "Clean blood is the instrument of health and the fountain of happiness" or, as the Bible states it, "The life of all flesh is the blood thereof." Whatever the system we employ, we produce results only as we purify the blood and clear the system of poisonous encumbrances.

Let us pause here a moment and see what scientific basis we have for the hypothesis that impure blood is the cause of disease, or that, "The life of all flesh is the blood thereof."

For centuries mankind has been searching for the cause of disease. Not content with taking the Biblical statement, and deducting therefrom, pathologists have advanced one theory after another, only to see each give way and weaken. At present, medical doctors are almost universally working on the germ theory of disease. But the germ theory is already weakening and is due for being thrown aside. Dr. Fraser of Canada and Dr. Powell of California have experimented with billions of germs of all varieties, but they have been unable to produce a single disease by the introduction of germs into human subjects. 'Dr. Waite tried for years to prove the germ theory, but he could not do so. During the World War an experiment was conducted at Gallop's Island, Massachusetts, in which millions of influenza germs were injected into over one hundred men at the Government hospital, but instead of the men taking influenza, the only change in them was "increased appetite and more vigorous health."

Dr. Fraser found that in many cases of diphtheria and other diseases the germs did not appear at the outset of the disease, and in some patients the germs did not make their appearance at all.

What, then, is the purpose of germs? Germs are scavengers. When you see flies swarming around a garbage can you don't say that the flies brought the garbage, but that the garbage attracted the flies. The case is the same with germs. The fermentation of poisonous acids and alkaloids in the human system attracts germs, because they feed upon it. The nature of the toxin and its localization determine the character of the disease. When an epidemic breaks out there has been a considerable number of people in a locality who have eaten the same kind of food, lived under similar conditions, been subjected to the same climatic and atmospheric changes, and these factors have brought about an identical fermentation of toxins in the bodies of such persons and manifested the same group of symptoms. That is why we have epidemics.

Let us very briefly deal with the other theory of the cause of disease, one that has attracted rather wide attention. That is the theory that "subluxations" at the spine cause disease. These "subluxations" cause the bones to impinge the nerves, so say those who advocate this theory. However, we have found by dissection that the nerve where it passes through the opening between the vertebrae is from one-third to one-twelfth the size of the opening, that it is surrounded by a vaseline-like fatty tissue, and that no pressure would be possible at that point, even if the disk between the vertebrae were reduced to nothing. Why, then, do we sometimes have tenderness and contraction at a spinal segment? Simply because the morbid matter that has localized in an organ or tissue has set up an irritation there, and this irritation is transmitted along the nerve to the related spinal area, and it there produces a condition of contraction and hyperthesia. When the vertebra is "adjusted" (that is, pushed against) a stretching of ligamentous and muscular tissue results and an increased irritation is produced which is transmitted back to the organ or tissue affected where it in turn brings about a marked stimulation which sometimes causes the organ or tissue to throw off its original irritant. We see a parallel to this in cases of "sick stomach." If a person eats something which slightly "sours" in the stomach it will make him feel "upset," but if it "sours" greatly he will immediately vomit it up and then feel better.

This demonstrates why it is that so-called "straight" chiropractors sometimes accomplish results, and it will also indicate the reason why they so often fail.

There are several other theories of the cause of disease but space forbids their discussion.

To get back to our real cause of disease, we find that fullness of life means absolute freedom from disease. Disease in any form causes a limitation of life. Therefore, when disease (limitation of life) is present, there is some change in the blood, because "The life of all flesh is the blood thereof."

Naturopathic researchers have shown that wrong habits of eating, sleeping, working and recreation increase the intake of poisonous acids and alkaloids and at the same time so weaken the eliminative functions that these toxins are not thrown off. They therefore float in the bloodstream and eventually are deposited in some organ or tissue, causing disease to develop. Dr. Cummins shows that arterio-sclerosis, rheumatism and calculi are caused by accumulations of uric and oxalic acids in the blood. Bright's Disease, dropsy, ulcers and necrosis are brought about through the accumulation of uric and sulphuric acids. When carbonic acid combines with uric acid in the blood, cell asphyxiation is brought about causing anemia, tuberculosis, chlorosis or pneumonia. And, similarly, all other diseases have their origin.

Isn't is remarkable that man should experiment and theorize for so many centuries in an effort to find the cause of disease, and then, after all his labors, should be brought back to the Sacred Word revealed by God?" [1].

Dr. Lahn and the Causes of Disease

The following are considered to be the causes of disease by Henry Lahn, M.D. (an iridologist) and includes a few comments from Samuel Hahnemann and Sebastian Kneipp:

The diagnosis from the eye is giving us full enlightenment in regard to the state of the acute or feverous as well as of the chronic diseases, and will show that the latter are caused by organic derangements. Furthermore we are taught that aside from epidemics and blood poisoning the causes of disease are :

1. Inherited impurity of the blood.

2. Irrational care of the new-born, viz.:

    a) Improper food during infancy if the

child cannot be nursed by the mother; if the infant is fed with cow's milk, it should be given *uncooked* and *undiluted,* as it contains less solid nourishment than mother's milk. The thinning of the milk is always burdening the digestive organs and causes catarrh of the stomach and the intestines.

b) The body is hindered by the warm, relaxing bath to get rid of the inherited impurities of the blood.

3. False treatment of the milk-scurf ; by this skin disease the vigorous body tries to eliminate the inherited impurities. The suppression of the vital action by fats, oils, ointments, warm baths, etc., always weakens the body which is thereby encumbered with morbid matter and checked in its proper development. Milk-scurf which is thus falsely treated causes the blackening of the rim of the iris like other skin diseases (with the exception of scabies or crab-lice) if treated in the same irrational manner. From the standpoint of the diagnosis from the eye we therefore take all such skin diseases for subordinate kinds of milk-scurf.

4. Vaccination, by aggravating already inherited deteriority of the blood, hinders the body in every instance to eliminate the morbid matter and always prevents the iris from getting a lighter color. [Lahn's note: While objecting to every kind of vaccination because of the dangerous effects; it must be said that the injuries produced by 2 and 3 are often equal to those of vaccination. There was a case where milk-scurf had been suppressed by application of cream, and soon a yellowish rim formed around the pupil, the eye grew darker and critical affections of the heart and brain set in.]

5. Suppression of the scabies by ointments, shown in the iris by the sharply edged, red-brown spots already mentioned above.

6. Allopathic maltreatment; it is the cause of new and aggravated diseases, the consequences of medicine poisonings…

At all times and by all thinking physicians it has been observed and acknowledged that the suppression of skin-diseases is always followed by more serious diseases, and men like Theophrastus Paracelsus and his contemporaries Prospero Alpini and Quercetanus, and over 200 years ago the Italian Bonomo, have raised their warning voice against this fatal practice.

Hahnemann, seeking the causes of chronic diseases and their difficult cure, supposed that in most instances, "the healing is impeded by formerly suppressed scabies." His own observations and those of many others showed that chronic diseases appeared after a quick suppression of scabies by external remedies, and this circumstance led him to take a certain morbid matter which he called Psora for the cause of many deep-rooted evils.

The diagnosis from the eye shows us that his view is perfectly right, and that those homeopaths who did not agree with Hahnemann's theory, on account of the discovery of the mite (1786), were wrong.

Allopathy treats scabies, like all other skin-diseases, with salves and soaps containing mostly tar, sulphur, and mercury, and at the same time admits that patients thus cured (?) "get afflicted with stiff joints and have even become unable to move their limbs." We can complete the list of injuries caused by the allopathic treatment of scabies by adding the unfailing proofs of a deep-going corruption of blood and lymph: over-sensitiveness against colds, predisposition to catarrh and inflammation with more or less fever, in the last stages: serious ulcers and tumors, hot and cold gangrene, and cancer.

In fact, every experienced practitioner of the natural method of healing has often had occasion to observe the injuries following the suppression of scabies (i.e. interfering with the action of the skin by means of salves, soaps, and similar preparations). Pastor Kneipp makes the following statement:

"The abominated evil 'scabies' can do much harm on the surface, but still more inside of the body. It is to be deplored that remedies are used which instead to cure (i.e. remove the cause of the evil) are most detrimental to the organism and become the source of endless misery and suffering. Who knows all the fatty salves prepared with sulphur, alcohol, and other mixtures? They all have one thing in common. They perfectly close the pores of the skin, and by forming a greasy crust they almost completely stop the absolutely necessary perspiration which is thus held back in the body, causing many and often deadly diseases. This is not exaggerated but very grieving, especially if one knows how easily and quickly scabies can be cured by natural means.

"A well-grown man, 28 years of age, once sought my counsel, and his appearance reminded me immediately of a worm-eaten piece of wood. He could nowhere find relief, nobody knew what really ailed him. I asked him: 'Have you ever been afflicted with scabies in your younger years?' He affirmed my question; 'but,' he added, 'I was cured within three days.' That is not the way I want to cure, God forbid!

"Just in the cure of such loathsome diseases which most distinctly reveal the presence of foreign and poisonous matter in the system must uphold the principle: Everything in the body that does not belong there must be expelled from it! To practice the contrary would be like planting vermin into the clothing, or rabbits and mice into the field. But all applications which bring forth, extract, and remove poisonous matter from the body and at the same time strengthen the organism vigorous action, assist nature in her wise and beneficial course.

"After a water cure of six weeks the skin disease was perfectly healed, and the patient was finally able to choose a vocation. He still enjoys the best of health, and his stubborn sickness has vanished without leaving any traces."

The treatment of scabies according to the natural method of healing is the same as that of other skin-diseases: do not prevent the patient from scratching which brings sooner forth the eruptions, as the itching is always a plain hint of nature; a strictly non-irritating diet, water as beverage, and pure air will effect a speedy recovery. As to treatment of the skin, we recommend, according to need, cold baths, washings of body wholly or partly, about two or three applications daily, the first soon after rising, the second in the forenoon, the third in the afternoon and in the evening before retiring an air-bath of about ten minutes duration. If there is no opportunity for baths or washings, the skin can be cooled by covering it with wet linen, which may be renewed after an hour or two, as soon as the linen gets dry and the skin begins to burn again. The homeopathic remedy for scabies is sulphur.

After such general treatment the scabies like any other skin-disease comes out fully and wholly and generally begin to heal after the third or fourth day of the appearance. The temporary constipation will give way to copious evacuations; the urine will lose its sharpness, and the complexion which long before the appearance of the disease showed a somewhat grayish cast, will begin to get clear and rosy.

Warts, corns, etc., are to be regarded as diseases and have to be treated as such. We have observed how the wrong treatment of these evils by caustics, erasion, excision, etc., was followed by serious other ailments, for instance jaundice. All such morbid thickenings of the skin are removed without danger by the following simple remedy. Cut an onion through the middle and put in vinegar for twenty-four hours; take off the single coats and tie one onto the surface of the corn during the night; after repeating this every evening for one week, the thickenings can be removed painlessly. Interior homeopathic remedies are dulcamara, hepar sulphur, lycopodium. Like all other patent medicines, all so-called "corn-killers " are useless. [2]

Dr. Tilden and the Cause of Disease

Some of the most extensive writings on toxemia as a cause of disease are from Tilden (beginning in chapter 2):

Medical science is founded upon a false premise, namely, that disease is caused by extraneous, outside influences and that his affliction may be permanently "'cured" or palliated by drugs. As the term "medical" means pertaining to medicine or the practice of medicine, so has the use of "remedies" come to carry the idea of "curing," healing, correcting or affording relief. But in real truth, all so-called "therapeutics" are administered without any clear understanding of cause.

These words medical, medicine, disease and cure have become so impressed upon our inner consciousness that they now shape our thoughts and beliefs. So arbitrary and uncompromising are these beliefs that new schools and cults are forced to stay within the prison yard of these restrictions if they would hope for a public hearing. So it is that they may describe an impinged nerve to be the cause of some pathology. But they do not trouble themselves to find out why one impinged nerve "creates" a pathology whereas another does not.

Nor does the psychologist trouble himself to explain why worry may cause disease in one person but in another, does not. Nor why hope in one subject heals but not in another. Nor why faith does not always heal. They beg the question by declaring there was not faith enough, etc. Alas, no fool is a bigger fool than the fool who fools himself.

So we seek why it is that all new schools of thought hark back to their source —"demon germ"—and to the concept that disease is a real entity. With this idea firmly fixed, is it any wonder why even the best research comes to naught, why even the most spectacular discovery soon proves to be only one more mistaken belief?

What hope is there for medical science to ever become a true science when the entire structure of medical knowledge is built around the idea that there is an entity called disease which can be expelled when the right drug is found?

It is intention[al] to portray the common, everyday foibles of "scientific" medicine concerning disease and cure so that people will readily be able to identify them as the absurdities which they really are, so that they will come to know that they have been hoodwinked into false beliefs by the blare and trumpeting of pseudo-science. Then [to] describe the only worked-out, rational explanation of the true cause for so-called diseases. …this [shall be done] by contrasting the mythical old with the rational new, hoping in this way to prompt a few to initiate their own independent thinking and experimentation. The claptrap, tomfoolery, idol worship and medical superstitions of a deluded society may then be cast into the blessed limbo of forgetfulness. And the road will be paved for a healthy, more glorious fulfillment of man's infinite destiny—a destiny restricted only by man's imagination, self-discipline and right-thinking!

Until toxemia was discovered and elaborated… into a philosophy, there had been no real light shed upon disease, its cause and purpose. So-called "causes" and "corrections" have been and are a hodge-podge of guesswork and speculation which has confounded the best and most industrious medical minds in every generation.

Today, as never before, the brightest minds in the profession delve into research work in an effort to find the true cause of disease. Yet they are doomed to disappointment. We begin to understand why. All the best work which has ever been done searching for cause commences with effect. Certainly no reasoning mind can believe that an effect is its own cause! Today no one believes in spontaneous generation. The remnant of this belief was annihilated through the discovery of germs as the cause for fermentation. This was a discovery so profound that it created a frenzy in the medical world, And, as is the case with every epidemic of frenzy, mental poise was lost. The germ was accepted as the primary cause of disease. No one bothered to note that in order for a germ to exist it has to have a house to live in a— "house" which is created by the toxic and pathological pollution of the body, by systemic poisoning which creates the proper germ culture. Instead, everyone was swept off his feet. And, as is true in all sudden changes of mass belief, it was dangerous not to agree with the mob spirit. So it was that opposing or conservative voices were suppressed or ostracized.

The germ frenzy was fierce for two or three decades. But now it is becoming a thing of the past. Hopefully, it may soon become a dead letter.

Cause for disease is being looked for everywhere. No less a person than the late Sir James Mackenzie in *Reports of the St. Andrews Institute for Clinical Research,* Volume 1, declared, "The knowledge of disease is so incomplete that we do not even know what steps should be taken to advance our knowledge." At another time he wrote, "Disease is made manifest to us only by the symptoms which it produces; the first object in the examination of a patient is the detection of symptoms; and, therefore, the symptoms of disease form one of the main objects of our study."

The Value of Symptomatology

Sir James, when living, was probably the greatest clinician of the English-speaking world. Yet he had not outlived the medical superstition that disease is a positive entity, and that the way to find disease is to trace symptoms to their source. But if a symptom is traced to its source, what of it?

A pain is traced to its source, and we find that it comes from the head. But the head does not cause the pain. Then we find that there are symptoms of hyperemia—too much blood in the head. The pressure from too much blood in the head causes the pain. Then pressure must be the disease? No.

Then too much blood is the disease—hyperemia? Certainly too much blood in the head was a cause. But what caused the congestion? We find that pain is a symptom. Pressure causes pain. Pressure too is a symptom. Too much blood in the head causes pressure. Too much blood in the head is also a symptom. Pain, pressure and hyperemia are all three symptoms. In time the walls of the blood vessels weaken and the pressure ruptures one of the vessels. Hemorrhage into the brain causes death from apoplexy. Is the ruptured blood vessel the disease? Is hemorrhaging into the brain the disease? No, it is only a symptom. Is death from hemorrhage the disease?

If the hemorrhage is not severe enough to cause death but does produce some form of paralysis (and there can be many kinds), is paralysis a disease? Haven't we been traveling along quite a chain of symptoms in the journey from headache to paralysis. Yet we have not found anything to which all these symptoms point as disease. And, according to the requirements of Sir James Mackenzie, disease is made manifest to us only through symptoms! Here we have a chain of symptoms beginning with pain and ending in hemorrhage and death or paralysis without having discovered any indication as to the true cause. Nor will any other symptom—chain, such as stomach symptoms ending in pyloric cancer, give any more indication of the disease at its various stages than did the foregoing illustration.

The first indication which we have of any chain of symptoms is discomfort or pain. In any stomach derangement we have pain, more or less aggravated by food. Catarrh follows or, more often, precedes it. Or there may be that which we call inflammation or gastritis. Gastritis continues with a thickening of the mucous membrane. A time comes when there is ulceration. This will be called a disease, and is recognized as ulcer of the stomach. But actually this is only a continuation of the primary symptoms of catarrh and pain. The ulcer is removed, but the symptoms of inflammation and pain continue. Other ulcers will follow. This state eventually emerges into induration or hardening of the pyloric orifice of the stomach. When this develops, there is more or less of an obstruction to the pyloric valve outlet which, in turn, produces occasional vomiting. Then, on thorough examination, cancer is found.

When we analyze the symptoms from the first pain and catarrh in the stomach to the final denouement as cancer, we again encounter just another chain of symptoms. The first symptom to be noticed is pain. On examination we find a catarrhal condition of the stomach. But this catarrhal condition is not a disease. It is only a symptom. Catarrhal inflammation continues with the thickening of the mucous membrane, leading to ulceration. Nor is ulceration a disease only a continuation of the inflammatory symptom. Removal of the ulcer does not "cure" the "disease;" it only removes a symptom. These symptoms continue until there is a thickening and induration of the pyloris which is called cancer. But we really have not discovered anything, which approaches the true cause-merely a chain of symptoms from beginning to end.

By removing the cancer, the question of what the disease is has not been answered. Since cancer is the end-symptom, it cannot be the cause of the first symptom.

Any other so-called disease can be illustrated in the same manner. Pain and catarrh, as a rule, are the first symptoms which call a physician's or patient's attention that something is wrong. Yet, as we have seen, pain and catarrh are not the disease. And when the cause of the pain is discovered, this too proves merely another symptom—not the disease. The pattern follows true in all cases.

It is no wonder that diagnosticians become perplexed in their search after disease, for they have confounded symptoms and disease. The fact of the matter is, it is impossible on any ending of a chain of symptoms to say, "This is the disease." We have shown that headache, or pain in the head, is not a disease. We likewise pointed out that hemorrhage or apoplexy is not a disease, but only a continuation of the primary symptoms.

Said Mackenzie, "Disease is made manifest to us only by the symptoms which it produces." This statement tacitly infers that there are diseases and symptoms and that through symptoms we may find disease. But when we trace symptoms to disease, we are in the dilemma of the mountain climber who climbs one mountain only to find that there are other and higher peaks, on and on and on.

That Mackenzie was baffled in his search for fixed disease is indicated by the following (which is quoted from the reports cited earlier):

Many diseases are considered to be of a dangerous nature, and many attempts are made to combat the danger, with, however, no perception of its nature. This is particularly true with epidemic diseases, such as measles, influenza, scarlet fever, and diphtheria. As a consequence, proposals have at different times been put forward to treat individuals who suffer from these diseases upon some general plan, without consideration of the peculiarities of the individual case-and thus we get that rule-of-thumb treatment which is shown in the indiscriminate use of a serum or vaccine.

During influenza epidemics there is always a cry for a universal method of treatment, and attempts are made to meet this cry in the shape of so-called specifics and vaccines.

When a great authority declares that dangerous diseases are combated without any perception of their nature—and that, too, in spite of the germ theory— it should be obvious to thinking minds that the germ theory has been tried and found wanting. Yet when something must be done and nothing better has been discovered, he suggests, "serums and vaccines may be used indiscriminately."

Medicine rests upon a sound, scientific foundation. Anatomy, physiology, biology, chemistry and all collateral sciences which have a bearing on the science of man have been advanced to great perfection. But the so-called sciences of symptomatology, disease, diagnosis, etiology, and the treatment of disease go back to superstition for their foundation. We see the incongruity of jumbling real science with delusion and superstition. Disease is believed to be an entity; and this idea is followed by another equally absurd; namely, the idea of "cure." Around these two old assumptions has developed an immense literature which confounds its creators.

Truth as Famous Men See It

When a man's knowledge is not in order, the more of it he has, the greater will be his confusion. —Herbert Spencer.

Confusion worse confounded is the only explanation which can be given to the theory and practice of medicine. Of course it is hoary with age and is one of the learned professions. With much just pride can the rank and file point to its aristocracy—its long list of famous dead as well as living physicians. What has made most of them famous? The same attributes which have made others famous, in and out of the professions—namely, personal worth and education. Franklin was not a physician; yet he was as great as any and could use his grave manner in advising the sick as well as those not sick. He appeared to have a sense-perception for truth; and… this discrimination is the leading if not the distinguishing trait which has divided and always will divide the really great from the mediocre majority. These discriminating leaders are the yeast which raises all of humanity. This is the quality of character that could not be found in all Sodom and Gomorrah.

There was another discriminating mind in the eighteenth century—another Benjamin, who also was a signer of the Declaration of Independence. He was Benjamin Rush, a physician and luminary who brought distinction to medical science. He was larger than his profession. He left seeds of thought which, if acted upon by the profession, would have organized medical thought and prevented the present day confusion. He left on record such golden nuggets as:

Much mischief has been done by the nosological arrangement of diseases ... Disease is as much a unit as fever ... Its different seats and degrees should no more be multiplied into different diseases than the numerous and different effects of heat and light upon our globe should be multiplied into a plurality of suns.

The whole materia medica is infected with the baneful consequences of the nomenclature of disease; for every article in it is pointed only against their name ... By the rejection of the artificial arrangement of diseases, a revolution must follow in medicine ... The road to knowledge in medicine by this means will likewise be shortened; so that a young man will be able to qualify himself to practice physic at a much less expense of time and labor than formerly, as a child would learn to read by the help of the Roman alphabet, instead of Chinese characters.

Science has much to deplore from the multiplication of diseases. It is as repugnant to truth in medicine as polytheism is to religion. The physician who considers every different affection of the different parts of the same system as distinct diseases, when they arise from one cause, resembles the Indian or African savage who considers water, dew, ice, frost, and snow as distinct essences; while the physician who considers the morbid affections of every part of the body, however diversified they may be in their form or degrees, as derived from one cause, resembles the enlightened philosopher who considers dew, ice, frost and snow merely as different modifications of water, and as derived simply from the absence of heat.

Humanity has likewise much to deplore from this paganism in medicine. The sword will probably be sheathed forever, as an instrument of death, before physicians will cease to add to the mortality of mankind by prescribing for the names of diseases.

There is but one remote cause of disease ... These remarks are of extensive application, and, if duly attended to, would deliver us from a mass of error which has been accumulating for ages in medicine; ...the nomenclature of diseases from their remote causes. It is the most offensive and injurious part of the rubbish of our science.

The physician who can cure one disease by a knowledge of its principles may by the same means cure all the diseases of the human body; for their causes are the same.

There is the same difference between the knowledge of a physician who prescribes for diseases as limited by genera and species and of one who prescribes under the direction of just principles that there is between the knowledge we obtain of the nature and extent of the sky by viewing a few feet of it from the bottom of a well and viewing from the top of a mountain the whole canopy of heaven.

[One] would as soon believe that ratafia (a liqueur or cordial) was intended by the Author of Nature to be the only drink of man, as believe that the knowledge of what relates to the health and lives of a whole city, or nation, should be confined to one, and that a small or privileged order of men.

From a short review of these facts, reason and humanity awake from their long repose in medicine, and unite in proclaiming that it is time to take the cure of pestilential epidemics out of the hands of physicians, and to place it in the hands of the people.

Dissections daily convince us of our ignorance of the seats of disease, and cause us to blush at our prescriptions... What mischief have we done under the belief of false facts... and false theories! We have assisted in multiplying diseases. We have done more—we have increased their mortality.

I shall not pause to beg pardon of the faculty for acknowledging, in this public manner, the weakness of our profession. I am pursuing Truth, and while I can keep my eye fixed upon my guide, I am indifferent whither I am led, provided she is my leader.

Oliver W. Holmes, M.D., was a man who gave dignity and respectability to the profession. He was a literary man and from his beginning to his end was always larger than his profession. He once said, "I firmly believe that, if the whole materia medica could be sunk to the bottom of the sea, it would be all the better for mankind and all the worse for the fishes." *Breakfast-Table Series* will be read by the intelligent people of the future, who will know nothing of Holmes' fight for women against the dirty hands of herd-doctors and their consequences—puerperal fever.

Aequanimitas will keep Osler in the minds of intelligent people when Osler's *Practice of Medicine* will be found only in the shops of bibliomaniacs. Such men as Osler keep the dead weight of mediocre medicine from sinking into oblivion by embellishing medical fallacies with their superb personalities and their literary polish.

Throughout all the ages the finest minds have sensed the truth concerning the cause of disease and this has bulked large against medical insanities and inanities.

A very striking picture of the medical herd was made by "Anonymous" in his essay of "Medicine" in "Civilization in the United States."

It has been remarked above that one of the chief causes of the unscientific nature of medicine and the antiscientific character of physicians lies in their innate credulity and inability to think independently. This contention is supported by the report on the intelligence of physicians recently published by the National Research Council. They are found by more or less trustworthy psychologic tests to be lowest in intelligence of all professional men, excepting only dentists and veterinarians. Dentists and veterinarians are ten percent less intelligent. But since the quantitative methods employed certainly carry an experimental error of ten percent or even higher, it is not certain that the members of the two more humble professions have not equal or even greater intellectual ability. It is significant that engineers head the list in intelligence. In fact, they are rated sixty percent higher than physicians.

This inside disparity leads to a temptation to interesting psychological probings. Is not the lamentable lack of intelligence of the physician due to lack of necessity for rigid intellectual discipline? Many conditions conspire to make him an intellectual cheat. Fortunately for us, most diseases are self-limiting. But it is natural for the physician to turn this dispensation of nature to his advantage and to intimate that he cured John Smith, when actually nature has done the trick. On the contrary, should Smith die, the good physician can assume a pious expression and suggest that despite his own incredible skill and tremendous effort, it was God's (or nature's) will that John should pass beyond. Now the engineer is open to no such temptation. He builds a bridge or erects a building, and disaster is sure to follow any misstep in calculation or fault in construction. Should such a calamity occur, he is presently disqualified and disappears from view. Thus he is held up to a high mark of intellectual rigor and discipline that is utterly unknown in the world the physician inhabits.

The critic appears to think that "one of the chief causes of the antiscientific character of physicians lies in their innate credulity and inability to think independently." Presumably he means that the physicians cannot think independently; for if medicine, scientific or unscientific, could think at all, it might have thought its way out from this present day muddle.

The only thing that saves all physicians from the above indictment is that they are not examined on the cause and treatment of disease. If average physicians pass low on "trustworthy psychologic tests," it does not speak very well for the higher education which put so many medical students out of business a few years ago. But these psychological tests may be fitted to educational standards which are assembled with intelligence left out. Intelligence, like the *cause* of *disease,* is a force in nature that can be used under the proper environments; but it cannot be monopolized to the exclusion of all mankind. Gladstone in youth was passed upon by the Psychological test of his teacher and pronounced incorrigible; yet at eighty-six he was wielding an ax and translating Virgil.

Scientific Tests

People should not take to heart too seriously verdicts resting on scientific tests, since a very large part of the integral is scientific assumption and presumption. The New York Life Insurance Company turned me down more than fifty years ago.

"Anonymous," whoever he is, writes well; and as that of an iconoclast, his style is quite fetching. But, to save his bacon, it was well that he criticized from ambush; for he would make an excellent target. This type of person is as vulnerable as any Standard A type of professional man.

He shows his medical length and breadth when he says, "Of all the dreadful afflictions that plague us a few may be cured or ameliorated by the administration of remedies." That was said by medical men now one and two hundred years dead and with no more aplomb than that of the physicians of today in the literary class of our "Anonymous."

"Dreadful afflictions" do not "plague us." If we are plagued by disease, it is of our own building; and all we need do to get back to comfort and health is to quit building disease; then our subconscious self gets busy cleaning house.

"Anonymous" could not have made a statement that would have been more perfectly one hundred percent wrong. He says, "A few may be cured." That is a mild statement coming from one of the ambushed Caesars of scientific medicine. It can be presumed that he means there is a contingent possibility that a few can be "cured." This is false; for "afflictions" or disease cannot be "cured." Nature—our subconscious—has a full monopoly on the power to heal. Healing is nature's prerogative; and she could not, even if she would, delegate the task to physicians or to the academies of medical science.

What a glorious legacy vouchsafed by the powers that be! What a sad plight humanity would be in if medical commercialism had a monopoly on healing or "curing" the sick! But medical commercialism does very well, however, by vending its camouflage "cures" of all kinds. But when mankind awakens to a full realization of the truth that throughout the hoary centuries we have been buying false remedies from monopolistic pretenders, then ancient Aesculapius will be unfrocked and thrown out of business—staff, snake, and all.

"Anonymous," fearing the statement, "A few may be cured," was too strong, added the modifying phrase "or ameliorated;" which, in medical parlance, means palliated, relieved, etc. Such temporary relief is, in reality, the whole truth concerning so-called "remedies" or "cures." One day the great truth will be realized that healing or the power to throw off disease is entirely within the body itself and is a function of the subconscious. And when this truth is vividly realized, we will know better than to throw a monkey wrench into the machinery (through the use of drugs, serums, vaccines, surgery, feeding to keep up strength, etc.). We will no longer pollute the body or adopt heroic measures of "amelioration" which will only contribute to our future misery and disability. Rather we will adopt the only safe and sane style of living which leads to good health and a clear mind.

There is no "cure." "Amelioration" merely increases the **toxemia** and builds the so-called disease.

A delicate woman became [Tilden's] patient after suffering from migraine headaches for twenty-two years. She had taken remedies in varying degrees from twenty-two different physicians—a few widely known, one a neurologist of more than national fame. Most told her that there ,was no cure, but that with menopause (or "change of life") the headaches would cease. This was a "bum" guess. For she declared that her suffering had been greater than ever before the past two years, since her menstruation had ceased. Just how much the psychological suggestion that she would not get well for a given period of time, which was made by fifteen or twenty physicians, may have had in prolonging her headaches, it is impossible to predict. But we do know that drug palliation is always inclined to enervate and to build **toxemia.** She had further been treated by morphine hypodermics. This is fiendish. There should be a law against such malpractice but the ruling medical majority novor handicap themselves with prohibitory laws.

[Tilden's] prescription to this suffering lady was a simple one. No more smoking was to be allowed in the home (her husband was an inveterate smoker). Stay in bed and fast until one of the periodic paroxysms of headache had been missed.

The paroxysms had been coming weekly, beginning on Tuesday and leaving her prostrate until Friday. This patient had only one paroxysm under my care. The husband became very enthusiastic. [Tilden's] wry comment on his outburst of rejoicing was, "Your smoking combined with the prescribed drugs caused her unnecessary suffering for nearly a quarter of a century."

Drugging pain of any kind checks elimination and prevents the human organism from cleaning house. In this case of migraine, the physician slammed shut the doors of egress with drugs and then barred them with morphine. The prescription reversed the order. All eliminating doors were opened. The result was that she never had another headache. Of course, changes were prescribed in eating and other habits afterwards. People who have no bad habits are never sick.

About the same time... another woman came who had weekly paroxysms of migraine for sixteen years. Like the first case, she had been medicated by many physicians and told that she need not expect relief until after the change of life. This woman, too, had only one paroxysm after giving up her drug palliation and making a few changes in her daily habits.

Here, then, were two patients with a "dreadful affliction," which was kept "dreadful" by a senseless and criminal medication—and that, too, by physicians holding degrees from Class A colleges.

So we see, migraine is not cured. And if doping, as these two cases were doped, is *ameliorating*, then the dictionary definition of *ameliorating* should be changed to *toxifying*.

Crises

According to the toxin philosophy, every so-called disease is a crisis of toxemia (self-poisoning). This occurs because toxin has accumulated in the blood above the toleration point. The crisis or so-called disease (call it cold, flu, pneumonia, headache, typhoid fever, etc.) has been precipitated as an extraordinary means of elimination—a need precipitated because the overworked normal channels of elimination have been unable to handle the overload. Nature is endeavoring to rid the body of toxin. Any treatment which obstructs this effort at elimination complicates the problems and baffles nature in her self-healing efforts.

Drugs, feeding, fear, and keeping at work are all among the factors which prevent elimination. A cold is driven into chronic catarrh. Flu may then enter the scene to help rid the body of *toxicity*. Then pneumonia may follow with possibly a fatal ending if elimination of the poisonous secretions is checked by drugs. We already know what happens to headaches. Typhoid will be forced into a septic state and greatly prolonged, if the patient is not killed.

The above illustrates what happens when "cases are cured or ameliorated." But how different the story's ending is when the attending physician *knows* that every so-called disease is just a complex of symptoms which signify a crisis of **toxemia**—nature's house cleaning! For nature can succeed admirably if not interfered with by vendors of poison. Such efforts to destroy an imaginary entity lurking somewhere in the system only accomplish two things: both the vendor's profits and the patient's woes are mightily increased.

But it is a real pleasure for the conscientious physician, who knows that he cannot "cure" anything, to watch nature throw off all these toxic symptoms. All that is necessary is that he do a little *watchful waiting* and *keep hands off*. The patient will be comfortable most of the time. When asked how he is, he generally replies, "I feel all right. I am comfortable." Patients never answer in that way when drugged and fed. Yes, when nature is not hindered by officious professional meddling, sick people can truthfully say when well over a crisis of house cleaning, "I had a very comfortable sickness." Nature is not revengeful. Great suffering and chronic and fatal maladies are created by the incorrigibility of patients and the well-meaning but belligerent efforts of the physicians who fight the imaginary foe without ceasing. People are so saturated with the idea that disease must be fought to a finish that they are not satisfied with sensible, conservative treatment. Something must be done even if they pay for it with their lives. And tens of thousands do just that every year. This willingness to die on the altar of medical superstition is one reason why no real improvement is made in fundamental medical science. When people are ready for enlightenment (instead of medication, vaccination and immunization), the knowledge and the means are ready for them.

Is there nothing for a physician to do? Yes, of course! He should enter the sick room with a smile and a cheerful word, free from odors and neat and clean. He should be natural and free from affectations. He should not relate how many confinements he officiated the night before or how many thousands he has had in the past ten years. Professional lobbying is not appropriate for the sickroom. Patients should have confidence in their physician. But if he does a lot of medico-political lying, the patient will know it; and this sloughs confidence.

He should advise something warm for the feet; perfect quiet; no food, liquid or solid, and positively no drugs but the water desired; a warm bath at night and as often necessary for comfort. Rest, warmth, fresh air and quiet conducive to healing. Finally, the physician should educate his patient into proper living habits so that future crises of toxemia may be avoided.

When this regime is followed and nature is allowed full control, then the pessimistic state of "Anonymous" "that few diseases may be cured or ameliorated" should be changed to read, "All acute, so-called diseases will disappear and the patient will stay well if only he will practice self control by changing the enervating habits which brought on the crisis of toxemia." When this is done, so-called chronic diseases will never arise.

All Diseases Were Once Innocent

Cancer, tuberculosis, Bright's disease, and all chronic diseases were once innocent colds. They were "ameliorated." They returned and were again "ameliorated." This occurred again and again. Each recurrence was accompanied by greater enervation and a greater constitutional toleration for toxin-poisoning. Greater quantities of mucous and submucous tissue were requisitioned by the body to assist in eliminating the toxin.

Research is being carried on vigorously in an attempt to find the cause of disease, the conception of disease being that it is an entity. But in truth, all so-called diseases are merely increasing symptom complexes due to the repeated crises of toxemia. They have no independent existence. As soon as toxemia is controlled, the diseases disappear, unless an organ has been forced by innumerable crises to degenerate. Even organic change, when the organ is not destroyed, will be overcome by changing the style of living and getting rid of the cause—crises of toxemia.

To find the cause of cancer, start with enervation (generally brought on by stresses, junk foods, etc.), **toxemia** (brought on by the foregoing), irritation (caused by the poison), inflammation (the result of prolonged irritation), ulceration (inflammation causing the tissue to break out into "sores"), induration (hardening of the tissue) and, finally, cancer. To seek the cause of cancer through consideration of the end-product only (as is the prevailing procedure with popular cancer research), is like looking for the cause of man yet ignoring his embryonic life, conception, childhood, adolescence and manhood.

All symptoms of so-called diseases have but one origin. All diseases are one. Unity in all things is nature's plan. The human body is a wholistic entity and must be treated as such.

Herd Beliefs

Few, if any of us, realize what man's potential really would be if the handicaps with which he has handcuffed himself were removed. Many of these handicaps which stunt his growth are old beliefs and herd instincts.

The toxemic *philosophy is* founded upon the truth that there is no such thing as a cure. In this view, it disagrees radically with all the so-called curing systems. Every pretense or promise of cure in all lines of therapeutics is false. This cannot be grasped by all minds until sufficient thinking has been done so as to allow the idea to sink in. Convention and superstition now has the floor. And these enemies of progress and enlightenment are unwilling to sit down and listen to the other side. Many of us learn slowly, some not at all, still others of us are mentally put to sleep by truth.

There are ox cart minds in every generation. [Tilden has] confronted medical superstition of all kinds all [his] life. Many compliment [Tilden] on [his] clear reasoning on medical subjects. But just let [him] cross the border into their ethical, moral and theological preserves and they are both quick and vociferous in reminding [him] of [his] trespass. [Tilden's] own profession calls [him] an infidel—a word that fills the elect with abhorrence. But who is an infidel? Isn't he one who rejects a senseless convention? Didn't Christ repudiate the Pharisees?

The average mind prefers the old interpretation of words to any "new-fangled" definition. Until the world agrees on one dictionary, one Bible and one God, the tempest in the teapot of misunderstanding will continue to ebulliate…

Of course, God made man. He made everything. But why not find out just how He made him? Surely there is as much "glory to God" in discovering how man is made as there is in accepting an infantile interpretation which to date has taken us nowhere. When we understand how man is made, we shall begin to understand the laws of his being. And it will not be necessary for him to die of apoplexy, stone in the gall bladder or kidney, hardening of the arteries, or of any other so-called disease which is brought on through breaking the laws of his body and mind.

In doing our duty to our children, should we teach them the laws of their being and how to respect them? Or should we let them go on in the old way, break the laws of their being and ruin their health; then finally call a surgeon who will cut out "God's mistake"? Think it over. But if you're too fanatical to think, then pay a surgeon to cut out the *effects of* wrong living and let the cause continue.

Let Us Reason Together

Let us do a little homely reasoning. We are inclined to be awed by the word *infinite.* The *infinite is* limitless. But to our limited comprehension, it is a relative term and ambiguous. As we grow in experience, our once more restricted understanding takes on extended dimensions. Every person's understanding *of infinite is* restricted by his own imagination and awareness and varies from every other person's. We cannot think in terms *of* the limitless, and we should not try. But *if* we know the analysis *of* an atom *of* salt, we know the analysis *of* all the salt there is in the world.

This is true of all elements. If we know the analysis of a pound of butter, we know the analysis of all butter. If we know everything about one man, then we understand everything about all men. This micro-macro analogy—that the small unit is created on the same pattern as the larger unit, or that man is created in God's image and likeness—is the major key in our understanding of the universe and of the world around us.

So we should keep our feet on the ground—stay on earth—and be satisfied that all worlds are like our own.

How to Measure the Infinite

So we see how it is that through the intensive study of a part we learn about the larger whole. If we know everything about one disease, we know everything about all diseases.

When we tell the reader about **toxemia,** then he should know about all diseases. For **toxemia** is the basic cause of all diseases.

Instead of beginning at the top of any subject, we should start at the beginning. But en route on our journey from *cause* to *effect,* we may encounter some road blocks. Let us recognize that we all view the world through our own unique structure of information and belief, which we have come to regard as being true. But let some new information come along which shatters our preconceptions! Then our entire outlook is shaken at its roots, our house of belief is divided against itself, and we fall into confusion. Now it becomes necessary to readjust our thinking if we would conform with this new knowledge. Now comes the important decision. Either we timidly decide not to "upset the applecart" and to live in doubt concerning the knowable, accepting the unknowable based upon the prejudice and bias of "the faith of our fathers." Or we make the bold decision to restructure our "house of knowledge" so as to include this new information, however devastating. And we plunge fearlessly ahead in pursuit of Truth (some may prefer to call this God) "come hell or high-water."

Every truth squares itself with every other truth. Every department of science and reason blends into a unit. The laws of life are those of the cosmos. The laws of the universe are the laws of God. Every step must be a block of truth or God, the goal, will be sidestepped. Behold the head-on collision of the Christian world and the wholesale massacre that took place during the First World War. All this was due to undigested truth. The world is full of truth. But mental indigestion, due to bad habits and wrong food combinations, is universal.

Many think they know what [Tilden] means when [he] uses the word **toxemia**, having referred to the dictionary for its definition. But let those who would know the meaning look here—not in the dictionary.

Toxemia, the Basic Cause of All So-Called Diseases

So as to clarify our understanding and make our thinking more precise, let us compare definitions.

A Standard Dictionary definition reads: *"Toxin Poisoning—Toxin: Any of a class of poisonous compounds of animal, bacterial and vegetable origin—and poisonous ptomaine."*

On the other hand, a good definition of **toxemia** and **crises of toxemia** might read: *In the process of tissue-building (metabolism), there is cell-building (anabolism) and cell—destruction (catabolism). The broken-down tissue is toxic. In the healthy body (when nerve energy is normal), this toxic material is eliminated from the blood as fast as it is evolved. But when nerve energy is dissipated from any cause (such as physical or mental excitement or bad habits) the body becomes weakened or enervated. When the body is enervated, elimination is checked. This, in turn, results in a retention of toxin in the blood—the condition which we speak of as toxemia. This state produces a crisis (which is really nothing more than heroic or extraordinary efforts by the body to eliminate waste or toxin from the blood). It is this crisis which we term disease. Such accumulation of toxin, when once established, will continue until nerve energy has been restored to normal by removing the cause. So-called* **disease** *is nature's effort to eliminate toxin from the blood. All so-called* **diseases** *are* **crises of toxemia.**

It is important to note that **toxemia** does not really occur until after poison has entered the bloodstream—in other words, **toxemia** results only when the normal eliminative functions fail to carry off the **toxic** waste so as to maintain that balance which is required for health. Putrescent food resulted in ptomaine poisoning only when the eliminative functions failed to carry off the **toxicity.** Food or poison in the intestines is still on the outside of the body. A suppurating wound, ulcer or chancre is on the outside of the body (outside of the bloodstream). If septic (blood) poisoning occurs, it will be because the waste products are not allowed to drain—to escape. Even vaccine fails to produce septic poisoning because its poison is discharged on the surface—outside of the body. Occasionally the waste products are forced to enter the blood because of faulty dressings; then septic poisoning and death follow.

The Deadly Germ

It should not be forgotten that unobstructed, free drainage from wounds, ulcers, canals or ducts keeps them nonpoisonous. The *deadly germ* on the hands, lips, drinking cups, hanging straps of street cars—in fact, wherever found—is not deadly until it gets mixed up with man's deadly and filthy physical and mental habits. There are people who cannot be taught cleanliness; they either scrub their bodies raw or neglect them to the point of ripe fetor. It is an art to wear clothes and maintain a state of cleanliness conducive to health. Venereal and skin diseases, including the eruptive fevers, are fostered by clothes. There is something more than prejudice, fanaticism or partisanship behind my reiterated allusions to the congeneric relationship of syphilis, vaccination and smallpox. This relationship would have been discovered long ago had it not been for the big-time, big business commercialization of vaccine. Is it likely for a multimillion dollar industry which yields huge profits to become convinced that they are engaged in the wholesale syphilization of the population? Such would not be in keeping with our worship at the altar of profit-making.

The *deadly germ* must be mixed with retained, pent-up waste products before it becomes metamorphosed into its deadly **toxic** state. The dog or other animal licks the germ from his wound. When the "deadly germ" is asculated into the mouth and from there into the stomach, it is digested and eliminated. The normal secretions of the body, both outside and inside, are more than enough to do away with all the "deadly germs" which fall to the lot of each person.

Normal persons are deadly to all germs and to all parasites which are peculiar to the human habitat.

Normal people are equipped to handle the problems of life head-on. They have innate and built-in resources which, if exercised properly, will get them out of every difficult situation. Immunization and vicarious atonement are both cowardly dodges—a vain effort to avoid confronting the problems of life in a manly fashion.

Were we to recognize, as we should, that our troubles are of our own making, then we would not waste our time or stunt our growth by looking for some man or some vaccine which will absolve us from our sins. Truth exposes the germ fallacy.

"Cures" and immunization are the products of a civilization that does not civilize. Creedal religion is a "cure" and an immunization for those who would be good if evil did not betide them.

Self-control and a knowledge of the limitations of privileges brings to us the best in life. Then, if we are content to live in one world at a time and to meet our problems as they come, we shall have the best preparation for the tomorrows. If we live well today—live for the health of mind and body—we need not worry about germs that may come tomorrow… They do not know that the fear which they inculcate is more to be dreaded than the object of their warning. Fear does a thousand times more harm than any other one cause of toxemia.

Nature goes her limit in the prevention of absorption of any and all poisons. The indurated wall built at the base of ulceration is a conservative measure—it is to prevent absorption. In matters of prevention, nature sometimes goes too far and builds tumors and induration so dense as to obstruct circulation. Then degeneration takes place with slow absorption of the septic matter. This poisoning takes place very insidiously. It is called cachexia and among the names given to this pathology are syphilis, cancer, or (if of the lungs) tuberculosis.

This may be thought a great digression from toxemia. But, as all pathological roads lead to Rome—the unity of all diseases, no apology is necessary.

The Medical World Still Looks for "Cures "

The medical world still looks for "cures" for disease, notwithstanding the obvious fact that Nature makes her own repairs. All that Nature requires is an opportunity for exercising her own wonderful faculties for self-healing.

A few years ago a sick doctor offered a million dollars for a cure for cancer. If he had known the cause of *all* disease instead of having been "scientifically" educated, he would not have died. Cancer is the culmination of years of abuse of nutrition and of years of toxemia which resulted from faulty elimination. Forcing the bowels to move is an old and conventional method for so-called elimination. This gets rid of the accumulation in the bowels by causing an extra amount of water to be thrown out by the kidneys and bowels. But this forcing measure adds to enervation through overstimulation. Furthermore, elimination proper (e.g., the elimination of waste products from the blood, the source of all disease-producing toxins) is inhibited. The most powerful and best method for eliminating is through a fast. In other words, let Nature rest, for she needs no so-called "cures." To rest means: *stay in bed, keep a poised mind and body, and fast.* Nature works without handicaps. Do not let fear created by the old fear-mongers poison your mind by such spurious and miscreant threats as, *It is dangerous to fast. You may never live through it.* Alas, these bewildered and befuddled wiseacres do not even know the vast difference which exists between fasting and starving!

Here is a rejoinder which you might save for those killjoys who are afraid to allow their patients to fast: *You know, or think you do, that people who are forced to stay in bed because of injury never do well and that this is especially true of old people. But why is this true?* **Only because they are overfed.**

Germs as a Cause for Disease

Germs as a cause of disease is a dying fallacy. The bacteriological deadmarch is on and those with their ears to the ground can hear it. Intuition is forcing the active medical minds to fortify against the com-ing revulsion. And they are buckling on the armor of endocrinology. Endocrinology, focal infection, autogenous and synthetic remedies, vaccine and serum immunization are some of the high points in the science of medicine today. But there is a lack of fundamental unity to the system, and nature abhors chaos just as much as she does a vacuum.

Toxemia accepts the germ (organized ferment) just as it does the enzyme (unorganized ferment). Both are necessary to health.

[Tidlen's] theories have received but little attention except from plagiarists. Only a few, a very few, physicians know what [Tilden] stands for. These few, however, are enthusiastic and have proved to their own satisfaction that the theory has a universal application. Many *attempt* to work **toxemia** along with their own little two-by-four pet curing system (a means of "petting" personal pride), but it will not work. **Toxemia** is big enough for the best in any man.

What more can be asked by any physician than a philosophy of cause that gives a perfect understanding of the origin for all so-called disease? To know *cause* supplies even laymen with a dependable method for correction—an "immunization" which truly "immunizes." Dependable knowledge is man's salvation. When this may be had for as little effort as is required for a thorough understanding of the *philosophy of toxemia,* there is little excuse for any man, be he layman or professional, to remain in ignorance.

Toxin, the poisonous cause for toxemia, is a product of metabolism. It is constantly generated. But when nerve energy is normal, the toxin is eliminated as fast as it is produced.

The body is strong or weak, as the case may be, depending entirely upon whether the nerve energy is strong or weak. And it should be remembered that the functions of the body are carried on well or badly according to the amount of nerve energy generated.

Importance of Nerve Energy

Without nerve energy, the functions of the various organs of the body cannot be carried on. Secretions are necessary for preparing the building-up material to take the place of worn-out tissue. The worn-out tissue must be removed—eliminated—from the blood as fast as it is formed or it accumulates and the system is poisoned for this is **toxic.** This is a most important source of enervation.

Elimination of the waste products of tissue-building is just as necessary as the building-up process. These two important functions depend upon each other, and both depend upon the proper amount of nerve energy to do their job well. It behooves all people who would enjoy life and health to the full to understand how they may conserve their nerve energy, how they may learn to live conservatively and prudently. In this way, they will enjoy the greatest mental and physical efficiency and the longest life.

To the ignorant, thoughtless and sensual, these suggestions and advice may seem unnecessary—to be the preachments of a crotchety person. But it is the writer's belief that the more sober and thoughtful will welcome this knowledge. For this will help them to master both themselves and life. So far the masses have trusted their health and life to a profession that has failed to make good. Is not this self-evident, when the so-called masters of that profession are even now looking for the cause of disease? And is it not equally obvious that until the cause of disease is found, no dependable advice may be given for its avoidance?

Sixty-seven years of independent thinking, unbiased by sect or creed, have enabled me to discover the true cause of disease. And it is so simple that even a child can learn to protect himself against the alleged "diseases peculiar to children."

"These are times that try men's souls," said Tom Paine long ago. But if he were here now, perhaps he would change the line to read, "These are times that try men's nerves." Nerve energy and good money are the commodities that are spent very rapidly these days. Chasing the dollar causes great waste of energy; but it has been chased so much that it has developed wanderlust. Wanderlust is developed to such a degree that men enervate themselves catching up with a few dollars; they prostrate themselves upon the altar of money. There are many ways to use up nerve energy. All of us should strive to conserve all the nerve energy possible so as to meet the extraordinary demands of our harrowing 20th century.

Many bodies will become bankrupt before our nervous system adopts to the unparalleled demands of our Modern Age. Without nerve energy, the functions of the body cannot be carried on properly. Present day stress brings on enervation which, in turn, checks elimination. Then the resultant, retained toxins cause toxemia.

Everything which acts upon the body uses up energy. Even cold and heat require expenditure of nerve energy to adjust the body to these changes.

After middle life, those who would keep well and live to an old age should exercise care to keep warm and to avoid chilling of the body. Gourmandizing must be given up and self-restraint practiced in all of life's activities. Allowing the feet to be cold for any length of time or allowing the body to become chilled when a topcoat would have prevented it illustrate "leaks" which speedily drain away nerve energy.

As no provision is made for possible extra demands on energy at any given time, it becomes a matter of critical importance to learn how to conserve our nerve resources and how to build up more.

Conservation of Energy—The Greatest Step to Health Recovery

Now that [it has been] pointed out that **enervation** is the source of the only disease, **toxemia**, to which mankind is heir, it is easy to understand why the so-called "science" of medicine, as currently practiced, actually *causes* enervation. As such, it builds disease rather than correcting or ameliorating man's sufferings. Every so-called "cure" in its very nature causes enervation. Even drugs used to relieve pain wind up by causing greater pain and, sometimes, killing. Drugs used to relieve cough in pneumonia sometimes prove fatal. Removing stones from the gallbladder does not remove *cause*, for more stones form.

Rest from habits that enervate is the only way to give Nature an opportunity for healing. Sleep and rest of body and mind are necessary if the energy-level is to be maintained. Few people in active life rest enough.

Why Enervation Is the Cause But Not the Disease

Enervation per se is not disease. Enervation causes a slowdown in the elimination of tissue waste, causing toxic material to accumulate. The blood becomes charged with toxin, and we call this toxemia—poison in the blood. This is disease. When the toxin accumulates beyond the toleration point, a crisis takes place, which simply means that the body is eliminating the poison. We call the crisis disease, but it is not. The only disease is toxemia. What we call diseases are merely the symptoms produced as the body strives through heroic and extraordinary means to force the toxin through the mucous membrane.

When elimination takes place through the mucous membrane of the nose, it is called a cold—catarrh of the nose. When these crises are repeated for years, the mucous membrane thickens and ulcerates and the bones enlarge, closing the passage, etc. At this stage, hay fever or hay asthma develops. When the throat and tonsils or any of the respiratory passages become the seat of the crises of *toxemia*, we have croup, tonsillitis, pharyngitis, laryngitis, bronchitis, pneumonia,

etc. What is in a name? All are symptoms of the expulsion of toxin in the blood at the different points named and are essentially of the same character. All so-called diseases are merely crises of *toxemia* and evolve from just one cause—*toxemia.*

This description of *crises of toxemia* may be extended to every organ of the body. For any organ that is enervated below the average standard—from stress or habit, from work or worry, from injury or from whatever cause—may become the location of crises of *toxemia.* Symptoms vary according to the location of the crisis. From this observation we have come to the erroneous conclusion that each symptom-complex is a separate and distinct disease. Let these pages help dispel the abysmal darkness which has engulfed our population and the medical profession. Let the *philosophy of toxemia* bring us to the only rational conclusion possible: *that every symptom—complex goes back to one and only one cause for all so—called diseases—TOXEMIA.*

Let us "pound away" with more illustrations and detail so that this "disease"-freeing information will penetrate both the conscious and the subconscious minds. Let us attempt to throw off the crippling chains of slavery to a false and disease-causing doctrine—that specious concept of remedies and "cures." Only then will we be ready to build for ourselves through the unfettered means of the natural powers within us both new bodies and new minds.

The symptoms that are called *gastritis* (catarrh of the stomach) are very unlike the symptoms of cystitis (catarrh of the urinary bladder). Yet both are caused by crises of *toxemia.* Each is but a different location for the extraordinary and heroic efforts by the body to eliminate toxin from the blood.

It should be obvious to the discerning how completely illogical it is to treat catarrh of the nose as a local disease. Or to conclude, when these crises are repeated until ulceration takes place and the mucous membrane becomes so sensitive that rust and pollen produce the sneezing which we identify as *hay fever,* that these symptoms are actually a separate disease caused by pollen. Isn't it obvious that rest and total abstinence from food, liquid and solid (not water, of course) and changing our enervating habits will restore nerve energy? Then the elimination of toxin through *natural* (rather than *extraordinary)* channels will take place, and full health will return. And this state of health will remain permanent if only the erstwhile victim of hay fever or other so-called disease will not wander from the path but instead stick with his reformed life-style.

The first elimination of toxin through the nose is called a cold. When this elimination is continuous with exacerbation, then toxin crises (fresh colds) and occasionally ulceration takes place. Then bony spurs may form and hay fever develops. All are symptoms of toxin elimination. The *cause* is the same from the first cold to hay fever. The catarrhal discharge which continues throughout the interims of fresh colds (crises of *toxemia*) is chronic catarrh and is named as such in medical literature. Deluded practitioners treat this locally as if it were an independent, fiendish entity, when the real truth is that the victim of so-called *chronic catarrh* keeps his system enervated by tobacco, alcohol, sugar and sweets of all kinds, coffee, tea, excessive eating of butter and bread, too much rich cooking, excessive eating of all kinds, too much sensual pleasure, etc.

Keeping the system enervated prevents full reestablishment of eliminative channels through the normal excretory organs. As time passes, the body becomes more tolerant of toxin. The "catching cold" propensity abates, and there are fewer crises of *toxemia* (colds). A greater number of the mucous membranes are requisitioned by the body to carry out extraordinary elimination (elimination through other than the normal channels). The entire body starts to deteriorate. So-called chronic diseases begin to manifest. In catarrh of the stomach, the mucous membrane takes on thickening, hardening, ulceration and cancer (all of which

are described in medical literature as so many different and distinct diseases!). But these symptoms are no more separated from their *one* cause than was President Washington derived from a different source from the boy George who cut down his father's cherry tree. Cancer was once the symptom-complex of a so-called cold. As the *philosophy of toxemia* explains, it grew to its final malignant stature through many crises of *toxemia.* The changing symptoms were merely the result of organic degeneration brought on by repeated crises of *toxemia.*

Every so-called disease has the same inception, evolution and maturity. Different symptoms result only because toxemic crises affect different organs of the body.

Treating the various symptom- complexes as distinct entities is fully as scientific and sensible as would be the salving of a dog's tail for its sore ear.

All diseases are the same fundamentally.

The cause traces back to toxemia which was caused when enervation prevented the normal eliminative system from performing its full function. Enervating habits of body and mind are the primary reasons for depleted energy—enervation.

Every chronic disease starts with toxemia and a toxemic crisis. These crises are repeated until organic change or degeneration takes place. The chain of symptoms which range from cold to catarrh to Bright's disease, to tuberculosis, cancer, syphilis, ataxia and all the other so-called diseases from beginning to end are all, each and every one, just the end-symptoms of the cumulative effects of crises of toxemia...

The Causes of Enervation

To understand disease, we must know the **cause.** Since **toxemia** is the **cause** of all disease and since **enervation** is the **cause of toxemia,** it behooves all who are sick and want to get well and all who are well and want to stay well to know what causes **enervation.**

A normal, healthy person is one who is poised (self-controlled) and who has no nerve-destroying habits. A self-controlled man is a man who is not kicked by habits, cuffed or driven.

Man is either the master of himself, or else his appetites and sensual desires are his master. If the former is true, then he enjoys health until worn out, and this should not occur before from ninety to one hundred and fifty years of age. If he is disposed to sensual activities yet has his habits more or less under control, he may live from sixty to ninety years. But if he is a sensualist, one who is controlled by his habits and passions, the story is a different one. He may sit up after bedtime to take a last smoke or to eat a lunch, he may get up in the night and smoke ([Tilden] knew a celebrated physician who used tobacco to secure sleep; he died at fifty-four years of age), or who takes a drink to quiet his nerves and make him sleep, or who goes the limit venereally—that man becomes irritable, grouchy and dies prematurely.

Excess transforms a man into a disgusting brute. The word brute is used here to express the state of one who is devoid of self-control. Those who begin with fine constitutions are often converted into neurotics who have left health and comfort far behind. For such, so-called comfort may mean only short periods at the best and these only through the influence of drugs or stimulants…

Just as with infants and children, many physical "diseases" of the worst possible description find their origin in subjective or psychological states or from the mistaken practices of our society. So that these prime causes for enervation and hence disease may be better understood and thus avoided, let us consider some examples and their consequences.

Overwork is said to enervate, but behind this charade lurk many bad habits who are the real killers rather than work itself. It is work done without the pleasure which comes from accomplishment which is the true enervator and disease-builder. Frustrations which originate from an unsatisfied mind, a desire for other duties before mastering the duties in which actually engaged, a desire for more pay without actually possessing a real desire to perform efficiently. We should work with our creative instincts. Just as we are created in the image of our Creator, so is our work in many ways an image of ourselves. Work should be performed for the joy of creation—not just for the sake of mere emoluments.

Dissatisfaction and overworked emotions are enervating. Worry, fear, grief, anger, passion, temper, over-joy, depression, dissatisfaction, self-pity, pride, egotism, envy, jealousy, gossip, lying, dishonesty, failing to meet obligations and appointments, taking advantage of misunderstandings, abusing the credulity of friends, or abusing the confidence of those who confide in us—all enervate and in time build chronic disease.

Business Worries. Business worries are a source of enervation. But the business—any business—is not in itself the cause for the worry. A work well done is a delight, and constructive work which delights is character-building. Similarly, work which is slovenly performed dissatisfies; but the slovenly worker rarely looks within himself to find the true cause of his discontent. It is our mode of living which brings on enervation with disease as its sequel. Worries looking for a "cure" generally look in the wrong place—only to produce more enervation. Business is what a man makes of it. A thorough understanding of business accompanied by honesty and industry removes worries and saves nerve energy. Worry does not create efficiency. Nor is inefficiency removed by worrying. Worry, lack of control over emotions, improper eating, stimulants—all build disease.

Nothing produces more poise than a thorough understanding of one's personal habits and occupation. Bluff and bluster might create an illusion of efficiency for awhile; but, as surely as the chickens come home to roost, the truth will out. Worry, even though camouflaged by a serene exterior, will ultimately cause a worker to break down and disease will be his lot.

Housewives who carry a burden of worry become enervated and lose health. Causes for their worry are found in the lack of control of the emotions, improper eating, bad care of the body, and inefficiency. Instead of resolutely going to work to remove defects, we are often drowned by them. An uncontrolled temper will sooner or later down its owner. Gossip is not an admirable quality; and, unless overcome, it will in time drive friends away. Envy and jealousy are cancers which eat out the soul of those who indulge them. What is left to love when the soul is gone?

When anyone, from indolence and health destroying habits, allows himself to gravitate below the standards expected of him by his friends, he should not be surprised if they run away from him.

Loneliness. Who are the people who are left alone? Often these are people who have lived selfish lives, people who have demanded entertainment when they should have been entertaining themselves. Happiness and entertainment must come from within-from a love of service, work and books. If this fountain of youth and pleasure is not found before old age creeps over us, we shall find ourselves alone. Even in the midst of a throng, we shall be alone, forever alone. What could be more pathetic?

Self-Indulgence. Self-indulgence is contrary to ethics and brings condemnation. What about the ethics of gluttons, what about their religion? Excess in everything follows on the heels of abnormal selfish indulgence. Coming under this heading are self-pity and vainly seeking for a "cure." We must take our deficiencies upon our own shoulders and acknowledge them fairly and squarely. Extravagant habits, even if there seems to be an inexhaustible supply of energy, ultimately produces a self-destructive morale. From this, like a relentless nemesis, runs the trail to premature death. Causes of death are given such names as heart disease, apoplexy, paralysis, kidney disease or suicide, but what is in a name? Such names only obscure the true cause which is, first, last and all the time, a selfish body and mind which has wrought its own retribution through destructive self-indulgence.

A study of Nature produces the illuminating truth that man, to long endure, must live for service—not through giving alms but through helping others to help themselves.

Self-indulgence in the use of stimulants, even in moderation, is a constant drain upon the nervous system. A time arrives when the last cigar, the last cup of coffee, or the last hearty meal snaps the vital cord. But why should this ending always be unexpected and a surprise?

Grief. Grief is enervating. Those who are weak and toxemic may be so prostrated by grief (unless put to bed, kept warm and quiet, and withheld food) that their own life may also be forfeited. Food taken under conditions of grief does not digest, but rather acts as a poison. Some people are made invalids for life by a great grief.

Shock. Shock, mental or physical, may prove so enervating as to kill by heart failure or to produce a permanent nervous condition. Wrong eating or overeating may prevent a return to health.

The shell shock which many soldiers suffered during the First World War was often converted into permanent invalidism through such enervating habits as tobacco or overeating.

Anger. Anger is very enervating. A daily shock of anger produces profound enervation. Tempers which "fly-off" at the slightest provocation ruin digestion and create nervousness. Unless controlled, epilepsy may evolve and cancer may end life. The chronic grouch is likely to build an ulcer or cancer of the stomach. Rheumatic arthritis, hardening of the arteries, gall-stones and premature old age may all come as the consequence of an undisciplined temper.

Egotism. Because of his self-love, selfishness, misanthropy and distrust, the egotist sees unfriendliness in all the acts of others—every hand is against him. This causes **enervation and toxemia** which lead on to many nervous derangements and even insanity. A misanthrope loves himself above everything and before everybody. The moment he breaks with his nearest and dearest friend, that friend's head comes off, figuratively speaking. The egotist hates all who fail to feed his vanity. Hate and anger are always on top, even when draped with a mocking smile when finesse or stratagem demands. Friendship, honor, and veracity all depart when self-interest is impinged upon or neglected. Men of this type have no gratitude. They demand everything and give nothing without an ulterior motive. Mild egotism may not go beyond a disagreeable or overbearing selfishness.

Selfishness. A selfish nature always looks after himself first. A common type of selfishness is interpreted as love of children. But when a son or daughter marries against the father's wish, disinheritance follows. Why? Because ambition or self-love is piqued. So-called love is more often selfish ambition than true affection. Such selfishness leads on to *enervation* and *toxemia.*

Ambition. Ambition of a selfish type brings on ill health, for it meets with so many disappointments. Even successful ambitions produce fruits which are often used to gratify sensual appetites thereby bringing on more disease. **Noble ambition** goes with self-control and service to mankind; health and long life are two of its rewards. But ambition for display and ostentation gives only evanescent gratification which dissolves like a rainbow-hued soap bubble and leaves behind an expensive bill in the form of wasted nerve energy.

Thousands of semi-invalid women bring on **toxemic crises as** their reward for giving dinners and an egotistic display of dress, home and furnishings. Women gratify such silly, stupid ambitions and pay for their thrills with broken health. Many waste more energy at an afternoon card party than they can renew in a week.

Envy. A begrudging nature is typical of envy of a low and disease-producing type. The man who possesses this kind of envy is a vandal. Given an opportunity, he will slip a monkey wrench into the machinery of those whom he envies—He will poison reputations by innuendo.

Who steals my purse steals trash: 'tis something, nothing; 'Twas mine, 'tis his, and has been slave to thousands; But he who filches from me my good name Robs me of that which not enriches him, And makes me poor indeed.
—Shakespeare.

When it is safe to do so, such a person will wreak even bodily harm against those whose merit towers over his. Contrasting to such despicable sentiment is a praise-worthy desire to equal the accomplishments of one admired. To rejoice in the success of others and to strive **to equal them** through success achieved by merit—such noble aspirations build a sound mind and a healthy body.

Love and Jealousy. According to Solomon, "Love is strong as death; jealousy is as cruel as the grave." Solomon should have known.

Shakespeare knew just about everything worth knowing up to his time. He said:

How many fools serve maddened jealousy! The venomed clamors of a jealous woman Poison more deadly than a mad dog's tooth.

The systemic poisoning of overwrought emotions has been known since reasoning began. But, aside from knowing that "a poison is generated in the system" from great anger, jealousy, hate and grief, the *modus operandi* has never been satisfactorily explained. Now this is made clear through the **philosophy of toxemia.** That the pathology of jealousy was clearly understood by Shakespeare is clearly evidenced by the words which he puts into the mouths of some of his characters.

Excessive emotion—jealousy, for example, or great anger—precipitates a profound enervation which inhibits elimination. This floods the blood with toxin and brings on a malignant *toxemia* in the form of toxin drunkenness; this, when occurring in people of a belligerent nature, causes them to run *amuck.* Murder, even several murders, are sometimes committed. Gentler natures may end the psychological storm through suicide.

Jealousy and unrequited love, when developing in a vicious, unmoral subject, may in time undermine the constitution through gradually increasing the state of *enervation* and *toxemia.* Catarrhal inflammations become worse with no hope of final recovery until the causes of enervation are overcome—namely, enervating habits of mind and body, of which jealousy is the chief.

A French sheepherder's daughter, being opposed by her father in marrying a lover, killed the parent while he slept by the campfire. A short time after the tragedy, some men came upon the camp and discovered the girl eating her father's heart which she had cut up and roasted in the fire. When discovered at her cannibalistic feast, she held up what was left of the heart and with a sardonic laugh declared, "He broke my heart and I am eating his."

Only a short time ago, the overwrought nerves of a jazz and alcohol-crazed girl forced her to kill her mother because the latter sought to oppose her subconscious demands for more stimulation.

When *enervation* and *toxemia* have reached such a peak as is typified by the two girls mentioned above, then civil and moral laws abdicate to subconscious laws. These, like cosmic law and order, are unmoral but run true to necessity. Psychological like physical cyclones are exceptions to the regular order. Yet they are true to basic laws of nature. Such savage powers, when aroused, have no scruples to gainsay. And they tear through order as ruthlessly as fiends.

Drunkenness. Prohibition was a beautiful ideal, but it merely substituted one social disease for another even greater. What mother would not rather have her son brought home from the corner grogship drunk than to see him escorted to jail handcuffed to a policeman?

Enervation and *toxemia,* when focused on the brain, bring out neurotic states with all kinds of symptom—complexes. Drunkenness substitutes for bank robbery and other outlawry. So long as food drunkenness retains its prestige with the professions (prescribed by doctors, babbled to us on Sundays, and deciding our brawls on Mondays), it will take more than statutes to enforce law and order. Most of our laws are made while the lawmakers themselves are drunk on food and tobacco.

Drunkenness and crime of all kinds are extraordinary modes of toxin elimination— ***Crises of toxemia.*** Enforcing temperance or control of crime are bound to fail in their objectives until we learn to restyle our lives in harmony with the laws of nature. This should be obvious to the student of nature. Wants are based upon subconscious needs. Sentiment or ethics have nothing to do with them. Our subconscious is neither moral nor immoral. It belongs to the Great Cosmos which is systematic, perfect in order, but unmoral. Intemperances of any kind force unnatural needs which, if not satisfied in the usual manner, may reap the whirlwind. Surgeons, laws and anodynes may perhaps relieve **effects.** But true health restoration *must* be based upon removing **causes.** Laws and drugs are quack remedies. The only true remedy is self-control. To gain poise and self-control, we must learn to understand the need. Then we may justly aspire for truly successful lives which are lived in harmony with the laws of nature.

Overeating and Gluttony. Overeating is a common and universal enervating habit; eating too much fat in creams, butter, fat meats, oils, rich pastries and sweets; eating too often; eating between meals; and checking the process of digestion by water-drinking between meals.

Food inebriety is more common than alcohol inebriety. The subconscious is as busy as a hive of bees substituting, antidoting, and in repairs; in substituting one stimulating excess for another (demanding whiskey, tobacco, opium, etc. as a substitute for gluttonous eating); in requiring thrills, shocks and sensual excesses as a result of food poisoning.

Ungratified sense demands are often appeased through food excesses or other stimulants. Then, goaded by nature as a consequence of self-poisoning, the harried victim of his own acts may run amuck.

The gluttonous build putrefaction in the bowels. Nerve energy is used up resisting systemic infection. The supply of blood needed for the surface of the body for the purposes of warmth is diverted to the mucous membrane of the gastrointestinal canal to neutralize poisonous material which is about to enter the system. The mucous membrane becomes turgid with blood, establishing a mucorrhea (excessive secretion of mucus). This is what we call catarrh. This secretion mechanically obstructs absorption of putrescence and also antidotes the poison from bringing the antibodies from the blood.

A battle royal is going on all the time in the intestines of the gluttonous. The subconscious rallies all the help it can muster. Finally, when the system is drained of its self—generated antidotes, the victim is sent by his subconscious to find alcohol, tobacco, coffee, tea, condiments and more food. Moral preachments and the prohibitory laws which are passed by solons who are drunk on toxin, bowel putrescence and tobacco result in ethical and legal monstrosities-unsightly miscreations who are whelped from the perversions of nutrition!

A driving desire for food three times a day spells **enervation.** Trouble is only a short distance away. The wise will take note and correct their appetites and their intake.

Perverted appetites are built by overeating, by eating rich food until appreciation is lost for staple or plain food, by the use of stimulants (alcohol, tobacco, coffee and tea), through using butter, salt, pepper and rich dressings, as a consequence of eating when we are not hungry (real hunger will take the plainest foods with relish), or eating when sick or uncomfortable, or eating at off hours or between meals, or just from eating too much.

Gossip. Gossips are always slanderers. Slanderers are always and forever potential liars. If they do not know that they are broadcasting lies, they are criminally careless in not endeavoring to find out whether the tale they are spreading is true of not. Gossip *enervates the gossiper.*

Gossips are always enervated for they live in fear of being discovered. Their secretions are always acid. They are inclined to pyorrhea and mucous membrane infections. They are slow to recover from catarrhal **crises of toxemia.**

Gossips are empty-headed slaves to their habits of slander and spite. They are malignant parasites which feed upon carrion. They are the lowest type of criminal-hell monsters who kill with their breath. They often die of cancer.

Sycophancy. Flatterers look like friends, as wolves like dogs (Byron). He hurts me most who lavishly commends (Churchill).

A real sycophant, like all people who are not honest, lives a life which enervates and which nature condemns early.

Dishonesty. Dishonesty eventually hardens the arteries. Then cancer terminates a miserable existence.

Religiosity. This is defined as the *morbidly pious,* who yet practice some of the foregoing described habits. The ending, again, is premature death.

A saving religion (be that Christian, Jewish, Moslem, Taoist, Shintoist, Buddhist, or what-have-you) could be described as one which frees the adherent from mental and physical habits which over-stimulate, enervate and intoxicate.

There is only one way to get rid of toxemia. We must rid ourselves of our enervating habits. Nothing else will work-be they "cures," prayers, drugs, surgery or whatever nostrum-honest or dishonest. Cause must be removed. Get rid of the cause and adopt a lifestyle which keeps you permanently free. Then health will return and abide perpetually." [3]

It should be added that, in these times, nutritional deficiencies and excesses (eating too much highly processed food) play much larger roles in illness than they did in Tilden's day.

References

[1] Cordingley, E. W. *Principles and Practice of Naturopathy.* Reprint from Health Research, Mokelumne Hill (CA), written 1924.

[2] Lahn, H. *Iridology: The Diagnosis of the Eye,* 6th ed. Kosomos Publishing, Evanston (IL), 1914.

[3] Tilden, J. H. *Toxemia Explained.* Reprint by Life Science Institute, Manchaca (TX), written circa 1926.

The Tree of Toxemia

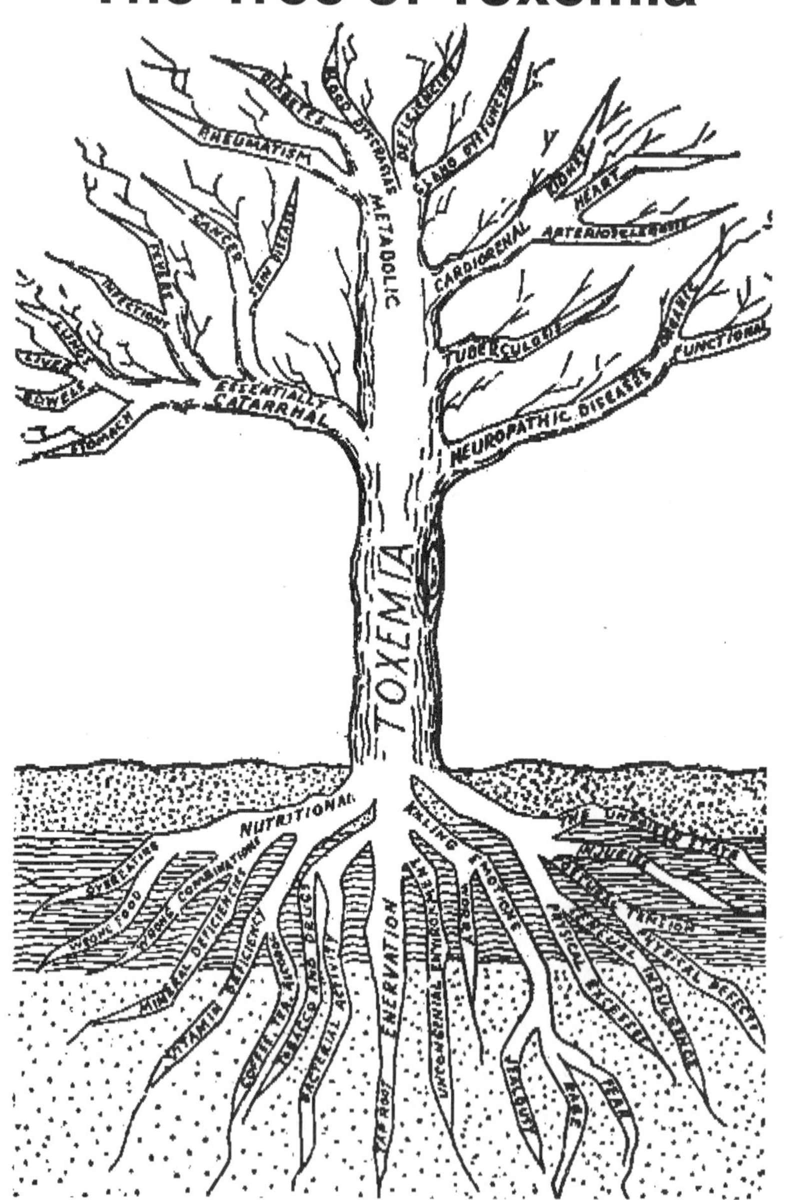

I have seen similar trees (showing causes of disease) in other writings. It may be that this analogy was developed from the story of the "Tree of Good and Evil" in Genesis or perhaps not. Either way, this tree shows how Tilden viewed toxemia as a cause of disease. I should also add that I have no idea what religion Dr. Tilden practiced and that I do not share several of his views that some would refer to as religious. I do however, like the fact that as best as he could, he gave detailed thoughts about how disease forms. Naturopaths do not just deal with symptoms—we are always looking for causes.

4 Laws of "Cure"

How do people become better? Natural health practitioners have had several ideas about how the body improves, which many of old referred to as the "laws of cure."

This first section was written by H. Lindlahr, a medical doctor who promoted natural therapies,

"This brings us to the consideration of acute inflammatory and feverish diseases. From what has been said, it follows that inflammation and fever are not primary, but **secondary** manifestations of disease. No form of inflammatory disease can arise in the system unless there is present some handicap to health which Nature is endeavoring to overcome and to get rid of. On this fact in Nature is based [the] claim to be the fundamental law of cure.

"Give me fever and I can cure every disease." Thus Hippocrates, the "Father of Medicine," formulated the fundamental Law of Cure over two thousand years ago. ...this law [is expressed] in the following statement: **Every acute disease is the result of a cleansing and healing effort of Nature.**

This law, thoroughly understood and applied in the treatment of diseases, will eventually do for medical science what the discovery of other natural laws has done for physics, astronomy, chemistry and other exact sciences. It will, by demonstrating the unity of disease and treatment, transform the medical empiricism and confusion of the past and present into an exact science.

Making a general application of the law, we deduce that all acute diseases, from a simple cold to measles, scarlet fever, diphtheria, smallpox, pneumonia, etc., represent Nature's efforts to remove from the system some form of morbid matter, virus or poison dangerous to health and life. In other words, acute diseases cannot develop in a perfectly normal, healthy body living under conditions favorable to human life. The question may be asked: If acute diseases represent Nature's healing efforts, why is it that people die as a result of them? The answer to this is: the vitality may be too low, the injury or morbid encumbrance too great, or the treatment may be inadequate or harmful, so that Nature loses the fight; still acute diseases represent an effort of Nature to remove the causes of disease and thus to reestablish normal, healthy conditions.

It is a curious fact that this fundamental principle of Nature Cure and Law of Nature has been acknowledged and corroborated by medical science. The most advanced works on pathology admit the constructive and beneficial character of inflammation. However, when it comes to the **treatment** of acute diseases, physicians seem to forget entirely this basic principle of pathology and treat inflammation and fever as though they were, in themselves, inimical and destructive to health and life.

From this inconsistency in theory and practice arises all the errors of allopathic medical treatment. Failure to understand this fundamental law of cure accounts for the confusion on the part of exponents of the different schools of healing science, and for the greater part of human suffering.

Nature Cure philosophy never loses sight of the fundamental law of cure. While allopathy regards acute disease conditions as in themselves harmful and hostile to health and life, as something to be "cured" (we say it suppressed") by drug, ice or knife, the Nature Cure School regards these forcible house cleanings as beneficial and necessary—so long as human beings continue to disregard Nature's laws. While, through its simple, natural methods of treatment, Nature Cure easily modifies the course of inflammatory and feverish processes and keeps them within safe limits, it never checks nor suppresses these acute reactions by poisonous drugs, ice, serums, antiseptics, surgical operations, suggestion or any other suppressive treatment.

Skin eruptions, boils, ulcers, catarrh, diarrhea, and all other forms of inflammatory febrile disease processes are indications that there is something hostile to life and health in the organism, which Nature is trying to remove or overcome by these so-called "acute" diseases. What, then, is to be gained by suppressing them with poisonous drugs and surgical operations? Such practice does not allow Nature to carry on her work of cleansing and repair and to attain her ends. The morbid matter which she is endeavoring to eliminate by acute reaction is thrown back into the system. Worse than that, drug poisons are added to disease poisons. Is it any wonder that fatal complications arise, or that the acute process is changed to chronic disease?

Does the Greater Part of Allopathic Materia Medica Consist of Virulent Poisons?

The statements made in the preceding pages are a severe indictment of so-called "regular" medical science, but they point out the difference in the basic principles of the old school of healing and those of Nature Cure philosophy.

The fundamental Law of Cure quoted in this chapter explains why allopathic medical science is in error, not in a few things but in most things. Their foundation, the orthodox conception of disease, being wrong, it follows that everything built thereon must be wrong also.

No matter how learned a man may be, if he begins a problem in arithmetic with the proposition 2X2=5, he will never arrive at a correct solution even if he continues to figure into all eternity. Neither can allopathy solve the problem of disease and cure so long as its fundamental conception of disease is based on error.

The fundamental law of cure explains also why the great majority of allopathic prescriptions contain virulent poisons in some form or other, and why surgical operations are in high favor with the disciples of the old school.

The answer of allopathy to the question, "Why do you give poisons?" usually is, "Our materia medica contains poisons because drug poison kills and eliminates disease poison." We, however, claim that drug poisons merely serve to paralyze vital force, whereby the deceptive results of allopathic treatment are obtained.

The following will explain this more fully. We have learned that so-called acute diseases are Nature's cleansing and healing efforts. All acute reactions represent increased activity of vital force, resulting in feverish and inflammatory conditions, accompanied by pain, redness, swelling, high temperature, rapid pulse, catarrhal discharges, skin eruptions, boils, ulcers, etc.

Allopathy regards these violent activities of vital force as detrimental and harmful in themselves. Anything which will inhibit the action of vital force will, in allopathic parlance, cure (?) acute diseases. As a matter of fact, nothing more effectively paralyzes vital force and impairs the vital organs than poisonous drugs, ice and the surgeon's knife. These, therefore, must necessarily constitute the favorite means of cure (?) of the old school of medicine.

This school mistakes effect for cause. It fails to see that the local inflammation arising within the organism is not the disease, but merely marks the locality and the method through which Nature is trying her best to discharge the morbid encumbrances;-that the acute reaction is local, but that its causes or "feeders" are always constitutional and must be treated constitutionally. When under the influence of rational, natural treatment, the poisonous irritants are eliminated from blood and tissues, the local symptoms take care of themselves; it does not matter whether they manifest as pimple or cancer, as a simple cold or as consumption.

The Law of Dual Effect

Everywhere in Nature rules the great Law of Action and Reaction. All life sways back and forth between giving and receiving, between action and reaction. The very breath of life mysteriously comes and goes in rhythmical flow. So also heaves and falls in ebb and tide the bosom of Mother Earth.

In some of its aspects this law is called the law of compensation, or the law of dual effect. On its action depends the preservation of energy.

The Great Master expressed the ethical application of this law when he said: "Give, and it shall be given unto you. . . . For with what measure ye mete it shall be measured to you again." Luke 6:38.

In the realms of physical nature, giving and receiving, action and reaction, balance each other mechanically and automatically. What we gain in power we lose in speed or volume, and vice versa. This makes it possible for the mechanic, the scientist and the astronomer to predict with mathematical precision for ages in advance the results of certain activities in Nature.

The great law of dual effect forms the foundation of healing science. It is related to and governs every phenomenon of health, disease and cure. ...the fundamental law of cure in the words, "Every acute disease is the result of a, healing effort of Nature", ...was but another expression of the great law of action and reaction. What we commonly call crisis, acute reaction or acute disease, is in reality Nature's attempt to establish health.

Applied to the physical activity of the body, the Law of Compensation may be expressed as follows: Every agent affecting the human organism produces two effects: a first, temporary effect, and a second, lasting effect. The second, lasting effect is always contrary to the first, transient effect.

For instance: the first and temporary effect of cold water applied to the skin consists in sending the blood to the interior; but in order to compensate for the local depletion, Nature responds by sending greater quantities back to the surface, which results in increased warmth and better surface circulation.

The first effect of a hot bath is to draw the blood to the surface; but the second effect sends the blood back to the 'interior, leaving the surface bloodless and chilled.

Stimulants, as we shall presently see, produce their deceptive effects by consuming the reserve stores of vital energy in the organism. This is inevitably followed by weakness and exhaustion in exact proportion to the previous excitation.

The first effect of relaxation and sleep is weakness, numbness and death-like stupor; the second effect, however, is an increase of vitality.

The law of Dual Effect governs all drug action. The first, temporary, violent effect of poisonous drugs, when taken in physiological doses, is usually due to Nature's efforts to overcome and eliminate these substances. The second, lasting effect is due to the retention of the drug poisons in the system and their destructive action on the organism.

In theory and in practice, allopathy considers the first effect only and ignores the lasting after effects of drugs and surgical operations. It administers remedies whose first effect is **contrary** to the disease condition. Therefore, in accordance with the law of action and reaction, the second, lasting effect of such remedies must be **similar** to the disease condition.

Common, everyday experience should teach us that this is true, for laxatives and cathartics always tend to produce chronic constipation.

The second effect of stimulants and tonics of any kind is increased weakness. Their continued use often results in complete exhaustion and paralysis of mental and physical powers.

Headache powders, pain killers, opiates, sedatives and hypnotics may paralyze brain and nerves into temporary insensibility; but, if due to constitutional causes, the pain, nervousness and insomnia will always return with redoubled force. If taken habitually these agents invariably tend to create heart disease and paralysis and ultimately develop the "dope fiend."

Cold and catarrh cures (?) such as quinine, coal tar products, etc., suppress Nature's efforts to eliminate waste and morbid matter through the mucous linings of the respiratory tract, causing retention of disease matter, thus breeding pneumonia, chronic catarrhs, asthma and consumption.

Mercury, iodin, salvarsan and all other alteratives, by suppression of external elimination, and even more so by their own destructive effects, create internal chronic diseases of the most dreadful types, such as locomotor ataxia, paresis, paralysis agitans, etc.

So the recital might be continued all through the orthodox materia medica. Each drug breeds new disease symptoms which are in their turn cured (?) by other poisons, until the insane asylum or merciful death rings down the curtain on the tragedy of a ruined life.

The teaching and practice of homeopathy, as explained in another chapter, is fully in harmony with the law of action and reaction. Proceeding upon its basic principle "Similia similibus curantur", or "like cures like"-it administers remedies whose first, temporary effect is similar to the disease condition. In accordance, then, with

the law of dual effect, the second effect of these remedies must be contrary to the disease condition, that is, "curative."" [1]

The view accepted by most homeopaths (which is similar to that developed by Dr. Hahnemann) is probably what is known as *Hering's Law* as espoused by this 19th Century homeopath, "cure proceeds from above downward, from within outward, from the most important organs to least important organs, and in reverse order of appearance of symptoms" [2]. The first portion of the law (cure proceeds from above downward) is believed to mean that if someone had pain in the shoulders, but now has it in the hips that healing is occurring [3]. The second portion of the law (from within outward, from the most important organs to least important organs) is believed to mean that improvement is occurring when psychological symptoms (within) symptoms improve even if physical (outward) symptoms (like skin) worsen. The third portion of the law is fairly literal that healing proceeds from the most important organs to the least important organs. The final portion (in reverse order of appearance of symptoms) has also been stated that "as healing progresses, symptoms appear and disappear in the reverse of their original chronological order of appearance. Homeopaths have observed that consistently their patients reexperience symptoms from past conditions. The time during which the patient has suffered from these symptoms range from six months to ten or twenty years before present treatment" [3].

My own views of "cure" are somewhat different (though consistent with traditional naturopathic philosophy). Unless strictly recommending a classical homeopathic remedy (and virtually nothing else), it is rarely found necessary to rely on any part of *Hering's Law*. Why? Because most of the people will report improvement most of the time (98.4% within 2-3 months, please see Appendix A). The primary times situations commonly referred to as "healing crises" arise when individuals have been advised to go off of caffeine or if they are fighting some type of parasitic or mycotic infection—these people will generally tend to have periods of discomfort (sometimes even after they have begun to improve).

Some naturopaths tend to work more on the physical level with clients, while others tend to focus more on emotional levels. Though undoubtedly some of the causes of enervation actually led to ill health (as is discussed in chapter 3), as a naturopath that is not the focus. Morality issues are critically important, but when people pay to see a naturopath, that is not why they think they are setting the appointment. However, practical suggestions along those lines when they seem to be required for the healing process are appropriate.

The basic view on the healing process is that if someone is ingesting something that is toxic to them, they need to eliminate it from their diet. This allows the body to detoxify and heal itself (vis medicatrix naturae). Since many seem to have nutritional deficiencies, one should recommend what the body needs for rebuilding. Thus healing is an elimination of toxins (when applicable), avoidance of future toxins, and nourishing the body so that it can heal itself. Although there is also divine healing, that is not the focus of this book and it will not be addressed here.

References

[1] Lindlahr, H. *Philosophy of Natural Therapeutics.* Lindlahr Publishing, Chicago, 1918.

[2] Vithoulkas, G. *The Science of Homeopathy.* Grove Press, New York, 1980.

[3] Cumming, S. and Ullman, D. *Everybody's Guide to Homeopathic Medicine.* J.P. Tarcher, Los Angeles, 1984.

5

Psycho-therapy or Mind-cure

It seems like many have gone from feeling there is little connection between the mind and body to believing that the mind can overcome any problem on its own. While even the Bible says that, "A merry heart does good, like a medicine" (Proverbs 17:22), it also suggests that herbs and other natural remedies are helpful (e.g. Revelation 22:2; II Kings 20:7; Jeremiah 51:8). There needs to be a balance in looking at the mind-body connection.

While having a positive attitude can greatly enhance the healing process, it alone is usually not enough for people with chronic health problems.

The Reasons?

Since by definition, the problem is chronic, the mind has obviously not overcome this problem on its own. The other reason is that if the body is deficient in some essential nutrient (such as iodine), no amount of thinking is going to create something out of nothing. Additionally in many chronic health problems, the mind and body is often crying out for nutritional support (especially for the endocrine or the immune systems).

The following was written by Dr. Kulkarni under the heading *Psycho-therapy or Mind-cure*:

There is no doubt that we can control the diseases both of body and mind by giving hopes and assurances to the patient. There are some who can fill others with hope and cheer and others who can not. An experienced nurse very often soothes the mind and relieves the sufferings of her patient. An experienced Ayurvedic physician very often quotes a suitable Sanskrit verse from the old authors and explains its meaning to his patient saying that a certain drug is an excellent remedy for his malady as some kind of humor is in excess in his body; then the patient feels cheered and confident of his cure, so that he feels considerably relieved in mind.

A patient very often feels that he is almost cured when a cheerful nurse assures him that she has seen worse cases cured and he would get all right in a very, short time.

A student of the author who is now practicing in Homoeopathy and Biochemistry told him that the verses composed by the author on Homoeopathic and Biochemic Materia Medica have been of great use to him. He cited some of the verses to three of his patients with the result that he inspired them with confidence and hope and they felt half cured of their maladies.

Dr. Lindlahr says—"Every thought and every emotion has its direct effect upon the physical constituents of the body. The mental and emotional vibrations become physical vibrations and structures. Discord in the mind is translated into disease in the body while the harmonies of hope, faith, cheerfulness, happiness, love and altruism create in the organism the corresponding health vibrations."

In *Vedant* philosophy it is said that we have in this, our physical body, one astral (ethereal) body which governs our mind; our will-power is dependent on it. First we must strengthen the will, then we must direct it towards what is good by fixing the mind on it and meditating on it. We should not expect nor attempt for too much in the beginning. The success in spreading religious beliefs is based on the perseverance and steadiness of the founders and those who attempted to spread them.

Forgetfulness and idleness are the enemies of our will, we should try to cultivate the memory by concentrating our will with etheric power and by-the-by success will be ours. It is now a well-known fact that though suggestions or psycho-therapy is not itself able to cure all diseases, it helps a good deal to cure many of them, chiefly nervous disorders and mental troubles.

"There are various terms," says Lowe, "with which most people are familiar such as Faith-cure, Christian Science-cure, Mental healing, Will-cure, Hypnotic suggestion, Curative mesmerism, etc. The basis of all these is etheric vibration influenced by the will of the person himself or of another for it is a demonstrated fact that the other penetrates every material substance without exception; an act of will being composed of etheric vibratory energy."

The following quotation from the Herald of Health April 1919 will show that the attempt of some persons to cure all diseases only with faith or suggestions is merely ridiculous.

Query: "Hallow John! I hear your father was cured of rheumatism by Christian Science."

Reply: "Oh no, he was cured of Christian Science by rheumatism."

Rheumatism, gout, migraine, neuralgia, sciatica, sprue, diarrhoea, dysentery, cholera, boils, abscesses, carbuncles, cancers, etc. cannot be cured by faith or suggestions alone; they need sunlight, water, diet, and sometimes suitable homeopathic medicines also which work according to the Law of Similars. Dr. Lindlahr and others also hold the same opinion. [1]

Dr. Lust stated, "Naturopathy agrees with Mental Science, Christian Science, New Thought, and other mental pathologies in that all disease is originally thought, but with Physical Culture, Sex Specialism, Dietotherapy, Hydrotherapy, et al. in that the manifestation is distinctly material."

Does this mean the mind plays no role in healing? Absolutely not. The mind is very important. It has been estimated that the mind alone can contribute to improvement to around 30% of the population [2].

People with positive attitudes, combined with proper intervention, usually report improvement quicker, report greater improvement, and (quite important for health care professionals) tend to follow recommendations better. Although naturopaths have helped many people who didn't think they could help by such care (usually they came in because a relative persuaded them to give a naturopath a try), it is much easier helping people who believe they can be helped.

Often, in people with chronic health problems, relapses occur. People with better attitudes tend to forge onward (although sometimes with difficulty) and continue with follow-up interventions until they again improve. People with negative attitudes tend to give up faster especially when improvement is not as immediate, long-lasting, or dramatic (or when relapses occur, although relapses do not occur for everyone).

People with better attitudes tend to be more understanding. For example, when it is recommended that someone go off of caffeine and they are warned that it may give them headaches for a few days (up to 11), those with better attitudes tend to stay off caffeine, while those with worse attitudes give up and go back to it. Those with better attitudes tend to get better faster (though not always). People with positive attitudes seem more willing to make positive changes in their lifestyles more than those who do not have positive attitudes.

For anyone (whether they originally had a positive or negative attitude), as the body begins to feel better, the mind takes note. The mind then works with the body to continue the healing process (unless the attitude is severely negative or distrusting). The mind then seems to believe that since the body is improving, it can validate and support the healing. This is an excellent occurrence which is frequently seen.

Relaxing and reducing stresses where possible also seems to help the healing process for many people (see chapter 15 on rest). Although for many, this is nearly impossible until their nutritional status has been sufficiently improved.

A word of caution is probably in order at this point. People with chronic fatigue, for example, often have a tremendous amount of pressure to finish various tasks that they sometimes delay due to their fatigue. In their zeal to accomplish these tasks, some will overexert themselves as they begin to feel better. This is a case of the mind-body connection being pushed a bit too far. It happens all the time. Naturopaths often try to warn clients about overdoing things as they first improve as even exercise (for some) can trigger a severe relapse [3].

Thus, the mind-body connection is important, but it is not the only factor in determining improvement for people with chronic health problems.

References

[1] Kulkarni, V. M. *Healing Through Naturopathy.* Reprint by B. Jain Publishers, New Delhi (India), originally written circa 1925.

[2] Stove, J. and Pellegrino, C. *Chronic Fatigue Syndrome: The Hidden Epidemic.* Harper & Rowe, New York, 1990.

[3] McCalley, K., et al. *Use of Exercise for Treatment of Chronic Fatigue Syndrome.* Sports Med, 1996;21(1):35-48.

6

Simple Rules Which Lead to Health

There are many books on how to have good health. Some better than others. In this chapter, rules of health that Herbert W. Armstrong espoused as well as some by me are discussed. Mr. Armstrong wrote:

Is bodily health important? Next to the salvation of one's soul, sound, vigorous bodily health surely is the most necessary and the most valuable treasure a man can achieve in this world.

The body is the temple of the Holy Spirit. It should be kept clean, sound and healthy. Unless one is really fit physically he is not in a position to render efficient service to the Lord's work.

Unless the body is fit and vigorously healthy, the mind is slowed down, energy lags, vitality is sluggish, and accomplishment is greatly handicapped. No one can be happy, except in health. No one can really enjoy living except in health. Good health is a treasure more precious than the world's most colossal fortune.

Very, very few are really vigorously healthy. You may not be actually sick or in pain—you may have no specific disease or disorder—and yet fall far short of that state of real bodily power and vigor and energy which is everyone's right.

Following are ten simple common-sense rules which, if followed will increase the bodily and mental vigor of any person by 100 percent. If you have thought you were enjoying perfect health, try these ten simple rules for a brief 30-day test. The result will amaze you. You will feel like a new person.

Vigorous, energetic health costs very little, if any, in money. You simply pay the cost in added effort. The results are worth many times the effort.

If you will adopt these rules and stick rigidly to them, you can guarantee yourself at least ten years longer life—accidents barred.

Especially the rule pertaining to daily rubdowns, will prove a guarantee for longer life. The physical trainer who was in charge of the physical condition of ex-President Taft conducted a nationwide investigation to learn the secret of long life. He interviewed and extensively questioned every person he could reach who had attained the age of 100 years. He sought the secret of living to be a hundred, if there was any one secret. The result of this research amazed him. Some attributed their long life to the fact they never had smoked, but others had been smokers. Some to the fact they were vegetarians, but others attained 100 while eating meat. Practically every one gave different reasons to which they, themselves, attributed their long life. But the physical trainer was surprised to find that there was only one thing which all in common had practiced, and to which virtually none of them gave any credit. Every single one of them had habitually taken daily rubdowns. The importance of the regular daily rubdown cannot be over emphasized. This does two things of paramount importance. First it invigorates the cells, and second it stimulates blood circulation.

If you can have the strength of will and the determination to put these rules into daily practice, and keep them up, you not only feel better, but will have a keener mind, clearer vision, and greater capacity both mentally and physically.

Here Are Ten Rules

1. Sleep — Be sure of good ventilation—**PLENTY OF FRESH AIR** in the bedroom all night, winter and summer. Some people still follow the old injurious fallacy of shutting up all the windows and doors tight at night. They are afraid they will take cold if they let in fresh air. They could not be farther from the truth, as any doctor or physician will testify. Those who sleep with windows wide open seldom have colds. Fresh air is **FREE**—and nothing is more vital to health, but avoid drafts striking you.

    Sleep on the side and never flat on the back, which overheats the spine and often leads to serious conditions. If possible sleep alone.

2. Arise — Get right out of bed the instant you awaken. Do not lie in bed, or turn over for a second sleep, no matter how tired or dragged down you feel. A second sleep dulls the mind.

3. Bath and rubdown — Take a regular morning shower bath if possible, making it short and snappy, ending with a vigorous rubdown. If no shower is available, take a tub bath at least two or three times a week. End with cold water, especially in cold weather. This closes the pores and prevents chilling and taking cold.

    If no shower is available, take a vigorous rubdown in the bedroom daily or twice daily, using a Turkish or bath towel or massage brush. Begin at wrists and feet massaging vigorously toward the heart. If the room is cold, just apply a little more energy—the vigorous rubbing will keep you warm.

4. Head rub and shampoo — Before leaving the bedroom, massage and rub the scalp vigorously with tips of fingers, suitable stiff bristle brush, or electric vibrator. This stimulates new circulation thru the scalp, makes the brain more active, and is the best guarantee there is against baldness. Shampoo the hair at least every two or three weeks. Be sure to use neutral, mild soap (imported castile is best) and rinse thoroughly.

5. Water — Immediately after breakfast, drink one or two full glasses of water. Start in with whatever you can drink, increasing it till you are able to take one or two full glasses. Soon you will crave it. Drink twice as much water through the day as you have been accustomed to doing, if you are an average individual. This morning glass of water is very important.

6. Breakfast — Avoid too heavy a breakfast. If you eat pancakes, eat but a few. Do not eat too many eggs, and never more than two or three times a week. Eggs are good food, but too many produce a sluggish liver. Avoid soggy, heavy foods. Eat some fruit if possible—especially grapefruit, oranges, etc.

7. Food — In the main, simply eat what you find agrees with you but be sure to get a reasonable amount of fruits, and leafy vegetables (lettuce, raw cabbage, spinach, etc.) and milk, every

day. Avoid meals loaded with meat, potatoes, beans, corn, etc., unless balanced with leafy vegetables and fruits.

For health's sake eat very little or none of the meats called "unclean" and forbidden under the Old Testament Mosaic law. Above all, eat slowly, and CHEW THOROUGHLY before swallowing. Avoid overeating. Most people eat twice what they should.

8. Elimination — Nothing is more vital to health than habitual regularity of elimination. Constipation is nothing but the penalty of lack of regularity. Pills will not **CURE constipation.** Nothing but the reestablishment of regularity of habit will cure it. For those suffering from this, it is advisable to resort to divine healing but be sure you deserve it by reestablishment of regular habits, preferably at a set time of day. Also regulate diet to aid this.

9. Breathing — At least three times during the day—preferably bed time, rising time and once during the day—go outdoors, or open all the windows and doors in the house, stand erect, chest out and shoulders back, and **BREATHE DEEPLY** several times. Inhale slowly through the nose, till lungs are completely full. Exhale through the mouth, till the lungs are entirely emptied of air. Repeat several times. Try to learn the habit of breathing deeply, taking in more air and more completely emptying the lungs at every breath.

10. Exercise — Few people past twenty-five get sufficient exercise, except those who are farmers, or get exercise through daily labor. Even in this case it is likely that only certain parts of the body are receiving sufficient exercise. Walking in the fresh air every day is good. For those who lead an indoor life, such sports as golf or tennis are splendid. Often bedroom exercises are advisable. Your body and muscles will not likely wear out, but can more easily rust out. Each individual must determine for himself what additional exercise, if any, he needs, as differing daily occupations naturally affect this.

It goes without saying that all forms of dissipation must be avoided if these 10 health rules are to prove successful. There are many forms of dissipation too: besides such things as drinking, smoking and keeping late hours.

Perhaps the most common form of dissipation in the average Christian home is coffee and tea drinking. People who would never think of smoking or chewing tobacco will drink several cups of coffee or tea daily, actually injuring their bodies through this dissipation more than thousands of smokers through tobacco. The heavy coffee drinker is sinning to a greater degree against his body than a light smoker. Scientific tests show that the normal individual in good vigorous health may drink one cup of coffee or one cup of tea, per day without noticeable physical affect. Some people cannot drink any without injury. But two cups or more, according to scientific tests, are sufficient to overcome the reserve of bodily "resistance" and produce noticeably injurious affects. The Bible lends advice here, too, when it tells us to be temperate in all things. [1]

Mr. Armstrong wrote some information on fasting which is included in chapter 20. Although Mr. Armstrong believed in divine healing, he also wrote, "If God is the Healer—the *only* real Healer— and if medical science came out of the ancient heathen practice of medicine-men supposed to be in the good graces of imaginary gods of medicine, is there, then, no need for doctors?

"If all people understood and practiced God's Truth, the function of the doctor would be a lot different than it is today. Actually, there isn't a cure in a car-load—or a train-load—of medicine! Most sickness and disease today is the result of faulty diet and wrong eating. The true function of the doctor should not be to usurp God's prerogative as a Healer, but to help you to observe nature's laws by prescribing a correct diet, teaching you how to live better *according to nature's laws.* In other words, to *prevent* sickness, not heal *after you* are sick! Unfortunately, most doctors today are woefully unprepared properly to advise patients about diet. They studied *medicine,* not *foods!*

"There are a few schools of 'healing' coming along today somewhat along this line, who work more with nature's laws, and not with drugs and medicines — the naturopaths, osteopaths and chiropractors, etc. These may and may not be good, largely according to the school from which they came and the ability of the man himself.

"There are other needed functions for certain types of doctors. Child-bearing, for instance, is *not* a sickness from which women need healing, but a natural thing ordained of God. It would seem but right that we should have obstetrical specialists, then, for specialized aid and care on such occasions.

"If something breaks on my automobile—something that can be fixed back either by myself or a specialist in a garage—do not just pray and do nothing, expecting God to do for you what you can do for yourself. If you break an arm, or other bone, it certainly is right to take it to a specialist and have him set it. He can't heal it, however. You should *trust* God to do that. So, you see, there *are* a number of functions which human doctors or physicians can rightly perform. But remember that *healing is,* after all, out of their line—only God can heal! Only God can forgive sin!" [2]

On the areas of food and nutrition, here are some additional points:

1. Organic food is considered the best.

2. Unrefined food is better than refined food (e.g. whole grains are better than refined).

3. People should eat at least two servings of fruit and three servings of vegetables each day.

4. Artificial sweeteners, artificial fats, hydrogenated fats, preservatives, artificial colors, etc. are not natural food.

5. Alcohol and meat should be consumed only in extreme moderation (if at all), excesses in this area are not healthy.

6. If an entirely organic diet is not possible, vitamin-mineral supplementation in moderation (i.e. not many times the body's needs) is a good idea if the supplements are actually food (please see chapters 22 and 23).

7. People should eat several times per day, even if a piece of fruit is the entire meal.

Rest and other principles that are covered in this and other chapters are also advocated.

References

[1] Armstrong, H. W. *Ten Simple Rules that Lead to Health.* In Early Writings of Herbert W. Armstrong. Reprint by Giving and Sharing, Neck City (MO), originally written in 1928.

[2] Armstrong, H. W. *Does God Heal Today?* In Early Writings of Herbert W. Armstrong. Reprint by Giving and Sharing, Neck City (MO), originally written circa 1928.

7 Naturopathic Assessment

Natural health care professionals utilize many different assessment techniques. This section will briefly discuss assessment techniques including the initial interview, family history, medical diagnosis, blood tests (infectious, CBC, endocrine, and specific nutrient), allergy tests, iridology, and reflex nutrition assessment. As a general rule, the assessment should not be limited to one technique. A minimum of two for each person is preferable. The maximum amount varies based on each situation and cost/time considerations should play some role.

The Interview and History

A technique that every health professional should use is the initial interview (some types of subjects covered are at the end of this chapter). During the interview it is important that the client tell his or her story. It should not be rushed if possible. Our initial interview (including our questions) lasts approximately fifty minutes. Some people are less talkative and need to be asked more ques-

tions. Whether or not a client is talkative, there are some pieces of information which need to be found out, such as symptoms and diet. Specifically it is helpful to know how long the client has been suffering, what was going on in his or her life when he or she first remembers having the problem, if he or she had been ill or traveling, when he or she feels worse, what he or she believes may trigger fatigue, and what, if anything, seems to help.

Taking a family history can be useful. Often a family history can reveal diabetes (which, to me, suggests an increased tendency towards hypoglycemia), thyroid problems (which suggests that nutritional support can be helpful in subclinical situations), asthma/allergies (which suggests that the patient probably has some type of allergy), trips to foreign countries (which sometimes can indicate possible parasite involvement), etc.

A useful assessment technique is to find out any medical diagnoses that one may have. Follow-up interviews are also important. Follow-ups provide an opportunity to see what worked, what did not work, and what could (or should be changed). Even with our high improvement rate, a significant percentage did not report improvement until 60 days after beginning to follow our recommendations.

Quantitative and Laboratory Tests

Although many people are overly concerned about information from quantitative and laboratory tests, these tests do have value. They are not as completely conclusive as some seem to feel. When in doubt, remember not to violate any laws and that everyone is different.

Blood tests are usually used to look for viral (as well as fungal) agents or antibodies, blood chemistry, endocrine levels, etc. [1] Comprehensive stool analysis can help locate parasites and some mycotic (fungal) organisms. [1] Saliva tests can reveal information about pH and are sometimes used to look for mycotic organisms. [1] Hair analysis (which is discussed further below) can give clues concerning mineral imbalances. [2]

Nutrient serum tests are useful, but limited. There are reasons to question the value of blood as a nutritional marker. Low hemoglobin or red blood count can indicate a deficiency of iron, vitamin B_{12}, or other nutrients, but does not necessarily indicate that supplementation is useful. It has been reported that various B vitamin deficiencies can exist while serum levels of these nutrients appear to be normal. This can especially happen when homocysteine levels are elevated. [3-4] Based on current knowledge, it is suspected that in the future, homocysteine levels will be considered more important than cholesterol levels. Elevations of folic acid can mask a vitamin B_{12} deficiency. Thus a normal chemistry panel looking at vitamin B_6, B_{12}, and folate acid probably cannot be relied upon to rule out deficiencies. [3-4]

Severe iron deficiency can reliably be determined using a blood test, but mild deficiencies/anemia is much more difficult to establish. This is because these people do not have the microhypochromic cells which are associated with severe deficiency. Thus, in some iron anemias, serum iron is not always diminished and serum ferritin concentrations can be normal in blood tests when a deficiency exists. [5]

Serum tests of total carnitine, free carnitine, and acytlcarnitine can be run. Higher serum carnitine levels correlate with better functional capacity. [6]

Endocrine hypofunction has been repeatedly speculated as causes for many chronic complaints. [7-9] Classical endocrine hypofunction, especially glucocorticoid insufficiency and corticotrophin releasing hormone (CRH), have been found by scientists at National Institute of Health (NIH) to exist in people with chronic fatigue syndrome. [10] Endocrine hypofunction is often determined by blood tests. One of the more common tests is a thyroid panel. In a typical thyroid panel, various hormone levels (T-3, T-4, TSH) are checked; from my personal nutritional perspective, many false negatives are reported. Others share this view. [11] However, this is probably a good time to distinguish "nutritional endocrine hypofunction" from "medical endocrine hypofunction." From a medical standpoint, one has thyroid hypofunction if a blood test demonstrates it. Nutritional thyroid hypofunction is different. If one has symptoms associated with hypothyroidism, reflex assesses that thyroid support is an issue, and responds positively to nutrition for it, it is acceptable to conclude that one has/had a nutritional thyroid hypofunction issue. Nutritional support for the thyroid tends to be temporary because it provides nutrients for the thyroid to rebuild (typically it is much longer for women,

especially if they take any form of estrogen); medical interventions for thyroid (such as synthetic T-4) tend to be permanent because instead of helping the thyroid rebuild, it is medically concluded that the thyroid cannot produce enough hormones on its own (thus artificial hormones are needed). This is an important distinction for all nutritional endocrine issues.

This separates a nutritional problem from a medical problem. In a nutritional situation, the endocrine gland reflex will appear to respond and rebuild. In a medical situation, the gland is apparently not capable of performing its normal functions, thus must be artificially supported (many people who supposedly needed synthetic thyroid have been, usually slowly, able to get off of it and have a normal thyroid panel). On the other hand, there are times when medical hormone support is necessary.

Hypotension (as well as hypertension) can usually be determined by simply taking someone's blood pressure. Often people who are severely fatigued or who tire after exertion, suffer from some type of nutritional hypotension. As a rule, this group responds well (and quickly) to nutritional support.

One should also try to look at such common sense information such as age, height, weight, gender, and body fat. All of these factors can be helpful in determining optimal recommendations. Body fat percentage is also helpful to monitor because often when people who wish to lose weight exercise, they gain muscle while they lose fat. If body fat is not monitored, it is quite hard to determine actual progress. In general, it is considered that changes in body fat percentage are more significant than changes in scale weight.

Allergy tests can be helpful for people with health problems. Immunoglobulin E (IgE) tests, although good for determining airborne allergies, are often of questionable value because they seem to result in many false negatives where food sensitivities are involved. [12] My clinical experience makes me somewhat skeptical of immunoglobulin G (IgG) tests because they appear to show too many false positives (some others seem to agree). [13] My personal preference is to use reflex assessment or pulse assessment to determine food and environmental factors which may be involved.

The Use of Hair Analysis

Hair analysis reports can provide some insight into mineral and toxicity issues. "Hair analysis is more correctly referred to as tissue mineral analysis of TRICHO (hair). This nomenclature distinguishes it from the hair analysis done in a beauty shop." [14] "As hair is synthesized in the follicle, elements are incorporated in the hair proteins with no further exchange or equilibrium with other tissues. In general, the amount of an element that is irreversibly incorporated into growing hair is proportional to the level of the element in other body tissues." [2] Some factors that can change this include hair treatments such as dyes, shampoos, conditioners, etc. Sometimes airborne and other pollutants can change this as well.

The following is a list of substances quantified in hair analysis:

Elements Considered as Toxic	Elements Regarded as Nutrients
Aluminum	Boron
Antimony	Calcium
Arsenic	Chromium
Beryllium	Cobalt
Bismuth	Copper
Cadmium	Iodine
Lead	Iron
Mercury	Lithium
Nickel	Magnesium
Platinum	Manganese
Silver	Molybdenum
Strontium	Phosphorus
Sulfur	Potassium
Thallium	Selenium
Thorium	Sodium
Tin	Titanium
Uranium	
Vanadium	
Zirconium	
Zinc	

It should be noted that several of the elements considered as toxic are also considered to be ultra-trace nutrients.

Biofeedback Based Assessments

The human body can help provide valuable information that can be used to assess needs and problems. Some include muscle testing (such as Reflex Nutrition Assessment), pulse testing, iridology, and biofeedback equipment. Of course, even symptomatic feedback (through follow-up consultations) is a form of biofeedback.

Reflex Nutrition Assessment, otherwise known as RNA, is an ancillary form of nutrition assessment. It is a technique used to assess nutrition status by observing the response of muscles under externally provided human-force. Although it is a controversial technique which is not accepted by many "mainstream practitioners," [15-16] it (and similar techniques) has been used successfully by many others. [17-23] It is an excellent way to determine nutritional deficiencies and sensitivities which are commonly found in people with chronic health complaints. (Reflex Nutrition Assessment is the subject of chapter 8.)

Pulse testing is another form of biofeedback. It is a technique which is helpful in determining food and environmental sensitivities and was developed by an immunologist. [24] Although it is not medically accepted that rises in pulse rate indicate a food sensitivity [24], it is medically accepted that foods which induce asthma can make the pulse rise after eating. [25] It can be an invaluable assessment tool. (Pulse testing is the subject of chapter 9.)

Iridology is an interesting form of biofeedback. Essentially, it is believed that by looking at signs in the iris and changes to those signs, that various aspects of health and healing can be assessed [26]. (Iridology is the subject of chapter 10.)

The use of electronic biofeedback equipment seems to be helpful for some problems. One study found that 35% with constipation had complete success, while 13% had partial success using biofeedback, [27] while another found that 92% reported at least some improvement. [28] One study found that combining biofeedback with physical therapy helped migraine sufferers [29] (for other approaches to migraines, please see the study in Appendix A). The value of biofeedback alone in improving blood pressure is unclear [30].

Some Interview Subjects

Most naturopaths have their clients complete a symptom survey form. Most interview the client for at least forty minutes on the first appointment (most first appointments will probably last about one hour).

Some questions asked may include:

a) How long have you had health problems?
b) What is your biggest concern?
c) What do you think may have caused/ triggered them? (It is remarkable how many people have a pretty good idea of one or more of the causes of their health problems)
d) When do you feel better and when do you feel worse?
e) Do you sleep well?
f) Do you have a family history of thyroid problems or diabetes?
g) What allopathic diagnosis do you have?
h) What do you normally eat in a typical day (meal by meal including snacks and desserts)?
i) Do you consume much salt?
j) What beverages do you normally consume?
k) What, if anything, seems to help?
l) Do you have any digestive difficulties?
m) Do you like or dislike hot/cold weather?
n) Do you perspire a lot?
o) Do you feel stressed or depressed?

One thing to teach doctors involved in natural health is, "If you do not listen to your clients, they will not listen to you!"

Most naturopaths write down what the client says. Believe it or not, clients who improve OFTEN forget problems they had when they first came in.

Some Things A Naturopath Should Consider

Feel the client's hands to see if they are cold. If the hands are cold, it may suggest heart and/ or thyroid involvement (adrenals and kidneys can also be involved, but much less often). Then perform reflex assessment of each of the appropriate reflexes.

If the environmental reflex goes, check them on various foods and environmental items. If it cannot be determined what bothers them, they will be provided a pulse form, such as is shown in chapter 9. Always recheck each reflex that appeared to have a problem and then recheck each reflex with the client holding the appropriate product for that reflex (there are many product options for most reflexes, but normally only one will be needed). If the reflex does not strengthen, try checking different products until at least one responds.

Naturopaths will run other tests they feel are appropriate. As a general rule, naturopaths should ensure that the client is not allergic to any of the ingredients or does not have objections (such as herbs tinctured in alcohol or glandulars for a vegan) to taking the products. A good naturopath will explain the product(s) as appropriate.

Most provide a written recommendation sheet as to what they suggest the client should follow (foods to avoid, supplements to take, acupressure instructions, etc. as indicated). Separate dietary instructions are sometimes also provided

When dealing with someone with chronic fatigue or fibromyalgia, it is sometimes appropriate to warn them that exercise or overwork can cause a relapse [31], so they should literally "try to take it easy." (Exercise is helpful for many, but at some stages of recovery it sometimes needs to be minimal.)

At the end of the first appointment, always ask if the client has any questions about anything done or has any problem or concern that was not covered.

It is important to schedule a follow-up appointment. Usually this is two to four weeks later. During follow-ups, ask about the symptoms they originally presented or wrote down on the symptom survey form. Some questions asked include:

a) How are you doing?
b) Are any symptoms better?
c) Are any symptoms worse?

Note: Sometimes people with chronic fatigue will tell you they feel no improvement, yet when you question them, you will find they have been more active, accomplished more work, had visiting relatives, etc. Therefore, it is good to ask what changes have occurred in their life since their last visit. It is also good to do many of the same things originally done in the first appointment and recommend they reduce, continue, or change supplements as appropriate. If there is a pulse form completed, review it and have the client avoid the suspected allergens/sensitive foods.

What to Try if Nothing Seems to Help

It is likely that no practitioner can clearly help all the people all the time. If, however, a client for whom the above does not seem to be fully helping, consider the following suggestions:

1. Suggest they consume at least two servings of fruit and three servings of vegetables each day (this is a valid suggestion for nearly everyone).

2. Suggest that they avoid bovine dairy and caffeine products

3. Suggest they take a food multiple vitamin/mineral formula (not a synthetic one).

4. Support the liver. The liver is the chemical factory of the body and if it is working better, eventually the rest of the body should be as well.

5. Suggest eating more frequently with smaller meals using more lower glycemic organic foods.

6. Suggest stress reduction techniques, including eliminating some of their daily tasks when practical (it also helps if they have the support of their family/ friends).

7. Fasting may be indicated (see chapter 20).

If the above is not at all effective, then it is possible that some infectious agent, sleeping problem, other toxin, and/or mental issue is present. Appropriate tests and intervention will then be needed. If it is partially effective, continue it until a more effective intervention can be developed, such as gradually increasing one supplement at a time to see if more improvement is noted.

One last comment about blood tests, even medical doctors know, "The glucose tolerance test is not reliable for evaluating most cases of hypoglycemia" [32].

Improvement (The Proof of Assessments)

Reported improvement is one of the best ways to determine whether any assessment technique is effective. Always interview people and perform reflex assessment,and incorporate information from any medical diagnoses, laboratory tests, and other sources as available. This is how our 98.4% success rate was obtained (it was calculated by adding up those who improved in the studies shown in Appendix A and dividing that sum by the total of those who followed the recommendations). Therefore, it is clear to me that measuring the totality of clients who report improvement vs. those who do not is perhaps the best assessment technique (at least for those who want to assess the effectiveness of any given doctor, as well as for any doctor who wants to measure the effectiveness of any assessment technique).

References

[1] Fischbach, F. *A Manual of Laboratory Diagnostic Tests,* 2nd ed. JB Lippincott, Phil., 1984.

[2] Quig, D.W. *Comprehensive Interpretations for Hair Analysis from Al to Zr.* Doctor's Data, West Chicago, 1998.

[3] Miller, S. *Old and New Rationales for Serum B12 and Folate Determinations.* Clinical Laboratory Sciences,1993;6 (5): 272-274.

[4] Motulsky, A., et al. *Nutritional ecogenetics: Homocysteine-Related Arteriosclerotic Vascular Disease, Neural Tube Defects, and Folic Acid.* Am J Human Genetics,1996;58:17-20.

[5] Fairbanks, V. *Iron in Medicine in Nutrition: 185-213.* In: Modern Nutrition in Health and Disease, 8th ed. Lea & Febinger, Phila,, 1994.

[6] Plisoplys, A. and Plisoplys, S. *Serum Levels of Chronic Fatigue Syndrome: Clinical Correlates.* Neurophysiology,1995;32 (3): 132-138.

[7] Burns, D. *Accumulating Scientific Evidence Supports Glandular Therapy.* Digest of Chiropractic Econ, Nov/Dec 1987: 74-79.

[8] Bland, J. *Glandular Therapy.* Circa 1989.

[9] Harrower, H. *Practical Organotherapy.* 3rd ed. W.B. Conkey Co.: Hammond (IN): 31-36, 1921.

[10] Popov, I. M., et al. *Cell therapy.* J. Int'l. Acad. Preventive Med,1977; 3:74-82.

[11] Edienaur, H. *Blood Chemistries.* Presentation at the 12th Annual Meeting of the American Naturopathic Medical Association, Las Vegas, Sept. 1996.

[12] Bindslev-Jensen, C., et al. *Food Allergy and Food Intolerance - What is the Difference?* Ann All,1994; 72(4): 317-320.

[13] *Measurement of Specific and Nonspecific IgG4 Levels as Diagnostic and Prognostic Tests for Clinical Allergy.* J. All and Clin Immunol,1995; 95 (3): 652-654.

[14] Leek, R. *Balanced Nutrition through Hair Analysis,* 4th ed. The Leek Corporation, Los Angeles, 1990.

[15] Kenny, J. J., Clemens, R. and Forsythe, K. D. *Applied Kinesiology Unreliable for Assessing Nutrient Status.* J Am Diet Assoc, 1988;Vol. 88.

[16] University of California at Berkeley Wellness Letter. *Allergic to Everything?* Berkeley: UC Berkeley, December 1991.

[17] Versendaal, D. A. *Contact Reflex Analysis and Applied Trophology.* Holland (Mich.), D.A.Versendaal, 1990.

[18] Shepard, S. *Healing Energies.* Provo, Bi-World Publishers, 1983.

[19] Thiel, R. J. *Clinical Trial on the Effects of Dietary Restriction, Homeopathy, and Combination Nutritional Supplementation on Symptoms Associated with Seasonal Allergic Rhinitis.* Dissertation. Union Institute, Cincinnati, 1993.

[20] Lewith, G.T. and Kenyon, J. N. *Clinical Ecology: A Therapeutic Approach to Understanding and Treating Food and Chemical Sensitivities.* Thorsons Publishers, Wellingborough (UK), 1985.

[21] Thiel, R. J. *Serious Nutrition for Health Professionals.* California Health Group, Arroyo Grande (CA)1995.

[22] Burr-Madsen A. *Body Polarity Reflex Analysis and the Nutritional Connection.* Thoth, Inc., Carson City,1992.

[23] Rosen, M.S. and Williams, L. *The Research Status of Applied Kinesiology, Part II: An Annotated Bibliography of Applied Kinesiological Research.* In: A. K. Review, 1991; 1(2): 34-47.

[24] Coca, A. *The Pulse Test.* Lyle Stuart, New York, 1967.

[25] Kunz, J. *The American Medical Association Family Medical Guide.* Random House, New York, 1982.

[26] Jensen, B. *The Science and Practice of Iridology.* Bernard Jensen, Escondido (CA), 1989.

[27] Gilliliand, R., et al. *Outcome and Predictors of Success of Biofeedback for Constipation.* Brit J Surgery, 1997; 84:1123-1126.

[28] Rao, S.S., et al. *Effects of Biofeedback Therapy on Anorectal Function in Obstructive Defecation.* Digestive Diseases and Sciences, 1997; 42(11):2197-2205.

[29] Marcus, D. A. *Nonpharmacological treatment for migraine: incremental utility of physical therapy with relaxation and thermal biofeedback.* Cephalgia, 1998; 18:266-272.

[30] *The sixth report of the Joint National Committee on Prevention, Detection, Evaluation, and Treatment of High Blood Pressure.* National Institutes of Health: National Heart, Lung and Blood Institute, 1997:PM8380.

[31] McCully, K., et al. *Use of Exercise for Treatment of Chronic Fatigue Syndrome.* Sports Med,1996; 21(1):35-48.

[32] Herbert, V. and Barrett, S. *Alternative Nutrition Therapies. In Modern Nutrition in Health and Disease,* 9th ed. Williams & Wilkins, Balt., 1999:1801-1810.

8

Reflex Nutrition Assessment

This chapter includes comments the author of ten makes to practioners to whom he teaches this technique. It is not intended to teach lay persons the technique.

Reflex Nutrition Assessment, otherwise known as RNA, is an ancillary form of nutrition assessment. It is a simple, non-diagnostic, experimental method of assessing the potential nutritional needs of the human body. RNA is a form of biofeedback that does not require expensive equipment and is considered to be experimental. It is a technique used to assess nutrition status by observing the response of muscles under externally provided human-force. Although it is similar to other forms of kinesiology, it has many unique applications and has been demonstrated to have a high degree of accuracy. In a sense, muscle testing techniques like RNA are somewhat of a combination of East meeting West (or like combining old and new). It is understood that Dr. Beardall (D.C.) developed one of the earlier techniques with the assistance of an acupuncturist and other individuals.

Performing RNA consists of performing at least two assessments. The first assessment is to determine if a reflex indicates a nutritional need and the second assessment is to determine which dietary or supplement approach can help fit that need. It is this combination of the two assessments which contributes to its high rate of accuracy.

How to Perform Reflex Nutrition Assessment

The most important concept to keep in mind is that all people are different. Because of this difference, all successful practitioners using RNA have learned that it is important to adjust their amount of applied force based on individual response.

Step 1: Have the subject hold an arm outstretched. This arm should be parallel to the ground. Tell the subject to resist any pressure that you may place on the subject's wrist.

Step 2: Place the three middle fingers of your hand on the top of the ulnar (dorsal/backside) side of the subject's wrist, just before the end of the forearm. Apply pressure against the subject's wrist; the subject's arm should be able to resist this pressure. Then maintain your hand's position without applying pressure.

Step 3: Place the palmer tip of the index finger on your other hand on the top base (bridge) of the subject's nose.

Step 4: Again apply pressure against the subject's wrist; the subject's arm should not be able to resist this pressure (this particular point is for testing purposes only; most people will not be able to resist your applied pressure while this point is touched).

You may wish to repeat steps 2 through 4 to get the "feel" for this technique.

Step 5: Again apply pressure against the subject's wrist; the subject's arm should be able to resist this pressure.

Step 6: Place the suspected allergen in the subject's hand while applying pressure against the subject's wrist. An inability to resist this pressure should be considered to be a possible sensitivity. For airborne allergens, also place the allergen against the lung reflex. For suspected foods, also place the allergen against the food sensitivity reflex. Inabilities to resist should be considered as possible sensitivities.

Step 7: Touch various reflex points in accordance with the subject's complaints. An inability to resist your pressure should be taken as a possible nutritional deficiency. Note any points that appeared to have nutritional deficiencies. One should often re-check reflexes. When re-checking, greater pressure should actually be applied to the points that the subject was able to resist and apply less pressure to the points that the subject was not able to resist. This is to ensure that the reflex response is not being misinterpreted. Another reason to re-check an individual is that this will give you the feel for assessing an individual. "Ideal" individuals (from a Reflex Nutrition Assessment standpoint) have sufficient strength to resist pressure when you are not touching a nutritionally-deficient reflex, but have almost no ability to resist pressure when you touch them at the top of the nose or at a point which indicates a possible nutritional deficiency.

Step 8: Recheck the nutritional deficiency reflex, except this time have the subject hold a possibly needed nutrient, food, or combination of nutrients. If supplements are involved, it is usually not necessary to take the supplements out of their packaging. Note which supplements restore the subject's ability to resist your applied pressure. If some nutrient, food, etc. only partially restores the subject's ability to resist your pressure, then you should check other supplements (for example, if the thyroid reflex is an issue you may wish to try some glandulars, kelp, and/or other herbs).

Step 9: You may, in conjunction with other forms of assessment, then wish to make various nutrition-based recommendations. Reflex Nutrition Assessment is not a diagnostic tool, but is presented as an interesting source of ancillary information for nutrition assessment. It is important to inform your subjects that most food supplements recommended should be taken at meals and that only one of any supplement should be taken the first day to reduce the possibility of any negative reactions to the supplements. All should be told to immediately discontinue any supplementation which they (or any one of their health professionals) feel may be causing some type of negative reaction.

How to Perform Reflex Nutrition Assessment on Difficult Subjects

There are several types of people which are difficult to check, but until you perform steps 1 through 4, it is nearly impossible to know in advance.

People who have no strength to resist step 1 are very difficult to check. In that case, it may be necessary to apply pressure to someone else instead. The "surrogate" holds an arm outstretched just like the subject would; and you (while touching various reflexes on the subject) apply pressure against the surrogate's wrist. Your touching both individuals at the same time maintains the electromagnetic connection. This is also a good technique to use for small children (sometimes it is easiest to assess children when they sit on the surrogate's lap). The other steps are the same.

General Reflexes

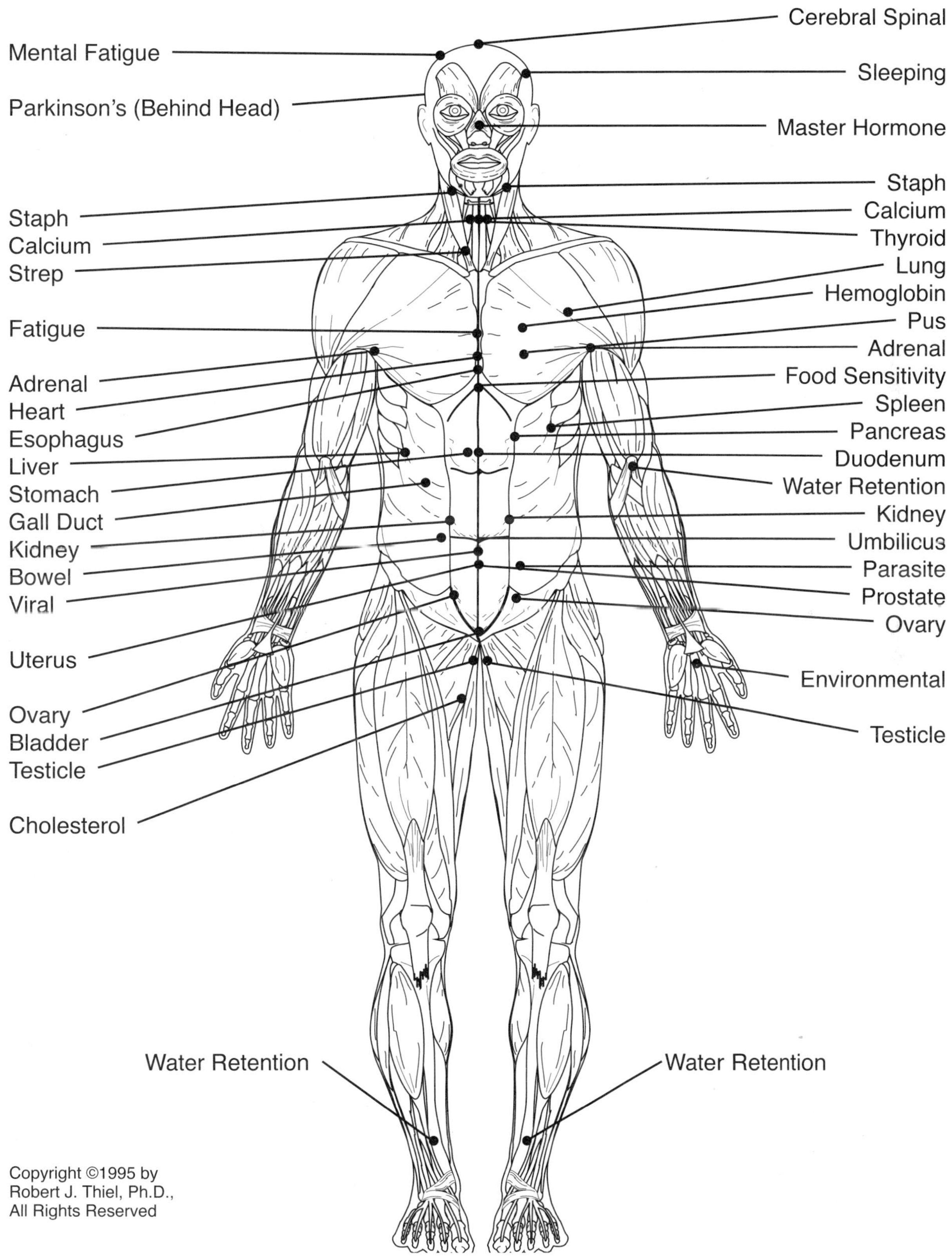

People whose arm continues to resist your pressure in step 4 are also difficult. This will happen about 5-10% of the time. If this occurs, first modify step 2—instead of touching the top of the nose with the palmer tip of the index finger, try the ulnar (dorsal/backside) side. If the use of the ulnar side of the finger results in the inability to resist your pressure, you will need to reverse the palmer/ulnar comments in this book. For some people, holding a bottle of something containing essential fatty acids for a couple of minutes will make it easier to check them.

If the previous approaches do not work, have the subject turn his or her head to the left and to the right. At each extreme, repeat step 4. If step 4 is successful, then have the subject keep his or her head in the appropriately turned position.

Special Notes on Foods and Environmental Sensitivities

Allergies and environmental sensitivities are major problems. Although supplementation can help, there is no substitute for avoiding foods to which one is sensitive. The methods used for isolating sensitivities are reflex assessment, elimination diets, pulse rate changes, oral history reports, IgG tests, and classic allergy (IgE) tests (although naturopaths cannot order this in California).

To reflex assess potential food or environmental sensitivities, simply place the suspect food/vial in the palm of the subject's hand while applying pressure against the other wrist. An inability to withstand the pressure is considered to be an indication of a possible sensitivity (this method only provides ancillary information and should only be considered an indication; and yes, not all sensitivities will appear using this method); other methods should be used to confirm (or deny) results obtained using this experimental technique. When foods are involved, also place the potential food/vial at the base of the sternum. If the sensitivity is not general, but may cause a digestive problem only, place the vial above the suspected organ. In the case of some type of fatty food, it may be placed over the gall duct.

Most people who have airborne allergies and/or environmental sensitivities also have food sensitivities. Avoiding suspect foods tends to reduce mucus production as well as increase tolerance to airborne allergens. There have been great results using this technique. Once you master the technique, you should too. Be aware that many considered to be "health experts" do not consider techniques such as this one to have any value [1-2]; however, the author and certain other practitioners disagree [3-9].

Special Notes on RNA

In addition to touching the heart reflex and checking it like most other reflexes, there is another way to check the heart reflex which some prefer. Have the subject clasp both hands with their arms fully extended in front of them. You then apply downward pressure to one or both wrists. If the subject is unable to resist this pressure, then it is an indication of a problem with the heart reflex—the related nutrition is the same as listed later in this chapter.

As mentioned previously, many authorities considered as health experts do not believe that assessment techniques similar to Reflex Nutrition Assessment can have any value [1-2]. Nor (like the rest of this book) have any of these statements been reviewed by the FDA.

Is Reflex Nutrition Assessment Scientific?

If scientific means "Is Reflex Nutrition Assessment based on physical scientific principles?", the answer is yes. If scientific means "Are the results of Reflex Nutrition Assessment repeatable?", the answer is yes. If scientific means "Does Reflex Nutrition Assessment add to our knowledge about our subjects?", the answer is yes. However, if scientific means "Do most health scientists currently accept this method?", then the answer is no. However, there are dozens of studies, summaries of studies, and clinical experiences which have demonstrated the application of the principles behind Reflex Nutrition Assessment (also see the studies in Appendix A).

Reflex Nutrition Assessment has certain similarities to other forms of deltoid kinesiology. Forms of kinesiology have generally been criticized by mainstream health practitioners. The primary reason normally given is lack of controlled data. Another problem is that the primary study that most of the "mainstream" seems to cite was a limited trial involving only 11 subjects [1], while ignoring other studies which appear to demonstrate the effectiveness of it and similar methods [5,9-16].

One problem with kinesiological techniques is that there are many variations of them [i.e. 3-9]. The skill of the practitioner plays a significant role in its reliability. The version of kinesiology the author has developed is Reflex Nutrition Assessment. It was based on previous researchers' as well as his clinical experience.

Reflex Nutrition Assessment is based on the naturopathic premise that each individual is unique. It is based on the naturopathic premise that generalized nutritional recommendations not only do not meet the optimal nutrition needs of every person, there is no conceivable way that they could. RNA is based on the premise that the human body is capable of recognizing some of its nutrient needs.

Biological Facts

The human body contains several hundred miles of nerves which are capable of conducting electromagnetic energy. Local current flow occurs (in the body) wherever there is an electric gradient. The resting electrical potential of cellular membranes varies from 5 to 100 millivolts (nerve cells have some of the highest resting electrical potentials). Once stimulated, the action potential of nerve cells lasts for approximately 1 millisecond. Each action potential triggers (via local current flow) a new action potential at an adjacent area of membrane. The local flow is just powerful enough to trip the adjacent membrane site past its threshold potential. In nerve cells, the membranes are normally initiated at one end of the cell and then propagate toward the other end of the cell. [17]

Approximately 90 percent of the cells within the nervous system are glial cells. Glial cells sustain the neurons (the other 10 percent of the nerve cells) metabolically, support them physically, and regulate ion concentrations in extracellular space. [17] Neurons are most likely to be the portion of the nervous system involved with RNA. Neurons are composed of dendrites, axon terminals, and the axon itself. The synapse is the connection between the axon terminals of one neuron and the dendrites of another neuron. A single motor neuron in the spinal cord receives approximately 15,000 synaptic endings, whereas one in the brain receives at least 100,000. Thus, nearly every part of the human body is connected directly (and always indirectly) to every other part of the body. [17]

RNA Explanation

RNA is believed to be based on neuron firings triggered by changes in either local current flow or changes in electromagnetic energy. It should be noted that electromagnetic energy is not fully understood by the scientific community. It is generally believed that electromagnetic energy holds atoms together. It is theorized that electromagnetic energy exists in wave form. It is known that electromagnetic energy travels 186,000 miles per second. But how electromagnetic energy works in, or affects, biological systems is not fully known.

Mainstream Science?

While in his Ph.D. program, the author debated whether to do a project of measuring, correlating, and "proving" the application of biological electromagnetic energy (Reflex Nutrition Assessment) or to conduct a clinical trial to improve the health of ill persons. As a naturopath being more interested in helping people improve their health than in esoteric explanations, the clinical trial was conducted which also demonstrated that Reflex Nutrition Assessment could be a valid indicator of improvement. It is futile to use the term "prove", because there is a great deal of bias within the mainstream medical-scientific community against methods which they consider to be alternative or "low-tech." Though initially somewhat skeptical of this method, every attempt was made to keep an open-mind about it.

Speaking of being open-minded, one should be aware of what could be called "mainstream scientific bias" throughout history. As science is able to reveal more and more data and explanations, it can be easy to chide and ridicule various scientific explanations of biological systems throughout recorded history which are now proven to be false. We must ask ourselves, "Do we now possess all true scientific facts?" Current explanations may become fodder for ridicule sometime in the future. In the not too distant past it was taught that blood in the arteries was red, but that the oxygen-deprived blood in the veins was blue—now of course that is not true (blood is always red [17]), but that was what was taught as a fact of mainstream science. We all must keep an open mind when reviewing new theories and programs and do the proper research to determine validity.

When looking into the sky, it appears that the Sun is going around the Earth every day and that the Earth is stationary. Until a few centuries ago, all of the mainstream scientific community believed that the Earth was the center of the universe and the Sun traveled around it. When telescopes became better developed, Galileo and others could prove (at least to themselves) that the Earth revolved around the Sun. In the early 1800's a German medical doctor, Samuel Hahnemann, theorized that acute diseases that caused epidemics had an identical cause that became infectious to which he referred to as a "brood of...excessively minute, invisible, living creatures" [18] ; Hahnemann was criticized by the mainstream for this (and much of his other work) because it was not consistent with "mainstream science." Decades later when microscopes were improved, Hahnemann's work which laid the foundations for proving the existence of germ organisms was accepted (Louis Pasteur, who lived in neighboring France, received the credit for it). There is a new device which is being tested to measure electromagnetism (for physics applications). Within a couple of decades this type of device will be perfected to the point that it will accurately measure the type(s) of electromagnetic energy that is the basis of RNA. We can either wait decades for this type of "proof" or try to help people now.

Reflex Nutrition Assessment is remarkably accurate. There is often improvement in symptomatic complaints, even in many situations where medical professionals have not had success (sometimes for decades). The improvement results correlate to reflex response.

Differing Types of Electromagnetism

It should be noted that Reflex Nutrition Assessment is also based on the premise that the type of electromagnetic energy emitted by the palmar and ulnar (dorsal/backside) portions of the hand are somehow different. Some chiropractors assert the palmar side emits a positively-charged form of electromagnetic energy while the ulnar side emits a negative form, whereas some other holistic practitioners believe that should be reversed, with the palmar side being negative, etc. This differ-

ence is important because some reflexes appear to only react to positive forms, others negative forms, others both, and for some others it varies. It should also be noted that reflexes are not medical conditions, nor do they necessarily correlate with any medical condition (even if the names are the same or similar to any medical condition).

Answers to Frequent Questions on RNA

You and others will have questions about RNA. It is first important that you understand the answers to these questions so you can explain them clearly. The greater confidence clients have in the tester and RNA, greater compliance will be encountered.

An often asked question is, "How can holding a bottle of supplements possibly strengthen me since the bottle is a sealed container?" The question assumes that the substances contained within the container cannot be emitting electromagnetic energy, which of course is untrue. The question also assumes that electromagnetic energy is larger than the intermolecular spaces within the container, which of course is untrue. The question also assumes that the human nervous system is not capable of recognizing or reacting to external electromagnetic stimuli, which, of course, is untrue [17]. It is true that few (if any) measurements of the influence of nutrient electromagnetic energy in biological applications have been measured by mainstream practitioners, but this does not disprove the potential application of Reflex Nutrition Assessment.

Another question asked is, "Why does touching a reflex with some portion of the hand cause a reduction in muscle strength?" This is an excellent question. One theory is that since all matter emits a certain amount of electromagnetic energy, that the assessor's body is giving off electromagnetic energy as well. When this electromagnetic energy comes in contact with the subject's electromagnetic energy, it interferes with the subject's reflex connection to the other parts of the body (which is normally checked at the wrist). If the reflex being interfered with is somehow nutritionally deficient, this interference is strong enough to reduce this connection. For reflexes without nutritional deficiencies, this interference is not strong enough to overpower neuromuscular control. However when it overpowers, the addition of an appropriate nutritional supplement appears to give off enough electromagnetic energy to more than offset the interference to which the assessor's body is contributing.

Again, it has been asked, "Can the RNA practitioner's thoughts, allergies, or health affect the results?" The answer appears to be yes. All RNA practitioners are different and a practitioner's health can sometimes affect results. If checking someone on a food that bothers the practitioner, one has to be very careful—normally assess that substance several times if you personally get a reaction. Remember that RNA is best used by practitioners who are open-minded pursuers of truth. Another key to RNA is continually challenging and reassessing results (plus comparing results with traditional health tests and data), as well as checking reflexes, supplements, etc. that are not as obvious. At the International College of Naturopathy, Dr. Dale teaches that those who perform a different version of muscle testing keep a particular homeopathic remedy (*Succinic Acid 30x*) on their person while testing to help insure "neutrality"—it may be that this physically affects the tester (which she says German researchers have confirmed, as well as the specific potency of 30x) or that it works as a reminder to the tester that he or she is to be "open-minded pursuers of truth."

Showing a subject the appropriate reflex in this book (or on a full size wall chart) can be helpful to establish your credibility in this area. New clients should be given a brochure which explains RNA and answers some of the more common questions. Even if clients act like they want help and will follow recommendations, well-meaning friends and relatives often will discourage them. This is where having a brochure that explains the technique often comes in handy. Compliance improves when a brochure can be provided.

References

[1] Kenny, James J., Clemens, Roger and Forsythe, Kenneth D. *Applied Kinesiology Unreliable for Assessing Nutrient Status.* J Am Diet Assoc, 1988;Vol. 88.

[2] University of California at Berkeley Wellness Letter. *Allergic to Everything?* Berkeley: UC Berkeley, December 1991.

[3] Versendaal, D. A. *Contact Reflex Analysis and Applied Trophology.* Holland (Mich.): D.A.Versendaal, 1990.

[4] Shepard, Stephen. *Healing Energies.* Provo: BiWorld Publishers, 1983.

[5] Thiel, R. J. *Clinical Trial on the Effects of Dietary Restriction, Homeopathy, and Combination Nutritional Supplementation on Symptoms Associated with Seasonal Allergic Rhinitis.* Dissertation. Union Institute: Cincinnati, 1993.

[6] Lewith, G. T. and Kenyon, J. N. *Clinical Ecology: A Therapeutic Approach to Understanding and Treating Food and Chemical Sensitivities.* Wellingborough (U.K.): Thorsons Publishers:10-40, 1985.

[7] Thiel, Robert J. *Serious Nutrition for Health Professionals.* Arroyo Grande (CA): California Health Group, 1995.

[8] Burr-Madsen, Angela. B*ody Polarity Reflex Analysis and the Nutritional Connection.* Carson City: Thoth, Inc., 1992.

[9] Rosen, Marc S. and Williams, Louisa. *The Research Status of Applied Kinesiology, Part II: An Annotated Bibliography of Applied Kinesiological Research.* In: A.K. Review, Vol. 1, No. 2: 34-47, 1991.

[10] Thiel, Robert J. *Chronic Fatigue Assessment and Intervention: The Result of 101 Cases.* ANMA & AANC J,1996;1 (3):17-19.

[11] Thiel, Robert J. *Nutrition-Based Interventions for Attention-Deficit Disorder and Attention-Deficit Hyperactive Disorder.* ANMA Monitor,1997;1(4):5-8.

[12] Thiel, Robert J. *Effects of Naturopathic Interventions on Symptoms Associated with Seasonal Allergic Rhinitis.* ANMA Monitor, 1997; 1(2):4-9.

[13] Thiel, Robert J. *Musculoskeletal Pain Relief for People with Arthritis, Lupus, and Fibromyalgia.* Townsend Letter for Doctors and Patients, 1997; 172:91-92.

[14] Thiel, Robert J. *Natural Interventions for People with Fibromyalgia.* ANMA Monitor, 1998; 2(2):6-8.

[15] Thiel, Robert J. *Natural Interventions for Migraine Sufferers.* ANMA Monitor, 1998; 2(3):5-9.

[16] Thiel, Robert J. *Bioelectrical Stimulation for People with Patterns Consistent with Certain Infections. ANMA Monitor,1998; 2(4):5-9.*

[17] Guyton A.C. and Hal,l J.E. *Textbook of Medical Physiology,* 9th ed. WB Saunders, Phil., 1996.

[18] Cummings S. and Ullman, D. *Everybody's Guide to Homeopathic Medicines.* JP Tarcher, Los Angeles, 1984.

9

Pulse Assessment for Sensitivities

The use of changes in pulse rate as a method of determining food and environmental sensitivities was the subject of a book originally written by Dr. Arthur Coca, M.D. in the 1950s. Dr. Coca noticed that certain foods, which differed by individual, tended to raise the pulse count of different people by different amounts. He noticed that some cases of diseases appeared to improve if a person avoided foods that raised his or her pulse very much. Dr. Coca theorized that many diseases could be positively impacted if people did not consume foods that had a substantial raising effect on their pulse rate. He claimed success with a whole host of diseases including hypertension, headaches, ulcers, neurasthenia, diabetes, sinusitis, angina, asthma, indigestion, epilepsy, and hemorrhoids [1].

Dr. Coca and others have speculated that the pulse rate can help determine food and environmental sensitivities [1,2]. The use of pulse testing is not intended to diagnose class one food allergies or traditional inhaled allergies (an IgE or similar test would need to be performed). Although this is not a generally accepted technique, it should be noted that food sensitivities do not seem to be well understood. Toxicologists Bodin and Cheinisse state in their book, *Poisons*, that "The wide field of individual sensitivity, whether of an allergic nature or not, is still incompletely explored" [3]. It is interesting to note that one symptom medically associated with asthmatic attacks is an increased heart (or pulse) rate [4].

Dr. Coca claimed that some foods would give "that tired feeling." He felt that people with allergic tiredness (such as would be caused by food sensitivities) were normally miserable and often had recurrent headaches. He also felt that nutrient deficiencies could cause fatigue [1].

Several years ago the author started using the pulse test method of determining potential food sensitivities. A sensitivity to pickles and processed mustard was discovered. No problem with cucumbers, dry mustard, or vinegar was apparent, but there is simply something in those particular processed foods that is bothersome. In addition, other tested sensitivities include a few others such as oats. Other than oats, it is not sure why those particular foods have a negative effect, but there is personal evidence that they do. (In the case of oats, the author's mother informed him that he began eating solid foods at around one week of age and oats at around two weeks of age. She said that he always appeared to be hungry and she fed him what he seemed able to eat. It is now believed that early introductions of solid foods seem to increase the incidence of food sensitivities, including allergies.)

Other people have tested sensitive to a wide variety of other foods. The most common ones include cow's milk, caffeine-containing products, oats, wheat, white sugar, eggs, black pepper, soy products, shellfish, and artificial sweeteners.

The pulse test has many advantages over other techniques. It is performed on foods that one actually eats in the combination that one actually eats them. The subject actually performs the test (this is also a disadvantage sometimes). It is easy to do.

How To Perform Pulse Tests

First, the subjects will need to find their pulse. They will need to find it with one of their fingers, not the thumbs. The pulse can normally be felt about one to two inches from the palm of the hand on the wrist on the side which is under the thumb. Some people, especially heavier people, prefer to feel the pulse that is located toward the front of the neck on either side of the windpipe (on the carotid artery). (Actually, the neck pulse is a little easier for most people, but it is a somewhat less private method of taking one's pulse than is the wrist method. Privacy may be an issue, because sometimes people eat certain foods only in restaurants and prefer not to draw attention to themselves by pulse testing.)

Second, they need to be able to count the pulse beats. They must take their pulse for a full minute. Please do not allow them to take their pulse for only fifteen seconds and then multiply that number by four as a "shortcut." If they do, they will only "shortcut" the results; speed impairs the accuracy.

The accuracy rate varies by the individual, but with practice, it has been speculated that it may be as high as 80 percent or more. [5] Unlike certain other methods of determining food sensitivities, this one is easy to do and can be used when someone suspects they may be eating something that bothers them (for instance, at someone else's home).

For best results, it is important that your subjects record the results of their pulse testing. This is important because only this way can you determine if there is a pattern in the results. It is probably also the best way to remember the results. For your convenience, a copy of a form that you can use to record your results is included on the following page.

Although this book is copyrighted, you are given legal permission to copy the "pulse test" form for your own non-commercial use (you can copy it but not sell it or put it in any book you may write).

It is recommended that patients first take their pulse just prior to rising out of bed in the morning. This will probably be their lowest pulse reading of the day. (If not, that will be covered later in this chapter.) After getting ready for breakfast, and immediately before eating or drinking anything, they should take their pulse for one minute. They should record the results in the "before" box, as well as the time. They should begin eating. They are to note the foods (and beverages) in the "foods" column. Forty-five minutes later, they should take their pulse again and record the results in the "after" box. (Please note that this is forty-five minutes after they first took their pulse, not forty-five minutes after they have finished eating their meal.) They are to do this same routine for other meals or snacks that they wish to test. Although the form is set up by day and includes spaces for a variety of eating habits, it is not always essential that patients take their pulse ten times on any given day. Frequently people have told me that they wondered if certain foods bothered them and then they pulse tested those foods. Approximately half the time the suspected foods have been a problem, the other half have not. Please do not assume that because everyone else seems to consider some food to be "healthy", that it is healthy for everyone. It may be making them quite ill and tired or at least making their airborne allergies or environmental sensitivities worse. A small amount of the food is usually sufficient to raise the pulse if someone is sensitive to it. A small amount of food also has the advantage that it may not bother them so much if they are sensitive to it. However, a small amount of a true allergen can still result in anaphylactic shock, so patients should not intentionally consume foods that they may truly be allergic to for any reason.

Reviewing the Results

You need to review the written pulse test records. A good rule of thumb is that if a food raises a pulse seven or more beats per minute, it is possible that the patient was sensitive to something in that food. (For example, one could be sensitive to an insecticide or preservative spray on strawberries, but not to the berries themselves.) Reductions in pulse rate are not as significant, but some people who are sensitive to alcohol sometimes show a reduction of five beats (or more) per minute. Other people find that no food raises their pulse, while some find that every food raises their pulse—these and other results make interpretation complex and your training and experience will be critical for proper interpretation.

Most will pulse test entire meals, as opposed to single foods, but this can cloud the results. Some foods seem to decrease the pulse rate of certain people; if such a food is taken with a food that increases one's pulse rate, the two may cancel each other out. From a practical standpoint, though, it is much easier to pulse test an entire meal. If you review pulse results often enough and use a little bit of deductive reasoning, the foods that raise the pulse will become much clearer. You can always individually test any foods suspected to be the problem.

Pulse Results

The pulse should be taken for a full minute at a time (do not press with your thumb) and while sitting. Before arising and at bedtime, it should be taken while lying down. Please list the foods you are eating next to each meal. It is not necessary to list all the ingredients within each food. Also, please note any other exciting causes you may have experienced near the times you took your pulse such as shock, cigarette smoke, exercise, etc.

Remember take your pulse for a full minute and finish immediately before eating your meal. Take it again 45 minutes after you BEGIN eating. If it takes you more than 45 minutes to eat your meal, take your pulse 15 minutes after you finish.

Please feel free to write your pulse results on regular paper once you fill out this form.

	DAY 1			DAY 2			DAY 3		
	List Foods Eaten	Time	Pulse	List Foods Eaten	Time	Pulse	List Foods Eaten	Time	Pulse
Before Arising									
Breakfast									
+plus 45 min.									
Snack									
+plus 45 min.									
Lunch									
+plus 45 min.									
Snack									
+plus 45 min.									
Supper									
+plus 45 min.									
Snack									
+45 min.									
Upon bedtime									

Other factors (if any):

____

____

____

The foods found to be problematic most frequently include bovine dairy, caffeine containing "foods", wheat, oats, refined carbohydrates, and soy. For more information on some of these items, please review the studies in Appendix A.

Checking Non-Foods

Thus far, this chapter has mainly discussed foods. The other area in which pulse testing is helpful is with particulates and other substances in the air—especially in one's house.

If you use the complete pulse test form, your clients will be noting their pulse count before they rise in the morning, throughout the day (before and after meals), and when they first lie down to sleep at night. The pulse rate should be lowest before arising in the morning. The simple act of getting out of bed and walking around after a night of rest is enough to raise most people's pulse.

Now, what if the pulse rate is not lowest in the morning before rising? There are many possible explanations, but the one most relevant here is that while they were sleeping something in their environment probably raised the pulse rate. In cases like this, it can be suspected that during the night the person must be breathing in something that causes the rise.

Different people are affected by different things. For some, it may be house dust, dander, smoke, pollen, or something of which their room is constructed (such as dry wall or paint).

The first suggestion is to see what happens if they sleep in another room, in another bed, on another pillow (a newer one, preferably without a pillowcase), AND in their own home. Do not recommend that they first try a hotel room. Hotels have a tendency to use strong cleaning materials on sheets and pillowcases which can make some people ill. If the pulse is lower in the morning after trying a different sleeping place with different bedding, this will help you reduce the suspected causes of their pulse-rising problem.

The next night, they should sleep in the same "new" location, except this time put their usual pillowcase on the pillow. If the morning pulse is higher, you probably can conclude that the pillowcase or its cleaning (or lack thereof) is contributing to the problem. You do need to know, though, that it is likely that more than one item could be contributing to the problem. Through trial and error and repeated testing, you have a good chance to get a handle on some of those items that may be bothering your clients.

Most people keep their pillows for quite a few years. Pillows have a tendency to collect dust and dander. Most pillows are not machine washable. Since the face is probably quite close to the pillow all night, it always seems logical to consider pillows to be a prime suspect for raising your patients' pulse. Beds, sheets, curtains, wall tapestries, carpet, and other bedroom furnishings can all be factors. Some people have found that they have attained relief by covering their bedding (mattresses and pillows) with plastic covers which are available through certain medical supply houses. You may wish to recommend this as well, but economically speaking, use the pulse test first to help narrow down potential items. A wise investment may be a new machine-washable pillow; when dust and dander build up on it, simply wash it.

Speaking of purchasing pillows, the subject of "hypoallergenic" ones merits a few comments. Hypoallergenic pillows (and hypoallergenic hotel rooms for that matter) do not guarantee that someone will not be bothered by them. The term "hypoallergenic" seems to indicate that pillows, for example, are not made of goose feathers. If the particular polyester material they are stuffed with bothers someone, they will not find them "hypoallergenic", they will find them to be a nightmare.

Some people who are bothered by their pets will report a raised pulse if the pet has been on their lap. First, the patient takes their pulse in a clean pet-free area. Then they get their pet and stay around it for 10-45 minutes. They then take their pulse again. By the way, variations of this technique can be used to check to see if any particular room in their house, their office, or even certain stores will raise the pulse. It can also be used to check various household chemicals, but, of course, caution is advised.

Emotions

Foods, bedding materials, and particulates in the air are not the only items that can increase pulse rate. Anger, fear, excitement, and other emotions can increase it as well. That is why our pulse form asks them to list any other exciting factors that may have been involved (including shock, cigarette smoke, exercise). If you suspect that a subject's emotions affected the results of a test, you should probably have them re-tested again at a later time.

Other Information

A question that is frequently asked about food sensitivities is, "Can I ever eat the foods to which I am sensitive again, without having health problems?" The answer depends. It seems that the longer the sensitive food is avoided (beyond several months), the less sensitive the body becomes to it. As a general rule, it seems to take between six months and three or more years to become "desensitized" to a particular food. Also, it is not clear if this desensitization is permanent. To be safe, one should never eat a food which they have been clinically diagnosed as allergic too and should always try to avoid foods to which they may be sensitive. If after three years someone wishes to begin consuming the sensitive (as opposed to allergic) foods, they should consider consuming them in small quantities, infrequently, to avoid "re-sensitizing" themselves to them.

In rare cases, consumption of foods can cause anaphylactic shock (with peanuts perhaps the most dangerous food), which can lead to death. Do not risk anaphylactic shock.

Although the pulse test method of determining sensitivities does not have widespread (if any) support among immunologists, some doctors have reported having positive experiences with it [1,6]. Clinical experience suggests that many people who have had environmental problems for years, which did not respond well to more conventional treatments, have been helped by avoiding those substances that caused their pulse to substantially rise.

The pulse rate may have additional value as well. According to the American Heart Association (AHA), the normal resting range for pulse rates is 50 to 100 beats per minute (children normally have higher rates). Various studies have indicated that men with a resting pulse rate of more than 80 beats per minute have a much greater risk of cardiovascular-related death compared to those with much lower rates [7]. An abnormally high pulse rate is often due to an allergy or an infection (including chronic infections that go undetected through conventional assessments).

The use of pulse testing has worked successfully for many naturopaths. It is a non-invasive assessment technique that can be quite individualized.

Reference

[1] Coca, Arthur. *The Pulse Test.* Lyle Stuart: New York, 1967.

[2] Bodin, F. and Cheinisse, C. *Poisons.* World University Library: New York, 1970.

[3] Airola, P. *How to Get Well.* Health Plus Publishers: Sherwood (OR): 1989.

[4] Kunz, J. *The American Medical Association Family Medical Guide.* Random House: New York, 1982.

[5] Lewith, G. T. and Kenyon, J. *Clinical Ecology: A Therapeutic Approach to Understanding and Treating Food and Chemical Sensitivities.* Thorson's Publishers: Wellingborough, U.K.: 1985.

[6] Chaitow, L. *Asthma and Hay Fever.* Thorson's Publishers: Northamptonshire (UK): 1990.

[7] Williams, D. G. *Be Still, My Beating Heart.* Alternatives, 1999;7(23):177-179.

10

The Eye as the Window into Health

Many do not know that looking into the iris and other parts of the eye can reveal information about one's health. The best known proponent of iridology (the assessment of health by examining the iris) must currently be Dr. Bernard Jensen. His book, *The Science and Practice of Iridology* is studied by some naturopathic students. [1] However, before Dr. Jensen, there were of course others who have used the eye as the window into assessing health. Dr. Peczely is generally credited with developing the science of iridology [1,2], although there were undoubtedly others who had long used the human eye to assess health. Peczley believed "that allopathically treated diseases darken the color of the eyes." [3] Although the iris is not the only portion of the eye that can aid in health assessment, it will be the focus of most of this chapter.

Iridology was defined by Dr. J. Haskell Kritzer as follows: "Iridology is a science revealing pathological and functional disturbances in the human body by means of abnormal spots, lines, and discolorations of the eye." [4] Dr. Jensen adds,

Toxemias and where located, activity of each organ, glandular conditions, and drug poisonings are accurately identified. Chemical imbalance, miasma, congestion, constitution, and the ability to get well all show in the eyes. Iridology does not name diseases. The purpose of iridology is to determine the location of inflammation, the stage of inflammation, how it was caused, and the steps necessary to overcome it. [4]

It is felt that through looking at changes in the iris that one can determine whether an organ is worsening or improving, can determine anemias (though not the actual blood count), the constructive ability of the blood, can detect environmental strain, determine nerve force, the presence of germ life (though not the specific pathogen), nutritional problem, and other aspects associated with health. [1,2] Since prevention is the best 'cure', iridologists believe that people can be warned about problems in time to prevent the development of medically detectable diseases. [1]

Most iridologists are naturopaths or chiropractors, though others in the field of nutrition sometimes use it. [5] Some iridologists feel that a nearly complete history of past illnesses can be seen through the record left in the iris. [1,5] Even the Bible states, "The light of the body is the eye; if therefore thine eye be single, thy whole body shall be full of light. But if thine eye be evil, thy whole body shall be full of darkness" (Luke 11:34).

Over 300 years ago, it was written,

Shepherds judge the diseases of their sheep by the lines and other signs of the eye. In man, signs near the iris indicate diseases of the lungs and chest, also cough. If children have sound flesh in the inner angles of the eye, it means health; if these angles lie deep and devoid of flesh, it means disease or death. If the white of the eye is turning into blue and is veined, it indicates diseases of the sexual organs. [1]

Interestingly, is that one of the pioneers in using the eye to assess health was Peter Johannes Thiel [ed. note: Quite possibly a relative to the author, although it could not be verified.] The following was written by Peter Johannes Thiel in 1905, but was translated into English by Dr. F.W. Collins in 1918.

The Colors in the Iris

In the white of the eye, all colors are blended into white, as in the sunlight. But the white of the eye may show abnormal colors; the red of the arteries in active congestion and inflammation, the yellow of bile in liver diseases, the blue of veins in passive congestion, etc. And there are practitioners who can recognize still other diseases by the white of the eye, as we shall see later. We are only concerned with the iris of the eye.

The clearer, purer and denser the blue or brown, the less diseased is the body. When the blue merges into gray, or brown into green, a different state of affairs arises.

Every state of passive congestion, from the most insignificant black and blue spot to the decay of an entire limb, is accompanied by sluggishness and cloudiness of the blood, by a fall in temperature, and a feeling of pressure, and registers itself in the iris as a shadow, ranging from the finest shading to a black spot. Every dry chronic catarrh, as a chronic nasal catarrh, dry cough, "dullness" in the ear, dry vaginal catarrh, constipation, etc., signifies blood stasis, anaemia and lowered temperature, and registers itself in the eye as shadows. It is well here to call attention to the dark ring due to anaemia, found in the iris at its attachment to the sclera.

At first [Collins] only looked for the real dark, almost black spots, which signifies a positive interruption of the circulation. These were caused by some form of external violence, as from a blow, a stroke, a push, a fall, a tear, a cut or an operation, etc. On account of such an injury from external violence, this science was discovered. When a small boy, the future Dr. Peczely sought to extricate his hand from the claws of an owl; in doing so he broke its leg and noticed in the eye of the owl the sudden appearance of a black

mark running perpendicularly downward from the center. He bandaged the owl's leg and observed on numerous occasions when the bird returned, that the spot in the eye never disappeared. Only, when in later years Dr. Peczely observed similar signs in his own patients, he remembered this occurrence; and thus was the science of "The Diagnosis of Diseases by Observation of the Eye" discovered.

It is quite as astonishing to the patients as to the observer if, at the first glance at such spots with their light borders, one can diagnosis and locate fresh wounds, scars, healed and unhealed; operations, etc. It often happens that the patient no longer remembers the occurrence. Usually his memory returns during the examination or soon thereafter. Thus [Collins] had the following experience: During one of my lectures a patient would not admit that he had received an injury to the spine; eventually he confessed that at the battle of Koeniggraetz, on account of a severe injury to his spine, sustained through a fall from his horse, he had to lie in Nazareth for several weeks. He thought that had happened too long ago to be of any significance. As is so often the case, [Collins] had to teach this individual that these eye signs never disappear.

Is it any wonder if the beginner in this art, after a few successful diagnosis, makes the search for these light and dark spots his hobby, and after many blunders eventually turns his back to all our teachings and becomes our most aggressive opponent? An added difficulty is the fact that many patients insist upon having their past injuries diagnosed. Thus, at one of my lectures, [Collins] had the following painful experiences: ...[it was] pointed out to one man that he had haemorrhoids, stasis of blood in the rectum. He at first denied it in spite of the evidence, but finally acknowledged that he had undergone a severe rectal operation on account of haemorrhoids and a rectal fistula. [Collins] found only a very insignificant shadow that was almost hidden by other neighboring and distant evidences. But more of this later. At another time, in the presence of an audience, an elderly woman insisted upon having her trembling hand diagnosed: another, her broken ankle. Both cases were not easy to recognize, because of the presence of a great number of other signs. ...at first, such cases often discouraged [Collins], until ...the limits of the possibilities of our art [are recognized]. Therefore, all beginners should guard against the temptation of carrying on such work as sport.

The Formations in the Iris

Still more important than the colors, is the arrangement of the fibers in the iris. If the fibers were only blood vessels, they would spread over the entire iris like a net. But the ring around the pupil, which we will later recognize as the stomach area, shows, in most eyes, smooth parallel threads running in a direction at first angles to the margin of the pupil, like the radii of a circle. In a person with a normal, healthy stomach, these fibers are equidistant from one another, like the spokes of a little wheel surrounding the pupil. The healthier the body, the straighter is the course of these radiations to the white of the eye. The distance between the rays is necessarily increased the further they extend towards the periphery. The spaces between are filled in by other branches, like the feathers on a quill. The denser this fiber formation, the greater the muscle tissue of the body, the firmer the skin and the inner and outer mucous membranes. The looser and more widely separated are the fibers, the looser the structure of all the organs of the body; looseness of the skin and flabbiness of the muscles, sluggishness of the pores of the skin (in winter continual chilliness, in summer constant sweating), continual feeling of tiredness, softening of the bones (in children ratchets), torpidly of all the glands and all the organs and an inclination to dilatation (scrofula, emphysema of the lungs, dilatation of the heart, enlargement of the spleen in leucaemia, Bright's disease, varicose veins, nervous prostration, softening of the brain, etc.) The position of these signs shows us which particular organ is suffering from this loss of vitality.

Next we must consider these formations by themselves. They arise through a union or a separation of the fibers in the upper layers. When they unite they form thicker fibers which are raised above the surrounding tissue, and are more brightly illuminated by a light from external sources, and therefore appear brighter.

The Abnormal Colors and Formations in the Pupil

Abnormal colors in the pupil arise through a cloudiness in the cornea, a cloudiness of the aqueous humor, in cataract and in albinos. The transparent cornea surrounds the entire eye, acting as a protection to it. It also covers the sclera or white of the eye. In front of the iris it is raised like a watch glass over the face of a watch. Through the presence of foreign bodies, its transparency may be impaired. In such cases the vision is obscured, as if one were looking through a haze. If such foreign bodies or abscesses lie in front of the pupil, the latter changes from a deep black, found in normal eyes, to a gray color. The various tissue layers, which surround the eye, contain a black pigmented layer directly behind the vascular choroid. No rays of the sun can penetrate this layer and illuminate the interior of the eye. In a similar way the photographer darkens the interior of his apparatus and throws a black cloth over his head to keep stray beams of light away from his camera. Only those rays of light that have passed through the lens in front should fall upon the photographic place. In a similar way, only that light should read the retina that has passed into the eye through the pupil. The pupil, in a healthy eye, appears black because of the dark pigmented layer lining the interior of the eye ball. In those cases where this pigmented layer is absent, the light rays penetrate the sclera and choroid and cause irritation of the retina. This light, striking the blood vessels, causes a red reflection. This red reflected light passes out of the eye through the pupil, giving the latter a reddish hue. Such people are called albinos. The pigmented layer of the hair and skin is likewise lacking in these people, for which reasons they seem to have such delicate white skin and white hair. We find similar conditions in white guinea-pigs and white mice. Because of the lack of protection of this pigmented layer, the albinos are very sensitive to light and weather conditions and to mental influences.

If the black pupil turns gray, we must find out whether the cloudiness lies in the cornea, in the aqueous humor, or in the lens in back of the iris. We can readily determine this by directing a ray of light into the eye, by means of a magnifying glass or pocket flash light. The aqueous humor is a fluid, as clear as water, situated between the cornea and iris. It becomes turbid very easily. The lens lies directly behind the pupil and iris and, like a burning glass, its duty is to gather together the rays of light and focus them as an image upon the retina. Through changes in its elasticity, it causes near-sightedness and far-sightedness; through cloudiness, it causes cataract formation. This begins as a mistiness of the cornea, so faint as to be difficult to recognize; but is easily recognized in the beginning of its formation through our examination. It reveals other conditions usually associated with it: lack of bodily secretions, stasis of the blood, low grade of metabolism and sluggishness of digestion. In the early stages it can be prevented from developing and be cured by a thorough nature cure, relieving the congestion in the head by sitz baths and light and air baths, and more especially by the curative powers of odic force.

In a more advanced condition its maturity can be hastened by increasing the congestion in the head. It can not be operated upon until the lens has become hard and total blindness has developed.

...these abnormal colors in the pupil [are described] at some length because patients so frequently seek advice from the eye specialist about these matters.

Let us now consider the pupil in health. The pupil is the gate of vision and at the same time the safety valve for a very strong light. When looking into darkness, the pupil of the healthy dilates as far as possible in order to take in as much light as possible to render the vision clearer. It is a well-known fact that at night cats have very large pupils, and therefore, see so well at these times, whereas, during the day, their pupil is narrowed down to a mere slit. In a strong light the sphincter of the pupil contracts involuntarily, otherwise an overabundance of light would blind the retina, and through repeated irritation cause amaurosis.

We often notice a large widely dilated pupil in persons in whose eyes were instill drops of atropine, for an operation, or even for a brief examination. Through this drug the pupil is artificially dilated and permits the operator to make a long and uninterrupted examination of the interior of the eye. By means of this poison, which is obtained from the thorn apple and deadly night shade, the sphincter of the pupil weakened, not only during the short time of the operation, but more or less permanently; the pupil remains dilated, the light that enters the eye is not sufficiently cut down, and the gradual development of blindness all too easily brought about. The women in the southern countries use atropine that they may have a pitch black bewitching eye. How easily, from the blinding rays of the sun in these warmer countries, can blindness ensue.

The sphincter of the pupil should always retain its mobility. The greater its power of contraction and dilatation and the more this is stimulated by light from without, and not from irritation of the nerves within, the greater its power of vision, and the more normal is the work of all the organs of the body. A person whose pupils contract well in a strong light, and dilate well at night time, will have skin pores that contract well in the cold that will prevent the body from freezing; in warm weather these pores will dilate and the skin, through the evaporation of its secretion, will enable the body to cool off; his digestion will be good; his metabolism active. The sphincter muscles of the stomach and intestines, of the urinary bladder and of the gall bladder will work normally and regularly—in sort, all the activities of his body will be well regulated. Such eyes we will find in all people who live according to nature, as foresters and farmers, and especially children who are allowed to play in the open.

If we find in children wide, sluggish pupils, we must bear in mind inherited weakness, many diseases in childhood, and more especially worms. The small pinworms rob the sphincter of the anus of its tone, the round and especially the tapeworms weaken the tonicity of the entire intestine. Digestion and metabolism are sluggish and the sphincter of the pupil is likewise sluggish.

Large sluggish pupils denote bodily weakness. The wider the pupils, the nearer the body is to death, provided the tonicity of the pupillary muscles can not be recovered by a natural mode of living. Such pupils dilate very little in the dark, and contract to an insignificant degree when light enters the eye. In order to detect the degree of sluggishness, [Collins] instruct[s] the patients to cover their closed eyes with their hands, then quickly notice the size of the pupils as they take their hands away, and then [Collins] direct[s] the rays of an electric pocket lamp into the eye. Sunlight or lamplight may be used in a similar way if the rays are focused through the pupil by means of a magnifying glass used as a burning glass. The pupil of a healthy person will suddenly contract to a small size and bear the light pretty well. The sluggish pupil will only contract a little, but the eyelids will close tightly and a flow of tears will be evidence of the irritation produced.

Through irritation of the eye to a greater or lesser degree, one can determine the grade of nervous instability.

[Collins] consider[s] the observation of the pupil the very best method for determining the nervous state of an individual. The pupil of a healthy person remains the same size in the same light and does not interfere with the examination by dilating and contracting alternately. And a person of a weaker constitution, whose nerves may be weak and dulled, but who does not show any nervous instability, has sluggish pupils that do not change their size in an unchanging light. The hypersensitive nervous individuals not only open and close their eyelids continually, but more particularly their pupils are constantly contracting and dilating. A change in the intensity of light is not the cause of this, but rather the nerves of the eye, which are closely related to the whole nervous system…we will come to recognize the pupillary ring as the area of the nervous system. The nervous individual may seek to master his hyper-irritability in the presence of the examining physician. He can hold in check his expression and his actions. With a certain amount of training, he may be able to quiet an over-active heart. Therefore, he may be able to deceive the physician in regard to his nervous condition. But he cannot control the contractions of his pupil, so he cannot deceive the eye examiner.

Mention must still be made of the fact that near-sightedness and far-sightedness have an influence upon the size of the pupil, something that the eye examiner must learn and consider. And further, operations upon the iris cause the development of abnormal formations in the pupil. One should guard against mistaken diagnoses of this condition… [Collins] want[s] to take every opportunity to emphasize the damage caused by mercury in any form, and the advantages of treatment according to the principles of nature therapy through ashes, sun baths, sitz baths, sweat cures, etc.

The Eye Signs of Disease and the New Ray Researches

How is it possible that the areas of the various organs in the iris are arranged according to their position in the body? The eye has no direct nerve communication with each individual organ, and is not actually involved in diseases of the various organs. The "materialistic" gentlemen believe in the transmission of power only through channels that can convey such power, as, for example, through the blood vessels, nerves, or at least through oscillatory waves that can be demonstrated, counted and measured.

Reichenbach, with his teaching of odic force as energy in the form of rays, has now, after a silence of one hundred years, suddenly come to life again, due to two new discoveries; one, the wireless telegraphy; the other, the discovery of the invisible rays. Who is the greater master, the discoverer of the first steam engine or the discoverer of the innumerable improvements upon it? Who has rendered the greater service to mankind, the first discoverer of the invisible odic rays, or the investigator of innumerable varieties of invisible rays? Just as it is hardly possible any more to discover new elements, so will it be with new rays. Then one will come to realize that according to the laws of the conservation of matter and energy, the various elementary substances are only transformations of one original element, material or substance, whatever one may choose to call it. In a similar way we will learn that all the rays, like all other forms of energy, are only transformations of one original form of energy. It will further be shown that all these changes take place under the influence of the two antagonistic poles. Not only have magnetism and electricity their double polarity, that is, a male "positive" (+) and a female "negative" (-) pole, but also heat, light, gravity, and all other forces like odic force and the new rays. Likewise, all the elements and all bodies, the earth and all the heavenly bodies, and the solar system have their male or positive and their female or negative pole. All transformations of energy, as light into heat, electricity, magnetism, odic force, the forces of attraction or repulsion, etc., take places according to the laws of polarity. Reichenbach has already pointed out that the human and animal bodies, the plants, crystals and stones have antagonistic poles in their length, breadth and thickness. Also, man and woman, the male and female species in animals and flowering plants, all confirm the theory of polarity.

Reichenbach named the unknown force of radiant energy that is invisible, and only to be recognized by very sensitive people in a dark room, after the god of the Germanic people, Odin or Od. Therefore, in my pamphlet, "German Method of Healing by Odic Force Instead of Swedish Massage," and in the first edition of this work, [Collins has] retained the name Od. After the discovery of the invisible ultra-violet rays, which lie beyond the violet end of the spectrum, as well as the invisible but otherwise entirely different X rays, other investigators have more recently carried their study of the invisible rays still further. A more detailed consideration of these discoveries and their significance in regard to life itself and in regard to the eye-signs of disease, is better reserved for my more complete edition. The researches of Bequerel must, however, be considered here. He found out that even our body emits N-rays, and that they emanate from the nerve centers. He acknowledged the value of Reichenbach's discovery and confirmed the results of his investigations.

What the industrious Reichenbach described in his now rare two-volume work, "The Sensitive Person," has since been confirmed by later investigations. It is deserving of mention that to this day investigators seek to elaborate upon, and to apply to other branches of research, Reichenbach's original discovery of radiant energy. But this by no means detracts from the significance of Reichenbach's Odic Force.

The Eye Signs of Disease and the Methods of Nature Therapy

Peczely and Liljequist, founders of "The Diagnosis of Diseases by Observation of the Eye," were homeopathists. In the homeopathic movement of the past century this method of diagnosis' played a very important role. For what could plead more eloquently against the large allopathic doses of drugs, and in favor of the small homeopathic doses, than the demonstration of the residual poison in the iris? And then the homeopathic physicians held a conference which sounded the death knell of the possibilities in, and the usefulness of, this method of diagnosis, much to the detriment of their movement. This is proven by the large number of recruits we have made along the lower Rhine who are practicing this science and using it as an aid in spreading the knowledge of the methods of nature therapy. Nothing else has made Pastor Felke's "Method of Healing" so popular and famous along the lower Rhine but his carefully studied diagnoses from the eye. Felke was considered the keenest practitioner in the world.

Then [Collins] appeared with [his] little book and photographs describing the diagnosis of diseases by observation of the eye. None of the Felke, Kneipp, homeopathic or any nature therapeutic society along the lower Rhine troubled themselves about the great expense incidental in arranging for these illustrated lectures. These lectures were very well attended, and became most efficient in spreading the doctrine of curative methods in accordance with the laws of nature. The medical profession recognized its significance, for they felt impelled to prosecute, in every possible way, this popular "Eye Diagnosis." They likewise attacked my book, my lectures, my activities, and even my very person. They tried, above all, to give the death blow to nature therapy methods, since at the trial of Tilsit they sought to prove that the "Eye Diagnosis" was pure humbug and a swindle. Schroeter was foolish enough to walk into a trap when he took the matter into the court.

Every practitioner of this method of investigation must know how easily the investigation is influenced by one's emotions and frame of mind. It is not a simple mechanical reading of letters, but a difficult interpretation of living movable signs, a sort of "reading between the lines." It is not so much a question of certain external symptoms as it is a question of the investigation of the underlying cause; a comparison of related areas, colors and formations; a question of reasoning and judgment. It requires considerable practice to arrive at conclusions quickly, and a great deal of discretion, composure and proper frame of mind in order not to go astray. [Collins] usually refuse[s] to make cursory examinations, referring such cases to [his] free Wednesday afternoon clinics at Lebensheim. There [his] organization is complete, and [he is] not disturbed; besides, there [Collins has his] glass. ...seldom [is the glass used] for magnifying purposes... [but] to illuminate the eye. An electric pocket lamp gives [Collins] very good service for the same purpose. For beginners, however, a good magnifying glass is strongly to be recommended. This glass need not have the lines of the areas marked upon it, as is found in Schroeter's ill-famed glasses. Such a crutch for the beginner was an impediment for those further advanced.

While the nature therapy societies of the Rhine and Westphalian group gave undivided recognition to the "Diagnosis of Disease by the Eye," the leading organizations and most important periodicals of the nature therapy movement, for some unknown reason, remained cool toward us, if they had not already turned against and condemned us. The "Deutsche Warte," the leading paper of the movement, and with it many other natural therapy periodicals found it necessary to reject our methods of examination, since it did harm to their movement. [2]

The more things change, the more they stay the same! Is it any wonder that there are still arguments in our profession? Isn't the debate about health supposed to be about improving people's health and not about control, power, or the advancement of one group at the expense of truth?

An examination of this (or any iridological chart) will reveal that there are a tremendous number of points in the eye. In order to be more certain as to the particular part of the body which is being affected, many modern iridologists take photographs of the iris. [1]

Although Peter Thiel had his own view about how iridology might work, a different view has been put forth by others:

> The iris is a center for countless tiny blood vessels, muscle fibers, and nerves (imbedded in the four pigmented layers of the iris), which are linked with every part of the organism via the autonomic nervous system. In an unhealthy body, toxins are deposited in the iris, irritating nerve endings and leaving a record in the iris of the condition of overworked organs: Signs of ill health are visible as cloudy patches, dark spots, and lines [4].

Essentially, the darker the spots, the more severe the health condition is believed to be [4]. The reverse is also believed to be true—the lighter spots become, the better the affected tissue/organ is believed to be doing [4].

What Might the Signs in the Iris Mean?

Dr. Jensen has written,

> The perfect eye shows no flaws—no holes, no inherent weaknesses, no distortion of fibres, no deposits, and is a perfect color...One who analyzes from the standpoint of the cause and effect relations in natural law, will be able not only to recognize the disorders which are represented in the iris, but will recognize the progress of correction, and will observe and follow healing signs as they become manifest in the iris...In iridology, the important fundamental is the appearance in the iris of signs that new tissue is replacing old tissue [1].

One of the oldest charts, originally produced in English, used for iridology.

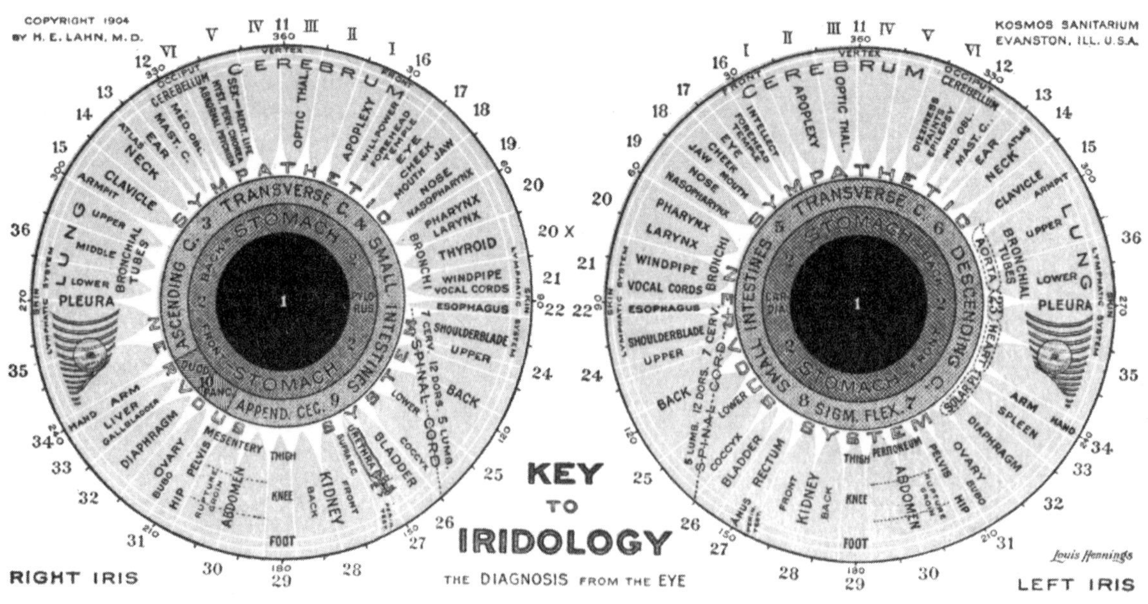

90

The following interpretation of signs and lines in iridology was adapted from work done by T. Kriege:

WHITE signs in the iris themselves can indicate inflammation or overstimulation. The whiter the signs, the more acute, inflammatory and sometimes painful is the organ. "If the condition becomes chronic, then the originally white sign changes to blue-white, dirty-white, yellow, or even brown" [6]; this chronic situation is one which is usually the result of deposition of toxic wastes and residues. White signs are actually only white in blue or gray irises, in brown eyes there is a lightening of the brown iris tissue.

DARK iris signs suggest under-stimulation, diminished function, and enervation (for more information on enervation, please consult chapter 3). The color tends from gray to dark gray. Dark iris signs indicate a chronic state from over-relaxed tissue.

BLACK iris signs suggest a loss of substance. "They originate from the destruction of the second layer of the iris" [6].

COLORED signs may be yellowish-red, brown, black-brown, or any other shade. "They lie mainly in the deeper iris layers" [6]. They are sometimes referred to as toxin-flecks since they indicate toxins.

SHORT WHITE lines are considered to be a sign of inflammation.

LONG WHITE lines, which cross the paths of the organ areas on the iris, are considered to be indications of neuritis or neuralgia. If they are zig-zig, they are considered to indicate cramp-like pains.

DARK lines are considered to be an indication of nervous weakness.

WHITE or YELLOW-WHITE flakes and clouds are considered to be signs of acute or chronic inflammation of the mucous membranes.

WISPS of any color are large and not intense. "White wisps are signs of an extensive tissue-inflammation" [6] (other colors may indicate rheumatism or other systemic problems). Dark wisps indicate that an organ has become weak through reaction (such as the uterus).

DARK SKIN zones indicate a suppressed excretion.

SIGNS OF POSSIBLE IMMINENT DEATH: "(a) A black-wedge sign in the heart area (b) Completely solid black scurf rim (c) A perpendicular-oval pupil" [6]. (The scurf rim is the outer edge of the iris [1].)

There are other signs and interpretations, and those interested in iridology should study books such as those listed as references at the end of this chapter.

The usefulness of iridology is still questioned today [5], but at times it is a helpful adjunct. It is known by modern scientists that the iris is affected by antioxidants. [7] It is also suspected that iris freckles is a risk factor for developing uveal melanoma. [8]

Although utilizing some iridology in my office (using a special magnifying lens), in most cases it is easier (and perhaps more accurate) to use other forms of assessment. Also, the evidence is not totally convincing that the precise pattern is consistent on all eyes. If someone's eye shows the points as shown on the previous chart, it seems logical that someone else's eye may have the same points shifted a few degrees. It can be suspected though that there actually is some physical connection between the eye and the other parts of the body and suspect that some type of electromagnetic energy is conveyed (although full acceptance of the odic force hypothesis may be questionable). Nevertheless, iridology has been found to be an occasionally helpful adjunct to some of my assessments. It is a technique to which all naturopaths should have exposure.

References

[1] Jensen, B. *The Science and Practice of Iridology.* Bernard Jensen Enterprises, Escondido (CA), 1988.

[2] Thiel, P. *The Diagnosis of Disease by Observation of the Eye.* Reprint from Health Research, Mokelumne Hill (CA), Originally written in 1905, translation copyright 1918 by F. Collins.

[3] Lahn, H. Iridology: *The Diagnosis from the Eye,* 6th ed. Kosmos Publishing, Evanston (IL), 1914.

[4] Kulvinskas, V. *Survival into the 21st Century.* 21st Century Publications, Woodstock Valley (CT), 1975.

[5] Herbert, V. and Barrett, S. *Alternative Nutrition Therapies. In Modern Nutrition in Health and Disease,* 9th ed. Williams & Wilkins, Balt., 1999:1801-1810.

[6] Kriege, T. *Fundamental Basis for Irisdiagnosis.* As translated by A.W. Priest, 1969. Camelot Press, London.

[7] Marshall, G. *Antioxidant Enzymes in the Human Iris: An Immunogold Study.* Brit J Opthamol, 1997; 81:314-318.

[8] Horn, E., et al. *Sunlight and the Risk of Uveal Melanoma.* J Natl Can Inst, 1994; 86(19):1476-1478.

11

Light and Color

Light has been recommended therapeutically for quite a long time. In the second century A.D., the physician Aretaeus recommended that "lethargics are to be laid in the light, and exposed to the rays of the sun." [1] Ancient Sanskrit writings describe the body as being composed of seven energy centers, called chakras. "These chakras, located at the sites of the major endocrine glands and corresponding to particular states of consciousness and personality types, were responsive to or ignited by different color." [2] Even modern medical doctors admit, "We know from the days of tuberculosis that ultraviolet light has a beneficial and healing effect." [3] "Photobiology is based on the interaction between optical radiation and living organisms. Specifically, the science of photobiology involves the study of how the infrared, visible, and ultraviolet portions of the electromagnetic spectrum influence biological processes." [4]

Naturopaths, of course, like light—natural light (although we will use other lights if indicated). Decades ago Dr. Kulkarni wrote:

Sunlight

The influence of sunlight upon the vital processes has been recognized from the earliest times. The old Greeks and Romans employed the sun-bath or insolation very frequently in the treatment of chronic maladies of all sorts. The natives of the South Sea Islands and other primitive peoples still utilize this powerful agent in the treatment of the sick. The natives of the *Terre celiente* of Mexico have long practiced exposure to sunlight on the sea-beach partially covered with sand, as a treatment for syphilis, the patients thus treated being made to drink large quantities of infusions of leaves of various sorts while exposed to the sun. The natives of Haiti are said by M. Delow to employ similar practices (Kellogg).

All physicians place the highest value upon exposure to the sun by an out of door life as a means of stimulating the nutritive processes of the body in many chronic disorders such as anaemia, tuberculosis, and in convalescence from fevers and other similar condition. The value of the sun-bath as a therapeutic measure will be readily appreciated by noting the facts respecting its remarkable physiological influence which must be very largely attributed to the actinic rays although a share of it must be attributed to the calorific effect of the sun's rays (Kellogg). The sun-bath is a more valuable and practical exciting measure; it owes its properties to the three sets of rays of which it is composed viz. thermal, luminous and actinic or chemical rays. The thermal and luminous rays are directly stimulating to the cells of the tissues, causing a development and accumulations of heat while the actinic rays act upon the nervous system in a most powerful manner.

The Sun-bath or Insolation

Sunlight is one of the most powerful of all hygienic and curative agents. As a hygienic measure it is of inesteemable value in the destruction of dangerous microbes, most of which are unable to resist the action of the direct rays of the sun for more than a few minutes. Sunlight is thus the most important of all disinfecting and sterilizing agencies. The value of sunlight in the maintenance of health is well shown in the dwarfed development or rapid deterioration of plants deprived of its stimulating influence. In eaves, mines and other places from which the light is excluded plants with the exception of the fungi do not grow or if they do, very quickly die never attaining maturity. Animals also are dwarfed and become sickly under these conditions (Kellogg). In hospitals a larger percentage of recoveries occurs on the sunny side than on the shady side of the ward.

Physiological effects—The sun's rays not only influence the skin, but pass through the skin into the body exciting and stimulating the cells and tissues. The surface circulation is greatly accelerated, free perspiration occurs, the heart's action is increased and the activity of all the vital functions is promoted. In many cases the patient experiences very pronounced sensations of langour and drowsiness during the bath and not infrequently falls asleep. The effects of the sun-bath are practically identical with those of the electric light-bath. Sunlight may be properly regarded as not only a source of radiant energy in the form of heat but as a powerful tonic through its actinic rays. Its calorific or heating rays may be isolated by placing a red glass screen between the sun and the patient so that the actinic rays are filtered out. For tonic effects, the caloric rays may be separated by employing a blue glass screen in like manner.

Sun-bath is taken by lying on a mat in a perfectly nude state and by exposing the whole body to sunlight. Sensitive persons who get headache or who feel dizziness may protect their heads with a large green leaf, preferably of a plantain tree or any other plant or with a wet cloth of green or blue color. It should be taken for a period from 30 to 60 minutes or even longer till the patient perspires freely. After a sun-bath he should take a hip bath to cool the system and it should be followed by a brisk walk in the sun to have reaction and to obtain normal temperature of the body. The best time for a sun-bath is from 10 a. m. to 3 p. m. Those who are not accustomed to it should, in the beginning, take the sun-bath in the mild sunlight only.

Partial sun-baths—these are taken with the best results in case of nodules, tumors, indurations, painful parts, internal or external growths, ulcers, open sores, boils, abscesses, carbuncles, cancers, etc. The author [Kulkarni] has tried sun-baths directly or through green or blue glasses in such diseases and found even the worst pain of cancer eased by it. He has also given sun-bath to the abdomen of typhoid patients with best results. Diarrhoea, dysentery, tabes mesenterica have yielded very satisfactorily to these sun-baths when judiciously administered to the abdomen of such patients.

Therapeutic applications—The sun-bath is useful in all cases of malnutrition, anaemia, inactivity of the skin, chronic dyspepsia, worst cases of neurasthenia, indigestion, chlorosis, rheumatism, diabetes and obesity (Kellogg). The ancient made great use of the sun-bath in the treatment of the sick. According to Plutarch, Diogenes, the renowned Athenian cynic, was in his old age accustomed to lie in the sunshine for the purpose of recruiting his energies, a custom which according to Pliny was common among the old men in Greece. It is stated that Diogenes valued his sun-bath so highly that when called upon by Alexander, who offered to render him any service in his power, he replied, "Only stand a little out of my sunshine" (Kellogg).

Caution—Those who are not accustomed to sun-baths are likely to get sunstroke or heat stroke if they are exposed to strong light for a long time. Such sensitive persons should expose themselves only for five minutes in the beginning and the duration should be increased gradually to one to two hours. The head must be protected with green leaves and the body must be protected with a green or blue sheet made wet if necessary. [5]

The Value of Sunshine

In the United States, natural hygienist George J. Drews wrote:

All vegetable-life utilizes sunshine in the process of anabolizing inorganic matter into organic material. Every ray of light, heat and energy derived from burning or oxidizing organic fuel is freed sunshine that had been imprisoned in the organic molecule by vegetable anabolism. The very existence of vegetable life depends on sunshine. Animal-life is not so far removed from vegetable life that it can do without sunshine. Instinct prompts the fish and wild animals to bask in sunshine. Even the mole basks where the sunshine can penetrate a thin layer of sandy earth. Nature did not cover the human body with a dense coat of hair: Why? It would take a volume to explain why the law that perpetuates the fittest, should have selected the nude human animal. After a little sane reasoning, the reader will agree with me that Nature fully intended that the human body should be exposed to sunshine and air for chemical reasons. The function of chlorophyll in plants is to transmute inorganic matter into organic matter by the aid of sunshine.

THERE ARE CELLS IN THE TISSUES OF THE HUMAN SKIN WHOSE FUNCTION IS ANALOGOUS TO THAT OF CHLOROPHYLL and this stands to reason when there are, actually, some lower animals whose tissues contain chlorophyll granules. It is a proven fact that the skin absorbs solar energy. It has also been proven that the perspiration gathered during a solar bath is composed largely of uric acid and other waste poisons; whereas, that gathered during hot-air or steam baths is composed mostly of blood serum. Sunshine therefore draws the blood to the surface, vitalizes the skin and stimulates its respiratory and eliminative functions: thus relieving the overworked lungs, liver and kidneys. Furthermore, sunshine, by supplying the proper energy, stimulates every function of the body to normal activity. What is more important in preventing disease and restoring health, vitality and strength? Natural food, fresh air and sunshine are the infallible factors in preventing and curing consumption. There is nothing like sunbathing for those who are emaciated from any disease. Every seeker of health is advised to take a nude sun-bath every day, and if your neighbors object, wear a single open mesh garment through which sunshine can penetrate.

Doctor Babbitt has summed up many facts bearing upon the power of sunlight to augment strength, beauty and intelligence. Those races who go partly or wholly nude in the sun demonstrate their superior strength and physical development. No race that swathes in sunproof, airproof garments can compete with the nude Dyaks, Ahts, Kaffirs, Arabs and Fuegians for strength, speed and endurance.

Sunshine, fresh air and proper exercise are as essential as natural (unfired) foods for gaining and maintaining health, vitality, strength and beauty. Some very thoughtful women keep the blessed health-giving sunshine out of the house because it bleaches the carpet. Does this sound consistent?

When you tan very quickly it indicates that you should take plenty of sun-baths to eliminate the poisons in your system until the tan leaves and the beautiful pink color of healthy blood remains on the whole body. Remember that THE CHLOROPHYLL-LIKE FUNCTION IN THE SKIN HAS THE POWER. WHEN AIDED BY SUNSHINE, TO CHEMICALLY, TRANSMUTE INORGANIC ELEMENTS AND POISONS INTO ORGANIC AND USEFUL ELEMENTS AS IS DONE IN THE LEAF OF PLANTS. [6]

It is true that all life (if for no other reason than to produce food) needs sunlight. The occasional sunbather should be cautious about sunburn.

Light Today

Light problems are probably on the increase, as Dr. John Ott wrote in 1973,

> As man has become more industrialized, living under an environment of artificial light, behind window glass and windshield, watching TV, looking through colored sunglasses, working in windowless buildings, the wavelength energy entering the eye has become greatly distorted from that of natural sunlight. [7]

With the advent of "energy efficient" buildings and the internet, it is probable that even less natural light is available today. Normal incandescent light bulbs produce a fairly broad spectrum of light which is deficient on the blue side of the spectrum, whereas fluorescent lights "typically produce a rather distorted spectrum of light, which contain only a limited portion of the total spectrum." [2]

The author's house and barn contains windows and skylights (animals need natural light too, though they are all outside during most of the day). He also uses what is known as full spectrum lights in both home and office. Getting light as natural as possible promotes optimal health. So many spend too much time indoors—this is unnatural. Thus, by letting sunlight in and using full spectrum lights, this can help make up for the natural light depravity that is so common today.

The human eye sees less than 1% of the total light spectrum. Unlike sunlight, ordinary incandescent light contains virtually no ultraviolet light. [2] Although there is a great deal of controversy surrounding the risks and benefits of ultraviolet light, it seems that many involved in the therapeutic use of light see far more benefits than risk from using it. [2,3,7] Dr. David Grimes believes that it is sunburn, and not sun exposure, that is the major cause of skin problems. He has accurately stated, "...sunburn is to be avoided, but incidental sun exposure by simply being in a sunny environment at a low latitude or high altitude is beneficial for health." [3] Dr. Ott seems to suggest that problems associated with ultraviolet light may actually be related to the use of prescription as well as tinted glasses. [7] He has also suggested that light from televisions and regular (not full or broad spectrum) fluorescent lights may be harmful. [7] Interestingly, he reports that one study found that calcium was absorbed better in an environment with mock sunlight than one with fluorescent lights. [7] This seems reasonable since vitamin D production is stimulated by natural sunlight. [8]

In addition to the fact that the office itself is lighted with full spectrum lights, sometimes the author uses red light for some with arthritis and other problems of the joints. The particular light "is a light emitting device (LED) that produces light with similar characteristics to that of a helium-neon laser. This is the wavelength, power, and photonic energy used for over 30 years throughout the world for acupuncture point stimulation." [9] Although it is not a laser, "it has demonstrated to perform equally, if not better, than more costly lasers. The purity and power of the light causes a biophotonic stimulation of any area of the body where light is placed in just a matter of seconds." [9]

One of the more interesting cases the author has had involved a boy who had no circulation to his left knee (according to medical professionals who also said he would never regain circulation there) who regained feeling after several weeks of application. People who had stiff fingers and joints have also been helped to regain some degree of motion. This light "has proven itself to be extremely effective in temporary pain control," [9] though it is rarely used for that purpose. It is suspected that this type of light helps in at least two ways—it may increase localized vitamin D production, thus aiding in the utilization of calcium and, perhaps more significantly, providing "biophotonic stimulation", it sends a signal to the body that the tissue being lighted should be treated as normal as opposed to abnormal tissue. This is consistent with the work of Dr. White who found that red light was a nerve stimulant. [10] Thus, natural detoxification and healing may be stimulated in an area that the body has apparently (through autoimmune conditions such as arthritis) considered to be semi-foreign. If this is correct, then the therapeutic use of light may have major ramifications in improving human health (especially since there seems to have been an explosion in "autoimmune" disorder).

Light has often been used to help people with depression, even nonseasonal major depression. [11-14] In a clinical trial, the majority of women with premenstrual depression reported improvement after being exposed to bright light (>2,500 lux, 2 hours each time) twice per day (morning and evening) [15]; the investigators seemed to feel that the light's affect on circadian rhythm may be the reason for the improvement. [15] It may be that light eases depression (whether or not the depression is premenstrual) by raising serotonin levels. [13] Because of this, it is believed that light may also help people with obsessive-compulsive disorder. [13] For winter depression, studies support the idea that "full spectrum light, or light that includes a balance of both visible and UV wavelengths, is necessary for successful therapy." [4] Dr. Zane Kime has written that a series of exposures to sunlight can decrease resting heart rate, blood pressure, blood sugar, and lactic acid in the blood, while increasing energy, strength, endurance, stress tolerance, and the ability of blood to absorb and carry oxygen. [2] Light may even help with bulimia nervosa (about 1/3 with bulimia also have Seasonal Affective Disorder, see later in this chapter). [16]

Dr. Grimes has found a link between lack of sunlight exposure and hypercholesterolemia and coronary heart disease. [17] He believes that an increase in sunlight, including the ultraviolet portion of the light, is protective against coronary heart disease [17]; he speculates that sunlight deficiency suppresses immunity and thus allows for a greater progression of the disease. [17] He also notes that vitamin D and cholesterol are chemically similar, that sunlight is required for vitamin D production, and that cholesterol levels are lower in the summer (a time of higher sunlight) than in the winter. [17] He speculates that the metabolism of squalene (which is a precursor of both vitamin D and cholesterol) into vitamin D or cholesterol is affected by whether or not there is sufficient sunlight. [3] Research done on chickens suggests that the cholesterol in eggs can be cut be 25% if the chickens are in an environment with full spectrum light instead of other forms of artificial lighting. This is consistent with my own observation that eggs our chickens lay (and our chickens spend most of the daylight hours outside and have a window and skylight when in the barn) appear quite different from those bought in a store (and this is even true when we are comparing our brown eggs to commercial brown eggs). This, combined with Dr. Grime's research, [17] suggests that in a nation where so many people spend so much time indoors, that lack of sunlight may be why so many Americans have problems with cholesterol.

Research by Dr. Ott suggests that hyperactivity, fatigue, irritability, and attention deficit problems could be worsened with regular fluorescent lights while behavior and academic performance could be improved with full spectrum lighting. [2] whereas another study he performed suggested that fixing radiation leaks from television sets improved behavior and hyperactivity. [2]

One of the most commonly known light-depravity conditions is Seasonal Affective Disorder (often referred to as SAD). It causes depression and mood swings in affected individuals. [11] It probably is most common in Scandinavia, Alaska, and other areas which have darker than usual winters. About 60-80% with SAD show improvement when exposed to 10,000 lux light for 30 minutes per day [1] (full spectrum light seems to be the best for this [4]). The primary side effects (when they occur) associated with light therapy are mild and include insomnia, blurred vision, headache, agitation, and nausea. [1] For depression associated with SAD, Dr. Anna Wirz-Justice claims, "Light is as effective as antidepressant medications are, perhaps more so." [16] It should be noted that tryptophan depletion may also be a factor in SAD. [12]

Light may also be able to help people with certain types of sleep disorders, in order to help normalize circadian rhythm [16,18,19]. It was reported in the *Journal of the American Medical Association* that light therapy is gaining acceptance in the treatment of circadian sleep disorders, circadian disruptions associated with jet lag and shift work, bulimia nervosa, and depression. [16]

Color

"Chromo-therapy is a method of the treatment of disease by the use of radiant colors." [10] Color is derived from light and is a form of radiation. The wavelengths of visible light range from around 400 to 760 nanometers starting from violet to indigo, blue, green, yellow, orange, and ending with red. [4] Some research has suggested that blood pressure, pulse rate, and respiratory rate tend to decrease after exposure to green, blue, and black light while they tend to increase with red, orange, and yellow light [2]. Many maternity wards use blue light (450 nanometers) for the treatment of hyper-bilirubinemia (neonatal jaundice)—it was found in

1968 that babies exposed to full-spectrum light or blue light for several days had bilirubin levels reduced to safer levels. [2]

Dr. George Starr White was one the leading exponents of "chromo-therapy" in the past. Based on his research, it was concluded,

The color rays must be applied directly to the skin, and not through clothing, and the colors must be pure and not intermingled with other colors. The therapeutic action of colors thus applied has been found as follows:

RED has a stimulating effect of blood and nerves. It is indicated in tuberculosis, anemia, physical exhaustion, paralysis, and all debilitating conditions. CONTRA-INDICATED in inflammatory, feverish, or excitable conditions.

YELLOW AND ORANGE are nerve stimulants. They are valuable in constipation, impaired digestion, and pelvic disorders in women. CONTRAINDICATED when there is an over-excited system.

REDDISH-ORANGE is valuable in cancer and other malignant growths.

GREEN is quieting and soothing upon the nerves and body generally. It must be a true green and have no tendency toward yellow.

BLUE AND VIOLET are nervines, astringents, febrifuges, and sedatives. They soothe the nerve and vascular systems, and are good where there is inflammation or nervousness. Indicated in hemorrhage, cerebro-spinal conditions, neuralgia, and rheumatism. [10]

Research by Dr. John Anderson indicated that blinking red lights at different speeds, stopped 72% of migraines within an hour, and even 93% of whose migraines did not stop reported feeling better. [2] Baker-Miller pink (same color as some bubble gum) has been proven to calm nerves in minutes and is used in areas of many prisons for that purpose. [2] Research by Dr. Ott showed that plants who had an ultraviolet filter over natural light (which restricted some of the wavelengths of the light) choroplasts, which had been functioning in an orderly pattern, changed to a disorderly and even immobile pattern, thus showing that color can affect plants at the cellular level. [7] Red and white lights may be able to improve the performance of athletes. [2]

Each color has a different wavelength range than other colors (actually each has been defined by the Commission Internationale de l'Eclairage [4]). Photon energy varies as well as can be seen in the chart below.

Thus it is clear that each color is different from every other color and thus can reasonably be expected to have different influences on biological organisms—including humans!

Spectral Band (color appearance)	Wavelength Range	Photon Energy (eV)
Red	760-610 nm	1.63-2.03 eV
Orange	610-585 nm	2.03-2.12 eV
Yellow	585-575 nm	2.12-2.16 eV
Yellow-Green	575-530 nm	2.16-2.34 eV
Green	530-495 nm	2.34-2.50 eV
Blue-Green	495-485 nm	2.50-2.56 eV
Blue	485-465 nm	2.56-2.67 eV
Violet	465-380 nm	2.67-3.26 eV
Non-Visible Light:		
Infrareds	1000-760 nm	1.63-.001 eV
Ultraviolets	400-100 nm	3.10-12.4 eV [4]

References

[1] Lam, R., et al. *Light Therapy for Depressive Disorders: Indications and Efficacy.* Mood Disorders, Systemic Medication Management,1997;.25:215-234.

[2] Lieberman, J. *Light Medicine of the Future.* Bear & Company, Santa Fe (NM), 1991.

[3] Grimes, D. *Coronary Artery/Heart Disease, Cholesterol, and Sunlight.* In Clinical Pearls. ITServices, Sacramento, 1998:298-300.

[4] Brainard, G. *The Healing Light: Interface of Physics and Biology.* In Seasonal Affective Disorder and Beyond. American Psychiatric Press, Washington (DC), 1998:1-44.

[5] Kulkarni, V. M. *Healing Through Naturopathy.* Reprint from B. Jain Publishers, New Delhi (India), originally written circa 1925.

[6] Drew, G. A. *Unfired Food and Trophotherapy.* Reprinted by Health Research, Mokelumne (CA), originally written 1912.

[7] Ott, J. *Health and Light.* Devin-Adair, Alpharetta (GA), 1973.

[8] Holick, M. F. *Vitamin D.* In Modern Nutrition in Health and Disease, 9th ed. Williams & Wilkins, Balt., 1999:329-345.

[9] *The Relief-Light.* Micro Digital Technology, Mesa (AZ), circa 1998.

[10] Cordingley, E. W. *Principles and Practice of Naturopathy.* Health Research, Mokelumne Hill (CA), Originally written 1924.

[11] Lam, R.W., et al. *Seasonal Affective Disorder and Beyond.* American Psychiatric Press, Washington (DC), 1998.

[12] Ghardian, A., et al. *Efficacy of Light Versus Tryptophan Therapy in Seasonal Affective Disorder.* J Affective Disorders, 1998;50:23-27.

[13] Modica, P. *Serotonin Rise May Explain the Effects of Light Therapy.* Med Trib, Feb 20, 1997:8.

[14] Kripke, D. *Light Treatment for Major Depression; are We Ready?* In Seasonal Affective Disorder and Beyond. American Psychiatric Press, Washington (DC), 1998:159-172.

[15] Parry, B. *Light therapy of Premenstrual Depression. In Seasonal Affective Disorder and Beyond.* American Psychiatric Press, Washington (DC), 1998:173-191.

[16] Lamberg, L. *Dawn's Early Light to Twilight's Last Gleaming.* JAMA, 1998; 280:1556-1558.

[17] Grimes, D. *Sunlight, Cholesterol, and Coronary Heart Disease.* Qtr J Med, 1996; 89:579-589.

[18] Wesson, V. and Levitt, A. *Light Therapy for Seasonal Affective Disorder.* Seasonal Affective Disorder and Beyond. American Psychiatric Press, Washington (DC), 1998:45-89.

[19] Hayakawa, T., et al. *Trials of Bright Light Exposure and Melatonin Administration in a Patient with Non-24 Hour Sleep-Wake Syndrome.* Japanese Soc Sleep Res, 1998:259-260.

12
Air, Ozone, and Breathing

An area where naturopaths and allopaths have tended to agree (most of the time, except when many allopaths used to encourage smoking) is that polluted air is dangerous. Naturopaths have generally found positive uses for ozone; however, allopaths have some (but usually less) uses for it.

The first portion of this chapter was written decades ago (so some of the comments will no longer apply) by G. Frank Scholl, a medical doctor, who felt that clean air was an essential part of "preventative medicine." What is of additional interest is that he mentions air as a "blood purifier," a naturopathic term. Dr. Scholl wrote as *The Vital Necessity of Air:*

Value of Pure Air—There are some things in nature of which we take but little cognizance, probably from the fact of their apparent simplicity. Pure air, pure water, pure food are essential and fundamental to good health and health to happiness, so we see that our very lives depend upon the exercise of principles which we neglect to study and understand, possibly on account of other and manifold duties. But nature's laws are invariable, and the time comes when dire results follow a disregard of first principles. Anyone will admit that pure, unadulterated food is necessary to health. Food is converted into blood, which having circulated through the body is unfit for further use until purified.

Air a Blood Purifier—It is through the medium of the air, with its life-giving oxygen, that the blood is purified. It, therefore, follows logically that air and pure air is necessary to health and, other things being equal, the health will be imperfect in proportion to the impurity of the air we breathe. It should be our aim to learn much of so important a condition of health in order that we might, so far as is possible, avoid disease.

Necessity of Pure Air—Not only is pure air of value to preserve a state of health, it is an absolute necessity. It is true that some persons with strong wills and capacious lungs can perform the feat of holding the breath, but if they endeavor to prolong the experiment from a minute and a half to two minutes, the need of breathing becomes so intense that control over the muscles of the chest is lost and a deep inspiration must be drawn in spite of resolutions to the contrary. If the access of fresh air to the lungs is absolutely prevented by external force, death speedily takes place, the fatal result occurring in from five to fifteen minutes. This latter condition is present in hanging and drowning and in some forms of croup in children. Four minutes is the limit of time a person can be deprived of oxygen and live…

Qualities of Pure Air

Composition—In speaking of pure air, we refer to a standard condition of air. The air is a mechanical mixture of elements. As ordinarily met with at the surface of our earth, pure air, when analyzed, is found to be composed of seventy-nine parts of nitrogen and twenty-one parts of oxygen to every one hundred parts of air. It contains also a considerable quantity of watery vapor, a trace of ammonia, and from three to six parts in ten thousand of that deleterious gas carbonic acid. Oxygen is the active element. If a candle be held in oxygen it would burn more brightly than in ordinary air, and so our own lives, if lived in an atmosphere of oxygen, would be more quickly spent. Our tissues would be quickly used up. Nitrogen, which forms so large a proportion, acts simply as a diluent; of itself it cannot support life, and a lighted candle held in nitrogen gas is quickly extinguished. Carbonic acid gas, or, as it is called, carbon dioxide, is normal to the extent of .04 percent, and though it is useless to animals, it is quite as necessary to plant life as is oxygen to us.

Localities of Pure Air—As air is rendered impure by respiration, the purest air is found in those localities farthest removed from human habitation, i.e., on the mountain tops and upon the ocean. When there is a tendency to disease or during recovery from a disease, residence in the mountains or at the seashore is of distinct benefit.

In order to understand how it is that the breathing in and out of the air of a room in time vitiates it, it will be necessary to explain some points of the anatomy and physiology of the respiratory tract—and the act of respiration.

Respiratory Tract

Anatomy—The respiratory tract is made up of the lungs and the air passages leading to them. The air passages comprise the larynx or voice box, the trachea or windpipe, and the bronchial tubes—two in number—which are branches of the trachea.

The Larynx—The larynx is situated at the upper part of the trachea and presents in front the prominence known as Adam's apple.

The Trachea—The trachea or windpipe is four and a half inches long and extends from the larynx to about the middle of the breast-bone or sternum, where it divides into the two bronchial tubes.

The Lungs—The lungs, two in number, are situated in the cavity of the thorax or chest, one on either side of the heart. The lungs are made up of lobes, and the lobes are made up of still smaller divisions called lobules or little lobes. These latter are quite small, one one-hundred and twentieth of an inch in diameter, and they represent the ultimate divisions of the bronchial tubes, which have ramified and subdivided like the branches of a tree. Surrounding each lung and lining the cavity of the chest is the pleura, an inflammation of which constitutes the disease known as pleurisy.

Physiology—The larynx, trachea and bronchial tubes admit the air to the lungs. The larynx, in addition to this function, is the organ of voice, being supplied with the vocal cords. Voice is produced by the outgoing air setting these cords into vibration. The air cells, of which the lungs are composed, are the meeting places of the air and the blood for the purpose of the exchange of oxygen and carbonic acid.

Heart Functions—The heart, which is a thick, strong muscular bag, pumps the blood through the lungs as it goes round and round through the circulation, at the rate of about sixteen hundred pints of the vital fluid every hour. These sixteen hundred pints of blood, by being spread out in the fine network of delicate tubes in the walls of the air-cells, get rid of nearly sixty pints of carbonic acid, and absorb rather more than sixty pints of oxygen in that length of time. Upon this gaining of fresh oxygen and getting rid of stale carbonic acid unceasingly, our very lives depend, for, as demonstrated in hanging and drowning, if this interchange of the gases in the blood is interrupted for even the space of a few minutes death is the effect.

Unceasing Heart Pumping—Whilst life continues, night and day, our hearts must go on pumping dark, purple, venous blood into the lungs, to be there purified and changed into red arterial blood by losing its carbonic acid and gaining fresh oxygen, which is carried to every part of our bodies, as has been just explained, conveying everywhere its own new and vigorous life. Night and day, too, quite as unceasingly, must the lungs do their part, by pumping in fresh air to furnish this requisite supply of revivifying oxygen; and, what is almost equally important, they must pump out the air which has been partly deprived of its oxygen, and has received in its place the worn-out and now deleterious substances got rid of by venous blood. This constitutes the pulmonary circulation in distinction to the circulation of the blood through various parts of the body for purposes of its nutrition which constitutes the systematic circulation.

Respiration—The lungs, which contain the air, are not active in the act of respiration. The chest cavity enlarges by the contraction of the diaphragm and the elevation of the ribs and sternum so that the chest is enlarged in its vertical, its transverse and its antero-posterior dimensions. With this enlargement, the pressure from without is greater than the pressure from within, and the air rushes in, thereby distending the air vesicles. In expiration, the chest-cavity diminishes in the diameters in which it has been increased, and, as a result, the air in the lungs is subjected to pressure, and consequently rushes out. The air that passes in and out with each respiration is called tidal air, and is equal to twenty cubic inches of air. But, after an ordinary inhalation, it is possible, by the exercise of a little effort, to breathe in still more air, to the extent of one hundred cubic inches. This is called the complemental air. After an ordinary expiration, it is still possible to breathe out air to the extent of one hundred cubic inches. This is called the supplemental or reserve air.

Residual Air—After all effort to expel air from the lungs, there still remains about one hundred cubic inches, called the residual air, from the fact that it resides in the lungs. But we must not get the idea that this residual air is unchanged, for it is ever being purified.

Frequency of Breathing—The respirations vary from fourteen to eighteen per minute. They are greater during infancy and childhood. It is then during respiration that the fresh air, laden with oxygen is carried to the blood to give to the blood its oxygen, and to receive in its place carbonic acid. But the air does not meet the blood directly. On the outer side of the air cells we have the air, while distributed on its inner side we have the small blood vessels or capillaries which have carried the blood to the lungs. So that separating the air from the blood we have: first, the walls of the air cells, and second, the walls of the capillaries. But these two are so thin and delicate that the exchange can readily take place through them.

Impure Air

The Impurities of the Air—The light of modern research has enabled us to know much of atmospheric conditions conducive to disease and health, the latter particularly engaging our attention at this time. The impurities of the air are first, suspended substances and, second, gaseous substances. The suspended substances are particles of almost every known substance, the most important being sand, dust, soot, pollen, micro-organisms of all kinds, particles of food and clothing. The gaseous impurities are carbonic acid, whenever, it exceeds .05 percent; carbon monoxide; sulphur dioxide; sulphuric, hydrochloric and nitric acids; hydrogen sulfide, ammonia and its compounds, and organic vapors from decomposing animal and vegetable matters.

Action of Impurities of the Air—The solid impurities act by clogging up the air vesicles, thereby interfering with their function. They may of themselves be causes of disease, as in the case of micro-organisms. The gaseous impurities act first, by virtue of their own toxic or poisonous properties and, second, by the fact that they take the place of the necessary element, oxygen. Carbonic acid is normal to the extent of .04 percent. As before mentioned, air that we inhale contains twenty-one parts of oxygen and seventy-nine parts of nitrogen to every one hundred parts of air. On the other band, expired air contains sixteen parts of oxygen, five parts of carbonic acid and seventy-nine parts of nitrogen. If, now, we should be placed in a room where the air is unchanged, the air inhaled contains a greater percentage than .04 percent, and is consequently impure…

Chronic Effects of Air Poisoning—The chronic effects of long-continued breathing an air which is but moderately polluted are seen in a general deterioration of the strength, appetite and digestion, a pallid dyspeptic appearance from want of renewal of the blood.

Bacteria in the Air—Bacteriology has explained the cause of many diseases. The air is everywhere laden with them. They enter our bodies through the respiratory and digestive tracts. If our vitality or resistance is sufficient to withstand their invasion, we remain in a state of health; but, when the vitality is lowered for any reason, the bacteria invade the system and disease results. The bacteria present in the atmosphere are not, as a rule, actively disease producing. Those that do produce disease are found particularly where the discharges of diseased animals have been allowed to collect and dry. These excretions become pulverized and are subsequently carried about in the air we breathe. The dried expectoration of cases of tuberculosis, of influenza, and occasionally of pneumonia, produce these diseases in this manner. The boards of health in various parts of the country are fast coming to the conclusion that expectoration upon the sidewalks, in the street cars, in public halls, and so forth, is a menace to the public well-being. In hospitals, patients suffering with tuberculous disease are obliged to expectorate in special cups or paste board boxes, which are kept covered and subsequently destroyed. Similar measures might be adopted in private practice.

Evil Effects of Exposure to Draughts

Cold Air—Cold air, and especially cold, moist air, is so often a factor in the production of disease that the consideration of this constantly impending danger to health and its hygienic treatment by the means of suitable clothing is very important.

Clothing—Contrary to the popular notion, clothing gives no heat. It is by the motion of the air that respiration is possible. Impure air is diluted by pure air, and then rendered purer.

Ozone

Among the invisible ingredients of air sometimes found in considerable quantity, but not always present in any appreciable amount, is ozone.

Origin of Ozone—Ozone is made up of three atoms of oxygen, whereas free oxygen is made of but two atoms. It is therefore concentrated oxygen, and by loss of one of its atoms it is converted into free oxygen of two atoms.

Importance of Ozone—As yet, the researches of medical chemists only enable us to state that the test of Shoenbein indicates that ozone is more abundant in pure than in impure air; in. greater quantity at the seashore than in the interior, and in mountain air than in that of plains; absent in the center of large towns, yet present in their suburbs; deficient in the air of a hospital ward, yet plentiful in the atmosphere outside.

Ozone in Pine Woods—Dr. Nicholson of Michigan, found in a long series of observations that ozone was more abundant in a pine forest than in the open country during the summer, but less abundant during the winter; less abundant in coal-pits and over swamps than in the open country, and less abundant in the night than in the day.

Property of Turpentine—The results of these investigations in regard to the air of pine woods are in accord with the statements of Dr. Schreiber of Vienna, who declares that the turpentine exhaled from pine forests possesses to a very high degree the property of converting the oxygen of the air into ozone, and this fact perhaps explains why a continued residence among the balsamic odors of the pines has long been credited with a favorable influence in cases of consumption. The test for the presence of ozone in the air, consisting of paper which has been soaked in starch and iodide of potassium, or iodide of calcium, is not reliable.

Ventilation

Importance of Ventilation—Having reviewed the serious derangements to health that impure air might occasion, it behooves us to consider some preventive measures to ward off disease. The great remedy against impure air is, of course, proper ventilation…

Dust in the Air as a Cause of Disease

Solid Particles Dust of various kinds floating in the air, and often occurring in such minute particles that it can only be recognized in a bright sunshine, or by the aid of a beam of electric light, as Professor Tyndall has shown, is far more potent a cause of disease than is generally supposed.

Danger of Saliva-Loaded Dust—Although affections of the stomach and bowels are often induced by the introduction of particles of injurious dust swallowed with the saliva, diseases of the lungs are chiefly to be dreaded when air loaded with substances which are mechanically or chemically noxious find their way to the delicate mucous membrane which lines the recesses of our pulmonary organs. Bronchitis, catarrh and acute or chronic pneumonia, the latter often running on into one form of consumption, are especially to be guarded against in persons who are liable to be forced to inhale dust of various kinds…

Modern Improvements—In recent years, many improvements have been made in machinery. Factories made sanitary, workmen protected from dangers of all kinds, laws enacted compelling owners of factories to protect workmen; so that at the present time the operator and mechanic does not have the many dangers to contend with he formerly had. In many places illustrated lectures are given, educating him to avoid certain dangers and conditions in connection with his work [1].

Although that decades ago, farm machinery and factories were changed to reduce air pollution, the fact is that air is polluted. Air pollution is more of a problem now (as far as the entire planet is concerned) than it has ever been.

Trying to avoid breathing polluted air is one thing all should do, the other is to (of course) breath clean air. Dr. Kulkarni, who advocates breathing exercises has written, *Breathing Exercise, General and Psychic*, which is as follows:

Fresh Air and Proper Breathing

"Good air is an important element in a natural way of living and healing" (Platen).

If pure blood is the sustainer of life—fresh air is the purifier and supporter of blood; not only do both our lungs but also all our pores inhale fresh air constantly and supply oxygen to our blood if we allow them to do so. Therefore it is very necessary that we should spend as much of our days and nights as possible in fresh air only. A human being is an air animal; he needs continuously fresh air for his skin as much as for the inner side of his lungs. Without food and water an animal can live for some time; but without air it cannot even live for a few minutes. In impure air a man will die or will find his health impaired. Hence, it is very necessary that we should always live in and continuously breathe pure air. Impure air cannot be made worth inhaling by perfumes, scents of roses, Eau de cologne or by fumigation with odorous substances as they will make the air further unfit for inhalation; Nature wants us to inhale pure air, rich with oxygen, the life-supporting element.

Kind Nature has supplied us with pure air bountifully; but where shall we breathe it? If we go to public roads there the air is contaminated with offensive smell of the tar which is spread all over the roads for the facility of the motor car drivers and the felicity of the motor car owners. Offensive gases are often ejected from their motors. Restaurants are full of the strong odor of spices and of vapors produced by frying which excites a terrible cough. Public buildings, lecture halls, theaters, workshops, colleges and schools are full of effluvia and tobacco smoke. Public gardens are filled with smoke and dust proceeding from flour mills and cotton mills and railway engines. Even in the so called non-smoking compartments of the railway trains, we get the smoke blown on us; there too we are oppressed by the smoke of tobacco and sparks of fire coming from smoking compartments, which often burn our clothes. Old persons, young men and tender boys and even budding young women are seen smoking and offering cigars and cigarettes to their friends and the atmosphere surrounding them is found full of nicotine poison and the gas produced from igniting matches.

Pet monkeys have been seen smoking cigars with gusto. Boys either offer us a cigar or ask us to give one to them or claim matches from us to light their cigars; and if we tell them that we do not smoke, they do not believe us, as they are under the impression that smoking is an essential need of human beings. Our public buildings have become nicotine dens. Almost every building on the high road possesses one country tobacco-shop and more than one shop selling European cigars. No restaurant is considered up-to-date unless it can supply costly cigars. Some allopathic doctors recommend smoking for dyspepsia and flatulence instead of recommending some exercise or a change in diet.

Some *Unanee Hakeems* prepare a special scented tobacco for chewing and smoking with the addition of musk, amber, and other substances which cause sexual excitement in the beginning and sexual weakness and depression, nervousness, scurvy, pyorrhoea, etc. later on. Without knowing its after-effects many rich persons make use of it freely and suffer from its consequences. There is no wonder, therefore, that the percentages of illness and mortality are higher in towns than they are in villages. At this rate the atmosphere in towns will, in the course of time, get so much contaminated as to become unfit for the inhalation of human beings and with a little exaggeration, we may say, that it may cause suffocation even to the birds of the air from the smoke we emit from this globe.

It will be interesting to find how the most eminent modern writers on hygiene agree with the most ancient medical writer, Charaka, regarding the use of pure air. See chapter 1 Regarding Charaka's views. (1) "Health is only possible when to other conditions is added that of a proper supply of pure air." (2) "Air is the prime supporter of life and health, even life itself is dependent upon its purity." (3) Statistical inquiries on mortality prove beyond a doubt that of the causes of death which are usually in action, impurity of the air is the most important. (Parkes)

Inhale slowly, always through the nostrils prolonging the act as much as possible and filling the lungs, the lower as well as the upper parts with air; then give less time to exhaling and let every exhalation be forcible and accompanied by an abdominal movement which will aid in emptying the stagnant cells in the lower part of the lungs. (Hunter)

General Breathing Exercises

I. Breathing for Heart and Lung Stimulation
    (1) Stand erect facing the sun with hands at sides.
    (2) Breathe in slowly and steadily.
    (3) While breathing, gently tap the chest with your fingertips.
    (4) When the lungs are full, retain the breath and rub the chest with your own palms.

II. Breathing for Rib Strengthening
(1) Stand erect facing the sun with palms touching the ribs.
(2) Inhale a complete breath slowly.
(3) Retain the inhaled air for a short time.
(4) Rub your ribs gently with your palms while exhaling.

III. Breathing for Expansion of Chest
(1) Stand erect facing the sun extending both arms forward on a level with the shoulders.
(2) Inhale a complete breath till chest is full.
(3) Retain the air as long as possible and stretch the arms sideways straight with the shoulders.
(4) Then exhale rubbing the chest forcibly with your own palms.

IV. Breathing Exercise for Preserving Health
(1) Stand erect facing the sun, stretch both hands at sides, inhale deeply and exhale slowly; then raise the arms up until palms touch each other and rise up on the toes as high as possible. Inhale while rising up and raising hands and exhale while lowering the heels and hands slowly and steadily.
(2) Stand erect facing the sun, rub the chest with your right palm and inhale deeply; then exhale slowly and while exhaling clap the chest with both the palms.

V. Breathing Exercise for the Sick and the Invalids to Recoup Health
(1) Lie on your back on the ground well-cleaned for this purpose or on a carpet; stretch your head towards the north pole and your hands above the head and raise your knees. Then breathe deeply and steadily several times. While inhaling raise the abdomen as high as possible and draw it in as deep as possible while exhaling.
(2) Lie on your back and stretch both the hands on both sides. Inhale slowly and deeply filling in and emptying the lungs freely. Do this several times. Then turn to the left side and do the same, then turn to the right side and do the same.

Natural Breathing

Deep breathing is natural and entirely involuntary among those who do not overload the stomach or do obey Nature's demands. It is one of the organic functions carried on by bodily forces entirely independent of the lung activity. It purifies the blood, strengthens the heart with the oxygen inhaled, quickens the circulation of blood, distributes highly oxygenated vitalizing blood all over the body, increases the vitality and establishes immunity from disease.

Correct breathing supplies more oxygen to the blood, circulates it properly and purifies it, which can be clearly observed by clear and bright complexion, while the blood of those who breathe imperfectly is bluish, darkish, and lacking in oxygen which can be observed by livid or pale complexion.

Proper breathing not only improves one's health but also mental powers and clearsightedness. It also enables one to have a control over the passions and insures immunity from disease.

The air on the sea-shore contains .090 percent more oxygen than the air of the town. While the air in the town contains about 0.05 percent of carbonic acid, the air on lofty mountains contains more of oxygen and carbonic acid and less of organic matter than the air in districts while the atmosphere of the town contains diminished proportion of oxygen.

"A proper supply of pure fresh air" says Dr. Ruddock "is essential to the preservation and enjoyment of life and health, by breathing an impure atmosphere the vital energies are slowly but surely impaired."

Air loaded with "effluvia" says Bernan "from the lungs, skin, and clothes even of a healthy individual is offensive to a certain extent, but from that of a person in a state of disease prevented by the walls and ceiling from escaping is in the highest degree deleterious arid loathsome."

Physical Breathing Exercises

Pranavayu or oxygen enters the body chiefly through the nostrils and also through the pores. Hence the necessity of exposing the whole skin to pure fresh air and bright sunlight and also inhaling the air through the nostrils and not through the mouth. The breath taken through the left nostril creates negative electromagnetic currents on the left side of the body, while the breath taken through the right nostril creates positive electromagnetic currents on the right side of the body.

If a person has got the faulty habit of breathing through the mouth or if he suffers from frequent attacks of catarrh, polypus, formation of crusts, etc., the right method of breathing may be established and other troubles cured by practicing psychical breathing exercises prescribed in the Yoga philosophy under the heading of Pranayama. [2]

Ozone and Hydrogen Peroxide

Dr. Koch found that therapeutic use of ozone and other forms of oxygen were helpful for people with cancers, skin conditions, and a whole host of health problems. [3] Some companies supply something they call "vitamin O", which is not a vitamin, but is a liquid (or sometimes powder) which is intended to release oxygen within the body. Hydrogen peroxide formulas are used for similar purposes. [4]

Actually, according to one source, [4] the Food and Drug Administration has regulations which state that mouthwash should have hydrogen peroxide in it. It is naturally found in rainwater and some foods. Fruton and Simmonds' *General Biochemistry* mentions that microorganisms possess an electrical charge when found in liquid and that hydrogen peroxide (H_2O_2) takes electrons away from germs and viruses and kills them [4]. This is similar to what Dr. Koch has claimed. [3] Ozone, too, has been found to destroy a variety of microorganism. [4] Although some feel that the use of hydrogen peroxide and ozone borders on fraud [4], water in Los Angeles County is now purified with ozone.

The U.S. Environmental Protection Agency believes that indoor air pollution is a major problem. Certain air cleaners are manufactured to provide ozone at levels that are intended to approximate the ozone levels in outside clean air. There seems to be more ozone at the beach and in forests [1] and those areas seem to be good places to breathe. It makes sense to have inside air more like outside air. The lifestyles of most Westerners simply keep them inside too much.

There may always be controversy about ozone, but clean air is (and should be) an important principle of health for everyone. Exterior air is also polluted by many substances, including small particulate matter. Because of this, people (whenever possible) should live in areas where the air is fit to breathe.

References

[1] Scholl, B. F. *Library of Health.* Historical Publishing, Phil., 1931.

[2] Kulkarni, V. M. *Healing Through Naturopathy.* Reprint from B. Jain Publishers, New Delhi (India), originally written circa 1925.

[3] *Chemistry's Victory Over Disease.* Koch Laboratories, Detroit, 1941.

[4] McCabe, E. *Oxygen Therapies.* Energy Publications, Morrisville (NY), 1988.

13 Sound and Music

Sounds, such as music, are soothing, yet sometimes stimulating or even irritating vibrations. Music can help aid the healing process and just make life more pleasant. Viktoras Kulvinskas has written, "The harmonies and rhythms present in music heal and stimulate the subtle bodies of people... Music is truly medicine for the soul. Music induces emotional states by creating certain vibrational activities within the astral and mental bodies." [1] Humans are not the only ones who can benefit from pleasant sound—animals, and even plants, have been known to respond as well.

Some feel that music rhythms essentially organize the body. Some believe that music therapy is a medium through which the organization is "regained by linking the brain, body, and music." [2] Changes in brain waves due to music exposure (specifically converting from theta to alpha or beta rhythms) have been measured with an EEG for coma patients. [2] This same report showed that even improvised singing may offer help for comatose patients. [2] Another study found that combining relaxation breathing techniques with soothing music resulted in lower cardiac complications for people with coronary concerns. [3]

Music therapy has been found to help children who were developmentally delayed—it seemed to improve their hearing and speech, hand-eye coordination, and personal-social interaction. [4] Even though surgery is not really advocated, one study found that surgeons did a faster and more accurate job when they listened to music. [5]

Some reports indicate that music helps some sleep, remove stress, builds muscle tone (especially when singing), calms thoughts, and relieves some headaches. [6] However, what soothes one, may agitate another. Slow music tends to sedate us more than fast music, strings and woodwinds seem more soothing than trumpets or trombones, and many find the most relaxing music to be other than rock or jazz. [6] Some music professionals say music therapy works best when there are no lyrics on which to focus. [6]

Music and sound must help with loneliness— this may be one reason that people who are alone listen to music (or sometimes simply have the television on without watching it). It is believed that the sound of the voice may support the endocrine system and that music itself stimulates healing. [7]

Music and other "harmonic, rhythmic sounds" are believed to be the most useful for general support as is simply the human voice itself. [7] Tuning forks have been used to stimulate the healing process. Tuning forks, according to John Beaulieu, "provides a simple and effective method for activating the overtone series in meditation and healing. Listening to pure Pythagorean intervals is a method of attunement." [7] Tibetians have used older technology for similar purposes, while some moderns even use synthesizers. [7]

To use music, many find that they need to listen to a variety of pieces to determine what works best. [6] And for sleeping, some advise listening to the same piece each night (once you find which one works best for you). [6,7] To calm down, some suggest writing down feelings while listening. [6] Some suggest visualization techniques while listening or doing breathing exercises. [3,6] Music actually has been called one of the most ancient of healing arts. [7] Even the Bible talks about sound. The sound of a bubbling brook is likened to the fountain of wisdom (Prov 18:4) and when one is happy one is encouraged to sing (Jas 5:13).

Less Desirable Sounds

Modern research has uncovered some undesirable sounds, "Noise is an environmental pollutant derived specifically from the technological age." [8] Noise pollution is becoming an increasingly significant problem. It is believed that noise levels below 80 decibels are safe. [8]

Problems associated with excessive noise include hearing loss, disruption of work productivity, sleep disturbances, imbalances within the autonomic nervous system, and physical/mental disturbances. [9] Noise seems to increase accident rates, stroke, and cardiovascular disease. [8] Hearing damage can occur from music as well as from exposure to machinery. [9] "It appears that intermittent noise or changes in noise levels are more annoying than continuous noise of an equivalent energy level." [8] The ear, though, can recover some of its hearing ability when it is allowed to rest. [9] There is an anecdotal report that magnesium supplementation may help with noise intolerance, [10] but that does not mean it is recommended that people working in a noisy environment should take necessarily additional magnesium—ear plugs or avoidance of the noise is recommended.

References

[1] Kulvinskas, V. *Survival into the 21st Century.* 21st Century Publications, Woodstock Valley (CT), 1975.

[2] Aldridge, D., et al. *Where am I? Music Therapy Applied to Coma Patients.* J Roy Soc Med, 1990; 83:345-346.

[3] Guzzetta CE, et al. *Effects of Relaxation and Music Therapy on Patients in a Coronary Care Unit with Presumptive Acute Myocardial Infarction.* Heart and Lung, 1989; 18 (6):609-616.

[4] Aldridge, D., et al. *A Pilot Study of Music Therapy in the Treatment of Children with Developmental Delay.* Complementary Therapies in Med, 1995; 3:197-205.

[5] Allen, K. and Blasovich, J. *Effects of Music on Cardiovascular Reactivity Among Surgeons.* JAMA, 1994; 272 (11):882-884.

[6] Scofield, M. *Music Therapy: Melodies that Mellow.* In Everyday Health Tips. Rodale Press, Emmaus (PA), 1988.

[7] Harding, S. *More Noise or Sound Therapy?* Alt & Compl Ther, 1999; 5 (3):164-174.

[8] Godlee, F. *Noise: Breaking the Silence.* Brit Med J, January 11, 1992:1101-113.

[9] Bahadori, R. and Bohne, B. *Adverse Effects of Noise on Hearing.* Am Fam Phys; April 1993:1219-1226.

[10] Freidman, B. *Magnesium for Restless Sleepers.* Cordlandt Forum, 1992; 121:48.

14
Magnets and Electricity

Magnets and electricity are related concepts and may or may not work in a similar fashion. Dr. Kulkarni wrote,

Magnetism

We have different forms of magnetism such as metal magnetism, vegetable magnetism and animal magnetism. Metal magnetism is fully dealt with in every treatise on magnetism; vegetable or plant magnetism also repel similar and attract dissimilar magnetism of its kind; animal or human magnetism has also attracting and repelling properties. Those who have developed this power can, not only heal diseases but even fascinate living beings…

Magnetic Treatment

The principal rule to be observed by the physician when administering magnetic treatment is to place himself in such a position to the subject that opposite parts of their bodies come into juxtaposition, that is the right hand must touch or pass over the left side of the patient and vice versa.

When giving the magnetic passes in a sitting position, the subject should remain in a comfortable, relaxed and receptive condition. The more receptive and sensitive the subject, the more distinctly he will feel the magnetic vibrations like a mild current from an electric battery.

Magnetic passes must proceed from the head downward over the body, the hands returning in a sweeping outward, circular movement so as not to counteract the downward passes.

Positive and Negative Magnetism

Water may be charged with positive or negative magnetism as required by the character of the ailment; positive magnetism has an astringent effect upon the tissues of the body, while negative magnetism has a relaxing effect. Positive magnetism, therefore, would be in order for the treatment of chronic diarrhoea, while negative magnetism is most effective for the treatment of constipation.

In order to charge water or any other fluid positively, the left hand is placed under the vessel; while the right hand with fingers pointing downward and in close proximity to the fluid, makes circular passes. If a substance is to be magnetized negatively, the process would he reversed, that is the fingers of the left hand must do the charging. In like manner, fabrics and other substances may be charged magnetically (Lindlahr). [1]

Magnets have definitely became more popular in the 1990's. "Contemporary magnet therapy involves small, lightweight permanent unipolar or bipolar magnets in various forms for use in healthcare and self-help settings. Types of magnets include acubands, magnetic foil, jewelry, shoe insoles, magnetic mattresses, mattress pads, and pillows" [2]. Magnets are believed to stimulate lymphatic flow (which would help in detoxification), increase oxygen supply, encourage the healing of damaged tissue, aid in the management of M.S. symptoms, help with dental concerns, decrease inflammation (through its negative pole), and help the skin detoxify [3]. Modern research does support the concept that magnet therapy can result in pain-relief (though the results are not universal). However, a concern is that without nutritional intervention, magnets may work because they alter the location of internal minerals. This may help temporarily, but their long-term usage may pose a problem. Research still needs to be done in this area. The use of magnets alone without nutritional supplementation may not be the best course of action.

Some believe "that magnets are helpful in overcoming pain because they repolarize the body. This allows more nutrition and oxygen into the cells, and greater amounts of toxins out" [3]. It is claimed that magnets can help athlete's foot by increasing oxygen to the area and create "an environment that is not conducive to pathogenic organisms" [3]. Some, instead of using magnets, spray magnetically charged water over lesions, etc. [3].

Some believe the reason that people benefit from magnets is that by living in an industrialized society, our feet now have far less direct contact with the earth, and since we no longer have this regular grounding, magnets help fill in the gap. This theory does make some intuitive sense, but as mentioned many places in this book, there is not any one modality that is always helpful for everyone (though resting one day per week, as discussed in chapter 15, would be one exception).

Gary Null, Ph.D. has written, "Some words of caution: Do not sleep on a magnetic bed pad for more than 8 to 10 hours a night. Also, those practiced in this area explain that the body should touch the north, or negative side, of the magnet, as this produces healing effects. The southern pole, or positive side, is said to have the opposite effect, exacerbating pain and disease" [3].

Electrotherapy

Modern research has found (in a placebo-controlled trial) by sending an electrical impulse through a magnet, depressed people became less depressed [4]. On the other hand, there may be risks associated with electromagnetism. A Finnish study found that although there were no risks associated with the rate of depression for people who lived near high-voltage power lines, the risk of severe depression was 4.7 times higher for people who lived within 100 meters of one (though the actual number of people affected was quite small and possibly not significant) [5].

Decades ago, Dr. Cordingley wrote the following under the heading *Electro-Therapy*:

There is a considerable variety of electrical treatment appliances on the market, which deliver over a dozen different forms of currents, or modalities, to use the technical term.

Thus, we have the galvanic, faradic, slow, rapid and surging sinusoidal, high frequency violet ray, diathermy, and auto-condensation, which are the ones most commonly used...The sinusoidal current is known as an induced current, and in case of the rapid sinusoidal, is similar in some respects to the faradic, which latter is generated by magnetism in an induction coil, but differs from the faradic in that the voltage of the inducing current is higher and its undulations are smoother. My experience has been...at the faradic current is an excellent current for eliciting the spinal reflexes and the faradic equipment has the advantage that it can be carried around and used anywhere independent of the city current supply, because the faradic current can be generated by two or three dry cells.

The slow sinusoidal current has proven of value in constipation, a large pad being placed on the abdomen while a smaller one is placed opposite on the lumbar vertebrae. The even and slow contraction and relaxation produced increase peristalsis of the intestines and very often permanently overcome constipation in a relatively short time.

In various forms of paralysis, rheumatism, lumbago, and sciatica, all modalities of the sinusoidal, as well as the faradic, have proven of value. Where it is desired to affect a muscle, the usual way in which to apply the current is to place one electrode near the origin and the other near the insertion of the muscle.

The galvanic is the one polar electricity. That is, the current flows out at the positive pole, passes through the part of the body being treated, and then returns by the way of the negative pole. Some of the properties of galvanic current are as follows:

THE POSITIVE POLE	THE NEGATIVE POLE
Attracts Oxygen.	Attracts Hydrogen.
Accumulates Chlorine, Nitric, Phosphoric.	Accumulates alkal-hydrates of calcium, potassium, sodium, and Hydrochloric Acids. and am-monium.
Acid caustic.	Alkaline caustic.
Cicatrix hard, dry and unyielding.	Cicatrix soft and pliable. Dialates arterioles.
Stops hemorrhage.	Increases hemor-rhage.
Relieves inflamma-tion and pain.	Stimulates and irritates.
Hardens tissue.	Disintegrates tissue.

Because of these polar effects, it will be seen that it is of great importance using galvanism to properly place the pads. If the negative pad is placed where the positive pad should have been placed, the results are likely to be detrimental rather than beneficial. However, if the Naturopath will carefully analyze the condition he is treating, he should have no difficulty in placing the pads. For instance, in treating goitre, the purpose is to disintegrate tissue, therefore the negative pad should be used over the goitre, and the positive pad placed at the back of the neck or on the abdomen.

In case of extreme pain, as in cases of lumbago, arthritis, etc., the positive pad should be placed over the painful area, as the positive pole relieves the pain. If you are treating a sluggish liver, you place the negative pad over the liver and the positive pad opposite on the back, because the negative pad stimulates, and stimulation is what is wanted. If you are treating an ulcerated stomach, the positive pad should be applied over that organ, as the positive pole stops hemorrhage and relieves pain. If you will keep in mind the properties of each pole, it will be a rela-tively simple matter to properly place the electrodes for each case.

The galvanic current can be obtained by a machine made up of dry cells; directly from the commercial line if it is the direct current and a rheostat is used; through rectifiers if the alternating is the only avail-able commercial current; or through direct current generating equipment. Many regard the galvanic as the most useful of all currents, as it is the one physiological current. It is, indeed, a current of a wide range of usefulness, but nothing can re-ally displace the faradic and sinusoidal currents in some disorders.

The high frequency violet ray is a cur-rent that is soothing in its effects in many painful conditions, and it will frequently be found of benefit to use it after admin-istering a manipulative treatment to a very tender area. The violet ray has been grossly over-rated. Many manufacturers especially have advocated the use of the violet ray for every ailment to which the human family is subject and many disap-pointments have consequently resulted. However, as an adjunct treatment it has its uses, and in nervousness, headache, sleeplessness, and some other similar disorders. It has often proven of value even when used alone… Some of the below-enumerated effects are very slight in some cases, but still this current is ca-pable of producing each of these effects to a certain varying extent:

The High Frequency Violet Ray Current:

1. Increases oxidation and local nutri-tion.
2. Produces hyperemia in areas to which it is applied.
3. Adds oxygen to the blood.
4. Increases elimination of carbon dioxide.
5. Increases elimination of waste prod-ucts through the skin.
6. Increases the temperature where applied.
7. Locally germicidal.

8. Sparks to upper dorsal spine raises blood pressure.
9. Application at any area for 20 seconds to one minute with sparking is stimulative.
10. Application for 2 to 5 minutes with electrode held in contact is sedative.

The diathermy current is a heating current. It is used largely in rheumatic joints, gouty deposits, sciatica, lumbago, neuralgia, and neuritis. Lately it has come into use in the treatment of pneumonia with splendid results. Some enthusiasts advocate its use for nearly every disorder, and inasmuch as the essential part of the current consists in the production of heat in the deeper tissues, it can be seen that it would naturally be of value in all conditions which would be benefited by heat, and that applies to a wide range of ailments. It is applied much like the sinusoidal or faradic, two well-moistened felt pads, block tin or wire mesh electrodes being used.

The auto-condensation current, like the diathermy, is a high tension current, produced by a tesla coil and oudin resonator, which is used principally for the relief of high blood pressure. The patient sits or lies on their couch pad which is connected to one pole of the machine, and the circuit is completed through a handle which he holds in his hands. In my experience, this current is a sovereign remedy in high blood pressure. There is no other separate method... know[n] of that will lower the blood pressure as rapidly and effectively, as the auto-condensation current [6].

Especially impressive is Dr. Cordingley's comment "many disappointments have consequently resulted." This is because with electrical and other devices, the latest herbal "discovery", or the newest nutritional fad, many are often disappointed. No one intervention always works for everyone to restore health. Everyone is different and true naturopathy believes that interventions must be tailored to the individual, not the diagnosis. Many people do not seem to understand this though after being exposed to what can be called the "chemistry view" of human health (i.e. since the body consists of chemicals and chemicals always react in a consistent manner, if a new chemical is prescribed the problem supposedly will be addressed).

The author's recent research involving bio-electrical stimulation devices known as "zappers" may be the largest recent study on their efficacy. In it, 97.9% of subjects who had patterns consistent with chronic infections, underwent one or more zapping sessions, while also taking herbs, glandulars, and/or nutrients, reported improvement [7]. Thus, there is some efficacy in their use. A copy of the published study is included within Appendix A.

The earth contains many natural magnets (including magnetic north). There is electricity in the natural environment and even in the human body [8]. Both still may have use for naturopaths.

References

[1] Kulkarni, V. M. *Healing Through Naturopathy.* Reprint by B. Jain Publishers, New Delhi (India), originally written circa 1925.

[2] Horowitz, S. *Migraine: Magnets and Other Nondrug Therapies.* Alt & Comp Ther, 1999; 5(3):124-129.

[3] Null, G. *The Complete Encyclopedia of Natural Healing.* Kensington, New York, 1998.

[4] LaVoie, A. *Magnets May Help Battle Depression.* Am J Psychia, 1997; 154:1752-1756.

[5] Verkasol, P. K., et al. *Magnetic Fields of Transmission Lines and Depression.* Am J Epidemiol, 1997; 146(12):1037-1045.

[6] Cordingley, E. W. *Principles and Practice of Naturopathy.* Reprint by Health Research, Mokelumne (CA), written 1924.

[7] Thiel, R. J. *Bioelectrical Stimulation for People with Patterns Consistent with Chronic Infections.* ANMA Monitor, 1998, 2(4):5-9.

[8] Mederios, J. A., Pontes, F. A. and Mesquita O. A. *Is Colonic Electrical Activity a Similar Phenomena to Small-Bowel Electrical Activity.* Dis Colon Rectum, 1997; 40(1):93-99.

15
Rest and Sleep

Naturopaths have always been advocates of rest and adequate, natural sleep. Dr. Kellogg (whose famous brother marketed *Corn Flakes*) wrote the following under the heading *The Rest Cure:*

The importance of rest, as a therapeutic means in the treatment of certain forms of disease and morbid conditions, especially in surgical cases, has long been recognized by scientific physicians; but it is only within recent times that this most important of nature's various recuperative agents has been systematically studied, and a method of treatment, organized to which the term "rest-cure" could be appropriately applied. Mitchell was not the first, however, to present the subject in a methodical form. John Hilton, president of the Royal College of Surgeons, of England, had, long before, dwelt with much emphasis upon the importance of rest in the treatment of disease, and devoted a volume of considerable size to its proper employment in painful maladies. It must be granted, however, that Dr. Mitchell was the first to conceive a systematic treatment by rest combined with massage and a regulated regimen, a fact which has received world-wide recognition by the medical profession.

As a therapeutic agent, rest belongs in the category of natural agents, with exercise, diet, baths, etc. It is perhaps for this reason that it was so long neglected, as were also dietetics and hydrotherapy, which have only recently begun to receive the attention that their importance demands. Sleep, nature's great restorative, is the most powerful of all recuperative measures, for the reason that during sound sleep the nearest possible approach to perfect physiological and mechanical rest is secured. Rest, even during sleep, is not absolute; otherwise the life processes would cease, and death ensue. The advantages of the rest afforded by sleep are illustrated by many facts.

Both plants and animals require physiological rest. During its waking hours, which usually correspond to those of daylight, the animal expends energy in muscular and nervous activity. It gathers its food at the cost of more or less exertion, and otherwise exercises its powers in providing for its individual comfort or that of others. During sleep these expenditures cease, and the energies of the body may be solely employed in the repair of the injuries and losses which have occurred during the hours of waking activity. It is during sleep, when the force of the vital powers is thus concentrated upon the organism itself, that both animals and plants make the principal part of their growth.

Physiological and mechanical rest has long been known to be the best means of promoting recovery in cases of injury, and it is equally valuable in recruiting depleted vital energies or in repairing a breach in the continuity of the tissues. In cold climates, trees and plants take physiological rest during the winter months; while in warm countries, a similar rest is afforded by the dry season. The water-lily of Egypt flourishes in the canals during the wet season, when they are filled with water for irrigating purposes, but disappears utterly during the dry season, when the canals are empty, and their beds so dry and hard as to be used for roadways. When the floods come down the Nile, and the water flows into the canals, the lily, recuperated by its rest, blooms again. During the brief summer season of the Arctic regions, flowers and plants spring up after their long sleep, and attain maturity in a shorter period than in any other part of the world.

Another evidence of the universal necessity for rest is afforded by the fact that plants while in bloom, in many instances, exhibit evidences of sleep very similar to those shown by animals, closing their leaves or their flowers when the sun approaches the western horizon.

Growth and exercise are in opposing relation to each other. It is true that exercise promotes growth, but the growth does not occur simultaneously with the exercise. On the contrary, during periods of vigorous exercise, growth is checked. Increased oxygenation and improved elimination resulting from exercise are means of systematic invigoration which promote growth, provided the exercise be not carried to an extreme. By too great exhaustion of the bodily forces, growth is lessened.

In the child, growth may be said to be chiefly confined to periods of rest and sleep. The full development of the body having been obtained, repair takes the place of growth. Incessant activity, which must necessarily be accompanied by the loss of sleep, produces a rapid waste of tissue, as well as anaemia from a diminution both in the number of corpuscles and in the haemoglobin, or coloring matter, of the blood. Sleep promotes tissue production and repair.

Rest is necessary for the viscera as well as for the brain, the nerves, and the muscles. A viscus, as the liver or spleen, when at work, increases in size, from the unusual amount of blood circulating through its vessels. The diameter of the liver increases during digestion from half an inch to an inch. It is for this reason that the spongy viscera of the abdomen are each surrounded by an elastic capsule, which contains both muscular and yellow elastic fibers. The pressure, of this elastic covering, constantly acting upon the organ, promotes its return, to a state of physiological rest as soon as the demand for its activity has ceased.

Even the brain enlarges during activity. The thick skull does not permit an actual increase in the volume of the brain as a whole, but nature has provided an arrangement by which an enlargement of the active parts may occur. The large lateral ventricles which occupy the interior of the brain on each side are constantly filled with cerebro-spinal fluid. The optic thalami and the corpora striata, the most active portions of the brain, are so placed that they project into the ventricles. When distended with blood, and thus enlarged, as they are during activity, these bodies project farther into the ventricles, displacing a quantity of the cerebro-spinal fluid, which passes through the foramen of Monroe, the third ventricle, the aqueduct of Silvius, the fourth ventricle; the cerebro-spinal opening in the floor of the fourth ventricle; and the sub-cerebral spaces, into the vertebral canal. When the activity ceases, the pressure of the cerebro-spinal fluid causes it to return to the lateral ventricles, thus keeping them constantly filled, and providing suitable support for the blood vessels of the adjacent nerve structures. It has been shown that when the cerebro-spinal fluid is not present in the lateral ventricles, the brain cannot be injected without rapture of these vessels.

The rhythmical activity of the chest is another means of securing the return of the brain and the viscera to a state of rest after activity. The diminution in pressure which occurs during inspiration makes a strong draught upon the blood current in the direction of the heart, thus aiding especially the venous circulation of the brain and also that of the liver, as well as that of the other abdominal viscera.

Indications for Application of the "Rest-Cure"—More than twenty years' experience in the employment of the "rest-cure" in various forms has to the author amply demonstrated its value. It has been found especially successful in the treatment of the following conditions:

Chronic Pain—The rational treatment of painful maladies necessarily includes not only the recognition and treatment of the cause of the malady, but also mitigation of the pain itself, a consequence of the exhausting influence of long-continued pain, and the interference of this symptom with the normal processes of recuperation and repair. Rest and position are, in suitable cases, more effective in securing relief from pain than any of the ordinary sedative drugs, without rest. This is true of both local and general pains. The terrible pain of a felon [ed. note: a felon is a deep usually suppurative inflammation of the finger or toe especially near the tip or around the nail] may not infrequently be relieved to an astonishing degree by simply elevating the hand above the head. The pain of a rheumatic ankle sometimes disappears almost instantly upon the sufferer's assuming a horizontal position, with the foot elevated. The pain of an inflamed nerve, as in sciatica, yields prolonged rest more certainly than to any other treatment. The neurotic young woman who in an erect position suffers such intolerable spinal pain as to make existence almost unendurable, finds herself perfectly comfortable when in bed. Pelvic and abdominal pains often disappear as if by magic when the patient assumes a horizontal position. The relief thus afforded is often brought about by the removal of the tension upon the abdominal sympathetic nerve and its branches, which is secured by a reclining position.

In a majority of cases of this kind, some of the abdominal or pelvic viscera will be found displaced, or in a condition termed by Glenard "enteroptosis." When the patient is in an erect position, the stomach, liver, kidney, bowels—one or all of these organs—being in a pendant or floating condition drag upon the sympathetic in a way which may set up pain and morbid symptoms of the most varied character, and in structures either near or remote. Pain attributable to irritation of the abdominal sympathetic from the cause mentioned, may be locally expressed in any part of the body from the heel to the top of the head. Rest, in bed is a sovereign remedy for cases of this kind.

Emaciation—Progressive wasting of the tissues as indicated by a steady loss of flesh, is a morbid condition which sometimes proves most refractory to therapeutic efforts, especially when the means employed are exclusively of a medicinal character. There is, in fact, no drug which can be relied upon to secure a substantial and permanent increase in flesh. Emaciation is an evidence of a serious disturbance of nutrition; and when considerable in degree, or rapidly progressive, invariably demands a prompt and systematic application of the "rest-cure." An improvement in weight can be expected only as the result of an increase of residual tissue, or fat. This requires, first of all, an improvement in digestive activity, which may involve an increase in either the quantity or the quality of the digestive work done. Not infrequently, patients complain that, although they have a good appetite, and eat large quantities of food, they nevertheless steadily lose in flesh. In these cases, a thorough-going examination of the stomach fluid obtained after a test meal, shows the coefficient of digestive activity to be low—in other words, the quality of the digestive products is [sic] so poor that they are, in large part, useless for the purposes of nutrition.

Successful treatment of these cases requires, next after an improvement in digestion by which a larger amount of tissue building material can be taken in, a careful economizing of the vital resources. As far as possible, the activity of the bodily powers must be concentrated upon the building up of the individual. All external expenditures of energy must be cut off.

Food is consumed in the body in three ways only—for heat production, force production, and tissue building. The food elements consumed in heat and force production cannot be deposited as tissue, or, at least, cannot be retained; consequently the amount of nutritive material used in this way should be limited to the smallest amount possible. In no way can the vital resources be thus economized so effectively as by the aid of the "rest-cure."

Fever—In all cases in which there is any considerable rise of temperature or febrile activity, from whatever cause, rest is one of the most essential features of treatment. If the temperature rises daily three or four degrees above normal, the patient should be kept in bed. If the elevation of temperature is not more than one or two degrees, the patient may spend a part of the time only, in bed; the balance of the time be may be dressed, if he desires, but should recline upon a cot, rolling-chair, or hammock. In this way, the great waste of tissue which always accompanies fever may be very materially lessened, and the intensity of the febrile action greatly diminished. Rest in bed is one of the most valuable of all the means which can be utilized in the treatment of pulmonary tuberculosis, or consumption, during febrile paroxysms.

The necessity of rest is well recognized in the treatment of typhoid fever and other acute febrile maladies, but its importance in the treatment of pulmonary consumption is often over-looked. In the last-named disease, the patient should be put to bed whenever the temperature rises above 101 degrees.

Neurasthenia—This condition, commonly called nervous exhaustion, is one in which the "rest-cure" has achieved some of its most important and remarkable triumphs. The value of the "rest-cure" in the treatment of neurasthenia has come to be so thoroughly recognized that it is by some considered almost a panacea. This view is an extreme one; nevertheless, mechanical and, as far as possible, physiological rest of the brain and nerves is, for many cases of this kind, most important as a requisite for recovery. This is especially true of those cases of nervous exhaustion sometimes encountered in young men and women who have led aimless and idle lives, and whose morbid condition is the result of a mental and physical stagnation rather than excessive work. In the case of overworked and worried persons, especially those in whom the decline of health has been accompanied by a loss in flesh, the "rest-cure" is indicated as a therapeutic measure of the first importance.

The Opium, Cocaine, Whisky, and Tobacco Habits—In the treatment of these poison habits [Kellogg has] found rest a most valuable accessory means. The man or woman who has long been addicted to such a habit will invariably be found in a state of nerve exhaustion, and it is this condition of the nervous system, and the veritable cyclone of nerve symptoms which arises from it as soon as the toxic agent is withdrawn, so that the patient, becomes conscious of his real condition, which renders the management of these cases so difficult. A person habituated to the use of any poison cannot be considered cured until the nervous system has been restored to a normal and well-balanced state. If the drug is simply withdrawn, and the patient left with a nervous system shattered by its pernicious influence, he will, in a majority of cases, find himself utterly unable to resist the importunities of his worn-out and pain-racked nerves for their accustomed solace. The morbid condition which constitutes an ever-present incitement to the perpetuation of the habit must be removed before the patient can be regarded as cured. "Rest-cure" is as valuable in the treatment of this form of nervous exhaustion as any other.

Another very important reason for the employment of the "rest-cure" in these cases, is the absolute control of the patient which it secures. The patient who has been long accustomed to the use of opium or cocaine, and even in some instances alcohol or tobacco habitues, require every possible assistance in getting through the first few days after the complete withdrawal of the accustomed drug, whether it is gradually taken away or suspended at once. In order to receive all the assistance possible from a rational system of treatment and by the aid of a trained nurse, the patient must remain in bed; for, during this period, he will require an application of some sort not only every hour but almost every moment, to quiet his clamoring nerves, as well as to while away the weary hours and beguile his mind into a normal channel. [Kellogg has] found the "rest-cure" of great value in the treatment of a large number of cases of the opium habit and other forms of drug addiction.

Gastric Ulcer—In this disease, there is not only marked wasting of the body in a majority of cases, in consequence of the disturbance of nutrition occasioned both by the ulcer itself and by the morbid condition of the stomach which precedes it, but there is also a local destruction of tissue which is aggravated by exercise. The irritability of the stomach and the highly excited state of the solar plexus render exercise upon the feet, in many of these cases, extremely painful, such exercise often giving rise to most distressing paroxysms of pain and gastric crises. By rest in bed, the patient's forces are economized; nutrition is improved; and more favorable conditions for recovery are secured.

Gastric ulcer is usually a consequence of long-continued hyperpepsia. Exercise upon the feet has a marked tendency to increase the hyperpepsia and thus promote the development of the ulceration; while mechanical rest has an opposite effect. In most of these cases, it is also necessary to give the stomach complete physiological rest by withholding altogether the administration of food by the mouth, and administering only specially prepared foods by means of the rectum. While the nutrition is thus restricted, absolute rest in bed is most important as a means of preserving the forces of the patient.

Hemorrhage—After severe hemorrhage from any cause, as from the lungs in pulmonary disease; from the uterus in cases of fibroid tumor or other diseases of that organ; from the rectum, in consequence of ulceration or bleeding hemorrhoids; or from any other cause whatever, a more or less prolonged rest in bed is of the utmost importance as a therapeutic measure, and is in the highest degree conducive, to the replenishment of the blood. In a number of cases of this kind the writer has noticed, during rest, an astonishingly, rapid restoration of the haemoglobin and a return of the normal blood count.

Diseases Peculiar to Women—While many diseases peculiar to women are the result of neglect to properly develop the muscles, especially those of the trunk; nevertheless, in a large number of the morbid conditions from which they suffer, a short course of "rest-cure" may be employed with very great advantage. This is especially true in all inflammatory diseases of the ovaries and uterus. Severe cases of uterine and vaginal catarrh are also greatly benefited by rest in a recumbent position. The effect of position upon the circulation of dependent parts is readily shown by noticing the change which occurs in the circulation of the hand when lifted above the head from the usual position by the side. If the veins are much swollen, as is likely to be the case when the arm swings by the side, it will be observed that instantly when the hand is raised above the head, or even to the horizontal position, the fullness disappears, and the skin of the band becomes blanched. This is not simply the result of gravity acting upon the blood, but is due chiefly to a decided contraction of the blood vessels in the hand. A like change occurs in the pelvic viscera. The swollen state of the blood vessels induced by the vertical position must greatly aggravate any pathological condition of the uterus or its appendages when congestion, either active or passive, is a prominent feature of the morbid state. The writer has frequently been told by patients that vaginal or uterine catarrh was always greatly increased during or after exercise upon the feet, and has seen such discharges disappear entirely during prolonged rest in bed, evidently as the result of the diminished circulation secured by the recumbent position.

Prostatic and Bladder Disease—The remarks which have been made with reference to diseases peculiar to women are equally true with reference to acute disease of the bladder, urethra, prostate gland, or the genital glands in men. An acute cystitis, urethritis, or prostatitis will be more readily benefited by rest in bed than by the employment of any other means. The same must also be said of orchitis, a disease which not infrequently resists treatment with great obstinacy, with out tile advantage of the recumbent position. In many cases of chronic disease of the bladder, in both men and women, "rest-cure" is of paramount importance as a therapeutic measure.

Bright's Disease of the Kidneys—The various pathological conditions of the kidney included under title term "Bright's disease" not infrequently demand rest in bed as a necessary condition for a cure of the disease, or even an arrest of its progress. This is especially true of acute inflammation of the kidneys. In this disease, there is a lessened ability of the kidney to eliminate poisons; consequently, the disintegration of tissue which occurs as the result of exercise upon the feet necessitates increased eliminative work on the part of the kidney. Exercise on the feet, and even sitting or standing, also involves greater activity of the heart and a higher arterial tension. An abnormal increase in arterial tension may be, in itself, sufficient to cause the appearance of albumen in the urine. It is evident, then, that in cases of acute inflammation of the kidneys, whatever tends to increase the arterial tension must aggravate the disease; and, on the other hand, the lessened arterial tension induced by rest in a horizontal position must favor recovery. In a somewhat extended experience in the treatment of this disease, the author has found rest an exceedingly valuable accessory.

Disease of the Heart—In the history of a case of organic disease of the heart, the first morbid condition of grave character which requires the attention of the physician, is often over-compensation. The unusual amount of work required of the organ induces an excessive development of the heart muscle, and this excessive cardiac activity results in a variety of disturbing and often alarming symptoms. There is no way by which the heart's action can be so quickly and so safely quieted as by means of rest in the recumbent position. There is no drug which is, even in a small degree, a substitute for rest, in cases of this kind.

In cases of cardiac insufficiency, rest in bed is equally as valuable as in cardiac hypertrophy with overaction of the heart. When the heart has become so weak as to be unable to maintain the circulation, the relief from work afforded by rest in the horizontal position, enables the heart to recover itself, be that, after a few days or weeks, as the case may require, the normal balance of the circulation is established; the heart, no longer distended and embarrassed with blood from which it has lost the power to empty itself, recovers its tone; the pulse becomes fuller and stronger; the cyanosis disappears; the swollen limbs return to their normal size; and the respiration is no longer embarrassed.

Nervous or Mental Irritability or Excitability—For certain cases of extreme nervous or mental excitability bordering on acute mania, and especially in cases of acute maniacal excitement, rest in bed, accompanied by appropriate treatment, is a measure of such great advantage that [Kellogg] should feel very loth indeed to undertake the treatment of cases of this sort without its aid. Rest in the horizontal position not only lessens the waste of tissue resulting from abnormal nervous or mental excitement, but secures to the patient the isolation and quiet which may exercise in a high degree a calming influence upon his over-excited nerves.

The Significance of Pain—In the selection of cases to which the "rest-cure" should be applied, it is necessary to understand clearly the significance of pain. Not infrequently, the pain experienced is very remote from the part which is the real origin of the pain, and to which, accordingly, the therapeutic measures should be directed.

In the employment of the "rest-cure" as a means of relieving pain, it is very important to distinguish between pains which are purely local in character and those which are of reflex origin. Local pains, or those originating in the parts where they are felt, if involving but a small portion of the body, may require rest only of the part itself. But sympathetic, or reflex pains generally, require complete rest. This is true, for example, of the intercostal pains connected with pleurisy, either acute or chronic, or adhesions of the pleura resulting from inflammation. The pleura and the overlying tissues are supplied with branches from the same sensory nerves. This fact should always be kept in mind, and should lead to a careful examination of the lungs in cases in which thoracic pains are experienced.

Quite a large proportion of all external pains are connected with disease of the viscera. Pain between the shoulders or above the lower angles of the scapulae, a very common chronic pain, indicates some disturbance of the fourth, fifth, and sixth spinal nerves. The nerve centers from which these nerves originate are those which chiefly give rise to the great splanchnic or visceral nerve, which is distributed to the stomach, liver, pancreas, and intestines. Its branches are also closely interwoven with the solar plexus and the lumbar ganglia of the sympathetic. It is consequently clear that the pain described may readily be produced by disease of the stomach, intestines, pancreas, liver, or some other viscus; and a careful investigation will usually show a prolapsed stomach or liver, a floating kidney, sagging of the bowels, or several of these conditions associated, whereby an abnormal and nerve-irritating condition is induced, affecting the branches of both the sympathetic and the splanchnics.

One-sided pain is, as a rule, an indication of a one-sided disease, while bilateral pain indicates a morbid condition affecting both sides. Even in cases arising from disturbance of the viscera, this rule holds good more frequently than might be expected. Migraine affecting one side of the head is, in the experience of the author, frequently connected with extreme hyperaesthesia of the lumbar ganglion of the same side. If both ganglia are affected, the patient will say that the attacks occur simultaneously upon both sides, or extend from one side to the other. In these cases, the greatest tenderness will usually be found in the lumbar ganglion of the side upon which the pain first begins. In cases in which the attack begins in the back of the head, extending thence upward over the whole head, both ganglia are usually found equally affected. In cases of pain arising from visceral disease, rest in bed for a week or two at the beginning of the treatment is a measure of very great advantage. At the conclusion of the period of confinement in bed, care should be taken to keep the organs in position by a properly adjusted supporter and appropriate applications of abdominal massage.

Disadvantages of the "Rest-Cure"—It should never be forgotten that rest in bed involves certain disadvantages, against which careful provision must be made. Man is naturally an active animal; and habits of regular, systematic exercise are essential to the maintenance of the integrity of the vital functions. Absolute rest in bed, without the employment of proper preventive measures, is, in itself, sufficient in many cases to provoke grave morbid conditions. The muscles, of course, rapidly deteriorate under the influence of inaction, but this is a matter of small importance compared with the injury sustained by the liver and other viscera. It is a common observation in surgical wards and hospitals that a healthy man confined in bed from fracture of a limb, becomes bilious, sometimes even jaundiced, ill consequence of interference with the functions of the stomach, liver, and bowels. The unpleasant effects of rest are readily understood when the important influence of exercise upon the viscera is recognized.

Exercise necessarily involves increased chest activity. The lungs constitute not only an air pump by which oxygen is supplied to the body, but, at the same time, exercise a most important influence in assisting the circulation and thus the functional activity of the stomach and liver.

The diaphragm not only acts as a great lymph pump, but by compression of the stomach and liver during the act of forcible inspiration, it exercises these important organs, and by promoting absorption, aids in emptying the stomach of its contents; while, by mechanical compression, it empties the liver of bile, and hastens the passage of the blood through its capillaries.

Perhaps more important still is the effect of exercise upon the general system in promoting the complete oxidation, or burning up, of the waste matters which are continually accumulating in the tissues through increased absorption of oxygen, and by draining off the poisonous waste substances prepared for removal from the body, and hastening their transportation to the liver, kidneys, lungs, bowels, and skin, through which they make their exit from the body. Diminished respiratory activity alone may be responsible for a congestion of the stomach and liver resulting in stomach and intestinal catarrh, infectious jaundice, and inactivity of the liver and bowels.

The horizontal position may also result in injury on account of the congestion due to the mechanical accumulation of blood in the dependent parts. Pneumonia not infrequently results from lying continuously upon the back during a course of typhoid fever or some other disabling malady. Even cerebral congestion may result from the horizontal position.

These and other disorders, the nature of which may be inferred from what has been said in reference to the influence of rest in producing these morbid conditions, may be prevented by the adoption of proper measures, the most important of which are massage and manual Swedish movements. The utility of massage in these cases need not be argued, as it is apparent at once that it may be made, to a very large extent, a substitute for exercise, without expending the nervous energy of the patient, or making any large draughts upon his vital resources.

These facts give massage a value which cannot be overestimated. It is a means by which the patient may receive the benefit of exercise without effort on his part; and in most cases in which "rest-cure" is required, massage must also be employed as a complementary measure. A few exceptions only need be made. These are so important, however, that they must not be overlooked. First of all, it must be remembered that in febrile conditions, or at least in all cases in which any considerable degree of febrile activity exists, massage must not be applied, for the reason that it increases heat production. In most cases, bathing and rubbing must be employed to a greater or less extent; but care should be taken to avoid all manipulative measures except stroking and centrifugal friction, the tendency of which, as regards heat production, is the opposite of all the other processes of massage. In the employment of the "rest-cure" for the relief of pain due to visceral prolapse or other diseases of those organs, manipulation of the diseased viscera must be avoided except so far as may be necessary for replacement; but massage to the limbs and other parts of the body may very wisely be employed, since, when administered in this manner, it operates most efficiently as a derivative measure.

In acute Bright's disease of the kidneys, massage must be avoided, or at least should be confined to the gentlest measures, for the reason that the kidneys are crippled, and it is desirable that their work should be restricted as much as possible within safe limits. A vigorous application of massage may suddenly throw into the circulation so large a quantity of toxic and excrementitious substances as to overwhelm the kidneys and create an increase of irritation, the result of which might be disastrous. Stroking and centrifugal friction are the only appropriate measures for cases of this kind until after there has been a marked diminution in the activity of the disease, as shown by a decrease in the production of albumen and an increase of urea, or a marked rise in the coefficient of toxicity.

In cases of excessive nervous and mental excitability, massage must be used only when great care is taken to select the right measures, and the treatment in such cases must be administered with unusual skill. The lighter measures of massage only are admissible in these cases. Percussion must generally be altogether interdicted. Gentle, deep kneading and centrifugal friction are most appropriate measures, and these should be employed derivatively.

Among the most valuable preventive measures to be employed In massage when administered in ordinary cases of "rest-cure," should be mentioned abdominal massage. Massage of the stomach, bowels, and liver aids greatly in counteracting the evil effects of rest upon these viscera, and in facilitating the processes of digestion and elimination, in fact promoting all the functions of the organs named, as well as those of the kidneys.

Another measure of greatest importance, in addition to general and abdominal massage, is to be found in lung gymnastics, which not only greatly aid the functions of the liver, stomach and other viscera, but also relieves the brain of blood, thus preventing cerebral congestion, and promotes elimination. Breathing exercises also promote the formation of blood, thus preventing anaemia, and greatly aiding the oxidation and elimination of waste matters. These exercises are valuable not only in ordinary cases, but in fevers, Bright's disease, and, in fact, in every case in which the "rest-cure" is employed, except acute pleurisy and pulmonary hemorrhage, in which, of course, it is important to secure as great a degree of quietude as possible.

The employment of lung gymnastics in fevers is a valuable means of combating the depressing tendency of the disease and of preventing the pneumonia which frequently accompanies fevers of a low type. It also aids in lowering temperature, not only by cooling the blood, but also by assisting in oxidation and elimination of the toxic substances to which the rise of temperature is due.

Ewald measured the temperature of the stomach by a thermoelectric device, and found it to be, on an average, 1°F higher than in the axilla. By making the patient breathe forcibly, even with the mouth closed, the temperature of the stomach was reduced to half a degree less than the axillary temperature. When the patient breathed steam at the temperature of the body, this lowering of the temperature of the stomach did not occur, showing that the internal temperature may be lowered by bringing the blood into contact with an increased quantity of cool air through forced respiration.

This measure has not been employed in febrile cases as much as it deserves to be. It is, of course, important that the patient should be entirely passive. The increased breathing activity should be secured by movements executed by the masseur, who, by raising the arms from the sides and drawing them upward, will aid inspiration; then, by returning them to the sides, and compressing the sides of the chest, may aid expiration. Cyanosis, which so frequently accompanies febrile action when the temperature rises to a dangerous point, may be made quickly to disappear by this means.

Position is a matter also worthy of mention as a means of combating some of the evil tendencies of rest. In cases with a tendency to cerebral hyperaemia, the head of the bed should be raised, thus utilizing gravity as a means of securing drainage of the brain. This is especially important in cases of apoplexy, and the same measure should be employed in pulmonary hemorrhage. In hemorrhage from other parts of the body, resulting in anaemia, the opposite plan should be followed, the foot of the bed being raised. This measure should also be adopted whenever it is desirable to antagonize congestion or inflammation in the lower extremities. Pelvic pain due to disease of the ovaries or of the bladder, prostate, or rectum, is often greatly relieved by raising the foot of the bed, in connection with rest in the recumbent position.

From what has been said, it is evident that massage is practically indispensable as a complementary measure of treatment in connection with the "rest-cure," and that it may be applied in some form in all cases requiring rest, and in such a manner as to greatly increase the advantages which may be derived from the "rest-cure."

After-Rest Exercise—A point of very great importance, to which attention should be called, is that rest alone seldom results in a radical cure. Rest secures a symptomatic cure, but does scarcely more than this, except to provide conditions favorable for recovery. Other recuperative measures must also be employed in connection with rest. Massage has been shown to be an invaluable remedy for this purpose. The "rest-cure" is only a preparation for exercise-cure. The patient who has been put to bed, and who has been relieved of his morbid symptoms by the rest thus obtained, must be made capable of enjoying good health upon his feet. To be cured in bed is not sufficient, as few sick people desire to spend their lives there. The patient must be gotten upon his feet and enabled to endure at least an ordinary amount of exercise without injury, before he can be considered well. Neglect of this point has resulted in a failure to effect anything more than temporary relief by means of the "rest-cure" in perhaps a large proportion of all the cases in which this measure has been employed. Since this point has been considered quite fully elsewhere in this work, the reader is referred to what has already been said.

The author would, however, emphasize the importance of supplementing, in every case, a course of "rest-cure" with a course of carefully graduated exercises, by which the patient may be safely introduced to life under ordinary conditions. The author expects to be able to place in press at an early date a work in which will be given many such series of exercises adapted to different conditions [1].

What is surprising about Dr. Kellogg's writings is that he did not allude to the following statement,

> Remember the Sabbath day to keep it holy. Six days shall you labor, and do all thy work: But the seventh day is the Sabbath of the LORD your God: in it thou shall not do any work, thou, nor thy son, nor thy daughter, thy manservant, nor thy maidservant, nor thy cattle, nor thy stranger that is within thy gates: For in six days the LORD made heaven and earth, and sea, and all that in them is, and rested the seventh day: wherefore the LORD blessed the Sabbath day and hallowed it" (Exodus 20:8-11).

Also known as the fourth commandment, this may have been the world's first labor and health law. It is a law that Dr. Kellogg was familiar with because he was a Sabbatarian (Dr. Kellogg was a Seventh Day Adventist). [ed. note: The author is also a Sabbatarian and a member of the Living Church of God.]

The concept of rest also includes sleep. Decades ago Dr. Kulkarni wrote,

> Do not sleep during day time.
> Do not keep up late at night.
> Keep open all the windows of your sleeping compartment.

"Airy, well-ventilated, sleeping apartments" says Dr. Ruddock, "should be ranked as the most important requirement of life both in health and disease." Sleep in the open air or in a room where there is ample provision of fresh air will be more refreshing and invigorating than in a room where fresh air is not freely admitted. "The air of an apartment," he adds, "containing several human beings, if unchanged, not only becomes charged with carbonic acid gas, but also gets impregnated with animal particles which fly off from the skin and lungs and are so minute as scarcely to be detected by the microscope but capable of decomposition and which taken by the breath into the lungs, may be absorbed and may develop the worst forms of diseases."

If you suffer from sleeplessness do not take bromide of potassium, morphia, opium or chloral hydrate. They do not produce healthy sleep but they cause stupor and the patient gets up in the morning with exhausted feeling. A hot foot-bath is an effective measure for inducing natural and refreshing sleep [2].

Dr. Kulkarni is correct that most people should not sleep during the daytime. Light (and caffeine) suppresses natural melatonin levels which help regular circadian rhythms (the normal sleep cycle) [3]. Sleeping medications are a terrible thing for many. Many authorities believe that they can almost only work by upsetting natural sleep cycles, thus leading to an unusual form of unnatural control [4].

Although melatonin may be safer than most (if not all) other synthetic sleeping pills, naturopaths should not recommend hormones, whether they supposedly are natural or not. Isolated hormones are unnatural isolates. Just like taking thyroid hormones can lead to atrophy of the thyroid gland [4], the ingestion of synthetic hormones does not encourage the body to heal what is causing the sleeping problems in the first place (though they may help a little if the problem is not physical). Stress reduction techniques, eliminating caffeine, ensuring adequate calcium and magnesium intakes, consumption of foods/supplements high in essential fatty acids, exercise during the day, and perhaps the occasional use of herbs are safer and more naturopathic. Many improve their ability to fall asleep and remain asleep by consuming calcium food supplements, herbs (including those high in essential fatty acids), and even certain glandulars. Other researchers have shown that moderate daily exercise improves the quality of sleep [5] and that essential fatty acids can sometimes induce sleep [6].

References

[1] Kellogg, J. H. *The Art of Massage.* Modern Medicine Publishing, Battle Creek (MI), 1929.

[2] Kulkarni, V. M. *Healing Through Naturopathy.* Reprint by B. Jain Publishers, New Delhi (India), originally written circa 1925.

[3] Wright, K. P., et al. *Caffeine and Light Effects on Nighttime Melatonin and Temperature Levels of Sleep-Deprived Humans.* Brain Res, 1997;747:78-84.

[4] *Physician's Desk Reference,* 53rd ed. Medical Economics, Montvale (NJ), 1999.

[5] King, A. C., et al. *Moderate-Intensity Exercise and Self-Rated Quality of Sleep in Older Adults.* JAMA; 1997277(1):32-37.

[6] Yehuda, S., et al. *Essential Fatty Acids and Sleep: Mini-Review and Hypothesis.* Med Hypo, 1998;50:139-145.

16
Exercise

Dr. Kellogg has been credited as one of the most vocal advocates of exercise. Until the 20th century, additional exercise was not necessary for most. Why? Well, there were almost no cars and little machinery. Thus, most people did a lot of walking, plus did a lot of physical work. Also, until the Industrial Age, most people were farmers. Farming with modern equipment is hard work—farming without modern equipment is harder physical work. Just milking one goat in the morning is work (try it once for fifteen minutes and see how your wrists and fingers feel), let alone plowing many acres, hoeing crops, harvesting crops, carrying water to crops when needed, and taking care of animals is not easy. It did, though, get people exposed to natural light, had positive cardiovascular effects, and resulted in most people (over one hundred years ago) eating fresh, organic food much of the year.

Now most people "work" without needing to expend the tremendous amount of physical energy that our ancestors did.

Even in rural India, Dr. Kulkarni felt that exercise was both preventive and curative. Decades ago he wrote:

Exercise is the natural accompaniment of Naturopathy. It favors thermic reaction and imparts energy to the limbs and cheerfulness to the mind. Everything in this universe is in its proper motion and having its due exercise. Even the sun which we see daily as the largest and brightest luminary in the sky is always moving in its orbit on its own axis. All the planets are moving round it. The Earth we inhabit also is in its motion always like other planets. Trees, plants, creepers, and even the grass are always shaken by the wind. The more they are shaken, the stronger they grow and their roots penetrate deeper in the earth. The birds in the air, the beasts on land and the fishes in water are all moving about and having their proper exercise. Human beings also, who take proper exercise, get stronger and healthier and keep always free from disease.

Nature has so constituted us that regular and proper exercise is necessary to counteract the wear and tear of life. This wear and tear goes on from hour to hour and day to day and exercise is needed to rebuild the body and re-invigorate the mind every day.

Natural Exercise

(1) Regular open air work in bright sunlight until proper perspiration is induced is the best of all exercises for human beings; digging or tilling the ground for growing vegetables, fruits, flowers, watering the plants, etc. are the most suitable. Those who have no facilities for such work may take brisk walks in the bright sun till they perspire freely. While walking, the whole body should be erect with shoulders turned backwards; breathing should be vigorous and deep. A healthy young man may need to walk 6 to 12 miles a day; the convalescent, weak persons, and women should at least walk 3 to 5 miles a day.

Physical Exercise

Those who are required to work hard physically are inclined to think that they need no special exercise. This, however, is a mistake as all physical labor either outdoor, such as carrying loads, etc. or indoor such as work in factories, mills, etc. brings only certain parts of the body into action while the other parts remain inactive, and tends to unequal development which is injurious to the body. It is therefore advisable that such persons should take appropriate exercise to develop and strengthen the unexercised parts of the body. The author does not mean that they should go through an exhausting course of exercises such as heavy weight lifting, athletic feats, etc. but some mild health preserving exercises, which will promote normal development of all the parts of the body and preserve the health and prolong life.

General Rules for Exercise

(1) When taking any exercise we should face the sun…the brightest luminary of heaven so that we may draw some energy…

(2) While taking exercise by lying down we should direct our head to the north towards the Pole Star, the fountain of magnetism so that it may impart some magnetism to us.

(3) We should be bare-headed, barefooted and have on as little clothing as possible so that we come in direct touch with mother Earth and her life element fresh air so that we may obtain proper magnetism from her.

(4) Exercise should be taken when the mind and body are at ease and in open places such as gardens, court-yards, verandahs, spacious halls or rooms, near an open window or where there is an uninterrupted current of fresh air.

(5) Do not take any vigorous exercise when you are tired, nor take it until you feel quite tired, nor take it just before or soon after a meal.

(6) Undress yourself or wear a loose light dress so that it does not interfere with the free movements of the limbs and so that all the pores of the body are well-ventilated by the touch of fresh air.

(7) No apparatus is necessary while taking exercise. But those who feel the necessity may use light wands, clubs, dumb-bells or grip dumb-bells not heavier than one or two pounds.

(8) Begin the exercise each day with a few light movements and gradually try and make it vigorous increasing at the same time the number of movements. If any movements cause pain or uneasiness, do them only five times and increase the number gradually.

Caution—Very weak persons and those who suffer from asthma, palpitations, phthisis pulmonalis, tabes mesenterica, hernia, displacement of uterus, fall of rectum or those who are liable to apoplectic fits should not take vigorous exercises except under the supervision of an expert physician.

Head and Neck Exercise

(1) All proper movements of the head and neck strengthen the vital functions of the whole organism by toning up the muscles of the neck, chest and back. They also cure obstinate headaches, neuralgic pains, obstinate catarrh of the head and chest, dimness of sight, tonsillitis, all sorts of throat troubles, enlargement of cervical glands, etc.

Turning of the Head

(2) Make the neck tense and slowly turn the head toward the left and touch the left shoulder with your chin, then slowly turn the head towards the right side and touch the right shoulder with your chin breathing deep all the while; do it ten to sixteen times.

Rolling of the Head

(3) Place the left hand on the forehead and the right on the occiput and raise the head as high as possible. Then roll the head around as much as possible ten to sixteen times.

Bending the Head Backward and Forward

(4) Stand erect facing the sun, make the neck tense and then slowly bend the head backward and then bend it forward as much as possible. Repeat the process ten to sixteen times; breathe deeply during the procedure. Remaining in the same position you can twist the neck and bend the head backward.

Turning and Raising the Head

(5) Stand erect facing the sun and raise the head as high as possible making the neck tense as much as possible, and then turn the head to the left slowly then to the right steadily. Repeat this ten to sixteen times breathing deeply all the while.

Sustaining the Weight of the Body on Head and Neck

(6) Lie down on a carpet with the head and the occiput touching it, the head pointing towards the North Pole and the legs towards the South Pole; make the neck and back tense as much as possible and raise the legs up and stretch them towards the head so that the knees touch the forehead and the whole weight of the body rests on the head and neck; remain in this position as long as possible. Repeat the procedure five to ten times. This is an excellent exercise of the head and neck beneficial to those suffering from dim sight and neuralgic pains.

Chest and Lung Exercise

(7) Stand erect facing the sun, gently raise the arms, palms pointing upwards and stretch them out firmly as if trying to touch the ceiling; breathe deep 10 to 16 times; inhale while raising the hands and exhale while bringing them slowly down; this will improve the undeveloped shoulders, cure the flat or pigeon chest, large abdomen, hollow back, etc.

(8) Raise the arms and palms to be in a line with the shoulders and stretch them firmly outward and backward; the head thrown somewhat backward and the face pointing towards the ceiling; lift the chest and expand it with deep breath 10 to 16 times. This will broaden and strengthen the chest and shoulders and will cure palpitation of heart.

(9) Keep the arms hanging loosely at the sides and gently inhale, at the same time; raise the arms straight at the sides, when the lungs are full, raise the hands so that they meet and the thumbs touch one another and turn the face towards the ceiling. Then without holding the breath exhale gently sweeping the arms and hands downward and forward; make these movements slowly and gently; this exercise will cure pain in the chest, sleeplessness, nervousness, headaches, etc.

(10) Raise the hands up to the waist touching the back with the thumbs and bend forward toward the floor; bend 10 to 16 times. Inhale while bending, exhale while rising; do all this gently without effort; this gives strength to the abdomen and the back and cures dyspepsia, flatulence and constipation.

(11) Raise the hands backward touching the back, just under the shoulder blades. Then gently incline first the head then the body and bend the chest forward; expand the back and breathe deep 10 to 16 times. Then bend the back towards the chest, not towards the abdomen; breathe deep holding the waist firm and without bending; move the chest and neck thus and breathe deeply 10 to 16 times. This will strengthen the heart and the chest. This exercise is invaluable for women and those who lead an indoor life. These movements will improve the voice, cure tonsillitis, expand the chest, strengthen the heart and improve general health.

To Strengthen the Muscles of the Arms, Abdomen, Back and Waist

(12) Stand erect facing the sun; raise both the hands up above the head and

bend the body towards the back as much as possible. Then bend forward until the fingers touch the feet, keeping the knees straight. Do it 5 to 10 times twice daily morning and evening. After a few days bend more and more until you are able to touch the ground with your whole palms. Inhale deeply and exhale slowly.

To Strengthen the Functions of the Chest Stomach, Liver and Spleen

(13) Stand erect facing the sun; raise the right hand up above the head and the left stretching towards the left side only. Then bend to the left as far down as possible. Then assume the original position and raise the left hand up as above as possible keeping the right hand stretched straight towards the right side only and bend the body towards the right side as down as possible. Repeat the process several times. Inhale deeply and exhale slowly.

To Strengthen the Chest and Increase the Capacity of the Lungs

(14) Stand erect facing the sun; stretch both the arms backward so that the hands touch each other; try to bring the hands as high as possible raising them higher with each repetition; rise yourself up standing on the toes and fingers of the feet. Then stretch the arms forward so that the palms touch each other. Inhale deeply while raising the body and exhale slowly while lowering the toes and returning to the original position. Do so 12 to 20 times thrice or at least twice a day.

To Strengthen the Muscles of the Abdomen and to Reduce Extra Fat

(15) Stand erect facing the sun and keeping the hands on the hips; keep the feet about 6 inches apart. Then bend towards the right side as much as possible and then assume the former position.

Then bend towards the left as much as possible and return to the original position. Then bend yourself on the front side as much as possible slowly and steadily and assume the former position. Then bend the back backward slowly as much as possible and resume the original position. Repeat it several times. Inhale deeply and exhale slowly during the exercise.

Exercise for Abdomen and Waist

(16) Lie down on the ground the back touching the earth the head pointing towards the north pole and stretch the legs straight like sticks towards the south pole. Stiffen the abdomen and draw it in as much as possible; slowly raise the head without stretching the hands on the ground and without raising the legs and bend double so that the forehead touches the knees; if you can't do it touch the soles of both the legs with both the palms bending your waist, but without bending your legs. Then slowly lie down on the earth without resting the hands on the ground; repeat the process ten to sixteen times. This is an excellent exercise for the abdomen and waist. It cures constipation, dyspepsia, flatulence, lumbago, etc.

Exercise for Abdomen, Waist, and Buttocks

(17) Assume the position mentioned in the Exercise (16), then hold fast with both the hands the lower portions of your thighs so that the palms touch the above portions of the popliteal fossae keeping all the weight of the body on both the hips. Then make slow and steady movements like a see-saw. This is a good exercise not only for the hands, arms and legs, but it is an excellent exercise for strengthening the muscles of the abdomen, waist, hips, etc. It cures dyspepsia, lumbago, pelvic pains, sciatica, rheumatic pains in the knees, etc.

Exercise to Strengthen the Muscles of the Shoulders and Arms

(18) Lie down as directed in Exercise (16); then raise both the hands above the head and bring them flat on the ground; then raise the right hand slowly and steadily and stretch it down; then repeat the procedure with the left hand. Do it at least ten times with each hand; take deep breaths through the nostrils during this procedure; then stretch the hands straight, the right hand towards the right side, the left hand towards the left. Then raise the right hand slowly and stretch it over the left; and then take it back to its former position; then raise the left hand in the same way and place it on the right hand flat and then take it back to its former position; do so ten to sixteen times.

This exercise will not only strengthen both the shoulders and the arms but will also cure asthma, cough and palpitations by oxidizing the respiratory organs and strengthening the chest.

Exercise to Strengthen the Legs

(19) Lie down on the ground with the back touching the ground, the head directed towards the north pole and stretch the legs straight like sticks toward the south pole. Then slowly and steadily raise the right leg up as high as possible and then bring it down slowly till it touches the ground and do the same with the left leg without bending the knee. Repeat the process ten times or more with both the legs alternately. Then turn to the right side and do the some ten times. Then turn to the left side and repeat the exercise with the left leg ten times. Then lie flat on the ground, the abdomen touching the ground and raise the right leg slowly and steadily as much as possible and then bring it down and touch the ground with it. Then raise the left leg in the same way; do it alternately 10 to 16 times.

This exercise will strengthen both the legs and cure epididymitis and varicocele if other necessary measures are also adopted.

Exercise to Strengthen the Whole Body

(20) Sit down facing the sun, keeping both the feet 15 to 18 inches apart. Do not allow the hips to touch the ground. Then stretch the hands and keep the elbows on the legs just above the knees. Then slowly raise yourself up and stretch down the head as far as the ground, and raise it immediately and stretch the right knee as far as the ground and then briskly raise it up; stretch the head again down to the ground and raise it immediately and then stretch the left knee down as far as the ground and raise it briskly and stretch the head down as before. Then comes the turn of the right knee and then the head and then the left knee and so on. Repeat this procedure several times. First try 10 to 16 times then gradually increase the number to 100 or 150 or even more if possible. This exercise will cure all diseases and make one strong, hearty and hale. It also prevents all diseases if practiced daily twice morning and evening and if possible even at night before going to bed [1].

(Breathing exercises are also included in chapter 12.) There are many books on exercise, but what Dr. Kulkarni wrote gives the definite sense of exercise that some naturopaths had (and have).

Research has shown that exercise (including sometimes walking 2 miles per day) helps with sleep disorders, reduces risk of cancer and cardiovascular disease (the two leading causes of death in the U.S.), reduces cholesterol and triglycerides, can provide the benefits of hormone-replacement therapy (without the side-effects) for menopausal women, can help reduce fibroids, helps some with chronic fatigue, can help with arthritis (and neck and back) pain, can help those with lupus, can increase natural killer cells (improves the immune system), reduces stress, helps with obesity, increases life span, and more [2-4].

References

[1] Kulkarni, V. M. *Healing Through Naturopathy.* Reprint by B. Jain Publishers, New Delhi (India), originally written circa 1925.

[2] Hamilton, K. *Clinical Pearls in Nutrition and Preventive Medicine,* 1997. ITServices, Sacramento (CA), 1998.

[3] Hamilton, K. *Clinical Pearls in Nutrition and Preventive Medicine,* 1998. ITServices, Sacramento (CA), 1998.

[4] Null, G. *The Complete Encyclopedia of Natural Healing.* Kensington Books, New York, 1998.

17

Naturopathic Manipulation: Massage, Acupressure and Reflexology

The simple touch of one person to another can easily have a therapeutic effect. Naturopaths have taken that concept and developed it much further. Although many do not realize it, historically, and even in some localities today, naturopaths have been licensed under some massage statutes.

In addition to exercise, Dr. Kellogg was a leading proponent of massage. He wrote:

Massage has chiefly to do with the circulation of fluid in the veins and the lymph channels, since these are more readily accessible from the surface than the arteries.

Friction acts chiefly upon the superficial veins, while petrissage and other forms of deep kneading act upon the deeper vessels as well.

Indirectly, the portal and pulmonary circulations are also influenced by massage. Massage of the extremities, for example, especially if concluded with centrifugal friction, may relieve congestion of both the portal and the pulmonary systems.

Massage of the legs acts more directly upon the portal system, while massage of both extremities favorably influences the pulmonary circulation in case of congestion of the lungs. Massage of the arms and legs also acts derivatively upon the brain and spine. For derivative effects upon the brain, however, care should be taken to avoid such exciting procedures as percussion and reflex stroking.

Massage also has a powerful effect upon the circulation by promoting the action of the diaphragm, which serves efficiently as a pump in assisting the circulation, as well as in carrying on the process of respiration. M. Camus has shown by experiments upon dogs that the increase either of the rate or the depth of respiratory movement increases the flow of lymph in the thoracic duct. The same has been shown in regard to the blood circulation by numerous investigators.

The influence of massage upon the lymph circulation is especially worthy of attention. The lymph vessels drain the tissues of waste and toxic substances, and prevent clogging from wandering cells. Lymph channels are most abundant in the subcutaneous tissue and in the fascia which cover and lie between the muscles, so that these vessels are mechanically acted upon in massage, especially by friction and kneading movements.

That massage and exercise of muscles greatly increase the flow of lymph has been repeatedly demonstrated by experiments upon animals, as, for example, it was found that the flow in the lymph vessels of a dog's leg nearly ceased when the animal was quiet, but as soon as the limb was exercised or massaged, the flow of lymph began again (Reibmayr).

It has also been shown that the flow of lymph from a limb in a state of inflammation was very easily induced, and was seven or eight times greater than from a sound limb. A swollen limb was found to diminish during the flow of lymph (Lassar).

The same author has shown that massage of a lymph gland increases the outflow of the fluid. Deep massage applied to a limb diminishes its size. The central tendon of the diaphragm contains a large number of lymph channels. The diaphragm may be regarded as a great lymph pump, since by its rhythmical movement, the lymph channels are alternately dilated and contracted.

Hoffinger has shown that the absorptive power of the peritoneum is greatly increased by massage. In experiments upon rabbits, the peritoneum was found to absorb under the influence of massage twice as much water in an hour as without massage.

An experiment made by Mosengeil, an eminent German physiologist, graphically demonstrates the influence of massage in promoting absorption. The joints of rabbits were injected with ink. Massage was applied to some of the rabbits and not to others. In the cases subjected to massage, the swelling which was produced by the injection rapidly passed away. When the rabbits were killed, some months afterward, it was found that the ink had entirely disappeared from the joints which had been massaged, and was found in streaks between the muscles, and accumulated in the lymphatic glands, indicating the course of the lymphatic channels. In cases in which the joints were not massaged, ink was found in the joints, but none in either the muscles or lymphatic glands. This result affords a striking illustration of the value of massage in affections of the joints accompanied by exudate.

It is through its power to promote absorption that massage is of great value in the treatment of local oedemas, general dropsy, and ascites.

Effects of Massage upon Respiration
These effects may be thus enumerated:

*1. Increase of Respiratory Activity—*Massage, as does exercise, increases the depth of the respiratory movements. This is doubtless in some measure due to the reflex influence of massage, but must also be attributed in part to its effect in bringing into the circulation waste products requiring elimination through the lungs, and in increasing oxidation, or, CO_2 production, which necessarily accompanies the increased heat production resulting from the effect of massage upon the muscles.

*2. Increase of Tissue Respiration—*It should be borne in mind that the function of respiration is not confined to the lungs. Respiration begins and ends in the lungs, but the most important part of the process is effected in the intimate recesses of the tissues themselves.

Massage is certainly a most efficient means of increasing tissue metabolism, by which oxygen is absorbed by the tissues and CO_2, taken up by the blood. This process takes place chiefly in the muscles, through the oxidation of the glycogen, of which they contain one half the total bodily store. Hence it is that massage, by acting directly upon the muscles, increases the tissue respiration by promoting circulation and general tissue activity.

In thus promoting the depth of respiratory movement and the intensity of tissue respiration, massage profoundly affects all the bodily functions. Through the increased lung activity there, is also increased circulation, as the lungs materially aid the heart in the circulation of the blood. Increased activity of the diaphragm serves to pump both blood and lymph toward the heart with greater vigor. Digestion, liver action, and other of the vital functions come in for their share of benefit in the increased vigor and efficiency of the respiratory process. The functions of the brain are more easily performed on account of the more perfect movement of venous blood and the better supply of oxygen received.

The Therapeutic Applications of Massage

As it is not the purpose of this work to enter into an exhaustive consideration of all the different applications of massage, we shall scarcely do more than mention briefly those maladies in which this therapeutic measure has been found most conspicuously useful. It is, in fact, hardly necessary to devote any very great amount of space to the general considerations which alone may be appropriately treated under this head, since the concise resume of the physiological effects of massage which has already been presented, will, for the intelligent practitioner, serve as the best possible index to its therapeutic applications; while for the masseur, the more specific directions given in connection with the individual measures of massage will be of greater practical use.

Disorders of Nutrition—Ancient as well as modern physicians have regarded massage as a measure by which the general nutritive processes of the body may be influenced in a most powerful degree. The value of massage as a therapeutic means arises from its remarkable influence upon the circulation, the direct and indirect stimulation of the nerves and nerve centers, and its remarkable modifying influence upon assimilation, disassimilation, and all the processes of secretion and excretion.

Anaemia and chlorosis are more rapidly and permanently cured by massage than by any form of medication which has been proposed. In connection with a properly regulated dietary and suitable hydropathic measures, massage must be considered as the treatment *par excellence* for these maladies.

The writer has seen excellent results in a number of cases of myxoedema in which massage was the leading therapeutic agent employed. If not capable of effecting a radical cure in this disease, it must at least be accredited with the power to prevent a further advance of the malady, and as a means of securing a very decided symptomatic improvement.

In cases of exhaustion from excessive mental, nervous, or muscular work, general massage secures the most marked and satisfactory results, relieving the sense of fatigue in a most wonderful man-

ner, and in cases of muscular exhaustion, restoring muscular power in a remarkably short space of time.

Massage also exerts a decidedly quieting influence upon the nervous irritability and insomnia so commonly accompanying cerebral and nervous exhaustion.

The restorative effects of general massage act with much efficiency as a means of retarding the encroachments of old age, as well as in relieving the infirmities incident of that age, as well as in relieving the infirmities incident to that period. It may be justly considered as a very excellent means of prevention against arterio-sclerosis, especially if employed in conjunction with suitable exercise.

Diethetic Disorders—While not a substitute for regimen in the treatment of those maladies having their foundation in a morbid diathesis, of which obesity, chronic rheumatism, and diabetes are the three leading types, massage is certainly a valuable adjunct in the management of this important class of disorders. It is of special value in the treatment of obeslty, particularly at the beginning of a course, when the patient is too feeble muscularly to undertake the active exercises necessary to effect a change in his nutritive processes.

Massage is equally useful in cases of rheumatism in which exercise is impossible in consequence of pain, stiffness, or deformity, and also as a means of relieving pain occasioned by the first attempts at exercise.

Of equal value is massage in the treatment of diabetes accompanied by great weakness or exhaustion, rendering the amount of exercise necessary for the burning up of the surplus sugar impossible to the patient on account of the feeble, condition of his nervo-muscular apparatus. Finkler reports a large number of cases of diabetes mellitus in which great improvement was secured by massage. Zimmer has shown that vigorous muscles, even when at rest, destroy more sugar, than do feeble ones, a fact which is easily understood when we remember that the muscles are the furnace of the body, and are the chief seat of the vital combustion by which glycogen, or sugar, is consumed. Large and vascular muscles will naturally consume more sugar than feeble and anaemic muscles, just as a large furnace with a good draft will consume more fuel than a small furnace with a poor draft. Under the influence of either massage or exercise, the blood is made to go through the muscles; while in a state of rest it goes round rather than through them. Bouchard also has shown that exercise of the muscles increases the consumption of sugar, and thus diminishes the amount of sugar found in the urine in cases of diabetes. [Dr. Kellogg has] often had opportunity to confirm this observation in [his] own experience in the treatment of this disease.

In the treatment of muscular rheumatism, massage not only relieves the pain accompanying the disease, but also antagonizes the muscular atrophy which is one of its most constant results.

In the treatment of articular rheumatism, massage relieves the pain through its derivative action, and also promotes the absorption of effused inflammatory products, and restores lost mobility. Other observers as well as the author have found massage useful in arthritis deformans, and it has given excellent results in the arthritic neuroses which are so often the result of acute or chronic inflammation and injuries to the joints.

The consecutive or secondary fatigue which is so apt to occur in the employment of exercise in these maladies is more readily relieved by massage than by any other means [1].

Dr. Kellogg (and others) have felt that massage to the head could reduce balding [1]. Using a rubber-bristled brush in the shower or bath while shampooing can create a massage-like effect. Circulation to the scalp has to improve local nutrition. It could also be considered like a mini-reflexology treatment each day, even being used on the bottoms of feet. Using it all over is similar to a "daily rubdown" as was mentioned in chapter 5.

Spondylotherapy

Some naturopaths have used spinal concussion, otherwise known as spondylotherapy for decades. It was developed by Dr. Albert Abrams. Of this technique, Dr. Cordingley wrote:

By spinal concussion we either soothe or stimulate the spinal centers. Slow concussion, generally has a soothing or quieting effect upon the organs or tissues related to the spinal segment, while rapid strokes have a tendency to excite or stimulate. For Spondylotherapy a mallet or plexor and an applicator or pleximeter are used. There units are known as concussors and concussodes respectively. The plexor is a wooden or metal mallet, six to ten inches long, while the pleximeter can be made of a piece of rubber five-eighths of an inch thick by two and one-half inches square, hollowed out on one edge so that it will set astride the spinous portion of a vertebra, and the legs formed by such "hollowing out" are placed one on each transverse process of a vertebra…Concussion is applied by striking the pleximeter, which is first carefully placed upon the vertebral segment related to the organ or tissue it is desired to affect, with the plexor. The strokes are made at the rate of about two per second, are given rebounding, and are continued for from twenty to thirty seconds. Then there should be a period of rest for thirty seconds to permit the response of the reflex, when concussion is repeated for from twenty to thirty seconds. Ordinarily the period of concussion should be repeated three or four times [2].

Reflexology

Reflexology is a method of massage of the feet and/or hands in an attempt to stimulate the body to restore its normal (healthy) physiology. "Reflexology is an ancient techniques based on the premise that there are reflex points on the feet and hands that correspond to every muscle, nerve, organ, gland, and bone in the body" [3] (in this way it is similar to iridology, please see chapter 10). "Reflexology is a science which deals with the principle that there are reflexes in the feet relative to each and every organ and all parts of the body" [4]. It is believed that pressing on these reflex points can break up congestion and that this helps the nerves relax and return to normal [3,4]. Reflexologists also believe that "The body's bioenergetic flow—the harmonious alignment of bodily functions and nervous energy—it a prerequisite to good health; and reflexology allows us to experience the internal relationship between our body and our physical and emotional environment" [5].

Reflexology is sometimes confused with Reflex Nutrition Assessment (RNA), however the two are not related. Both methods may be utilized for health assessment, however of the two, only reflexology is therapeutic. Reflexology was probably first developed by the Chinese. Dr. William Fitzgerald took the Chinese method of "zone therapy" and further pointed out that pressure and massage on certain zones of the body seemed to help normalize physiological function, even if the zone was quite far from the part of the body where pressure was exerted [4,5].

The basic concept behind reflexology is that since there are ten fingers and ten toes, the body can be divided into at least ten zones [4,5]. And that these zones run from toe to head and that each of the fingers is also connected to a zone. What is of scientific interest is the fact that there actually are single nerve cells which run from the feet to the head [6] (and a total of about 7200 nerves in each foot [3]), thus having some biological collaboration of this method.

There are several different ways to determine the points to be manipulated with reflexology, but the discussion here will be limited to the main two. The first is to apply a deep rotating pressure from the fingertips to every portion of the bottom of the foot (including the toes and side of the foot or the hand and fingers), and when a sore or painful spot is located, that is the area that gets massaged. The other is to manipulate the portion(s) of the foot and/or hand which corresponds to affected portions of the body. Reflexologists consider the tips of the toes to be sinus reflexes, the area where the toes connect to the foot as the reflex for the eyes, the portion immediately below the eye reflex is the one for the ears, the area below the ear reflex is the lung as well as heart reflex (although the heart reflex is only on the left foot), the area below the lung reflex is for the liver and gall bladder, the center of the foot is the kidney reflex, the area below the kidney reflex is for the intestines, the center of the large toes is the pituitary reflex, the area where the large toe connects to the foot as the thyroid and parathyroid reflex, the area on the top of the foot where the toes connect is the lymphatic drainage reflex, area along the side of the foot are for the back, knee, hip and other reflexes [4,5]. Those who wish to practice reflexology should acquire a chart and instruction on the practice.

Reflexologists normally like to apply a strong massaging pressure on affected points for several minutes per point and like to do this at least once per week to promote faster healing [3, 4, 5].

Acupressure

While naturopaths do not insert needles like acupuncturists do, many utilize forms of acupressure. Remarkable results have been seen for neck, back, and shoulder complaints by using acupressure. In acupressure, fingertips are applied to acupuncture points [4]. The fact that it is finger pressure applied to Oriental acupuncture points suggests a relationship to reflexology (actually reflexology should be considered a form of acupressure).

In the 1800's, the French scientist Michael Faraday (the person who Invented the world's first electric motor) stated:

All school children know that all matter is composed of atoms, vibrating at different rates of speed to form different densities; but what we should also know is that all matter or any other substance—dense, liquid, or gaseous—owes whatever power it may possess to the type of electrical charge or vibration given off by that substance [7].

It is known that the body not only is electrical in nature, but that it has positive and negative poles (some feel that the heart and the left side represent the negative and the brain and the right side the positive) [7].

The heart is the generator for electricity in the body…Contact healing is a method of contacting the electrical centers of the body. Balance and order must be established before health becomes established…

Contact healing, or acupressure, also treats the various parts of the body which relate to various areas, glands, and organs" [7].

Pressure from the finger or thumb without the nail is called sedation, whereas pressure which includes the nail is called tonification [8]. In either case, 10-15 pounds of pressure is normally applied for 2-4 minutes. Sedation is used as a light stroking finger pressure massage. Tonification is used as a "boring circulatory movement with fingertip or finger nail, be careful not to break the skin!" [8].

One of the most remarkable situations the author has faced with acupressure involved an 83-year-old woman whose right arm was in a continuous spasm. Her right arm moved so much, she could no longer write. Her medical "specialist" told her she had a pinched nerve and that nothing could help. Sedation was applied to two points on the sides of her elbow. The spasm reduced enough so that she could write again. When she came back a month or so later, she still could write. It was quite amazing when you consider that it was accomplished with just the application of a little bit of pressure for less than one minute!

There are too many acupressure points to comprehensively list them in this book, however three will be mentioned: "There is an acupressure point used against anxiety or nervousness. Apply slight pressure to the indentation in the center of your breast bone, known as the sternum. Holding four fingers over the area opens up breathing and relieves tension" [3]. "Mild vibration to the stomach and bowels is often enough to benefit in 'sour' stomach and constipation, but care must be taken not to treat the viscera too vigorously by this method, as injury may result [2]. Research has found that "P6 acupuncture point stimulation seems to be an effective antiemetic technique"; thus applying pressure to an area near the center of the wrist reduces problems associated with morning sickness [9]. Sea bands accomplish the same purpose if out on the ocean in a small boat. There are many books available on the topic of acupressure which provide instruction and charts of all the acupressure points.

While acupressure has been called "acupuncture without needles" [7], there is another form called electro-acupuncture. Electro-acupuncture involves the use of an electrical device to send a signal to encourage the body to heal itself. British research suggests that it can be helpful for some with fibromyalgia [10]. An animal study suggests that certain heart conditions may benefit from some forms of electro-acupuncture [11].

As time goes on, we will see much more research which will document the benefits of various forms of naturopathic manipulation.

References

[1] Kellogg, J. H. *Art of Massage.* Modern Medicine Publishing, Battle Creek (MI), 1929.

[2] Cordingley, E. W. *Principles and Practice of Naturopathy.* Reprint by Health Research, Mokelumne Hill (CA), written 1924.

[3] Null, G. *The Complete Encyclopedia of Natural Healing.* Kensington Books, New York, 1998.

[4] Ingham, E. D. *Stories the Feet Can Tell Through Reflexology.* Ingham Publishing, Saint Petersburg (FL), 1984.

[5] Rick, S. *The Reflexology Workout.* Harmony Books, New York, 1986.

[6] Guyton, A. C. and Hal,l J. E. *Textbook of Medical Physiology,* 9th ed. W.B. Saunders, Phil., 1996.

[7] Houston, F. M. *The Healing Power of Acupressure.* Keats Publishing, New Canaan (CT), 1974.

[8] Schulz, K. *Finger Pressure First Aid.* Health Research, Mokelumne Hill (CA), 1982.

[9] Hoo, J. J. *Acupressure for Hyperemesis Gravidarum.* Am J Obstet Gynoc, 1997; 176(6):1395-1396.

[10] Deluze, C. *Electroacupuncture in Fibromyalgia: Results of a Controlled Trial.* Brit Med J, 1997; 305:1249-1251.

[11] Li, P., et al. *Reversal of Reflex-Induced Myocardial ischemia by Median Nerve Stimulation: a Feline Model of Electroacupuncture.* Circulation, 1998; 97:1186-1194.

18

Water and Hydrotherapy

Water therapies have been around a long time. Sebastian Kneipp (the one who helped save Benedict Lust's life) used hydrotherapy which ultimately led to the separate field of naturopathy (see chapter 1) [1].

Dr. Kellogg wrote the following about the history of hydrotherapy:

WATER is without a doubt the most ancient of all remedial agents for disease. This fact is evidenced by the frequent reference to its use in the earliest medical literature, as well as by the habits and customs of the most ancient peoples as brought to light more fully within recent years by the study of the old Assyrian and Egyptian records. The reason for this is clearly to be found in the fact that water is a means, not only usually found ready at hand, but one which adapts itself to almost every imaginable pathological condition in a remarkable manner, thus approaching more nearly to a panacea than any other known remedy. No other

agent is capable of producing so great a variety of physiological effects, no other is so universally present, and hence none is so readily adaptable for meeting the various exigencies and indications arising from accident and disease.

The ancient Egyptians, Hebrews, Greeks, Persians, and Hindus all employed water in the treatment of disease, as do the representatives of these peoples at the present time. According to a Chinese record dating back several centuries before Christ, a physician prescribed for a woman of that country one hundred affusions of ice-water, each followed by wrapping in a linen sheet, — a treatment in principle resembling the wet-sheet pack.

The *Tokio Medical Journal (1881)* states that the cold bath has been in use in Japan for nearly eight hundred years, especially among the native country physicians, and that nearly three hundred years ago a small treatise on the medical uses of the cold bath was published by Dr. Nakagami, in which it was especially recommended for acute mania, hysteria, asthma, and convulsions in children.

Among the Spartans of ancient Greece, cold bathing was made obligatory by law. The bath in various forms is also frequently referred to in Grecian mythology. Hippocrates evidently had an excellent understanding of the physiological properties of water, both hot and cold, which he employed in the treatment of fevers, ulcers, hemorrhages, and a variety of maladies both medical and surgical, giving many directions for its use which the experience of two thousand years has not improved upon. For instance, he directed that cold baths should be of short duration, and should be preceded and followed by friction; and he evidently understood the phenomena of reaction, since he records the observation that after a cold bath the body quickly recuperates its heat and remains warm, while a hot bath produces the opposite effect.

Under the Romans, the bath attained a very high degree of development. Emperors vied with one another in erecting magnificent public baths, capable of accommodating thousands of persons daily. In studying the interesting ruins of some of these structures at Rome and Pompeii, the author was astonished to find the perfection attained in every detail of the equipment of these ancient bathing establishments. Hot or cold water baths, hot-air and vapor baths, might be enjoyed at will.

Asclepiades employed water in nearly every form, hot and cold baths, douches, compresses, etc. One of his disciples, Antonius Musa, attained great fame by curing the Emperor Augustus of a chronic catarrh by means of the cold bath, as a reward for which his statue was ordered to be erected in the temple of Esculapius; but a lack of discrimination in the use of this powerful agent led to his downfall. Being called upon to treat the emperor's nephew, Marcellus, a popular favorite, he adopted the measures which had resulted so admirably in the cure of the athletic old soldier, but they proved too powerful for the effeminate youth, and he was prostrated to such a degree that he died soon after at Naples, where he had gone to receive treatment at the hot baths of Baiae. This enthusiastic apostle of hydrotherapy succeeded later in redeeming his reputation by the cure of the poet Horace.

Pastor Kneipp, the Bavarian water-cure empiric, a few years ago had a similar experience. Being called upon to visit the pope, who was suffering from chronic rheumatism, he was received with great honors; but the first cold bath given the aged prelate, entirely unaccustomed to such heroic treatment, occasioned such an exacerbation of his sufferings that the poor priest was peremptorily dismissed in disgrace. Had the patient been a sturdy young German peasant instead of a feeble Italian gentleman, the prescription might have succeeded better. A similar lack of discrimination, whether by a charlatan or a legally qualified practitioner, is always attended by disastrous results. The untoward effects thus produced should not, however, be attributed to scientific hydrotherapy, but must be charged to the stupid audacity of quackery, or to the lack of information or experience of the otherwise competent physician.

According to Pliny, the bath was almost the exclusive method of treatment employed in Rome during five centuries Celsus and other prominent Roman physicians highly extolled the bath in their works, Celsus later making it one of the three essentials of what he called a perfect therapeutic system, termed "apotheraphia", the other two being exercise and friction [2].

Dr. Kellogg further wrote the following under the heading *The Physics of Water, Air, Heat, and Light in Relation to Hydrotherapy:*

HOFFMAN, whose authority commands universal respect, declared water to be more nearly a panacea for all human ills than any other known agent. This fact which has never been disproved, is largely due to the peculiar physical properties of this very versatile element. Water owes its value as a therapeutic agent chiefly to three most remarkable properties: (1) Its great power for absorbing and communicating heat; (2) Its solvent properties, water being the one universal solvent; (3) the facility with which its physical state may be changed from a liquid to a solid or a gaseous form. These properties give to it the most perfect adaptability to the various modes of application which are required in hydrotherapy. It will be worthwhile to consider briefly each of these several properties, as follows:

Water absorbs more heat for a given weight than any other body, and is hence taken as the standard of "specific heat." A pound of water contains five times as much heat as an equal weight of glass; about ten times as much as the same weight of iron, zinc, copper, or brass; and thirty times as much as the same quantity of mercury, gold, or lead. The specific heat of the human body is nine tenths that of water.

The readiness with which water absorbs and communicates heat and the great amount of heat which it is capable of communicating, or storing, exactly adapts it for use in making thermic applications of either heat or cold to the human body. There is no other substance which is at all capable of replacing it for these purposes.

Because of the large amount of water entering into the composition of the human body, its specific heat is near that of water, viz., 9 degrees. A pound of water at 10 degrees will raise the temperature of one pound of iron or copper from zero to nearly 10 degrees. A quantity of water equaling the body in weight, losing 1 degree of temperature through contact with the body in a full bath, will raise the temperature of the body a little more than 1 degree, taking no account of any change in heat production or heat elimination.

In the solidifying and freezing of water a large amount of heat is rendered latent, as shown by the fact that a pound of ice in melting absorbs, without any elevation of temperature, heat enough to raise one pound of water 142 degrees in temperature, the temperature of the water from the melting ice remaining at 32 degrees or slightly above it until all the ice is melted.

Water, in passing from the liquid to the gaseous state, likewise absorbs a considerable amount of heat. The amount depends somewhat upon the pressure, but may be reckoned at about 950 heat units, or the amount required to raise 950 pounds of water 1 degree in temperature. The total amount of heat required to raise a pound of water from the ordinary temperature to that of steam is about 1130 heat units. This heat reappears when the steam is condensed at the ordinary temperature.

In hydrotherapy, water is most commonly used in its liquid state, but it is also employed in the form of ice, and in the form of steam, though as steam, water is never applied directly to the body. When steam is utilized, as in the Russian or vapor bath, the body is not actually exposed to steam, but to the fog or mist formed by the condensation of the steam through contact with the atmosphere. In a vapor or Russian bath, the patient is not heated by the steam, but by the hot air and the suspended particles of warm water which come in contact with the body. As the steam enters the air of the apartment from the steam-pipe or other source, it is at once condensed into a mist, giving up to the air the ten or eleven hundred heat units which it contains, and thus heating the air. A pound of steam is capable of raising from the ordinary temperature to 130 degrees eighty-seven pounds of air, or 1,100 cubic feet of air, the amount contained in an apartment 10 x 10 x 11 feet in size. One pound of steam applied to the body would be capable of raising the temperature of a man weighing 150 pounds nearly 8 degrees), or ten pounds of flesh to a temperature of over 212 degrees. It is for this reason that steam can not be brought in contact with the tissues without destroying them.

A pound of ice, on the other hand, is capable of removing from the tissues of the body with which it is brought in contact 142 heat units while melting. It will not, however, lower the temperature of the tissues below 32 degrees, unless its own temperature should happen to be considerably below the freezing point, which might be the case in very cold weather. It is apparent that in the use of ice, great care must be exercised in order to avoid damaging the tissues by prolonged contact.

The temperatures employed in hydrotherapy are practically within the limits of 3 degrees and 140 degrees F. Applications are occasionally employed at a lower temperature, and very hot water may sometimes be applied, at a temperature as high as 160 degrees, as a means of stopping hemorrhages; but great care must be used. Live steam has recently been suggested as a means of checking hemorrhage, and may possibly prove to be of service in this capacity. Vapor and hot air may be tolerated at higher temperature.

Water is a fairly good conductor of heat. Its conductivity is much greater than that of air, but far inferior to that of the metals. Copper conducts heat one hundred times better than water. As a conductor of electricity, copper is immensely better than water. It is for this reason that water at any given temperature, hot or cold, makes a much more intense impression upon the skin than does air at the same temperature. On the other hand, metals of all sorts feel colder or hotter than does water of the same temperatures.

Ordinary water is a good conductor of electricity, a fact which enables it to render valuable service in most percutaneous applications of electricity and in such combined procedures as the hydrofaradic, the hydrogalvanic, and similar baths. As before remarked, water is the one universal solvent. In the body, it is the medium by which the foods rendered soluble by digestion are conveyed to the tissues to be assimilated, and thus rendered insoluble, while the effete matters rendered soluble by disassimilation are dissolved and conveyed back into the blood current, to be acted upon or eliminated by the liver, the kidneys, the skin, and the other excretory organs.

It is interesting to note that sugar and peptone, the two chief constituents of digested food, are among the most soluble of substances. Carbonic acid gas, a product of the oxidation of carbohydrates and hydrocarbons, is also highly soluble in the saline medium which constitutes the serum of the blood. Urea, a product of protein oxidation, has a high degree of solubility in water. Uric acid, oxalic acid, and other abnormal products are, on the other hand, less easily soluble than the normal waste products, and hence, as has been shown by Haig, readily accumulate in the body, especially in those portions in which the circulation is least active.

Thus the value of water as a detergent agent, not only for the surface of the body but for its interior as well, is apparent. This is, indeed, one of the most important therapeutic uses of water. It may be applied by means of water drinking, the enema, or the coloclyster (this term seems to the author preferable to the French *entero-*

clyster), gastric lavage, and by subdermic injection of the normal saline solution.

Water in the liquid form readily lends itself to application to the body in numerous ways, both active and stable, by the different forms of immersion, compresses, douches of various sorts, etc. The ease with which its temperature may be varied, enables us to secure by its means every degree of thermic effect desirable, while its weight renders possible various mechanical or pressure effects which are also highly valuable, as will appear later in this work.

The relation of air to the thermic effects employed in hydrotherapy is perhaps less direct and important than that of water, yet it is by no means insignificant. Air as well as water is capable of absorbing heat. Although its specific heat is scarcely more than one fifth that of water, the ease and rapidity with which it circulates about the body, its continuous contact with the skin, the variability of its temperature, and especially the fact that it is concerned in the evaporation of moisture from the skin, whereby an enormous amount of heat is constantly removed from the body, render its relations as a thermic agent important.

The influence of the air upon the body depends not only upon its temperature but also upon the amount of water which it contains. A cubic foot of air at 32 degrees is capable of absorbing slightly more than two grains of water. A cubic foot of air at 96 degrees is capable of absorbing eight times as much, while air at 72 degrees absorbs four times as much, or eight grains. It is thus apparent that air which has had its temperature raised without the addition of moisture is capable of promoting evaporation from the skin to a high degree. This fact must be taken into consideration in the management of patients at the different seasons of the year. In the summer-time the air is often completely saturated with moisture, while in the winter-time saturation of the heated air indoors rarely if ever occurs, except by the aid of artificial means. The more completely saturated the air is, the less rapidly does evaporation take place. Patients are much more likely to complain of chilliness after baths in the winter than in the summer, for the reason that the extreme dryness of the air gives rise to rapid evaporation of the small amount of moisture left on the skin after leaving the bath-room giving rise to chilliness, and occasionally resulting in a cold. On this account, patients must in the winter-time be dried with special thoroughness before leaving the bath-room, and must afterward be particularly careful about exposing themselves.

The rapid rate at which heat is removed from the body is by evaporation when dry, warm air is brought in contact with it may be easily shown by a simple illustration: Suppose an apartment (20 X 13 x 10) contains 2,600 cubic feet of air at 96 degrees, the temperature out of doors being 32 degrees. The indoor air is capable of absorbing nearly fifteen grains of water, in addition to that which it already contains, for each cubic foot, or more than five and one-half pounds of water. The absorption of less than one half of this (two pounds) through evaporation from the surface of the patient's body will abstract from the body something like 2,000 heat units, and would be capable of reducing the temperature of the body more than 130, provided no heat was in the meantime produced. The same air, if saturated with water, would absorb little water, and would take very little heat from the body. The relation of different conditions of the atmosphere to the rate of evaporation from the skin is a question which should perhaps receive more consideration in connection with hydrotherapy than has generally been accorded it.

It is also important to note that the respiratory processes of both the lungs and the skin are diminished by an exceedingly dry atmosphere. Interchange of gases in the lungs is also interfered with by an atmosphere saturated with moisture.

Atmospheric pressure is likewise a matter well worthy of attention in connection with hydrotherapy. In institutions located at an altitude of several thousand feet above the level of the sea, this is of special importance, on account of the tendency to pulmonary congestion due to the rarity of the atmosphere. Under such circumstances, extreme care must be taken to avoid the application of the cold douche and similar measures in such a way as to provoke disturbance of respiration; in other words, cold applications must be made to the chest only with the greatest care, and after applications have been made to other portions of the body, so that the effect may be generalized.

Cold air produces a less intense sensation of cold than does cold water, for the reason that its ability to absorb heat is only one fifth as great, and its conductivity of heat is enormously less. The thermic effect produced upon the skin by an object brought in contact with it is due both to the specific heat of the object and to its conductivity. Iron, copper, and other metals are such excellent conductors of heat that they may feel colder than water at ordinary room temperature even though their specific heat is many times less.

Most of the effects of hydrotherapy are obtained by means of methodical thermic applications to the skin. In other words, the specific effects of hydrotherapy are not chiefly due to water per se, but to the impressions of heat or cold made by this agent when brought in contact with the skin. So far as these same effects may be produced by other means, precisely the same results may be obtained.

Heat and cold are relative terms, what is termed a cold application being simply one that is of a temperature a definite number of degrees lower than the so-called warm or hot application. The impression made upon the skin, as elsewhere remarked, depends not only upon the temperature of the application, but upon the relation existing between the temperature of the application and the temperature of the skin.

The science and art of hydrotherapy include not only applications of water in its various forms, but thermic applications made by means of hot or cold air, vapor, and various heated objects, also heat and light.

Various sources of heat may be utilized in making thermic applications to the human body for therapeutic purposes. While water is generally the most convenient agent, there are conditions to which it is not adapted, and in which other means may be more advantageously employed. Heated air, the vapor of water, or rather the fog resulting from the condensation of steam in air at a temperature near that of the body, the sun's rays, and lastly the electric ray may all be utilized. The use of hot air in the form of the Turkish bath dates from remote antiquity, and the hot-air bath and the vapor bath have been used by many primitive people. The electric ray is, however, one of the most interesting sources of thermic energy; and while only recently introduced to practical therapeutics, it is certain to prove itself of the greatest practical utility. Both forms of the electric lamp, the incandescent and the arc, may be utilized as sources of heat.

The sun's rays, which the electric ray closely resembles in its action as a thermic agent, have been utilized in the treatment of the sick from the most ancient times. The amount of heat received hourly upon each square foot of the earth's surface is about equivalent to that produced by the burning of a sufficient amount of coal to produce one fourth of a horse-power of mechanical energy. The physical and therapeutic properties of sunlight and of the electric ray will be considered at greater length elsewhere in this work.

This means has the advantage over others in that the rays of radiant energy received from a luminous source penetrate the skin and the tissues to a great depth, in fact, reaching without doubt, the very innermost portions of the body [2].

Dr. Kellogg was not the only advocate of hydrotherapy, most naturopaths and even many medical doctors used to recommend it. The following was written by Dr. Scholl:

Hygienic Use of Baths

Temperature of Baths—Coming now to the detailed consideration of water as applied to the human skin in the form of a bath, in order to accomplish the important hygienic purposes described, it is obvious, in the first place, that temperature has a powerful influence in this respect.

Cold Baths—The range of the cold bath varies more than that of any other kind, extending, as it does, from 84 degrees Fahrenheit down to 33 degrees of the same scale. The lower temperatures included between these limits would, of course, test the endurance of even the strongest to encounter safely the severe shock which is generally produced by the sudden application, and still more the prolonged immersion of the body in a water so near its freezing-point; but from 84 degrees to 74 degrees the reaction required is so slight that few persons who are not actually invalids are too feeble to manifest it.

First Effect of the Cold Bath—A shock is experienced throughout the whole nervous system, more or less severe, according to the lower or higher temperature of the fluid, and the contracting effect of the cold aids the spasmodic contraction occurring in the small blood vessels to drive the blood to the inner portions of the body, and allow the surface to become quickly chilled.

Second Effect of the Cold Bath—But if the cold is not too severe, or the individual is not exhausted by fatigue, or enfeebled by disease, a change in these conditions promptly manifests itself soon after leaving the bath, especially if the skin is rapidly dried by friction with some absorbent substance. The heart and pulse return to their normal rate of movement, the nervous system recovers from the shock which it has undergone, the blood flows back to the surface of the skin, and a glow of renewed warmth is felt throughout the entire body.

A Guide to Cold Bathing—This agreeable change in the condition of the circulation and the sensations is called the reaction, and constitutes our very best guide to the employment of cool or cold bathing. If the water of a bath has been colder than is adapted to the strength of an individual's constitution, reaction comes on but slowly, and several hours may elapse before the natural balance of the circulation is fully restored. In such a case, the bands, feet and nose remain chilly, and also cold to the touch of another person. The fingers, lips and indeed the whole face, has a bluish tint, and a more or less shrunken appearance. The pulse continues weak and slow, and languor and feebleness characterize all the movements. Of course, the method of deriving the greatest amount of benefit from these indications is for each person to cautiously test the power of his system to establish reaction, commencing with a bath of 70 degrees or 65 degrees, and gradually descending the scale of the thermometer, as he finds he is able to fully react from the depression produced by venturing among its lower depths.

Time for Cold Bathing—It is recommended by some authors to resort to cold bathing either about an hour before breakfast in the early morning, or else late in the evening just before retiring for the night. The early morning bath of this kind may do very well for some few people of unusually vigorous constitutions, but as a general rule the evening is a better time for such a test of strength; and for many persons the middle of the morning, that is to say, about three hours after breakfast, when the first meal of the day has been nearly all digested, and the system is fortified thereby to bear the shock and establish the necessary reaction after it, is decidedly preferable to any other period of the twenty-four hours.

When to Avoid Cold Baths—Under no circumstances should a cold bath be indulged in either immediately before or immediately after a meal, on account of the tendency which its inevitable shock will have to produce more or less disturbance in the process of digestion by congesting the stomach and intestines. Nor are cold baths suitable for individuals in either extreme of life, because both in infancy and in old age the power of developing animal heat is least efficient in its operations, and the reaction is accomplished slowly, or not at all.

No Cold Bath After Fatigue—Protracted labor or exercise, whether mental or physical, if so long continued as to leave the body suffering from feelings of great weariness or exhaustion, absolutely forbid the use of the cold bath. It was under these circumstances that Alexander the Great, of Macedon, nearly perished, from plunging after a long and fatiguing march into the icy current of the river Cydnus; an imprudence which, it is said, did actually prove fatal to the German emperor, the aged Frederick Barbarossa, at the head of his crusading army, seventeen hundred years later. In adverting to this latter event, an ancient author quaintly observes: "No wonder if the cold water quickly quenched those few sparks of heat left in him at seventy years of age."

Duration of the Cold Bath—The duration of a cool or cold bath must vary very much with the temperature of the water. When very cold the period of immersion should not exceed one or two minutes, whilst with water between 60 and 70 degrees, the duration of the bath may extend to a quarter or even half an hour; in every instance, however, we must be guided by the completeness of the reaction on coming out of the water.

Friction After Cold Bath—Energetic friction of the whole surface of the body after bathing is highly beneficial as tending to produce the necessary degree of reaction. Active physical exercise, as well as warm and stimulating drinks, likewise aid in accomplishing the same desirable result. Even when a person is accustomed to the daily use of the cold bath, any sudden reduction of strength, such as may result from intemperance in eating, an evening debauch, or excess of any kind, particularly of the sexual powers, or even over-exertion in walking or in field-sports, will forbid recourse to it the following morning.

River Bathing—Bathing in rivers is even more to be recommended than that in ordinary bath-rooms during the summer season, as the gentle exercise of walking to and from the river-side, and if swimming whilst immersed in the water, promote the reaction which is so conducive to health. Evil consequences are, however, apt to result from river-bathing, if the baths are too prolonged, if too violent exertion is indulged in, or if the rays of the sun over-heat the head of the bather. Dr. Bell states that he has seen continued fever, of some days' duration, and violent headache, with slight delirium, arise in boys who had thus imprudently exposed themselves.

Varieties of Cold Baths

Cold Sponge-Bath—There are various ways of employing water in cold bathing, according to the force of the current of fluid, the amount of surface to which it is applied, and so forth. Effusion and sponging are the mildest ways of using cold water as a bath, and there are few persons, not actually invalids, who cannot thus employ water, of moderately low temperature, with benefit. After the slight depression of the bodily warmth, produced by sponging with fluid of 60 or 65 degrees, of course but a mild reaction follows, but this is suitably proportioned to the feeble energies of debilitated persons. By a repetition of the process a greater endurance is developed, and colder water may ultimately be resorted to, with correspondingly increased advantage. The cool or cold sponge-bath is sometimes of great service in treating typhoid fever, and others of the eruptive diseases, as will be explained in the second part of this work.

The Shower-Bath—In a shower-bath, the water falls in divided streams, and thus, being generally distributed over the whole body, gives a severe shock to the system; such a one, should the fluid be of a low temperature, as only the most vigorous persons can endure.

The Cold Douche—The cold douche differs from the shower-bath in that the water of a douche is poured upon the surface of the body in a solid column, instead of a number of small streams. It is sometimes highly efficacious in reducing the violent excitement of delirious or insane patients, but, being a very powerful agent, should be used only with caution and close watching, never in the indiscriminate way customary in some so-called hydropathic establishments, from which it is said that more than one sudden death has been the lamentable result.

The Bath for Old Age—The advance into old age of those who, in the vigor of youth and maturity, have accustomed themselves to the regular use of the cold bath, does not necessarily interpose an obstacle to the continuance of the practice of bathing, provided the general health remains good. But if there be evidence of feebleness of the functions, or disorder in any one of the great systems of the body, such as the digestive apparatus, or the muscular system, so as to prevent the customary allowance of nutritious food or of exercise being taken, the cold plunge or shower-bath should be given up, and simple washing with cold water, followed by active friction, substituted in its place. Should even this prove rather too great a shock for the enfeebled powers of life, as may be evinced by want of prompt reaction subsequently, recourse to anything but the tepid or warm bath must be strictly prohibited.

The Water-Cure—The evidence in favor of great benefit being derived in suitable cases from the so-called water-cure, in the numerous hydropathic establishments of Europe and this country, is very convincing; and, in fact, it is probable that persons generally of great mobility of temperament, who are readily excited and readily depressed, and whose nervous system is soon exhausted by either bodily or mental efforts, will often find relief in the systematic use of a moderately cool or cold bath.

Objection to Hydropathy—The difficulty is with establishments of this kind that, being carried on as business enterprises, their proprietors are not withheld, by any philanthropic considerations, from looking at every case which applies to them with an eye to business, and recommending their particular cure to all possible patients, except where they are very sure that positive injury will result from the treatment. It is therefore advisable, in every instance, to consult some reputable physician, who is not devoted to any exclusive system or dogma of medical practice, before submitting oneself to the powerful agencies of water as applied by hydropathic practitioners.

Cold Bathing Removes Heat—Dr. Bell judiciously remarks that there is a class of people who suffer from a sedentary life, devotion to the desk in business, or to study, and complain of troublesome heat and dryness of the hands, and sometimes of the feet, with accelerated pulse and thirst; their appetite is not good, nor their sleep sound or refreshing. Though their systems be actually weaker than usual, yet is there morbid activity of the skin, owing, in part, to the vessels of the integument not relieving themselves by free and regular perspiration. Cold bathing, by moderating cutaneous excitement, and relieving the perspiratory organs, removes the unpleasant feeling of heat and dryness; and, by sympathy, produces nearly correspondent effects on the stomach.

The Flesh-Brush and Exercise—The use of the flesh-brush and exercise in the open air are, it may be supposed, powerful auxiliaries to the measures just recommended.

Cold Bathing for Rheumatism—There are many persons who, though enjoying what is often called full health, are liable to colds, rheumatic pains and stitches from any slight exposure to cold or moist air. Their vascular and nervous systems are both tolerably excitable, and they are readily thrown into perspiration from even moderate exercise or warm apartments. In them, it is desirable so far to regulate the functions of the skin as to moderate its stimulation, and prevent the consequent debility which follows this state. Cold bathing accomplishes this purpose, and keeps the skin in a less constant condition of excitement, renders it less liable to sweat so freely from exposure to external warmth or by active exercise, and, of course, prevents the subsequent languor and susceptibility to morbid and enfeebling agencies. It would be a great mistake, in such a case, to talk of the tonic action of cold bathing. Its beneficial operation is evinced here at a time when no stimulus or tonic is admissible, and in habits sanguine and plethoric, on which nearly similar effects with those from cold bathing would be produced by a moderate bleeding, reduction of the usual quantity of food and diluent drinks.

Hygienic Application of Warm Baths

Temperature of Warm Bath—When the water used for bathing has a temperature of from 92 degrees to 98 degrees Fahrenheit, it produces upon the skins of most people the sensation of warmth, and although water of this degree of heat is usually employed chiefly for cleansing purposes, yet it has hygienic properties of a sufficiently marked character to render it worthy of especial notice. Since water is a much better conductor of heat than air, and especially than confined air, as much caloric is extracted from the human body when immersed in water which is only a few degrees lower than the average human temperature, as by air of much greater relative coldness.

Effect of Warm Bath—The warm bath diminishes the frequency of the pulse, especially when it has been greater than natural, and this effect is almost exactly in proportion to the duration of immersion. It also renders the respiration slower, and diminishes the temperature of the body, relaxes the muscular fibre, increases the bulk of the fluids by absorption, or perhaps only by restricting evaporation from the skin, removes impurities from the surface, promotes desquamation and renewal of the cuticle, lessening the hardness of the nails and indurations of the epidermis.

Separation of Outer Skin—The separation of the outer layers of the scarf-skin or epidermis, which may often be seen floating in small, whitish fragments upon the bath water, is due to two causes. In the first place, it is softened by the water, and so rendered more easily removable by slight friction; and secondly, it is in part pushed off by the increased fullness of the blood-vessels underneath. A humorous writer has compared the epidermis which covers the whole surface of the body to a tight shirt, and a dirty cuticle, therefore, to a dirty shirt which is gotten rid of by the aid of a bath.

Take Short Warm Baths—A prolonged daily use of the warm bath is apt to cause eruptions on the skin similar to those which managers of water-cure establishments pronounce critical and of the greatest advantage in certain diseases of the nervous system.

Warm Baths Soothe the Nerves—An immediate and very agreeable effect of the warm bath is to soothe a nervously excited condition and promote sleep, which to many people is peculiarly refreshing when procured by this means.

Time to Take Warm Baths—The best period for taking a warm bath is about an hour previous to the mid-day meal, because then the disturbance of the circulation will have time to pass off before food is introduced into the stomach, and the secretion of the gastric juice and other fluids necessary for digestion will not be thereby interfered with.

Duration of Warm Baths—The duration of a warm bath ought not to exceed in ordinary cases half an hour, although in the warm water-cure of Leuk, in Switzerland, patients sometimes remain in the tepid fluid five hours in the morning and three hours in the afternoon, with alleged benefit. In the Leuk bath, persons breakfast from little floating tables, which afterwards serve to support books and newspapers for their amusement, and it is said that the Emperor Charlemange used to hold prolonged levees whilst immersed in his warm bath at Aix-la-Chapelle, which was supplied by one of the numerous thermal springs of that famous city.

Warm Baths in Acute Diseases—The relaxing and soothing influence of the warm bath is an invaluable aid to the treatment of many acute diseases, and being, as a general rule, devoid of danger in its application, is a remedy peculiarly adapted to domestic practice, particularly among children before the skilled physician, who should always be sent for immediately when a person is attacked with any acute disease, has time to arrive. Its prompt remedial effects may often be observed in bilious colic, in painter's colic induced by the poisonous influence of lead, in spasmodic croup, in infantile convulsions, in mental excitement bordering on delirium or even violent maniacal frenzy, and in many other diseases, as will be more fully explained in the second part of this book.

Hot Baths

Temperature of the Hot Bath—The hot bath is so designated if the water employed is above the natural blood-heat of about 98 degrees Fahrenheit, and may range as high as 110 degrees, above which it is seldom safe to use water over the whole surface of the body. Of course, habit will often enable a person to endure the local application of water having a much higher temperature than this without injury.

Effect of Hot Baths—Hot baths are decidedly stimulating, and rapidly produce redness of the skin with quickening of the pulse and respiration. Perspiration is poured out upon the face in great abundance, the mind becomes dull and inattentive, and, if the immersion is unduly prolonged, vertigo and apoplexy may supervene. One experimenter lost, during the short space of eight minutes, in a bath of the temperature of 113 degrees, about a pound and a half of his weight. Even a hot foot bath of 110 degrees is stated in one case to have quickened the pulse from seventy-seven to ninety-two, and to have caused some headache in about half an hour. In another instance, a foot-bath of 113 degrees raised the pulse from sixty to one hundred and five beats per minute in, five minutes, and flushed the face, but without bringing on headache.

Where Danger Lies—The hot bath ought therefore to be employed cautiously or not at all by persons of sanguine temperament, and those of robust or plethoric habit of body, especially if there is any hereditary tendency to apoplexy in their families.

Where Good is Derived—This powerful remedy is, however, capable of doing good service in conditions of torpid, sluggish circulation, dry and cold skin, feebleness of muscular movement, and a low grade of sensibility; but great care must be used not to mistake this state of the system In an individual naturally weak and phlegmatic, or enfeebled by old age or chronic disease, for the languor of the vital processes which is produced by acute inflammation, or pressure of the blood upon the brain or upon the lungs.

When to Avoid Hot Baths—In suspended animation from sunstroke, apoplexy, insensibility from inhaling noxious gases, or from swallowing narcotic poisons, disastrous results might be, and probably would be, produced by the application of a hot bath.

When to Use Hot Baths—In exhaustion and torpor from exposure to intense cold, the hot bath, contrary to popular opinion on the subject, is a most valuable remedy. Some recent experiments performed in Russia, in order to determine what is the best way to resuscitate animals which have been subjected to such severe cold as to be almost fatal in its effects, gave the following results: Of twenty dogs treated by the customary gradual method of bringing them into a cold room which was slowly warmed, fourteen died; of twenty similar animals introduced at once into a warm room, only eight died; whilst of twenty in an analogous condition, which were placed at once in a hot bath, *all recovered.*

Local Hot Baths—Hot baths applied locally to small portions of the body only, have often proved beneficial in gout and in acute as well as chronic rheumatism, and are highly recommended by some authorities for the relief of piles, in certain affections of the kidneys, and in some female disorders. Sundry modifications of the hot bath, such as the Turkish bath, the vapor bath, and so forth, have, under certain circumstances, considerable value.

The Hygiene of Sea-Bathing

When to Refrain from Sea-Bathing—The long line of seacoast belonging to the United States, and the large proportion of our population which resides within a day's journey of the ocean, by placing a salt bath within the reach of many readers, render the subject of sufficient importance to be separately discussed. On paying a visit to the seaside, it is well to refrain from bathing, and indeed from exposure to the rays of the sun on dry land also, for a day or two if possible after arrival, or until the system becomes a little accustomed to the effect of the salt air and the surroundings. The rules already given in regard to the time of bathing, and especially as to not entering the water for an hour or so before or after a meal, ought to be strictly adhered to.

Duration of Sea-Baths—The time spent in the water cannot be prescribed with the same exactitude, since the proper length of a dip in the ocean varies very greatly with the temperature of the water and air, the vigor of the individual's constitution, his temporary condition of health, and so forth. But in the state of the circulation we fortunately have a general guide, which every one can readily consult for himself, and quickly determine when nature decides that the bath should promptly terminate. After the first shuddering inspiration, which is generally produced by the application of cold water to the bare surface of the body, with the quickened pulse and breathing which for a few moments accompany it, the pulse, the action of the heart, and the respiration all become slower for a short time, and then are again accelerated.

Signs to Stop a Sea-Bath— ...if immersion in the cold sea-water is too long continued, the pulse and the breathing are again reduced in frequency, a sense of chilliness comes on, and with this a slight blueness of the lips, and of the fingers underneath the nails, makes its appearance. The moment this is perceived, it should be accepted as an imperative order to quit the water at once and restore the lost activity of the circulation, which it indicates, by energetic friction of the surface with warm, dry towels as speedily as possible. As a general rule, from five to fifteen minutes is amply sufficient time to spend in the surf, and it is far better to err on the prudent side by coming out needlessly soon, than to prolong the bath until the teeth begin to chatter and the fingers have the shriveled, bluish-white appearance of a washerwoman's hand, thereby risking some serious internal congestion afterwards. When the water is unusually cold, and especially when the air is also chilly, a bath in the ocean, if taken at all, should be correspondingly brief.

*What Sea-Bathers Should Do—*In order to obtain the best results, a bather should enter the water whilst he is comfortably warm, and yet not in a free state of perspiration. It is a good plan to wet the head and breast first, or after wading only a short distance from the edge, for the purpose of avoiding the temporary fullness of the brain, which leaves some persons with a dull headache for several hours; also, if the sun is shining brightly, a bathing hat, or other protection for the head and nape of the neck, ought always to be worn.

*Adjuncts of Sea-Bathing—*Floating, diving and swimming are excellent ways of adding to the pleasure of the sea-bath, but the latter should not be indulged in when the surf is very heavy, when the tide is running out, or when there is a strong current nearly in a line with the margin of the beach, as the latter may diverge a little from the coast, and carry the bather too far out to sea before be is aware of his danger [3].

The author has visited Spa in Belgium (where the term spa comes from) and drunk of its waters. He has also done the same in Hot Springs, Arkansas. In Hot Springs, he also participated in a variety of baths, steam saunas, and other forms of hydrotherapy. The external hydrotherapies have been found to be quite relaxing. For historical reference, there are tours of older forms of hydrotherapy still given in Hot Springs for those who have interest in this area. Also, there are a couple of bath-houses still open. Although they do not do all the forms of hydrotherapy that were once done, they do offer a variety of them.

Internal Hydrotherapy

Dr. Kellogg and others have used colonics, enemas, douches, and other forms of water internally as well. Here is some of what Dr. Kellogg has written under the heading *Irrigation of the Colon—The Enema*:

This very useful procedure consists of the introduction of a quantity of water into the colon. The author employs the enema in three forms: First, the simple enema, the method of using which is well known; second, the *graduated* enema, a method devised by him a few years ago for the purpose of enabling persons who had become accustomed to the daily use of the enema to dispense with this very inconvenient procedure; third, the *coloclyster,* termed by the French, "enteroclyster," which consists in an enema taken in the right Sims's position or the knee-chest position, a long rectal tube being employed.

In the simple enema, the water is commonly employed at about the temperature of the body, or 98 degrees. Better results are obtained by employing water at 70 degrees F. The water is introduced by the aid of a syringe of some sort. Various excellent forms of syringes have been devised...

The temperature must also be adapted to the use for which the measure is employed. If for mere mechanical effects, a temperature near that of the body is proper. It is generally better to introduce the water gradually, so that the bowels may not be stimulated to contraction, causing the fluid introduced to be discharged before a sufficient quantity has been received.

While the water is being introduced, the patient lies upon his back, with the hips slightly elevated. If a strong desire is experienced to expel prematurely the liquid introduced, the difficulty may be overcome by asking the patient to resist the expulsive impulse strongly, if necessary by compressing the anus with a napkin for a short time, until the peristaltic movement has ceased.

In the employment of the enema, only such an amount of water as is necessary should be used. Many persons have been damaged by distending the colon so as to compel it to receive three or four quarts of water at once, as advised by a well-known empiric of New York City. On the very day of this writing the author has been called upon by a patient who was seriously damaged by following the advice of the charlatan referred to. The colon had evidently been stretched and dilated to such an extent that it had never returned to its normal condition, although considerable progress had been made in overcoming the obstinate intestinal inactivity caused by the habitual mechanical emptying of the colon.

In the application of the enema, great care must be taken to avoid the introduction of air into the bowels, as this may be a source of severe colic pain. It is also important that the quantity of water employed should be only sufficient to accomplish the purpose sought.

The enema may be usefully employed in the cases of feeble patients as a preparation for surgical operations. In such a case, the bowels should be first washed out, then two or three pints of water at 100 degrees should be slowly introduced into the rectum, the purpose being to increase the volume of the blood by absorption.

The warm enema (98 degrees to 100 degrees) may be usefully employed as a means of introducing water into the system in cases in which for any reason the patient can not swallow liquids without injury, as after operations, upon the stomach, in cases of *persistent vomiting* requiring complete gastric rest, in *hemorrhage* from the *stomach,* in *typhoid fever* with *gastric dila*tation, and similar cases. Absorption takes place from the intestine much more rapidly than from the stomach.

The enema is certainly most useful as a means of temporarily relieving chronic intestinal inactivity; but great care must be taken to avoid creating dependence upon it. However it is far better to be a slave to the enema than to "after-dinner pills."

A small cold enema is usually preferable to a large warm one. A pint of cold water maybe introduced into the rectum at night or before or after breakfast to be retained.

The warm enema soon loses its efficiency because of its relaxing effect upon the intestines. The tone of the muscular walls is gradually lessened from day to day, until the bowel may become enormously stretched. Large quantities of water should never be used, as they overstretch the bowel and produce atony. Three or four pints the limit for a daily application. The colon will hold a considerable quantity more than this, but should not be stretched to its full capacity under the relaxing influence of the warm water. The introduction of cold water into the small intestine is entirely free from this objection. Half a pint of cold water may be employed daily without injury, for the reason that the cold water energizes the muscles and nerves of the intestine. In the ordinary use of the enema, the temperature should be (80 degrees to 70 degrees).

In cases of extreme atony of the colon, the enema sometimes fails to produce evacuation, the water being in large part retained, in these cases contraction of the colon may be induced by applying a cold wet towel to the abdomen, lower back and perineum while the patient is at stool or by massage of the colon or by a small enema of very cold water.

Not the least valuable service rendered by this simple procedure is the post-operative management of cases of abdominal surgery. It is the author's custom to administer an enema immediately after the operation in all cases in which Stolz, in experiments to determine the antithermic effect of the cold enema in cases of *typhoid fever,* found that by the administration, at intervals of 5 to 10 minutes, of the enema at a temperature of 46 degrees, the pulse was slowed twenty to thirty beats, and the temperature as taken in the mouth was lowered 3.6 degrees.

The cold enema has rendered great service in the treatment of jaundice, as first shown by Krull. The author prefers the enema at 105 degrees to 110 degrees, followed by the cold enema (60 degrees). The cold enema is most effectual as a means of relieving *constipation* through its tonic effects upon the structures of the rectum and mucous membrane.

The Hot Enema—The hot enema, or hot irrigation of the colon, is a useful means of combating an inflammatory condition of the pelvic viscera. Hot-water introduced into the rectum and colon is brought nearer to the ovaries and other pelvic viscera than is possible in any other way. For this purpose, it may be administered three or four times a day, or if necessary once every three or four hours. The temperature should be 110 degrees to 120 degrees.

Reclus prefers very hot rectal irrigation (130 degrees) to vaginal irrigation or injection, in *congestions* of the *pelvic viscera.* It is of great value in the treatment of *prostatic inflammation,* causing disappearance of the swelling and pain and difficulty in micturition, often in a few hours, and in the majority of cases securing a complete cure of acute prostatitis in three to four days.

The hot enema is one of the most valuable of all hydriatic measures for combating *threatened collapse* in typhoid fever as well as in cholera and other conditions in which the vital failure is due to toxemia. The hot enema may even be used in cases of typhoid complicated by intestinal hemorrhage, and with marked benefit, when there is reason to believe that the patient is suffering in consequence of absorption of toxins resulting from the decomposition of retained blood clots. An immediate change in the aspect of cases of this sort is often apparent after freeing the colon of the fetid clots with a simple hot enema. The application should not be made while the hemorrhage is in progress, as the increase in arterial tension would involve serious risk. ...a day or two later the bowel may be washed out without apprehension. The coloclyster, or copious enema, is the most rational method of establishing intestinal asepsis, at least when combined with an aseptic dietary of farinaceous gruels, fruit juices, and systematic water drinking.

The hot enema (104 degrees to 115 degrees) may be used with great benefit for its relaxing effect upon involuntary muscular tissue, in cases of *hepatic* or *biliary colic.* It is found equally useful in quieting excessive *uterine pains* during *parturition,* and in combating *irregular contractions* of the uterus.

The large hot enema has for many years been employed by Cantani and Wonte in the treatment of colic and infantile diarrhea. These sagacious observers also recommend its use in intestinal occlusion and *pseudo-membranous* colitis.

The hot enema is one of the most helpful of all measures in surgical shock and other forms of *collapse.* It may be safely used in all cases of shock in which the skin is pale and the pulse weak. The temperature should be from 100 to 120 degrees. It should be followed by cold friction [2].

The author's personal experience with enemas is in conjunction with a 28 day juice fast, where enemas were used twice per day. It was a bit difficult at first, but ultimately was successful. Also, enemas have been used to help speed up the healing process for colds which are suspected to be allergy related.

What Type of Water to Drink?

There are many concerns and arguments about water. Here are some concerns from Dr. Scholl:

Water Precautions for Travelers—A wise precaution when traveling, especially in unhealthy districts or during an epidemic of any kind, is to drink none but boiled rain-water, which you can make sure has not been exposed to contamination by lead pipes, roofs or cisterns. To be effectual, the boiling ought to be continued briskly for half an hour or longer. Rain-water is preferable in limestone regions, because the hard water containing lime is partially or not at all improved in this respect by boiling, and gives rise to serious diarrhea in many of those unaccustomed to its employment. Such hard water is also probably one great cause of the very painful calculous disorders [3].

While most would have little objection with what Dr. Scholl wrote, Dr. Drews brought up a subject which is more controversial when he wrote:

Organic or Inorganic Water

Organic or Inorganic Water: Which is preferable? A very little common sense and reason will make this plain. We will first take rain water. This is the purest natural water that can be obtained as it contains only traces of aerial minerals and were it not for the dirt off roofs and the flavor of shingles, it would be more in demand. Artesian water is the very opposite, as it is saturated to its fullest capacity with inert soluble minerals which are often the source of trouble in the animal organism because they are hard to handle by the organs of elimination.

Shallow well and lake water has had a chance to deposit some of its burden of minerals. This is therefore the best source of common water.

Boiled water has only one advantage in that the germs of putrefaction have been destroyed. The deposit of stone in the kettle can only be considered as the load of the water that is evaporated.

Distilled water is chemically the purest, but in many cases even this is burdened with soluble metallic oxides from the sides of the still. Such metallic oxides are more injurious to the animal organism than the inert soluble minerals in common water.

The water of fruits and vegetables, i.e. fruit and vegetable juices, are laden to the utmost of capacity with organic salts and sugars. Some of these organic salts aid in the process of elimination by uniting with the waste material and thus rendering it soluble and elimitable. Organic water, therefore, has a two-fold eliminating capacity above mineral water. It has been proven that after eating watermelon, one may eliminate more water by weight than the weight of the consumed portion of the melon. This would prove that the organic salts in fruits, aid kidney elimination [4].

Now in this day and age, the best source of water is probably that naturally found in raw fruits and vegetables. There are some concerns about other points that Dr. Drews has raised. Well water and spring water have been the bulk of the water the author has drunk in the last 30 of my 40 plus years of life. Water from wells is natural for humans and is even recorded in the first book of the Bible as a proper water source (Genesis 16:7,14). Rain-water could be ideal, but modern air pollution makes me question that.

Regarding distilled water, without attempting to be controversial, the following statements should be taken into account:

- Although rain-water is naturally distilled, by the time it gets to the surface it is no longer distilled.

- Humans never naturally drank large quantities of distilled water (even when rain-water was purer than it is today, it was normally stored in wooden or other containers which leached).

- No one can be totally sure of the internal ramifications of distilled water for long-term use.

- Distilled water is the universal solvent.

- Distilled water does have short-term (and perhaps longer) therapeutic value for some people.

- Distilling water and then adding back inorganic minerals does not make it the same as natural water (please also see chapter 23).

There is also some controversy about how much water people should drink. Some natural hygienists have suggested that if people exclusively eat raw fruits and vegetables (which is not advocated long-term), they do not need to drink much water. Others have stated that people need eight or more glasses of water per day.

Heat does reduce the water content of foods. Therefore, it is conceivable that the more dry foods one eats, probably the more water one needs.

There will always be controversy associated with water and water therapies. However, it is good that water therapies were used by old-time naturopaths and are still used today.

References

[1] Burr-Madsen, A. *Natural Therapies, Module 1.* Gateways College, Shingle Springs (CA), 1996.

[2] Kellogg, J. H. *Rational Hydrotherapy,* 2nd ed. F.A. Davis, Phila., 1903.

[3] Scholl, B. F. *Library of Health.* Historical Publishing, Phila., 1931.

[4] Drews, G. J. *Unfired Food and Tropho-Therapy,* 3rd ed. Reprint by Health Research, Mokelumne Hill (CA), written 1912.

19
Clay and Mud

Naturopaths, ancient Egyptians, and other natural health practitioners have long used clays and various muds to support improved human health [1-3]. The German naturopaths Kneipp, Kuhn, and Felk all utilized it in their practices [2].

One of the more common clays used today is liquid bentonite whose active constituent is believed to possibly be montmorillonite. This particular clay is a volcanic ash [1]. It has been shown to attract and eliminate toxins [4]. It also appears to sometimes be effective for some forms of diarrhea [4] as well as in some forms of constipation [1]. In one study, using 2 tablespoons of bentonite in distilled water three times per day, it was found that 34 of 35 with diarrhea reported substantial relief [4].

It is most often recommended by this author for people who are bothered by airborne allergens [5]. Taking it for a few weeks each spring during allergy season can be extremely helpful. Many use it as part of a detoxification program. It has been written that, "All toxins and negative radiation are attracted to clay (a positive pole) and are eliminated out of the body" [1] and "Besides the colloidal properties of clay, it acts as a cleansing agent eliminating all noxious substances" [2]. Although some recommend that enemas be used when hydrated bentonite is taken internally [1], it has not been found that this is necessary (though it must be helpful for some). When used internally, some people have reported improvement for allergies, viral infections, parasites, mucous colitis, and even food poisoning [1]. It has been reported that some take it to try to prevent detection of illegal drugs in an employment screening, but it is not known if it helps in that situation.

It is believed that in addition to digestive concerns, because it has a positive pole, clay intended for internal consumption can cleanse, enrich, and purify blood [2]. It has been claimed that this affect can reduce the toxicity associated with radioactivity [1,2].

Bentonite can be swallowed in liquid form (such as Springreen #77), diluted in warm water. It does not taste good, nor does it taste bad. It essentially tastes "thick." It seems a little bit like chalk. Some people complain about the taste in their mouths, but most do not. Most seem to have no objection to the taste and most like what it does for them. Clays can be a helpful part of a detoxification program.

External Uses

There are of course external uses for mud and clay. Many apply clay as a compress or poultice [2]. Some believe that, "In the presence of clay, microbian flora disappear; in a clayish medium, pathogenic germs, that is to say parasitic organisms, cannot proliferate" [2]. Sebastian Kneipp often advised a mixture of clay and vinegar for mud packs and poultices [2] (vinegar is somewhat acidic and is often helpful for some types of digestive complaints). Some also recommend mud wraps for cosmetic and other purposes, "Fresh sterile mud has a wonderful aroma and consistency. It is filled with nutritional elements beneficial to help the body... [The] appearance and texture of your skin is left silky and smooth" [6].

Externally, clay is sometimes applied warm, cold, or at room temperature. It is sometimes left on for a few minutes or even overnight (normally longer for internal problems). When it is used on an over-active or naturally warm organ (such as the lower abdomen), it is supposed to be applied cold [2]. It will tend to become room temperature after a few minutes. Some like to heat clay in sunlight before use—warm clay tends to be used when the objective is to strengthen or revitalize an organ [2]. "In principle a clay application must not produce trouble or a sensation of pain" though sometimes it can worsen one before they improve (this same author has referred to the worsening of some experience as "apparent inconveniences") [2].

Dr. Lindlahr wrote the following under the heading *Mud and Clay Treatment*:

> **Certain localities in** Europe and in this country have attained considerable fame by the so called mud bath treatment. We tried this form of treatment for several years in one of our institutions but with indifferent success. The effect of the treatment is very much the same as that of the wet packs.
>
> The effect of the wet pack, poultice or compress is very much the same whether the material used be mud, clay, water, cottage cheese, flaxseed or any other mild acting substance. The beneficial results are brought about because the cool moisture in and under the packs or poultices relaxes the pores of the skin, draws the blood into the surface, relieves inner congestion and pain and promotes heat radiation and elimination of morbid matter.
>
> It has been found that on the whole the water applications produce fully as good results as mud, clay or other materials; besides, it has the advantage of being more cleanly and more easily applied. However, it is true that in many cases of chronic inflammation resulting either from internal disease, bruises or sprains, clay packs have proved of great benefit. The one advantage found in them is that this substance retains moisture and coolness much longer than a water pack or compress. They are, therefore, of special benefit in cases of subacute and chronic inflammations, of persistent soreness, and for all night packs or bandages.
>
> 1. **Clay Packs.** The best way to apply clay packs is the following: Take yellow, or still better, blue potter's clay, macerate in warm water until it is reduced to a smooth paste. When cold spread this with a wooden paddle or broad knife over a strip of cloth wide enough and long enough to cover the part to be treated, then surround the clay bandage with a few wrappings of toweling, flannel or other protecting material. The clay packs or bandages may remain in place until they become hot or dry.
>
> 2. **Mud or Clay Baths.** The mud or clay baths are applied in a manner similar to that of the clay packs but on a larger scale-to the entire body from neck to feet. The mud or clay must first be macerated and sifted so as to remove all pebbles, twigs or other foreign materials. The siftings are then mixed with hot water and reduced to a smooth paste. Mud or clay does not heat on the body as readily as a water pack, therefore it is best to heat the clay to 70 degrees F. before it is applied. The warm paste is spread on a sheet and this is wrapped around the body. One or two blankets, according to the warmth of the treatment room and the reactionary power of the patient, are then wrapped around the mud pack. The mud bath is applied like the full sheet pack…the only difference being that the sheet, instead of being wrung out in water is covered with a layer of mud or clay as described under clay packs.
>
> Care must be taken that the mud or clay used for such treatments is free from impurities. It should not be taken from localities contaminated by human refuse. The mud or clay bath is followed by a cleansing warm spray and rub, and finished with a quick tonic cold spray.
>
> While it is true that many people suffering from rheumatism and kindred acid diseases have found temporary relief by patronizing the popular mud bath resorts, it is also true that these "cures" are not permanent. The reason is that in these places practically no attention is paid to diet. The patrons live on the ordinary hotel and restaurant food which produces hyperacidity almost as fast as the mud baths reduce it.
>
> Neither do such patients receive the benefit of hydropathic, manipulative and

other natural methods. The result is that after resuming at home their accustomed mode of living, the "cured" patients soon again experience the old rheumatic aches and pains and other symptoms of hyper-acidity. Many of our patients suffering from such ailments had time and again tried the various mud cures, but experienced only temporary relief. It required the strict pure food diet, hydropathic and manipulative treatment, sun and air baths and the outdoor life to produce real and permanent cures. [7]

Just as naturopaths advocate food and natural vitamins (as opposed to isolated synthetics) [8], it seems that most using clay do not believe that chemical substitutes are as good as the real thing [2]. This probably is because all the working mechanism in clay are not known or understood. For example, it is believed that the more clay is exposed to sun, air, and rainwater, the more therapeutically active it will become since these allow the "clay to exercise its property of absorbing and storing a remarkable part of the energy of other elements, above all, the sun. It is possible that its particles, infinitesimally small, constitute its many condensers, capable of freeing withheld energy at the appeal of its opposite pole" [2] (more is discussed about light in chapter 11). For more information on the uses and precautions associated with clay, it is suggested to either read or acquire the books in references 2 and 7 as well as other available books on the subject.

References

[1] Tenney, L. *Health Handbook.* Woodland Books, Provo, 1987.

[2] Dexteit, R. and Abehsera, M. *Our Earth, Our Cure.* Citadel Press, New York, 1993.

[3] Null, G. *The Complete Encyclopedia of Natural Healing.* Kensington Books, New York, 1998.

[4] Damrau, F. *The Value of Bentonite for Diarrhea.* Med Ann District of Columbia, 1961; 30(6):326-328.

[5] Thiel, R. *Effects of Naturopathic Interventions on Symptoms Associated with Seasonal Allergic Rhinitis.* ANMA Monitor, 1997; 1(2):4-9.

[6] *Massage: The Art of Healing Touch.* Aroma Body Works, Shell Beach (CA), 1999.

[7] Lindlahr, H. *Practice of Natural Therapeutics.* Lindlahr Publishing, Chicago, 1919.

[8] Burr-Madsen, A. *Natural Therapies, Module 1.* Gateways College, Shingle Springs (CA), 1996.

20 Fasting

Naturopaths have long advocated fasting. In this chapter there are several positive views of fasting. The first from naturopath and natural hygienist, Dr. Kulkarni; the second from the natural hygienist, Dr. Drews (who also quotes Dr. Lust and Dr. Lindlahr), and the final one from the religious figure Herbert W. Armstrong.

Here is what Dr. Kulkarni wrote under the heading *Fasting:*

Fasting in these days has become very popular among some of the Naturopaths who consider it to be the only means of rational and natural cure for all diseases. Of course it is so for the ailments caused by over-eating or caused by errors in diet. Even in such cases, it is not beneficial to fast more than 48 hours; even during this period there is not the least objection to drink water of the tender coconuts or to chew sugar-cane-pieces and drink their juice. Fasting for several weeks as recommended by some of the Naturopaths further weakens the constitution of the patient which has already been weakened by disease. Besides, fasting for such long periods is not Natural. Even in the worst cases of indigestion, dyspepsia, acidity, flatulence, fevers, etc. [Kulkarni has] not ordered fasting for over 48 hours as there is no need to do so. Fasting is the best medicine. Of course, it is so for all those who have committed errors in their diet. Vitality of the patient is undoubtedly lowered by long fasting. Hence, either in acute or chronic ailments such a patient with lowered vitality and decreased activity will not be able to eliminate systemic poisons and waste products from the body though the elimination of such poisons from the body is very necessary both in health and disease.

Animals, wild or domiciled, as a rule do not take any food during illness. Even human beings do not feel any appetite during illness and have no inclination to take any food; they may be getting abnormal thirst due to the inflammation and heat caused by any acute illness but there is no desire for food. …clinging to their daily habits they persist against their inclination in taking food at the suggestion of their relatives and their attending physicians, as they are under the wrong impression that unless food is taken the patients might get weakened and their vitality be decreased. …Nature is the safest guide and neither the healthy nor the sick should take any food when Nature does not call for it, that is, when they have no appetite and when they have no desire for it. It is not the food taken but the food assimilated that supplies nourishment and the food taken unnecessarily when there is no appetite and the food undigested does, on the contrary, great harm by producing putrefaction and anto-toxin in the body.

Religious fastings of the Jains after sunset till sunrise next day and of the Hindus on Mondays and Thursdays for half a day and on Ekadashees once in a fortnight on the eleventh day after new moon and full moon for the whole day lead to keep them healthy without lowering their vitality in any way.

Such a fast for a short interval assists the body in eliminating wastes and disease products. It gives rest and renewed energy to the digestive organs and corrects defective nutrition.

Fasting for Curative Purpose

(1) Before commencing a fast the patient should keep his bowels clean by taking the enema daily at least for two or three days; he should also remain on milk and fruits during that period.

(2) During the fast a quick and friction bath should be taken every morning followed by a vigorous towel rub or massage all over the body.

(3) Daily exercise should be taken in proportion to the strength of the patient. Long walks with deep breathing are recommended.

(4) Whenever the patient feels hungry or thirsty a cup of pure water mixed with some fresh fruit juice may be taken. Tender coconut water or sugar cane juice is preferable.

(5) If the patient feels exhaustion and seems to lose his vitality he can break the fast by taking a cup of fresh milk and an easily digestible fruit. He should not take any hard indigestible food, salt, sugar, etc. at least for a week.

In indigestion, dyspepsia, gastritis, gastralgia, flatulence, flatulent colic, hepatitis, splenitis, enteritis, peritonitis, typhoid fever, dysentery, diarrhoea, sprue, cholera, etc. abstinence from food is very necessary till Nature calls for it. After a prolonged fast great care must be taken in resuming food. Sub-acid fruits such as sweet limes, oranges, grapes, apples, etc. should be taken first in small quantities, they must be masticated thoroughly and insalivated properly before they are swallowed; juicy vegetables such as lettuce, celery, radishes, cabbages, cauliflower, lady's fingers, etc. may be taken moderately; no spices should be added to them except onions, grated coconuts, and fresh lemon juice. The author's experience is that if we eat natural foods properly we are not required to fast for a long period.

A Naturopath should thoroughly acquaint himself with all the properties of every food-stuff and he should be able to instruct his patient what food will suit him and what food will not. He should also be able to know whether sun-bath) steam-bath shower-bath, enema, bandage, compress, or douche, will suit his patient's case. He should also know what sort of exercise or massage will help him most in eliminating poisons and waste matter from his patients' system. It is Nature that really heals; and the best physician only assists Nature in her healing efforts by helping her to eliminate systemic poison and waste-matter with the help of enema, sun-bath, steam-bath, etc. from his patients' body and never thwarts her progress in any way with poisonous drugs, injections, operations, etc. [1]

Here is what Dr. Drews wrote under the heading *Fasting:*

Nature often prescribes her own method of cure by taking away the appetite and craving for food. She even goes so far as creating an irresistible aversion for food. These signs should be promptly and religiously obeyed. Food should not be touched until there is a natural craving for it. When and as long as the patient has fever, no food should be offered him except plenty of water internally and externally. Foods simply add fuel to the already raging fire and create danger. Pure fruit juices and vegetable juices diluted with 50 to 75 per cent of pure water are Nature's best aid in counteracting and eliminating disease. Read the article on blood purifiers. A protracted fast is sometimes the best means of correcting perverted vital functions and disorderly proliferation. A fast of three to five days is the best means of increasing will power. It must be remembered, however, that unless you can absolutely vanquish the desire and craving for food during the fast, even in the presence of luscious fruit, you will indulge in dangerous starvation. During your fast you must not allow the presence of food to stimulate the flow of saliva or gastric juice. If you can not do this do not fast more than three days. During the second day you may be troubled with a very sick spell, but do not allow this to discourage you, as it is only a storm of adjustment and is on the third day followed by a sweet calm of lightness and clearness. If food is taken during the sick spell of the second day the beneficial effect is destroyed. Benedict Lust, N.D., says, "There is no disease that can resist a proper period of sane fasting scientifically employed," provided the patient has enough vitality and will power.

H. Lindlahr, M. D., says: "Fasting is a two edged sword which may do as much harm as good when promiscuously employed." Fasting is indicated in diseases caused by mistakes in diet; such as colds, catarrh, tonsillitis, obesity, rheumatism and incipient consumption. Some cults of the Orient advise fasting as a cure for old age. The process is to fast until the old and worn tissues are consumed in the effort to sustain life and then they partake of a selected diet to rebuild them a young body.

Fasting for health is absolutely useless as long as the intestines and colon are full of decaying and rotten faeces. During the week before the fast the patient should diet only on fruits, herbs and roots in order to give tonicity to the intestinal tract. The last day he should eat only lettuce or cabbage because this is most easily carried along by the peristaltic intestinal motion. Lettuce or cabbage is the least injurious if portions of it do remain in the intestines and decay. This seldom happens. Drink all the water you crave during the fast. Never break a fast abruptly. Eat very little the first day. Break the fast with oranges, watermelon or some other light and juicy fruit. In conclusion, do not undertake a fast of more than three days unless you are properly informed or have the care of a competent doctor. [2]

Herbert Armstrong wrote the included the following in an article which he titled *The Importance of Fasting:*

First, its connection with PHYSICAL HEALTH. Most people have come to believe today that it is NATURAL for people to be sick. THAT IS NOT TRUE! Sickness and disease are not natural, or accidental, but caused in every case by destructive habits. Sickness and disease cannot be eradicated until good habits—living according to NATURE'S LAWS as set in motion by the Creator—are substituted for bad ones. Bad habits of thought may be a contributing cause to sickness and disease or impaired health. Insufficient exercise, lack of drinking enough pure water, lack of deep breathing of fresh air, lack of sunshine, lack of sleep, faulty elimination, often contribute to poor health. But above all WRONG FOOD is the great outstanding cause. Few people realize this. Doctors seldom tell people this vital truth…

Voluntary abstinence from food for physical benefit or the cure of disease is as old as life upon this earth. Animals and birds instinctively fast as a means of restoring themselves to normal health whenever necessary. There is no such thing as a cure-all pill, drug, or medicine. But there is one thing that comes close to being a cure-all and that is FASTING. Especially is it the cure for such things as stomach disorders, constipation, rheumatic diseases, and the greatest help and often the cure for such things as kidney diseases, heart ailments, high blood pressure, skin diseases, asthma, anemia, and it is ALWAYS the thing to do in case of colds and fevers.

It was Benjamin Franklin who said "Feed a cold and starve a fever." But he did not mean one ought to feed a cold. He meant that IF one feeds a cold he soon will be starving a fever! The way to put out a fire is not to pile on more fuel. When you have a fever the body is on fire, and food is the fuel that makes it burn. If any member of your family has a cold or a fever, TAKE ALL FOOD AWAY at once! Give plenty of water. Give enemas twice daily, and warm sponge baths (not soaking in a tub) in a warm room twice daily. If you can give orange juice, or some other similar juice—which agrees with them—grapefruit, lemon, or tomato juice—that will do more good than harm. Give a glass of orange juice at a time, every two-to-four hours. [Armstrong] would not advise people inexperienced with fasting to go on a long fast of more than three, five, or seven days, unless they are under the care of a physician who understands and believes in fasting. And always remember this—if you have fasted two days or longer—this is IMPORTANT: In breaking a fast, do not start out with a full meal at once. Break it with two small pieces of buttered toast, toasted in the oven, HARD clear through, and a dish of about five stewed prunes. These should be soaked overnight before cooking, and then cook by just simmering, UNDER THE BOILING POINT, or steamed. If they are not boiled they will be plenty sweet, so add no sugar. Or, as an alternate, a dish of milk toast, but be sure the toast is toasted hard clear through. Second meal, two non starchy vegetables such as spinach, carrots, etc. - not potatoes or peas - along with a slice or two of hard toast and a little fruit (not rich canned fruit in syrup or canned with sugar). Then normal eating may be resumed by the third meal. [Armstrong has] been on a much longer fast, but [he has] studied fasting and spent a year, about 18 years ago, lecturing on diseases, diets, and fasting, and has had considerable experience putting many people through fasts. And [Armstrong has] never known one case where full results were not achieved! [3]

There are two common types of fasts: religious ones and health ones. Religious ones (for the author) tend to be around 24 hours (or more) and include no food or drink. Health ones can be a few hours to much longer (note: Some mainstream authorities believe that fasts longer than four weeks are potentially dangerous [4]. The longest one the author ever did was four weeks; the longest one his wife, Joyce, ever did lasted 40 days). The health fasts they have done are normally what would be called a "juice fast", where one drinks only water, fruit and vegetable juices (without combining the fruit and vegetable juices). Although there are benefits from fasting, they may not be quite as many as the earlier advocates have claimed (whether that is due to changes in food supply or other factors is not known). However, if one of many serious diseases that plague many in our society was contracted, more frequent fasting would be recommended.

References

[1] Kulkarni, V. M. *Healing Through Naturopathy.* Reprint by B. Jain Publishers, New Delhi (India), written circa 1925.

[2] Drews, G. J. *Unfired Foods and Tropho-Therapy.* Reprint by Health Research, Mokelumne Hill (CA), 1912.

[3] Armstrong, H. W. *The Importance of Fasting.* Reprint by Giving & Sharing, Neck City (MO), written circa 1940.

[4] Hoffer, L. J. *Metabolic Consequences of Starvation.* Modern Nutrition and Health and Disease, 9th ed. Williams & Williams, Baltimore, 1999:645-665.

21

Foods and Diet

There are many different views of what constitutes a proper diet. This chapter will attempt to touch on some of the prevailing views within the naturopathic community.

The first view was written by Dr. Royal Lee and Jerome Stolzoff:

There are certain basic facts relating to human nutrition that we believe are self-evident at this time. We offer them as follows:

1. The refining and processing of foodstuffs that has become so universal in all civilized countries has been done to improve the appearance, keeping qualities and competitive salability of foods without any regard to nutritional values. As a result of our high per capita use of such foods, we have a high incidence of certain deficiency diseases that are almost non-existent in countries where such food denaturation is not prevalent. (A list of such diseases is indexed in the chart following this article.)

2. Because of modem mechanized methods of food production, basic food commodities are today apparently far cheaper than they have been at any time in human history.

3. Because of the denaturation of foods, by refining and processing, we are overeating the fattening and energy-producing components, and literally starving for the vital vitamin and mineral factors in foods, (no less necessary to life than the fats, carbohydrates and proteins), which have become far scarcer and more difficult to obtain than at any time in the history of the human race. Actually our diets are excessively rich in the 'fuels' necessary for good health, but lack the 'spark' in the form of vitamins and minerals necessary to properly utilize them.

4. These vitamin and mineral elements are so complex and multiplex that their nutritional importance has been invariably discovered only by investigating the symptoms of physical degeneration and functional failures in animal and human subjects who were supplied with food lacking some of these essential elements. Further investigations have always shown that the lost material was so complex in its organic nature as to defy artificial substitution, if complete restoration was to be attempted. Where less than complete restoration was attempted, the results have been extremely unsuccessful.

5. Natural foods also are characteristic in being more satisfying to the appetite and are self-limiting in preventing a tendency to overeat. Honey is a good example;

children crave sweets and will invariably overeat if given artificial sweets such as commercial candy, but if given honey they will automatically limit their intake to that which is safe. In the case of devitalized or artificial foods there is either a total loss of appetite for the food in question after its use for a period of time, as has been noted in the case of buffer substitutes, or on the other hand, the substitute fails to satisfy the natural craving and overeating and obesity is the natural result.

6. Each animal species has its preferred and most favorable specialized food, to which it has become adapted over ages of experience. Therefore, no new food product or vitamin concentrate should be sold or recommended for human use until a background of experience has been accumulated by clinical tests or carefully observed use by competent investigators, to determine its specific nutritional values and effects. Violation of this cardinal principle has resulted, in some cases, in the creation of new pathological conditions more serious than the ones that were being 'cured.' [1]

The inevitable conclusion after the acceptance of the foregoing is that:

A. No food is safe, unless it is fresh enough to have retained most of its perishable vitamins. Spinach may lose all of its vitamin C in a week [2]; oranges in three months [3].

B. No food is safe, unless it has incurred no processing that would remove or impair its vitamin and mineral content. This eliminates pasteurized milk [4], white sugar [5], synthetic syrups, bleached flour, and practically all packaged cereals, shortenings, fats, etc.

C. No food is safe, unless it is free of any kind of synthetic adulteration, representing crude attempts to replace valuable organic constituents lost in processing. Wherever this has been attempted, the result has been found futile, and has proven to be actually dangerous. Tests made on dogs with white flour fortified with synthetic vitamins demonstrated that the fortified flour killed dogs quicker than the old white flour, unfortified [6]. That is why Canadian laws now prohibit the adulteration of bread or flour with synthetic materials of any kind. If the vitamin content is to be raised, it must be done by retaining the original factors, not by adding new ones of unknown effect.

D. No food is safe, unless it has a background of experience behind it establishing its value to the human family. Animal tests should be considered only as preliminary and suggestive indications of possible value [1].

The situation, no doubt, calls for some kind of legislative action to protect the public health. It also calls for a campaign of education on the part of makers of natural foods to call the attention of the public to the real facts, and to show the housewife how to get the most for her money in buying foods--not the most pounds of commodity, but the most nutritional value for the money.

Wheat, rice, and oatmeal have been selected as preferred cereals for human food. It is, no doubt, more than a coincidence that these grains are the highest in vitamin content. The food products richest in vitamins, over the ages, seem to have appealed most to our taste sense. The modem method of processing these cereals, however, has deprived us of the benefit of this long-established preference, It has cheated us by giving us the bulk food components--the starches and proteins of the cereals, without the vitally essential vitamins and minerals. As a result we may become obese, lowered in vitality and resistance to disease, lazy, and mentally and morally deficient. [7]

Dr. Lee and the author do not however, only advocate raw foods. Some of the early naturopaths, who are these days referred to as "natural hygienists" do. The most famous pioneer in this area probably was Dr. Drews. He wrote:

Those who are seeking for absolute health, longevity and refinement should understand that **the Body, Mind, Spirit and Soul are Absolutely Interdependent,** hence there is no sane mind, no spiritual perfection and no salvation of the soul without a healthy body. **Therefore the attainment of health is the first step toward the salvation (evolution) of the soul.** A healthy body can only be built and maintained with Nature's perfect (unperverted and unfired) food, pure water, fresh air, sunshine, exercise, restful sleep and a serene mental attitude savored with lofty aspirations.

It has been the earnest aim of the author to reintroduce a natural *health-sustaining, disease-resisting, disease-eliminating, brawn and brain-building* diet consistent with the present state of human evolution, civilization and refinement. A diet which shall promote further evolutionary progress on all the planes of the body, mind, spirit and soul. A diet physiologically and financially economical, artistic, inviting and delicious. All logical minds will agree with me that this can only be accomplished by feeding on natural food which contains all the elements for building a healthy body and which promotes all the natural functions of life.

Here it must be understood that cooked food is not natural because its chemical constitution is changed (perverted) by the destructive power of the applied high temperature. The sun energy (galama)

is dissipated. The volatile essences are exploded. The tonic elements (organic salts) have been freed, mineralized and neutralized. The proteins are coagulated. The starches are rendered so soluble that they enter the circulation undigested. The atomic arrangement of sugar is rendered incongenial and the oils are fused. Therefore, cooked food readily ferments and decays in the alimentary canal; besides, its consistency does not give the proper exercise to the organs of cominution, digestion and absorption; and it has a tendency to puzzle, confuse and pervert the alimentary functions--thus laying the foundation for disease.

Natural unfired food promotes all natural functions of the body. With natural foods, only, can be laid the foundation for the maintenance of a truly healthful and beautiful body, spirit and soul. By means of the natural tonic, detoxicating and eliminating elements in unfired food can Nature keep the body clean, cure all diseases of body and mind and eradicate immoral tendencles. It Is unnatural food which interferes with the natural metabolism of the system, which hinders and perverts natural growth, which retards recuperation and reconstruction, which produces anaemia and atonicity, which promotes disorderly proliferation, which causes abnormal craving and inebriety and which causes directly or indirectly nearly all the physical, mental and moral diseases and pains which ignorant, misinformed, deluded, ensnared and perverted humanity is heir to. Every attempt to improve on natural food by artificial means results in an absolute failure--it cannot be done.

Every unnatural thing or action in the realm of nature has inherent the cause of its own destruction. Hence, for every infection and malfaction nature has an acute reaction (crisis) which results in salvation for those who obey her laws, but interfere with that acute reaction by means of medicine or surgery, and it may disappear only to reappear in a later chronic or fatal reaction. "Interference perpetuates both good and evil" hence—"Resist not evil."

There is a "Beneficent Design" in unperverted Nature, but also a malefic design in perverted and artificial Nature.

Materia Panacea

Natural food, fresh water and live air in connection with plenty of sunshine, exercise and rest, is the only reliable "Materia Panacea."

No matter how civilized or infinitely refined man may become, natural food can always be served invitingly, temptingly beautifully and artistically without changing its wholesome chemical constitution. All natural food keeps pace with man in the progress of evolution and refinement, both by natural and human selection.

The hydropath, heliopath, aeropath, osteopath and homeopath can guarantee no permanent health, after they have assisted Nature to effect a cure, unless the patient will persist to feed on natural food and obey other hygienic laws. R. T. Trall, M. D. says. "Poisoning a person with drugs, because he is impure, is like casting out devils through Beelzebub, the prince of devils." The "Diagnosis from the Iris of the Eye" proves that drugs are the irritant poisons which produce chronic diseases.

Unfired Food
cannot produce disease
because it contains no
Inorganic Sugar
Glucose
Soluble Starch
and
Partly decomposed Protein
to saturate the blood
neither
Inorganic Salts
to irritate the nerves
nor
does it readily ferment
or decay
in the alimentary canal
to produce toxic elements.
Unfired Foods
properly selected

scientifically combined
and
judiciously administered
have harmless medicinal properties
and
true remedial value
for curing nearly all diseases
by supplying
the proper saline elements
in the organic form.

Man's Natural Food

The natural food of all animals is that food which appeals to their individual instinctive sense of alimentation and to which their tastebuds and digestive organs are adapted. Man's tastes are perverted by unnatural food and he pays the penalty submissively.

Man's natural foods are
- The Fruits,
- The succulent Herbs and Roots,
- The Nuts and
- The Cereals,
- which, in their natural (unfired) form appeal to his unperverted sense of alimentation.

Nature has supplied ample variety for each season to delight the senses and prevent monotony. Foods whose chemical constitution is changed by roasting, cooking, baking, fermentation, preserving, pickling and refining, are not natural and, therefore, cannot support and maintain health indefinitely. Every attempt to improve natural food by artificial means results in a failure. Animals have been fed on approximate foods, scientifically combined, and they died sooner than by starvation.

"Dainty and Artistic ways of serving Natural Food has a Usefulness beyond its Aesthetic Value."

Unfired Food Versus Cooked Food

Ninety-five per cent of indigestion is due to fermentable food and that means cooked food.

It is the nascent acid produced by the fermentation of cooked food that paralyzes the nerves that control the peristaltic muscles of the alimentary canal.

Unfired green herbs and roots when combined with flaked nuts (as prescribed under salads) cannot ferment in the stomach nor intestines and, therefore, cannot interfere with the peristaltic movement of the stomach or intestines.

The wholesome organic salts of unfired food are absorbed and their cellulose stimulates peristalsis (intestinal activity) whereas cooked cellulose aids fermentation and so retards digestion arid peristalsis. The harder the fibre of palatable herbs or roots the better for the stomach and intestines.

Sometimes gas is formed from the discarded mucus in the stomach and this must not be credited to the unfired food.

Do not blame the salads if you combine them with other inconsistent food material or cooked or baked foods at one sitting.

Natural foods do, not only, prevent and cure diseases but they also, often, awaken dormant chronic diseases (which gnaw at the core of life) to an active crisis in order to DEFEAT them and EXPEL them. When this happens the "Nature-Cure" is triumphant and the patient has nothing to fear but to help it along.

Human Progress

Only those can reach the Olympian heights of human excellence and human perfection who will get out of the ruts of perverted habits, who will cease to be their neighbors' apes, who will not be moved by the ridicule of the ignorant, who will seek to replace belief, faith and lazy credulity by proven knowledge, who will learn the truth from every source and demonstrate it; who will take counsel and hints from the wise and reason for themselves; who will always practice the best they know and thus live an exalted example to the world, and who will teach the truth to those who are willing to learn for self-improvement. The foundation to all reform is a natural, health sustaining diet.

Human Apes

Many good people who have not yet evoluted far beyond the ape will not be able to take advantage of the natural health diet until they can ape someone else, until it becomes a fad or until they are forced by disease, pain and misery. Don't be prejudiced by your perverted senses or by hearsay, but use your reason and find out for yourself. Don't hire the minister to think for you but develop your own brains by using them. Take a hint from the wise and improve it yourself.

Be Self-Made

Cultivate the best habits and practice self-mastery.

Ignorance And Sense

Don't boast of the disagreeable things you can eat nor display your ignorance in boasting of your health, retained in spite of eating unnatural foods, for you know not when Nature will call you to time. All natural food is relished by the unperverted palate as it comes from the hand of Nature. **Eat natural food to maintain and increase your physical and spiritual health** and avoid all food which ensnares the appetite with artificial flavors and chemically changed consistency. Don't rely on the likes and dislikes of your perverted sense of taste for selecting wholesome food nor blame the natural food when it painfully stirs up the filth in your system in order to displace it and eliminate it.

Digestive Fluids

Every natural food with an unchanged natural flavor as it comes in contact with the taste buds in the process of combination, stimulates the secretion of a special combination of digestive fluids which are best adapted to digest the food tasted. Cooking changes the flavor of foods and thus the new flavor becomes misleading to the function of secreting digestive fluids.

DISCHARGE THE COOK who knows only how to tickle, surprise and delight a perverted palate at the expense of health and **HIRE A TROPH** who knows how to combine and serve natural, health-sustaining foods in a dainty way.

PARENTS!—if you knew that every drug has an acute effect and also an opposite chronic effect which produces a drug disease later on and, provided you have the future welfare of your children at heart, would you not deem it extremely criminal to have them drugged?

Vaccination is the method employed to transmit, perpetuate and preserve the pox, syphilis and other infectious germs for future generations.

Human Perversity

Some people are so perversely civilized, so "would be" aristocratic, so imaginarily refined, so "goody-goody" mannered and so ridiculously delicate and dainty-mouthed that they dare not, and often cannot, eat natural foods; that natural foods choke them and that, even their ignorantly trained stomach revolts against natural foods. In this perversity; however, they are perfectly willing to be a fashionable sarcophag or necrophag (carrion eater); they are proud to be fashionably sick and pay a fashionable doctor and they have the wonderful courage to swallow the customary, most nauseating drugs irrespective of the dangerous after effects the expected cure may lead to. Unfortunately there are some good but uninformed people who would be true to themselves. These try natural foods with such suspicious fear of eating poison that they involuntarily arouse a reactionary and sympathetic revolt of the stomach, and others feel imaginary effects of poison and then they are sure that they cannot eat natural foods. Oh--what idiosyn-

crasies! Where is the will to be reasonably consistent with Nature?

Natural Food

The man that feeds on nuts and grains,
Crisp herbs and roots, sweet fruit and water,
Knows little of disease and pains
And of the many ills that bother,

His body well, his brain is clear.
His soul is full of every goodness.
He lives a life that knows no fear
Of Nature's' roughs, revenge and rudeness.

His passions are in harmony
With spirit, soul and better senses.
In consequence morality
Accuses him of no offenses.

Tobacco, coffee, meat and beer
And salt and pepper, wine and whisky,
Are words that harshly grate his ear;
He knows their use is low and risky.

From Cause to Effect

Unnatural food produces a diseased body; in this develops an unsound mind; this makes a foul character and this results in a ruined reputation and so involves an unhappy soul.

Best For All

A king can eat nothing better and a beggar nothing cheaper than natural food; it is the most wholesome for the rich and cheapest for the poor and can be served in such aesthetic and attractive manner as to become the dignity of the most refined and so simple as not to puzzle the most lowly without detracting from its quality or deliciousness.

A Warning

For the sake of humanity, never allow a doctor or anyone else to suppress an acute disease with drugs unless the patient is willing to take the consequences of worse disease that may follow later on as a return of the former disease in a chronic form or as a result of the poisonous drug.

For the same reason do not take (or advise to take) a drug or medicine prescribed by an allopathic doctor.

It is a proven fact that allopathic drugs either *palliate* by paralyzing the sense of pain or *suppress* the eliminating and healing activities by the introduction of a drug disease which in most cases turns out to be vastly worse than the disease suppressed. The poor, ignorant and helpless victims of some allopathic doctors are drugged for a half dozen or more (drug) diseases following one another until the patients are so full of virulent poisons that they are hopeless and then are pronounced incurable. Such allopathic doctors ought to be listed among criminals. Secondary and Tertiary Syphilis followed by paresis (softening of the brain) is the result of the mercurial drugs and salves used by allopathic specialists for men and women. They scare the patient with all kinds of dangers and guarantee quick cures, but they are not responsible for the effect of their drugs a year or five later…

Flesh A Stimulant

Flesh food is saturated with the waste products of muscle and nerve activities and ptomains. These are toxic poisons which intoxicate delicate persons like alcohol. When these poisons irritate the nerves controlling the heart, the blood pressure is raised with a corresponding sense of exhilaration which is followed by reactionary depression. The blood which is saturated with uric acid (the waste product of flesh food), is sluggish, thick and viscid. Every new addition of this waste poison liquefies the blood temporarily by chemical oversaturation. This process is contemporary with the increased blood pressure.

W. M. Cornell, M. D., LL. D., says that flesh food lays the foundation for inflammatory diseases, tends to produce a putrid diathesis and putrid diseases and also has a bad effect upon the mind, producing peevishness, fretfulness and an irritable disposition.

When the blood is saturated with the waste products of flesh it is fertile soil for cancers and for zymotic and bacterial infections. The food elements in flesh are wholly catabolized (i.e., worn out), and therefore up energy in metabolic changes instead of giving out energy.

Drugs

Any drugs which can kill or destroy parasites, microbes or miasms or which can suppress any disease or the healing crisis of a disease is a destructive poison. Drugs which are poison to microbes are also poison to the living cells in the human organism. To give a patient drugs is equal to increasing the quantity of poison his system is battling with. Nature cannot throw off two or more burdens more easily than one. Impurities cannot deterge impurities. If you harbor scavengers in your system quit supplying the filth and the scavengers will leave or starve. If your system is out of harmony, give Nature a chance to re-establish harmony and disease will be no more.

Blood Purifiers

There is only one natural and wholesome blood purifying medium and that is unfired vegetable juice and fruit juice. Such wholesome vegetables and herbs as contain the highest aggregate percentage of the positive (detoxicating) elements (Fe., Na., Mg. and Ca.) are best adapted for this purpose. The tables on food analysis will make this clear. All drugs concocted or decocted from vegetables or herbs by the thermal process (cooking) are unorganized and are often as dangerous as mineral or metallic drugs, because the system cannot utilize or eliminate them. These saturate the blood still more with useless (rather irritating or dangerous) matter instead of purifying it. All inorganic elements (except pure water and fresh air) that are not bound in an organic molecule are dangerous and a source of trouble whether they are used for food or remedies.

Unfired herb and fruit juices used as blood purifiers should be diluted with fifty percent (or more) of pure water. When the juices are too acrid or tart they may be diluted with sweet juices or flavored with honey (not sugar as it irritates the absorbent surfaces). Sugar is unorganized in the process of manufacturing and hence is most unfavorable for remedial purposes. The juices may be extracted by grating, macerating or by means of an "Enterprise Juicer."

Cold or warm infusions of sun-dried herbs can be used as a substitute. Soak the dried herbs from five to ten hours. Do not use scalding or boiling water. Why not eat such vegetables, herbs and fruits in their natural state or in the form of salads? Do that while you are well as a fortification. The sick and the convalescent person is generally too weak to eat the required quantity of such remedial foods. In order to get the prescribed quantity of the purifying elements they would have to fill up so tight that the stomach could not act nor digest the bulk. The problem is, to get the greatest amount of unquestionable good at the least expense of energy. Drink a cupful of the prescribed juices (Detoxyl), warm or cold, one hour before breakfast and take a fresh air exercise after it. Always drink detoxyl on an empty stomach, i.e., three hours after a meal and one hour before the next meal. The following list is in the order of efficiency:

- Swiss Chard stems
- Lettuce
- Strawberries
- Radishes
- Kohl-rabi
- Sorrel leaves and stems
- Rhubarb stems
- Cucumber
- Pineapple
- Orange
- Tomato
- Tangerine
- Grapefruit
- Apple
- Grapes

Blood And Nerve Tonics

Blood tonics are not far removed from blood purifiers. To properly tone the blood, nerves and vital tissues the whole list of organic tissue salts are indicated. Select judiciously of vegetables, herbs and fruits to suit the case. These may be prepared in the form of juices or salads. Study the lists under the various organic tissue salts and read the article blood purifiers...

The Life Of Food

We do eat live fruits, herbs, nuts and grain not to absorb their life to sustain our life but, in order to get the food material anabolized or organized to the highest perfection and stored with the greatest amount of sun-energy and before it has a chance to catabolize or disorganize and lose its store of energy in the process of decay or returning to inorganic life. The idea of absorbing life to sustain life is held in ignorance and superstition in the minds of those who are not yet fully ransomed from the cannibal of the past to the human. Life substance or magnetism can only be communicated or exchanged on the same plane of being. [8]

Natural Food-Stuffs, Their Constituents and Their Use

Dr. Kulkarni was also a natural hygienist. Here is what he wrote under the heading *Natural Food-Stuffs, Their Constituents and Their Use:*

Almonds contain oil, proteins and phosphorus, and are useful as a general tonic both to the body and brains.

Apples contain phosphates of calcium, potash and soda, albumen, chlorophyle, malic acid, lime, gum, sugar, etc., and they cure acidity, dyspepsia, colic, diarrhoea, disorders of liver and kidneys, such as gall-stones, and renal calculi. They are very useful for general debility.

Asparagus contains potash, phosphates of potash and soda. It is a diuretic and is useful for scanty urine palpitation of the heart and worm troubles.

Bananas or plantains contain phosphorus, iron, soda, albumen, starch, etc. The red contain more of iron and sugar and are good for anaemia and general debility; the yellow contain more of soda and are useful for constipation; the green contain more of potash and soda and are diuretic.

Barley contains starch, gluten, albumen, oil, salts and hordeic acid. It is a laxative, diuretic and tonic.

Cabbage contains sulphur, soda and iron; it is useful for coughs, bronchitis, asthma, warts and some skin diseases.

Capsicum or chili is a pungent stimulating medicine and not a daily food-stuff. It increases the secretion of saliva, gastric juice and every sort of liquid substance in the body just to have an after-effect or reaction. It causes burning in many parts of the body and great thirst later on. It contains iron, soda, and some acids; it is useful for chills, fever accompanied with chills, flatulence, stomach pains, rheumatism, etc.; it can stop toothache also temporarily if its tincture is applied to the seat of pain.

Carrot contains silicea, calcium and sodium salts and is useful for gouty patients as it eliminates uric acid from the system; it also prevents brick dust-like sediments in the urine. It brings the liver in proper order and cures gall-stone troubles also.

Celery contains iron and sulphur and is good for rheumatism and gout.

Cherry contains sodium salts and is useful for urinary troubles.

Chestnut contains fluorine, calcium, kalium and ferrum salts and is useful for blind piles, pain in the waist, hernia, congestion of liver, etc.

Cinnamon is a medicine and not a food stuff. It contains tannin, cinnamic acid, resin, sugar, and traces of potash. It is a remedy for flatulence, cancer, and haemorrhages of black blood.

Clove is also a medicine and not a food stuff, If moderately taken it cures dyspepsia; but in large quantities it has an opposite action. Externally it is useful for toothache and also for neuralgic and rheumatic pains.

Coconut contains phosphates of calcium, iron, potash and soda; it contains also milky and oily substance, albumen and a little starch. It is a valuable substitute for milk, ghee, cod liver oil, and all its preparations. It is very easily assimilated; more easily than milk and cod liver oil; the weak and the tubercular patients can safely make use of it both as food and general tonic. It is more strengthening than soups.

Currents contain iron, sodium and sugar; black ones contain more of iron than other sorts; they are cooling and a laxative and are useful for constipation, scanty urine, fever and anaemia.

Custard-apple contains soda, potash, sulphur and sugar. It is cooling and refreshing; it cures obstinate boils and carbuncles; the pulp prepared from its leaves can cure them sooner than a surgeon's knife and a doctor's poisonous mixtures.

Dates contain 20 percent pure sugar and some valuable phosphates, chiefly of iron. They prevent constipation and soothe the heart. They must be eaten with grated coconut as they are otherwise too sweet for the taste and are very heaty.

Figs are a laxative; they contain sugar, phosphates, gum, albumen, etc.

Flax or linseed contains acetic acid, acetate and muriate of potash. It is useful for congestion, inflammation, cough, etc. It promotes expectoration in coughs, consumption, tuberculosis, and is useful for hectic fever, night sweats, urinary difficulties, etc. One ounce of linseed, half an ounce of liquorice roots must be mixed in a pound of water and reduced to 8 ounces by boiling and taken with a few drops of lemon juice and a little honey. It is called linseed tea.

Garlic is a great disinfectant; it contains some strong odored acid. It cures obstinate sores and tuberculosis. Small pieces of garlic should be eaten with grated coconut and lemon juice. It can be used externally also.

Gooseberries contain citric acid, chloride of potash and sodium, gum, sugar, water and albumen. They are good for biliousness, constipation and dyspepsia.

Grapes are rich in sugar called glucose; they contain tannin, gum, tartrate of lime, magnesia, alum, iron, chloride of potash and soda, tartaric, citric and malic acid, etc. The rind or skin of grapes is astringent and constipating and the juice and pulp are laxative and they allay thirst and are useful for that reason in fevers and hot seasons. They are useful for children during teething and whenever they are constipated. They promote flow of urine and are useful in gout and rheumatism. Cancer patients will do well by eating a large quantity of them.

Hazelnuts contain sulphur, oil, protein, etc., and are useful for bleeding piles, haematuria and haemorrhages of dark blood from any orifice.

Honey contains glucose or grape sugar, phosphates, and some aromatics. It is the best substitute for sugar, jam, jelly, etc. and is useful in coughs, consumption of lungs, dyspepsia and also for boils and carbuncles.

Jackfruit is rich in sugar, albumen and calcium and soda salts. It is yellow inside when ripe and is laxative. Dyspetics should not venture to eat it in a large quantity as it is difficult to digest.

Jambools contain sodium salts and sugar and are useful for diabetes mellitus and diarrhoea.

Kajunuts contain soda, iron, and traces of silicea; both fruits and nuts are very heaty. The best time to eat the nuts is when they are tender.

Lemon contains potassium chloride, citrate malate, and tartaric acid; therefore it serves as an antibilious and antiscorbutic. It is also rich in vitamins. It cures spongy gums, scurvy, biliousness, dyspepsia, gout, rheumatism, constipation, sore throat, thirst, heart burn, lumbago and coughs simple or phthisical (sic). It is also, useful for liver and spleen troubles and may prevent malarial fever if continued long. It is also good for obesity and muco-colitis of long standing.

Lettuce contains potassium salts and is useful for sleeplessness.

Liquorice contains sugar, iron, sodium, etc. and is useful for coughs, and inflammatory conditions; it is a household remedy for coughs with linseed and lemon juice and for dry cough, bronchitis, asthma, pneumonia, etc. and also for boils, carbuncles, etc.

Maize contains calcium, iron and soda salts and starch which is easily turned into sugar. It is as strengthening as wheat though it contains less starch and more salts. It can be eaten with grated coconut.

Mangoes contain sugar and highly refined turpentine in them; they also contain iron, useful acid and they are useful for rheumatism, diarrhoea, diabetes, etc. Their seeds and rinds are astringent.

Milk serves both as food and drink. When fresh milk is not available, a cup of milk may be kept in boiling water for about 15 or 20 minutes and when it becomes tepid may be taken with or without fruit juice but without sugar. Milk is an excellent ingredient to quench thirst during illness, fatigue and in hot weather.

Millet contains soda, lime and iron salts, etc., it is nutritious and a laxative; It can be chewed and eaten when it is in its juicy condition. Its breads may be eaten with grated coconut or any fruits.

Oats (java) contain sodium, potassium, calcium and kalium salts; it is a very nourishing food. It is useful for diabetic patients as it contains sodium salts and less of starch than any other grain.

Onions contain sulphur, phosphorus, potassium salts, ammonia, phosphoric and acetic acids, citrate of lime, starch, sugar, ligumine and volatile oil, etc.; they are a household remedy for cough, bronchitis, scanty urine, colds, influenza, liver troubles, inflammatory conditions, gout, rheumatism, etc. They promote perspiration and circulation of the blood.

Oranges contain citric acid, citrate of potash, albumen, sugar, water, sodium and iron. In influenza, plague and dengue if they are eaten freely, they will prevent pneumonia and other troubles. It is a good remedy for dyspepsia, asthma, liver troubles, coughs, bronchitis, heart troubles, typhoid fever, etc.

Papaya (carica) contains sodium and calcium salts and is useful for dyspepsia, liver and spleen troubles; but is very heaty. Pregnant women should not venture to eat a large quantity of it.

Peach contains iron, gum, sugar and acids. It is a tonic and aperient and is useful for fever, and anaemia.

Pears contain nitric acid, pectose, gums, sugar, albumen and some valuable salts. Its external skin or rind is a laxative but the *inner portion* has the property of constipating the bowels. It is a very pleasant fruit. Its leaves can be made into an excellent toothbrush; they are better than all the tooth remedies in the market.

Peas and Beans contain, starch, albumen, sulphur, potash and calcium salts. They cause flatulence and uric acid. In small quantities, if well masticated and insalivated properly, and digested, they are nutritive and strength-giving.

Pineapple contains muriatic acid, a constituent of gastric juice and is useful for dyspepsia. It dissolves albumen and is a useful remedy in obesity, Bright's disease, diphtheria, etc.

Pomegranate contains sugar potash and sodium salts. It is an astringent food and is useful for diarrhoea, dysentery, sprue, worm troubles, etc. A strong decoction of its root-bark is an excellent remedy for tapeworm.

Plums and prunes contain potassium salts and sugar and are cooling and refreshing; they are gentle laxatives. They are useful in nervous diseases, irritability, dyspepsia, constipation, etc.

Potato contains citric acid, potash salts, phosphoric acid, starch and water. It is a very nutritious food. It can be used for poultices in indolent ulcers.

Radish is rich in soda and is a remedy for dyspepsia, piles, gall-stones, renal calculi, constipation, colic, etc.

Rice is rich in fermium salts, starch, etc., and is a good food in diarrhea, dysentery, fevers, etc. Its pericarp or bran is rich in sodium, potash and calcium salts and is a good remedy in constipation, dyspepsia, weakness and in some skin diseases.

Spinach contains ferrum salts. Some species contain ferrum and sodium salts and are good for dyspepsia, constipation, fever, urinary troubles, etc.

Strawberries are rich in citric acid, sodium salts and are a laxative. They are useful in fever, rheumatism, gout, etc. The leaves and roots are astringent and are useful for diarrhoea and dysentery.

Sweet lime (*Musami*) is an excellent food-stuff both during health and illness. It contains phosphates of calcium, iron, potash and soda. It also contains citric acid and citrate of potash; the fruit lasts even 3 or 4 weeks if properly preserved and is useful even in the worst type of typhoid fever, smallpox, dengue, influenza, cholera, constipation, colic and worm troubles.

Tomatoes contain citric and malic acids and also calcium and soda salts; they also contain phosphates of iron, oxalate of potash and sugar and are suited to anaemic and bilious patients but not to gouty persons.

Turnip contains sulphur, potassium and sodium salts; so it is an aperient and diuretic.

Walnuts contain phosphorus, phosphates of potash, calcium and magnesium and are suited to brain workers and persons of weak constitution; but they must be eaten very sparingly as they are very heaty and cause constipation; walnut oil is a remedy for eczema and other obstinate skin diseases. The tincture prepared from its rind cures obstinate eczema if taken in Homeopathic doses. Its unripe fruits are useful for worm troubles and the decoction prepared from its leaves (1 oz. to 10 oz of water) is a cure for sore throat, scrofulous ulcers, indolent sores, etc. One ounce of decoction is taken thrice a day. It is also used to wash obstinate and chronic sores.

Watermelon contains iron potassium and sodium and also a large quantity of sugar and water. It is an excellent fruit to quench thirst.

Wheat contains all the nutritive bio-chemic salts and phosphates required for the subsistence of the human body; calcium, iron, potash, and soda salts, water, fat, starch, albumen, etc. which are required for the human body are in wheat; so it may be styled as a perfect food for human consumption.

Man can sustain only on wheat for months and even years. Wheat among the cereals, milk among the animal food stuffs, plantains among fruits, and coconuts among nuts can be styled as perfect foods for human consumption. One can sustain on each of these for years without any other food and without losing energy.

Food cooked and uncooked

Why is disease so common and perfect health so rare? Because of errors in diet and in the mode of living. Civilization has introduced various fashions which ignore or break the laws of Nature and corrupt natural instincts of man.

Man's chief object and delight seem to be the cooking of food and mixing it with endless varieties of spices. Mixing changes the natural taste, cooking de-stroys the vitamins and life-sustaining and strength-giving properties, while spices make the food harmful to the general health of the consumer.

Is uncooked food less wholesome than the cooked? It is quite possible for human beings to maintain and nourish themselves on uncooked food and if properly taken it will make them healthier and stronger and keep them free from ailments.

Primitive races sustained themselves on raw and tender leaves, flowers, fruits and nuts. Famines turned them to roots and animal food, which of course required to be cooked or boiled; later on they cul-tivated cereals in the rainy season and preserved them for other seasons also. These they found hard to masticate with their teeth and began to boil them well. But these cereals can be made softer by hold-ing them in the mouth in small quantities and softening them with saliva or they may be soaked in water and made soft enough to be masticated well and swallowed after properly insalivating the liquefied grains which can be digested and assimilated more easily than the cooked ones. The cereals eaten in this way will supply more nutrition, more strength and better health and even a very small quantity will suffice to sustain human life.

More than 90 percent of human ailments are caused by errors in diet i.e., by eat-ing food not meant by Nature for human consumption. Uncooked food produced and ripened by Nature with the help of air, water and sunlight if properly eaten can prevent such ailments and promote health and strength and prolong life. [9]

Fruititarians and Food Combining

There are still many natural hygienists. Like most other naturopaths, they "oppose immuniza-tion, fluoridation, and food irradiation and eschew most forms of medical treatment" [10]. Some are also against homeopathy and some other modali-ties used by other naturopaths [8]. Perhaps the most extreme major group of natural hygienists are the ones who call themselves fruititarians (not all natural hygienists are fruititarians). They believe that cooking is carcinogenic, many herbs and spices are carcinogenic, cooking oils are carcinogenic, junk food (they include butter, which Dr. Lee [7] and others feel is not a health problem) is carcinogenic, and that all animal products are unwholesome whether cooked or raw [11]. Fruititar-ians do not even believe in eating vegetables—as T.C. Fry (a modern fruititarian) has written, "We do not require vegetables in our diet" [11]. Most fruititarians (including T.C. Fry) do eat some vegetables and some raw nuts in addition to fruit, but fruit is the bulk of their diet [11].

Fruititarians and other natural hygienists tend to be highly concerned about food combining. The concept is essentially that since different types of foods require different enzymes, etc. for digestion, it is more efficient to only eat similar types of foods at a time [12]. Although there is some truth to this concept, the body was designed to handle mixed meals (so apparently did Jesus who fed thousands with fish and bread, otherwise known as protein and starch, on at least two occasions (Matthew 14:17-21;15:36-38). On the other hand, many people who combine fruit (or fruit juice) with other foods (especially vegetables) develop flatulence. Fruits and vegetables should not be combined in the same meal with at least 1 hour spaced between them. Some have asked what is considered a fruit and what is considered a vegetable. Some, to be technical, can point out that squash, tomatoes, beans, and peas are "fruits" of their respective plants. However, for purposes of food combing, a fruit is something that is sweet and is normally considered to be fruit, thus all of the foods in the prior list are vegetables (as are avocados), whereas berries, melons, citrus, apples, plums, peaches, pears, bananas, grapes, etc. are fruits. Since lemons are not sweet, they (or usually their juice) can be combined with vegetables without a problem for most.

For people with highly sensitive digestive systems, proper food combining is more important. This means that protein foods are eaten by themselves or maybe with vegetables, that starches are eaten either by themselves or with vegetables, that dairy (if ever consumed) is eaten by itself, and that fruits are only eaten by themselves. Sometimes individuals are encountered who cannot combine melons with any other fruit. They can eat melon alone, but not in a mixed fruit salad which is commonly prepared.

The author's clinical experience has been that most with highly "sensitive digestive systems" actually have a pattern consistent with some type of chronic infection (parasitic or mycotic usually) and need to deal with that first (also see Appendix A). Once they do, food combining issues usually seem to become less of a necessary issue.

Dairy and Food Intolerances

There has long been debate in the naturopathic world about whether or not one should consume dairy products. T.C. Fry and others have long opposed the consumption of dairy [11]. Dr. Cordingley was in favor of consuming cow's milk and even recommends a milk therapy [13]; even Dr. Drews felt there was a place for natural milk from cows or goats. Dr. Frank Oski [14], Dr. Norman Walker (who lived to over 110) [15], and the author have favored raw goat's milk. Even the Bible says, "And thou shalt have goats' milk enough for thy food" (Proverbs 27:27). Without going into all the problems associated with commercial cow's milk, suffice it to say, the author does not consume it (with the exception of some cow's milk cheese, though mainly made from raw cow's milk). Raw goats' milk is hard to come by, though. It is understood that it is not available for legal sale for human consumption within California. Dr. Walker tells people who want their own goat milk to essentially be patient and if they want it enough they can get one some day [15].

Now, it is the author's clinical experience that everyone is not bothered by cow's milk. It is also his clinical experience that many are (please see the studies in Appendix A). Some people seem to assimilate the calcium, etc. from it, while it is suspected that others do not. Research suggests that most who have problems associated with cow's milk (usually referred to as bovine dairy products) yet still consume it on a regular basis, are not lactose intolerant (people who are lactose intolerant feel so bad from drinking it that they either do not or drink specially processed milk) but are bothered by one or more of its proteins. There are more than 25 proteins in cow's milk which can cause allergic reactions in humans [16]. The author's clinical experience suggests that people who are bothered by cow's milk sometimes suffer from asthma, frequent colds, insomnia, behavioral problems, diabetes, gastrointestinal upset, sinus conditions, ear infections, osteoporosis, and/or various forms of arthritis [16].

Caffeine is a problem for many [17]. Caffeine speeds up metabolism and affects mood, the natural hormone thyroxin speeds up metabolism and affects mood [18,19]. Many unknowingly use caffeine in an attempt to compensate for unknown low thyroid function (which can normally be helped through naturopathic nutritional interventions. Clinical experience suggests that women tolerate caffeine less well than men (though the author has seen no independent studies which prove this). The author's clinical experience also suggests that people who are bothered by caffeine sometimes have trouble losing weight, tire in the afternoons, have migraines, develop painful arthritis, get fibromyalgia, have gastrointestinal upset, have a greater tendency to develop tumors/ cysts (whether or not benign), and/or get other problems. The author personally does not consume any substantial amounts of caffeine (a list of "foods" with caffeine content is included in the migraine study in Appendix A).

Wheat is the "staff of life" as they say, but some cannot tolerate it. Sometimes this is due to an enzyme deficiency, thus enzyme supplementation can be helpful. Others cannot tolerate it for other reasons. Clinical experience suggests that problems associated with wheat include gastrointestinal problems, behavioral problems, and even sometimes severe mental health problems.

Oats are a great tasting high fiber food that has many health benefits—it even contains beta glucans [20]. Some, however, cannot eat them. They may not bother the stomach, nor cause any immediate reaction, however, if eaten for several days in a row, all the symptoms of a cold appear. This is true of many foods people are intolerant too—they do not always know the suspect food is a problem. Clinical experience suggests that people who are bothered by oats sometimes get chronic ear infections, frequent colds, fibromyalgia, joint pain, and other problems.

So much has been written about white sugar that this will be very brief. It is overly refined and does not have the mineral content that less refined sugar has [21]. It is a problem for diabetics and those with hypoglycemia. It reportedly can cause such a host of problems that will not be listed here. The artificial sugar substitutes are considered as worse (though rare use by people with certain health problems may be okay). The average American consumes 140 pounds of refined sugar and 25 pounds of artificial sweetener [22]. Sodas are the suspected primary way that most consume a lot of refined sugar and artificial sweeteners.

As mentioned in chapter 5, people should not intentionally consume artificial sweeteners, artificial fats, irradiated foods, artificial colors, artificial preservatives, and many other artificial additives. This does not mean that all the natural substitutes for these are necessarily safer either, but that common sense tells us that no one would intentionally eat those things if they were not mixed into other foods.

There are many, many other foods that can bother people (eggs, corn, peanuts, soy, etc. come to mind). Each person should be professionally assessed to see what they can tolerate and what they should avoid.

Diet

Unlike some natural hygienists and many in the "mainstream" believe, there is not one diet that is optimal for everyone. Genetics and other factors are involved. Everyone is biochemically unique, thus what works for one, does not always work for another.

The same day one may see someone who is overweight that does better on a high-protein diet while another is seen who does better on a low-protein diet. People who are hypoglycemic should eat five or more times per day, eat a lot of protein foods, and a lot of whole grains. People who tend toward gout sometimes benefit by avoiding most proteins and even switching to refined carbohydrates instead of whole grains (yes, it is terrible to have to recommend something like that, but the goal is to help them recover as quickly as possible).

Although most people feel that they have good diets, certain modern American concepts of a good diet are questionable. Specifically, it is not believed that eating hydrogenated fats (such as are found in margarine), low-fat milk (if one is bothered by one of the bovine milk proteins), artificial sweeteners/fats, and large amounts of white flour pastas, while avoiding good fats (such as are found in flaxseeds and olives) and sea salt (a source of iodine, but of course too much salt can be a problem), can help many people. Most would do well to eat at least three servings of vegetables and two servings of fruit per day (even the government agrees with me on this one [23]). Most should not eat meat more than once per day. Strict vegetarians tend to improve their health if they incorporate sea vegetables into their diet (many who come to my office seem to need iodine for their thyroids) as well as by eating from all the vegetarian food groups (it is amazing, but there are vegetarians who do not eat fruit and even some who eat few vegetables). Vegetarians need to be more careful about avoiding white flour products than non-vegetarians. Most people should eat at least three times per day, even if one of the meals is only a piece of fruit. Nearly everyone would do better by preparing their own foods, as opposed to buying them prepackaged and highly processed. Speaking of preparing food, olive oil is the best oil for cooking (many others are fine raw).

Organic fruits, grains, and vegetables (and goats' milk and meats for that matter) are best if they are fresh. It is very difficult to get truly fresh organic fruit. This will sound a bit heretical, but fresh non-organic fruit is sometimes better than old organic fruit (however, fresh organic fruit is best). Because fresh local produce is best, there is some basis for the concepts behind an initial (not long-term, rice only) macrobiotic diet.

Now, it should be noted that there are more concerns about non-organically raised foods since the first edition of this book came out. Furthermore, the increased amount of genetically-modified organisms (GMOs) in the food supply carries unknown risks that I have severe reservations about. Because of that, I strongly advocate that people try to consume as much organic produce, grains, and other foods as currently they cannot legally (in the USA at least) contain GMOs. GMOs (sometimes referred to as genetically-engineered foods) pose allergy and nutrient risks that I am not comfortable with (they also pose new risks on the food supply itself).

Note: The clinical use of nutrition, diet, and nutritional supplements is beyond the scope of this book. Some may wish to consult other works such as Balch's *Prescription for a Nutritional Healing* and my own book *Serious Nutrition: Incorporating Clinically Effective Nutrition into Your Practice* [24], which also contains symptom survey forms, certain protocols, and diets.

Although opposed to how most animals are raised for human consumption (thus disagreeing with what Dr. Drews wrote above about flesh as a stimulant), the author is not opposed to people eating animal products. Most people who do, though, seem to eat too much from this category. It should be added that the author does not eat shellfish. Two days ago, while at the beach for some sunlight and sea-bathing, the author read the warning sign that it is illegal to sell local shellfish for sale six months of the year, as it is considered to be dangerous. If it is considered dangerous six months of the year, that would not make one want to eat it the other six months of the year.

Regarding farm animals, they should be raised in a more humane environment than most now are. The author currently has his own chickens (also for eggs), turkeys, and goats (and may purchase a cow again). The consumption of less meat overall is better for the internal human environment (our bodies) and the external human environment (the earth). On the other hand, cows which are raised for food and which graze on the mountain sides around here are beneficial to the environment. The problem comes when they get sent away to feed lots (which should be considered improper and unnatural).

One question frequently asked is, "What do you eat?" Well, for breakfast normally an organic cereal with raw goat's milk. A fresh fruit snack in mid-morning or mid-afternoon (depending upon my schedule). Lunch is normally a whole wheat sandwich (with raw cheese or avocado) and a potato. Dinner is normally some type of meat (meat includes poultry and fish), starch (brown rice is a favorite), vegetables, and sometimes a salad (normally without salad dressing, but one can be used on occasion). In the evening, fruit, nuts, or a snack such as popcorn is consumed. Well water is normally drunk at home and spring water at the office. Beverages also include fruit juices and some alcohol (in moderation—never to the point of intoxication). Sometimes less healthy foods may be eaten, but in reasonable moderation. Some nutritional supplements are taken as well.

In conclusion, this chapter has shown several various naturopathic views of diet. There are now (and probably always have been) many views on what is the proper diet. As a general rule, the more natural the diet is, the better it is.

References

[1] *United States Department of Agriculture Yearbook,* Food and Life, pp. 12, 268, 151) 705, Government Printing Office, Washington, D. C., 1939.

[2] Eddy and Dalldorf, *The Avitammosis*, p. 171, Williams and Wilkins, Baltimore, 1937.

[3] Roberts, J. A., *Vitamin C in Citrus-juice Beverages and Canned Grapefruit Juice,* Food Research, 2:331-337, 1937.

[4] Jordan, E. O., A *Textbook of General Bacteriology,* Twelfth Edition, p. 691, W. B. Saunders Company, Philadelphia, 1938.

[5] Lewis L. R.. *The Relation of Vitamins to Obstetrics,* Am. J. Obstetrics and Gynecology, 29, 5:759, May, 1935.

[6] Morgan, Agnes Fay, *Science,* March 14, 1941.

[7] Lee, R. and Stolzoff, J. S. *The Special Nutritional Qualities of Natural Foods.* Lee Foundation for Nutritional Research, Milwaukee, 1942.

[8] Drews, G. J. *Unfired Foods and Tropho-Therapy,* 3rd ed. Reprinted by Health Research, Mokelumne Hill (CA), written 1912.

[9] Kulkarni, V. M. *Healing Through Naturopathy.* Reprinted by B. Jain Publishers, New Delhi (India), written circa 1925.

[10] Herbert, V. and Barrett, S. *Alternative Nutrition Therapies.* In Modern Nutrition in Health and Disease, 9th ed. Williams & Wilkins, Balt., 1999:1801-1810.

[11] Honiball, E. and Fry, T. C. *I Live on Fruit.* Life Science Institute, Manchaca (TX), 1990.

[12] Diamond, H. and Diamond, M. *Fit for Life.* Warner Books, New York, circa 1980.

[13] Cordingley, E. W. *Principles and Practice of Naturopathy.* Reprint by Health Research, Mokelumne Hill (CA), written 1924.

[14] Oski, F. A. *Don't Drink Your Milk.* Teach Services, Brushton (NY), 1995.

[15] Walker, N. *Fresh Vegetable and Fruit Juices.* Norwalk Press, Prescott (AZ), 1978.

[16] Whitaker, J. *Milk: The Ways It Does Not Do a Body Good.* Health & Healing, 1996; 6(3):6-7.

[17] James, J. E. *Caffeine Withdrawal and Cardiovascular Risk.* In Clinical Pearls 1997. ITServices, Sacramento, 1998:283-284.

[18] Spiller, G. A. *Metabolism and Physiological Effects of Methylxanthines.* In Caffeine. CRC Press, New York, 1997:225-231.

[19] Guyton, A. C. and Hall, J. E. *Textbook of Medical Physiology,* 9th ed. W.B. Saunders, Phil., 1996.

[20] Hallfrisch, J., et al. *Diets Containing Soluble Oat Extracts Reduce Urinary Malondialdehyde in Moderately Hypercholesterolemic Men and Women.* J Nutr Biochem, 1997; 8:497-501.

[21] United States Department of Agriculture. *Nutritive Value of Foods.* US GPO, Washington (DC), 1981.

[22] *Snacks.* Nutr Week, 1995; 25(41):6.

[23] Kennedy, E. *The 1995 USDA/HHS Dietary Guidelines: An Overview.* USDA, Washington (DC), 1995.

[24] Thiel R.J. *Serious Nutrition: Incorporating Clinically Effective Nutrition into Your Practice,* 2nd edition, Nazarene Books, 2012.

22

Natural and Synthetic Vitamins

The naturopathic standards drawn up at the Golden Jubilee in 1947 included the statements, Naturopathy...makes use of the healing properties of such natural agents as...organic vitamins... Naturopathy does not make use of synthetic or inorganic vitamins or minerals" [1]. This is actually fairly difficult to follow these days as most vitamin and mineral formulas contain synthetic vitamins and inorganic minerals (two companies whose products do not contain synthetic or inorganic vitamins are Doctors' Research and Springreen). In this chapter we will discuss natural and synthetic vitamins (minerals will be dealt with in the following chapter).

Irrespective of what is written in this chapter, it needs to be understood that mainstream "nutritional authorities" believe that synthetic vitamins are as good as natural ones. As amazing as it seems, they even go a step further by suggesting that only a quack would claim that natural (or organic) vitamins are better than synthetic ones" [2-3]. Interestingly, some of these same "authorities" have written that the body is designed to handle foods and should get its vitamins from foods [4,5].

"Vitamins are organic substances that are essential in small amounts for the health, growth, reproduction, and maintenance of one or more animal species, which must be included in the diet since they cannot be synthesized at all or in sufficient quantity in the body. Each vitamin performs a specific function, hence one cannot replace another. Vitamins originate primarily in plant tissues" [6]. *United States Pharmacopoeia* (USP) synthetic vitamin isolates are not naturally "included in the diet", they do not necessarily "originate primarily in plant tissues", nor have all of them been proven to safely and fully replace all natural vitamin activities (most have at least some vitamin activity though). USP vitamins are not food, even though they are often called "natural" and are sometimes added to foods. USP vitamins are synthesized, standardized chemical isolates [7]. In nature vitamins are never isolated: they are always present in the form of food vitamin-complexes [8-10].

Issues of Bioavailability

It is a scientific fact that the "bioavailability of orally administered vitamins, minerals, and trace elements is subject to a complex set of influences" [11]. Although some health professionals believe, "The body cannot tell whether a vitamin in the bloodstream came from an organically grown cantaloupe or from a chemist's laboratory" [4], this belief is misleading because it does not seem to consider the fact that there are multiple mechanisms which influence the absorption and utilization of most vitamins [5,11-25]). It also does not seem to consider the fact that nutrition scientists understand that particle size is an important factor in nutrient absorption even though particle size is not detected by chemical assessment (smaller size is generally better) [26]. Perhaps more amazingly it ignores the clear fact that, "The physiochemical form of a nutrient is a major factor in bioavailability" [27] (recall that nutrients in natural foods and USP vitamins are not always in the same physiochemical form [5,7,18,21,22,23,27-36]). Most USP vitamins are crystalline in structure [6,7,27], while most vitamins in food are not (and are actually present in a complex of carbohydrates, proteins, and lipids).

Electron microscopy indicates that isolated USP vitamins appear larger and have a crystalline appearance compared to vitamins in a natural food complex which have more of a rounded and smaller appearance.

Vitamins in Foods Compared to USP Isolates

Food Complex
Vitamin B-1

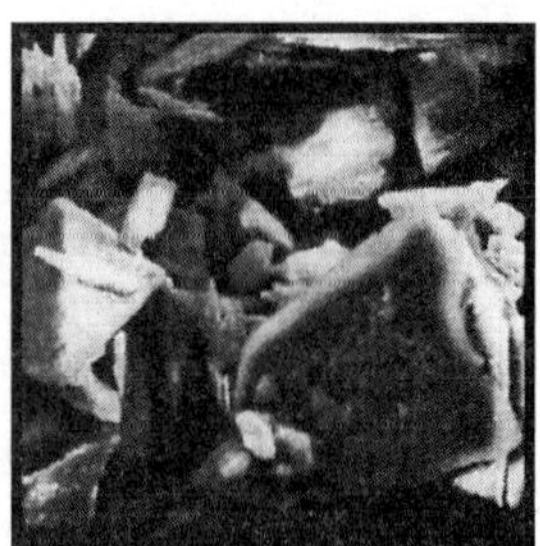

Isolate USP Thiamin
Hydrochloride

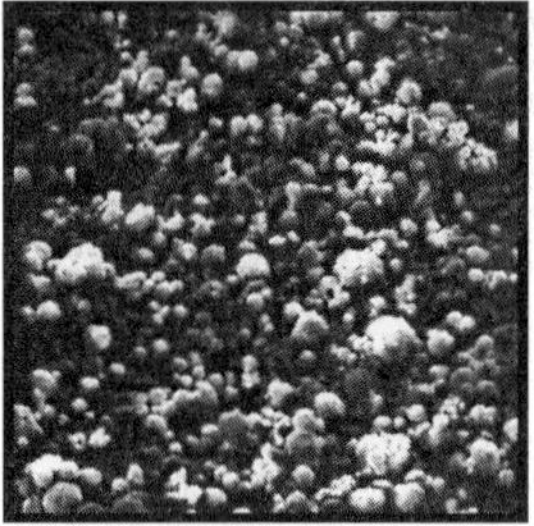

Food Complex
Vitamin C

Isolate USP
Ascorbic Acid

*Photographs from Electron Microscope
(all in the same magnification)*

Nutrition (like naturopathy), as a separate science, is a relatively new field, coming into existence only about 100 years ago, and then mainly because of food processing. Humans survived for thousands of years before synthetic vitamins were developed by consuming foods. These foods contained (and generally still contain) natural vitamins [18-23,37,38]. Natural food complex vitamins are in the physiochemical forms which the body recognizes. They generally are not crystalline in structure, contain food factors that affect bioavailability, and appear to have smaller particle sizes [37]. This does not mean that USP vitamins do not have any value (they clearly do), but studies (which may or may not conform to peer review standards) have shown that vitamins in natural food complexes are better than USP isolated vitamins [e.g.12-17,39-46].

Specifics by Vitamin

Some synthetic USP vitamins are analogues of the natural agents found to have vitamin action [18,32-36] (an analogue has similar, not necessarily identical properties). Some synthetic USP vitamin analogues have been shown to have no vitamin action [18,32,33], some can act as vitamin antagonists [20,33,34], and some can even produce deficiency symptoms of the specific vitamin they are analogues of [35] (the effects of the USP analogues differ by type).

Vitamin A The first naturopathic application of natural vitamin A was probably the use of liver by ancient Greek and Egyptian physicians for people with night blindness [18]. Vitamin A exists in foods primarily in the form of retinyl esters, and not retinoic acid [8,18]: it is not a single isolated chemical as synthetic vitamin A is. "The term *retinoids* refers to both retinol and its natural metabolites as well as to a large number of synthetic analogues that have structural similarities to retinol but may subserve only some (or none) of the functions of natural vitamin A" [18]. Most of the "vitamin A" in synthetic supplements are in a form which is not naturally found in food [18].

Some currently utilized synthetic retinoids are suspected of having potential for causing cirrhosis [47]. It has been reported that consumption of more than 10,000 I.U. per day of synthetic vitamin A increased the rate of birth defects, while consumption of natural vitamin A from foods (including betacarotene, a precursor) did not [48]. Retinyl acetate is the major synthetic form of vitamin A and is a vinyl or coal tar at one or more stages of processing (depending upon the manufacturer) [49]. An animal study found that synthetic vitamin A in the form of retinyl acetate significantly reduced vitamin E utilization [30]; this has not been shown to occur with natural vitamin A [i.e. 18]. An animal study concluded that a natural food complex vitamin A was probably less toxic than a synthetic USP form and was 1.54 times more absorbed into the blood [12].

Vitamin B1 The free vitamin B1 (called thiamin) is a base. When it is synthesized it becomes a solid salt such as thiamin hydrochloride or thiamin mononitrate [19]. Synthetically thiamin is usually marketed as thiamin hydrochloride or thiamin mononitrate [27] and is made from Grewe diamine (a coal tar derivative [50]) processed with ammonia and other chemicals [49]. No thiamin hydrochloride (often listed as thiamin HCL) or thiamin mononitrate is naturally found in food or the body (thiamin pyrophosphate is the predominant form in the body [51]) [27]. Yeast and legumes are excellent food sources of natural thiamin [51]. "Thiamin is rapidly destroyed above pH 8...the addition of sodium bicarbonate to green beans and peas to retain their color or to dried beans to soften their skins inactivates thiamin" [51]. High heat, x-rays, and UV irradiation also destroy thiamin [51,52]. Thiamin mononitrate tends to be used for food fortification since it is more stable under storage and processing conditions [27]. An animal study found that a natural food complex vitamin B1 was absorbed 1.38 times more into the blood and was retained 1.27 times more in the liver than an isolated USP thiamin hydrochloride [12].

Vitamin B2 The free vitamin B2 (called riboflavin) is a weak base. When synthesized it becomes an orange amorphous solid [53]. Some synthetic riboflavin analogues have very weak vitaminic activity [53]. Some natural variations, especially in coenzyme forms, occur in plant (including fungal) species [29]. Processing losses are usually not substantial but do occur as the result of leaching the light-sensitive flavins into water [53]; in addition, one study found that the pasteurization of bovine milk seems to reduce the bound form of riboflavin from 13.6% to 2% [54]. An animal study found that a natural food complex vitamin B2 was absorbed into the blood and was retained 1.92 times more in the liver than an isolated USP riboflavin [12].

Vitamin 'B3', Niacinamide "Niacin is a generic term...the two coenzymes that are the metabolically active forms of niacin (are)...nicotinamide adenine dinucleotide (NAD) and NAD phosphate (NADP)...Only small amounts of free forms of niacin occur in nature. Most of the niacin in food is present as a component of NAD and NADP... nicotinamide is more soluble in water, alcohol, and ether than nicotinic acid...many analogues of niacin have been synthesized, some of which have antivitamin activity " [20]. Niacinamide (also called nicotinamide) is considered to have less potential side-effects than niacin [20]; it also does not seem to cause gastrointestinal upset or hepatotoxicity that the synthetic time-released niacin can cause [55]. Beef, legumes, cereal grains, yeast, and fish are significant natural food sources of vitamin B3

[55]. Processing losses for this vitamin are mainly due to water leaching [56]. Synthetic niacin is usually made in a process involving formaldehyde and ammonia [49]. An animal study found that natural food complex niacinamide is 3.94 times more absorbed in the blood than USP niacinamide and 1.7 times more retained in the liver than isolated USP niacinamide [12].

Vitamin 'B5', Pantothenate Pantothenate was once known as vitamin B5 [57]. USP "Pantothenic acid consists of pantoic acid in amide linkage to beta-alanine", but the vitamin sometimes referred to as B-5 is not found that way in nature [22]. In food it is found as pantothenate; foods do not naturally contain pantothenic acid [22]. "Synthetic D-pantothenate, the active enantiomer is available as a calcium or sodium salt. However, multivitamin preparations commonly contain its more stable alcohol derivative, panthenol" [58]. Producing synthetic pantothenic acid involves the use of formaldehyde [49]. Organ meats, yeast, egg yolks, and broccoli are rich dietary sources of natural pantothenate [58]. Cooking meat and the processing of vegetables lead to significant losses of pantothenate (15-50% and 37-78% respectively) [58].

Vitamin B6 "An understanding of the various forms and quantities of these forms in foods is important in the evaluation of the bioavailability and metabolism of vitamin B-6"... one of the forms that vitamin B-6 exists is in the form of "5'0-(beta-D-glycopyransosyl) pyridoxine. To date only plant foods have been found to contain this interesting form of vitamin B-6" [21]. Yeast and rice bran contain more natural vitamin B6 than other foods [6]. The most common form in vitamin pills is USP pyridoxine hydrochloride which is not naturally found in food [59]. At least one synthetic vitamin B-6 analogue has been found to inhibit natural vitamin B6 action [34]. Synthetic B6 usually requires formaldehyde in its production [49]. An animal study found that natural food complex vitamin B6 was absorbed 2.54 times more into the blood and was retained 1.56 times more in the liver than an isolated USP form [12].

Vitamin 'B9', Folate The vitamin once known as vitamin M (and also vitamin B9 [57]) exists in foods as folate (also known as pteroylglutamate) [23]. Initially, natural food complex folate was given for people with a pregnancy-related anemia in the form of autolyzed yeast; later a synthetic USP isolate was developed [23]. Pteroylglutamic acid, the common pharmacological (USP) form known as folic acid, is not found significantly as such in the body and appears to be absorbed differently than folate [23]. Folic acid is not found in foods, but folate is [23]. Dr. Victor Herbert reports a study found "that consumption of more than 266mg of synthetic folic acid (PGA) results in absorption of unreduced PGA, which may interfere with folate metabolism for a period of years" [23]. Fortification with synthetic folic acid has been found to increase consumption for those who already have higher dietary intakes of folate more than those with lower intakes [60]. It is believed that fortification with synthetic folic acid may put a portion of the population at risk for vitamin B12 deficiency [61], yet all grain products advertised as enriched must (according to the US FDA) be fortified with folic acid [62]. "Foods with the highest folate content per dry weight include yeast, liver and organ meats, fresh green vegetables and some fruits" [23]. Food processing is a concern since "50-95% of folate in food may be destroyed by protracted cooking or other processing such as canning, and all folate is lost from refined foods such as sugars, hard liquor, and hard candies" [23]. An animal study found that a natural food complex folate was absorbed only 1.07 times more in the blood, yet was retained 2.13 times more in the liver than isolated USP folic acid [12].

Vitamin B12 Initially natural food complex vitamin B12 was given for people with pernicious anemia in the form of raw liver, but due to cost considerations a synthetic USP isolate was developed [63]. Cyanocobalamin (the common pharmacological/USP form of vitamin B12) is not found significantly as such in the body; it is usually present in reduced metabolically active co-enzyme forms (without the cyanide) often conjugated in peptide linkage [5,64]. According to Dr. Herbert (and others) vitamin B-12 when ingested in its human-active form is non-toxic, yet Dr. Herbert (and others) have warned that "the efficacy and safety of the vitamin B12 analogues created by nutrient-nutrient interaction in vitamin-mineral supplements is unknown" [5]. Some synthetic vitamin B12 analogues seem to be antagonistic to vitamin B12 activity in the body [33,35]. Most synthetic B-12 is made through a fermentation process with the addition of cyanide [49]. An animal study found that a natural food complex vitamin

B12 was absorbed 2.56 times more in the blood and was retained 1.59 times more in the liver than isolated USP cyanocobalamin [12].

Vitamin C There probably has been more controversy regarding vitamin C than any other vitamin. Ascorbic acid (AA) is not a synonym for vitamin C, though it certainly has vitamin C (antiscorbutic) properties (dehydroascorbic acid is the other biologically active form) [10,65]. Foods generally contain both biologically active forms of vitamin C [10,65,66], yet most synthetic vitamin C only contains isolated ascorbic acid [7,67]. Consuming five servings of fruits and vegetables per day will result in an intake of at least 210mg per day of natural vitamin C (the RDA is 60mg, though 200mg has been proposed) [66].

Although it has been written, "The bioavailability of vitamin C in food and 'natural form' supplements is not significantly different from that of pure synthetic AA" [10] this is simply not true. As "proof" this particular author cites two papers. The first citation is a study that concludes since serum ascorbic acid levels were at similar levels after various vitamin C containing foods and synthetic ascorbic acid were consumed, that the bioavailibility is similar [67]. The conclusions reached seem to ignore the fact that it may be possible that DHAA or other food constituents associated with natural vitamin C may have positive effects other than raising serum ascorbate levels. The second citation is a study that probably should not have been cited as it never compared vitamin C as complexed in food versus synthetic ascorbic acid (it compared synthetic ascorbic acid to Ester-C which is a commercial blend of synthetic ascorbic acid and select metabolites as well as to ascorbic acid mixed with some bioflavonoids) [68].

Interestingly it is known that, "Diets with high vitamin C content from fruits and vegetables are associated with lower cancer risk, especially for cancers of the oral cavity, esophagus, stomach, colon, and lung. In contrast, consumption of vitamin C as a supplement in experimental trials had no effect on development of colorectal adenoma and stomach cancer" [66]. Other studies seem to give a reasonable hint about the comparison of vitamin C in foods compared to isolated ascorbic acid [41,69]—they suggest that foods are superior. A human study found that a vitamin C complexed in food was absorbed 1.74 times more into red blood cells than isolated USP ascorbic acid [13], while another found it to be 1.35 times more absorbed into the plasma [14]. Also, it appears that vitamin C in citrus decomposes more slowly than plain synthetic ascorbic acid; whether this is due to bioflavonoids or other substances found in citrus is unknown [42]

A human study found that a food complex containing 500mg of vitamin C was 2.16 times more effective in reducing sorbitol in diabetics than was isolated ascorbic acid [43]. One study using 1000mg per day of vitamin C complexed in food showed an average decrease of 46.8% in protein glycation after four weeks [44], while a study using 1000mg of isolated ascorbic acid per day only had a 33% reduction in three months [70]. An animal study found that after one month of feeding, vitamin C complexed with food (it was not a simple mixture) induced a significant reduction of 77%, 66%, and 40% in plasma total cholesterol, LDL + VLDL, and triglycerides respectively and that USP ascorbic acid or bioflavonoids alone were ineffective (though isolated USP ascorbic acid did raise HDL); this same study also found that the natural food complex vitamin C strongly inhibited atherosclerosis [15]. Another animal study found that vitamin C complexed in food was 41% more effective than isolated ascorbic acid in decreasing galactiol when cataracts were present [45]. These studies strongly suggest that there may be multiple benefits associated with natural vitamin C that are not always apparent when only serum ascorbic acid levels are measured.

Vitamin D The history of synthetic vitamin D is a shocking one. Vitamin D is not an isolate, it "is a combination of substances" [25]; USP vitamin D forms are normally isolates. Foods contain complexed, not isolated, vitamin D. "The first vitamin isolated was a photoproduct from the irradiation of the fungal sterol ergosterol. This vitamin was known as D1...vitamin D obtained from irradiation of ergosterol had little antirachitic activity" [36]—in other words, the first synthetic vitamin D did not act the same as natural vitamin D.

"At the time of its identification, it was assumed that the vitamin D made in the skin during exposure to sunlight was vitamin D2", but it was later learned that human skin produced something called vitamin D3 [36]. It was first believed that provitamin D3 was directly converted to vitamin D3, but that was incorrect. The skin actually contains a substance commonly called provitamin D3; after exposure to

sunlight previtamin D3 is produced and it begins to isomerize into vitamin D2 in a process which is temperature dependent, with isomerized vitamin D3 being jettisoned from the plasma membrane into extracellular space. Vitamin D2 was used to fortify milk in the US and Canada for about forty years until it was learned that D3 was the substance which had better antirachitic activity, so D3 has been used for the past twenty years [36]. But vitamin D has many benefits which are unrelated to rickets: B and T lymphocytes have been shown to have receptors for vitamin D similar to those found in the intestines, vitamin D seems to affect phagocytosis, and may even have some antiproliferation effect for tumor cells [36]. It has not been proven that any single USP isolated form of vitamin D has all the benefits as natural occurring forms of vitamin D. (Also, since the vitamin D was not particularly stable, manufacturers used to put in 1.5 to 2 times as much of synthetic vitamin D as they claimed. This led to neonatal problems and hypercalcemia. [36].) New vitamin D analogues are still being developed: some which may have greater affects on calcium utilization [71], some even may be helpful for breast cancer [72]—but these really may be pharmacological, and not naturopathic, applications since these analogues are not food. In view of the historical errors in the supplementation with forms of vitamin D, it is reasonable to conclude that additional benefits of natural source vitamin D may be discovered, further distinguishing it from synthetic isolates.

Vitamin E "Synthetic and naturally derived alpha-tocopherol, and their ester forms, are commonly used in vitamin E supplements. These various forms give rise to isomer differences, ester differences and formulation differences that can affect their absorption and subsequent utilization" [30]. Natural vitamin E "as found in foods is [d]-alpha tocopherol, whereas chemical synthesis produces a mixture of eight epimers" [9].

An article in the Journal of the American Dietetics Association had a large headline which stated, "The natural and synthetic forms of vitamin E deliver equal health benefits to human beings" [73]. It was not a review article and it only compared isolated natural vitamin E to synthetic vitamin E for one application (it never checked vitamin E as complexed in food). Although it states, "Contrary to findings of studies conducted with animal subjects, human beings appear to be able to absorb the natural and synthetic forms as well", this conclusion was based upon one human study [74]. In it, subjects who received large amounts of natural or synthetic vitamin E had equal benefits in inhibiting the oxidation of low-density lipoprotein cholesterol (LDL-C). Although this study has value, it did not prove the premise of the article. Vitamin E has more beneficial effects on the body than simply inhibiting oxidation of LDL-C [75]. Three issues later in that same journal posted a smaller piece which stated, "The placenta, the fetal liver, or both are able to discriminate between natural (*RRR-*) and synthetic (*all-rac*) alpha-tocopherol; *RRR*-alpha-tocopherol is transported preferentially over *all-rac*-alpha-tocopherol...Maternal plasma and lipoproteins and cord plasma obtained at the time of delivery (after 5 to 9 days of supplementation) had higher concentrations of natural than synthetic tocopherol regardless of the vitamin E dose received", yet strangely it did not declare in large headlines that natural vitamin E was superior to synthetic vitamin E [76]. The study is consistent with the results of another human study which found that there was no difference in the absorption and secretion in chylomicrons of various tocopherols, but that there was a preferential enrichment of very low density lipoprotein with RRR-alpha-tocopherol [77]. These studies help demonstrate that although synthetic vitamins have some of the benefits of natural vitamins, they really do not replace all the benefits of natural ones.

It has been written that, "Vitamin E is the exception to the paradigm that synthetic and natural vitamins are the equivalent because their molecular structures are identical" [78] (vitamin E, of course, is not the only exception). "Synthetic vitamin E is produced by commercially coupling trimethylhydroquinone (TMHQ) with isophytol. This chemical reaction produces a difficult-to-separate mixture" [78]. A human study concluded that isolated "natural vitamin E has roughly twice the availability than synthetic vitamin E" [17] (synthetic vitamin E forms are analogues). A human study by Acuff (et al) found that isolated natural vitamin E was absorbed 3.42 time better than synthetic in cord blood during pregnancy [16]. An animal study suggests that isolated natural vitamin E has less tumorgenicity than isolated synthetic vitamin E [39]. A human urinary excretion study concluded that isolated natural vitamin E was 2.7 times better

absorbed than isolated synthetic vitamin E; this study suggests that it seems the body may want to rid itself of the synthetic as quickly as possible [46].

In foods, natural vitamin E is always found with lipids and other food substances [9]. Most so-called "natural vitamin E" is isolated from the food it was originally in and it is questionable to call it "natural" since it no longer really is a food. An animal liver study found that a natural vitamin E complexed in foods was 2.6 times more retained than isolated USP d-alpha tocopheryl acid succinate (which is the so-called 'natural form' once it is isolated from its food complex) [12]. Thus, it appears that isolated natural vitamin E is at least 2.7 [46] or 3.42 [16] times better than synthetic vitamin E and that natural vitamin E as complexed in food is 2.6 times better than isolated natural vitamin E [12].

Vitamin 'H', Biotin Biotin is a water-soluble vitamin once known as vitamin H. "Various biotin derivatives, analogues, and antagonists are known...Most of the biotin of natural products is protein bound" [79]. Crystalline USP biotin is not protein bound. Foods contain the "free, available form of biotin" which is usually protein bound [79]. Egg yolk, liver, and some vegetables are relatively rich in biotin [79]. Synthetic biotin is made from fumaric acid (trans-1,2-ethylene [50]) [49].

Vitamin K Many compounds have vitamin K activity, but at least one (K3, which has often been used in supplements) may be dangerous [31]. Vitamin K1 (phylloquinone) is how it exists in plants and "there are no reports of toxic effects of phylloquinone at 500 times its RDA" [31]. It is now recognized that menadione (the substance initially known as vitamin K3) "should not be employed any longer as a therapeutic form of vitamin K" (it can cause hemolytic anemia, hyperbilirubinemia, and kernicterus in infants) [31]. Dark green vegetables appear to be the primary food source of vitamin K [80]. There is another form of vitamin K that is found in the diet which is inadvertently formed during hydrogenation of oils called dihydro-vitamin K1; its relative bioavailability is still unknown [81]. However, since the consumption of hydrogenated oils appears to be dangerous [82], it does not seem that this synthetic form is as good to consume as the form naturally found in unprocessed food (phylloquinone). Believe it or not, some feel that this artificial type of vitamin K may be beneficial for human health [81].

Food Processing

"In the historic struggle for food, humans ate primarily whole foods or so-called natural foods, which underwent little processing...The nutrient content of food usually decreases when it is processed" [38]. Changes in the production and processing of food have resulted in multiple thousands of deaths in the U.S. [82-84]. A recent study found that tomatoes grown organically contain more natural vitamin C (and calcium) than "conventional grown" ones [85].

Food processing techniques can reduce the amount of every known essential vitamin [56]. The refining of rice reduced B-complex vitamins and initially led to deaths in Asia due to beriberi [4,19]. Even though synthetic USP vitamins are added to white rice, it does not contain the same nutrients as unpolished brown rice (nor does white flour contain the same nutrients as whole flour) [4,86]. The earlier refining of corn meal which reduced natural vitamin B-3 and amino acid levels was so devastating it produced around U.S. 7,000 deaths per year for several decades [84]. The refining of whole grains (including wheat, rice, and corn) has resulted in a dramatic reduction of their natural food complex nutrients [4,86]. The milling of wheat to white flour reduces the natural food complex vitamin and mineral content by 40-60% [86]. Various food processing techniques (including pasteurization of milk) reduce the available vitamin B6 in foods by 10-50% [86,87]. The recently introduced artificial fat *olestra* (also known as *Olean*) robs the body of oil soluble vitamins (vitamins A,D,E, and K) and carotenoid antioxidants (betacarotene, lutein, lycopene) [88-90]; the proposed "solution" is to add synthetic USP versions of the vitamins to *olestra* products [88-90]. Irradiation of meat and other foods "changes the characteristics of food" [27] and has been found to reduce levels of vitamins A, B1, B6, E, K, and other nutrient levels [6,27,91]. Unknown nutrients may also be affected from food processing. No one yet knows how the combinations of these more recent food processing techniques will effect human health [92], but it is not likely that they will promote optimal nutrition.

Reading the Label

There are essentially two types of vitamins sold in the U.S.; those found in a natural food complex and USP isolated ones. With the new supplement labeling law, it is in some cases even more difficult to determine if a vitamin is natural or synthetic. The fact that the label may in many places use the term 'natural' does not mean that any vitamins contained in it are natural. Labels that state the source is USP grade (or otherwise indicate they are USP vitamins) are synthetic/isolates. Labels that say the vitamins are in a food-base are almost always synthetic/isolates (essentially they are synthetics mixed with a small amount of food). Synthetic vitamins mixed with food are still synthetic, they are not the same as vitamins complexed in foods [28]. To verify this further, recently a small test was done where vitamin C complexed in food (in supplement form) was compared to isolated vitamin C mixed with food (in supplement form) with a device that measured oxydative reductive potential, this device confirmed the results of other studies (as well as clinical experience) that vitamin C complexed in food is better than synthetic vitamin C mixed with food.

If vitamins are from food, the label will almost always so state. Some chemical terms on labels will indicate that the true source of the vitamin is synthetic such as:

Vitamin Name	USP or Synthetic Name
Vitamin A	Acetate (palmitate is also usually a USP form [93])
Vitamin B1	Thiamin hydrochloride or Thiamin mononitrate
Vitamin B5	Pantothenic acid (pantothenate is what is in food)
Vitamin B6	Pyridoxine hydrochloride
Vitamin B9	Folic acid (folate is what is in food)
Vitamin B12	Cyanocobolamin (cobalamins are what is natural)
Vitamin C	Ascorbic acid (this is usually a USP)
Vitamin D	Most any single form other than the term vitamin D without a number
Vitamin E	Mixed tocopherols
Vitamin K	K3 or menadione (K1 or phylloquinone is what is in plants)

Generally speaking, if you find one of the USP types in the product, the rest of the vitamins are also synthetic/isolates. It seems that many companies want to obscure the fact that their vitamins are not the same as those naturally found in food complexes.

Understand that the primary reason that isolated USP vitamins were developed was cost [63]. A secondary reason probably was standardization (it is harder to standardize food), including stability [7,23,27]. Neither reason justifies placing USP isolates on the same health level as natural vitamins as found in foods. Synthetic USP isolates are not the same as natural vitamins complexed in food. Natural ones are superior and safer than the synthetics.

Synthetic vitamins are dangerous. Various studies indicate that folic acid, which is synthetic, seems to increase the risk of various forms of cancer [95]. A major study in the USA involving 37,882 women concluded that those that took multi-vitamin formulas died sooner than those that did not take them [96]. A major study involving 30,899 US adults found that those who took the usual synthetic vitamin and mineral formulas not only did not live longer than those who did not, they had greater risks of dying earlier because of taking non-food supplements—the study recommended nutrient containing foods [97]. The reality is that it is safe for humans to get their vitamins from real food or nutritional supplements that are only composed of 100% real foods.

And speaking of real foods, a paper that I co-wrote reported how food vitamins were much more effective in preventing the accumulation of advanced protein glycation end-products [98]. These glycation end-products are believed to be a major source of problems for those with Alzheimer's (they seem to cause it), Down syndrome (they seem to contribute to cognitive deterioration), and diabetes (they seem to cause some of the worst complications associated with that disorder).

Humans would not naturally eat many of the substances that are used in the manufacturing of synthetic vitamins. Humans are supposed to eat food [94] and receive their vitamins from foods—even the mainstream acknowledges this [4]. Most people can improve their health by eating health-building whole foods such as fruits and vegetables and whole grains (and consuming less refined carbohydrates) [4,99]. This alone can help increase the consumption of natural vitamins. Vitamin nutrition should come from food or from supplements which are as close to food as possible. Since no one knows everything there is to know about nutrition, it seems logical from both a historical and modern (and always from a naturopathic) perspective to consume vitamins in the forms found in natural food complexes and not to try to build health based on chemical isolates.

References

[1] Burr-Madsen, A. *Natural Therapies, Module 1.* Gateway College, Shingle Springs (CA), 1996.

[2] Barrett, S. and Herbert, V. *Fads, Frauds, and Quackery.* In Modern Nutrition in Health and Disease, 9th ed. William & Wilkins, Balt.,1999:1793-1800

[3] Whitney, E. N. and Rolfes, S. *Understanding Nutrition,* 7th ed. West Publishing, St. Paul, 1996.

[4] Whitney, E. N. and Hamilton, E. M. N. *Understanding Nutrition,* 4ed. West Publishing, New York, 1987.

[5] Herbert, V. and Das, K. C. *Folic Acid and Vitamin B12.* In Modern Nutrition in Health and Disease, 8th ed. Lea & Febiger, Phil.,1994:402-425.

[6] Ensminger, A. H., Ensminger, M. E., Konlade, J. E. and Robson, J. R. K. *Food & Nutrition Encyclopedia,* 2nd ed. CRC Press, New York, 1993.

[7] The United States Pharmacopeial Convention. *USAN and USP Dictionary of Drug Names.* Mack Printing, Easton (PA),1986.

[8] Olson, J. A. *Vitamin A, Retinoids, and Carotenoids.* In Modern Nutrition in Health and Disease, 8th ed. Lea & Febiger, Phil.,1994:287-307.

[9] Farrell, P. A. and Roberts, R. J. *Vitamin E.* In Modern Nutrition in Health and Disease, 8th ed. Lea & Febiger, Phil.,1994:326-358.

[10] Jacob, R. A. *Vitamin C.* In Modern Nutrition in Health and Disease, 9th ed. William & Wilkins, Balt.,1999:467-483.

[11] Schumann, K., et al. *Bioavailability of Oral Vitamins, Minerals, and Trace Minerals in Perspective.* Arzneimittelforschung, 1997; 47(4):369-380.

[12] Vinson, J., Bose, P., Lemoine, L. and Hsiao, K. H. *Bioavailability Studies.* In Nutrient Availability: Chemical and Biological Aspects. Royal Society of Chemistry, Cambridge (UK) 1989:125-127.

[13] Vinson, J. *Human Supplementation with Different Forms of Vitamin C.* University of Scranton, Scranton (PA).

[14] Vinson, J. A. and Bose, P. *Comparative Bioavailability of Humans to Ascorbic Acid Alone or in a Citrus Extract.* Am J Clin Nutr, 1988;48:601-406.

[15] Vinson, J. A, Hu, S. and Jung, S. *A Citrus Extract Plus Ascorbic Acid Decreases Lipids, Lipid Peroxides, Lipoprotein Oxidative Susceptibility, and Atherosclerosis in Hypercholesterolemic Hamsters.* J Agric Food Chem, 1998; 46:1453-1469.

[16] Acuff, R. V., Dunworth, R. G., Webb, L. W. and Lane, J. R. *Transport of Deuterium-Labeled Tocopherols During Pregnancy.* Am J Clin Nutr, 1998; 67:459-464.

[17] Burton, G. W., et al. *Human Plasma and Tissue Alpha-Tocopherol Concentrations in Response to Supplementation with Deuterated Natural and Synthetic Vitamin E.* Am J Clin Nutr, 1998; 67(4):669-684.

[18] Ross, A. C. *Vitamin A and Retinoids.* In Modern Nutrition in Health and Disease, 9th ed. William & Wilkins, Balt.,1999:305-327.

[19] Tanphaichitr, V. *Thiamin.* In Modern Nutrition in Health and Disease, 8th ed. Lea & Febiger, Phil.,1994:359-365.

[20] Swenseid, M. E., Jacob, R. A. *Niacin.* In Modern Nutrition in Health and Disease, 8th ed. Lea and Febiger, Phil.,1994:376-382.

[21] Leklem, J. E. *Vitamin B6.* In Modern Nutrition in Health and Disease, 8th ed. Lea & Febiger, Phil.,1994:383-394.

[22] Plesofsky-Vig, N. *Pantothenic acid and Coenzyme A.* In Modern Nutrition in Health and Disease, 8th ed. Lea & Febiger, Phil.,1994:395-401.

[23] Herbert, V. *Folic Acid* In Modern Nutrition in Health and Disease, 9th ed. Williams & Wilkins, Balt.,1999:433-446.

[24] Vinson, J. *Human Supplementation with Antioxidants.* Med Sci Res, 1992; 20:145-146.

[25] Holick, M. F. *Vitamin D.* In Modern Nutrition in Health and Disease, 8th ed. Lea & Febiger, Phil.,1994:308-325.

[26] Jenkins, D. J. A., Wolever, T. M. S. and Jenkins, A. L. *Diet Factors Affecting Nutrient Absorption and Metabolism.* In Modern Nutrition in Health and Disease, 8th ed. Lea & Febiger, Phil.,1994:583-602.

[27] Macrae, R., Robson, R. K. and Sadler, M. J. *Encyclopedia of Food Science and Nutrition.* Academic Press, New York, 1993.

[28] Turner, G. *Spectral Data Services.* Tests conducted Feb. 1993.

[29] McCormick, D. B. *Riboflavin.* In Modern Nutrition in Health and Disease, 8th ed. Lea & Febiger, Phil.,1994:366-375.

[30] Schelling, G. T, Roeder, R. A, Garber, M. J. and Pumfrey, W. M. *Bioavailability and Interaction of Vitamin A and Vitamin E in Ruminants.* J Nutr,1995;125(6):1799S-1803S

[31] Olson, R. E. *Vitamin K.* In Modern Nutrition in Health and Disease, 8th ed. Lea & Febiger, Phil.,1994:342-358.

[32] Kasai, T., Inoue, K., Komatsubara, H., Tsujimura, M. *Synthesis and Antiscorbutic Activity of Vitamin C analogue: L-threo-hex-2-enaro-1,4-lactone Ethyl Ester in the Guinea Pig.* Int J Vitamin Nutr Res,1993; 63(3):208-211.

[33] Ishida, A., Kanefusa, H., Fujita, H. and Toraya, T. *Microbiological Activities of Nucleotide Loop-Modified Analogues of Vitamin B12.* Arch Microbiol,1994; 161(4):293-299.

[34] Nakano, H., McMahon, L. G. and Gregory J. F. *Pyridoxine-5'-Beta-Glucoside Exhibits Incomplete Bioavailability as a Source of Vitamin B-6 and Partially Inhibits the Utilization of Co-Ingested Pyridoxine in Humans.* J Nutr,1997; 127(8):1508-1513.

[35] Tandler, B., Krhenbul, S. and Brassc E. P. *Unusual Mitochondria in the Hepatocytes of Rats Treated with a Vitamin B12 Analogue.* Anat Rec,1991; 231(1):1-6.

[36] Holick MF. *Vitamin D.* In Modern Nutrition in Health and Disease, 9th ed. William & Wilkins, Balt.,1999:329-345.

[37] Thiel, R. *Vitamins are Naturally Found in Food Complexes.* ANMA Monitor, 1999; 3(1):5-9.

[38] Bauernfeind, J. C. *Nutrification of Foods.* In Modern Nutrition in Health and Disease, 8th ed. Lea & Febiger, Phil.,1994:1579-1592.

[39] Nitta, Y., et al. *Induction of Transplantable Tumors by Repeated Injections of Natural and Synthetic Vitamin E in Mice and Rats.* Jpn J Cancer Res, 1991; 82(5):511-517.

[40] Ha, S. W. *Rabbit Study Comparing Yeast and Isolated B Vitamins* (as described in Murray RP. Natural vs. Synthetic. Mark R. Anderson, 1995:A3). Ann Rev Physiol, 1941; 3:259-282.

[41] Mack, A. *All Vitamin Supplements Not Created Equal.* Med Trib, May 21, 1998:17.

[42] Vinson, J. A. and Bose, P. *Bioavailability of Synthetic Ascorbic Acid and a Citrus Extract.* Ann New York Academy of Sciences, Vol 498. 525:526, July 1987.

[43] Vinson, J. A., et al. *In Vitro and In Vivo Reduction of Erythrocyte Sorbitol by Ascorbic Acid.* Diabetes, 1989;38:1036-1041.

[44] Vinson, J. A. and Howard, T. B. *Inhibition of Protein Glycation and Advanced Glycation End Products by Ascorbic Acid and Other Vitamins and Nutrients.* Nutr Bioch, 1996;7:659-663.

[45] Vinson, J. A., Courey, J. M. and Maro, N. P. *Comparison of Two Forms of Vitamin C on Galactose Cataracts.* In Nutrition Research, Vol 12. Pergamon Press, 1992:915-922.

[46] Traber, M. G., Elsner, A. and Brigelius-Flohe, R. *Synthetic as Compared with Natural Vitamin E is Preferentially Excreted as Alpha-CEHC in Human Urine: Studies Using Deuterated Alpha-Tocopherol Acetates.* FEBS Letters, 1998;437:145-148.

[47] Fallon, M.B. and Boyer, J. L. *Hepatic Toxicity of Vitamin A and Synthetic Retinoids.* J Gastro Hepatol, 1990; 5(3):334-342.

[48] Rothman, K., et al. *Teratogenicity of High Vitamin A Intake.* NEJM, 1995; 333(21):1369-1373.

[49] Hui, J. H. *Encyclopedia of Food Science and Technology.* John Wiley, New York, 1992.

[50] Haynes, W. *Chemical Trade Names and Commercial Synonyms,* 2nd ed. Van Nostrand Co., New York, 1955.

[51] Tanphaichitr, V. *Thiamin.* In Modern Nutrition in Health and Disease, 9th ed. William & Wilkins, Balt.,1999:381-389.

[52] Kimura, M., Itokawa, Y. and Fujiwara, M. *Cooking Losses of Thiamin in Food and Its Nutritional Significance.* J Nutr Sci Vitaminol, 1990; 36(S1):S17:S24.

[53] McCormick, D. B., *Riboflavin.* In Modern Nutrition in Health and Disease, 9th ed. William & Wilkins, Balt.,1999:391-399.

[54] Kanno, C., Kanehara, N., Shirafuji, K., Tanji, R. and Imai, T. *Binding Form of Vitamin B2 in Bovine Milk: Its Concentrations, Distribution, and Binding Linkages.* J Nutr Sci Vitaminol, 1991; 37(1):15-27.

[55] Cervantes-Lauren, D., McElvaney, N. G. and Moss, J. *Niacin.* In Modern Nutrition in Health and Disease, 9th ed. Williams & Wilkins, Balt.,1999:401-411.

[56] Williams, A. W. and Erdman, J. W. *Food Processing: Nutrition, Safety, and Quality Balances.* In Modern Nutrition in Health and Disease, 9th ed. William & Wilkins, Balt.,1999:1813-1821.

[57] Tenney, L. *Health Handbook.* Woodland Books, Provo (UT), 1987.

[58] Plesofsky-Vig, N. *Pantothenic Acid.* In Modern Nutrition in Health and Disease, 9th ed. William & Wilkins, Balt.,1999:423-432.

[59] Leklem, J. E. *Vitamin B6.* In Modern Nutrition in Health and Disease, 9th ed. William & Wilkins, Balt.,1999:413-421.

[60] Crane, N. T., et al. *Evaluating Food Fortification Options: General Principles Revisited with Folic Acid.* Am J Public Health, 1995; 85(5):660-666.

[61] Tucker, K. L., Mahnken, B., Wilson, P. W., Jaques, P. and Selhub, J. *Folic Acid Fortification. Potential Benefits and Risks for the Elderly Population.* JAMA, 1997; 276(23):1879-1885.

[62] Maurer, K. *Group Urges Increased Folic Acid Fortification.* Family Practice News, October 15, 1996:11.

[63] Mervyn, L. *The B Vitamins.* Thorsons, Wellingborough (UK), 1981.

[64] Weir, D. G. and Scott, J. M. *Vitamin B12 "Cobalamin."* In Modern Nutrition in Health and Disease, 9th ed. William & Wilkins, Balt.,1999:447-458.

[65] Vanderslice, J. T. and Higgs, D. J. *Vitamin C Content of Foods: Sample Variability.* Am J Clin Nutr, 1991; 54(Supp 6):1323S-1327S.

[66] Levine, M., et al. *Vitamin C.* In Present Knowledge in Nutrition, 7th ed. ILSI Press, Washington, 1996:146-159.

[67] Mangels, A. R., et al. *The Bioavailability to Humans of Ascorbic Acid from Oranges, Orange Juice and Cooked Broccoli is Similar to that of Synthetic Ascorbic Acid.* J Nutr, 1993;123(6):1054-1061.

[68] Johnson, C. and Luo, B. *Comparison of the Absorption and Excretion of Three Commercially Available Sources of Vitamin C.* J Am Diet Assoc, 1994;94:779-781.

[69] Weisburger, J. H. *Vitamin C and Disease Prevention.* J Am Coll Nutr, 1995;14(2):109-111.

[70] Davie, S. J., Gould B. J. and Yudkin, J. S. *Effect of Vitamin C on Glycation of Proteins.* Diabetes, 1992;41:161-173.

[71] Miyamoto, K., Murayama, E., Ochi, K., Watanabe H. and Kubodera, N. *Synthetic Studies of Vitamin D Analogues. XIV. Synthesis and Calcium Regulating Activity of Vitamin D3 Analogues Bearing a Hydroxlkoxy Group at the 2 Beta-Position.* Chem Pharm Bull, 1993; 41(6):1111-1113.

[72] Fioravanti, L., Miodini, P., Cappelletti, V. and DiFronzo, G. *Synthetic Analogs of Vitamin D3 have Inhibitory Effects on Breast Cancer CellLines.* Anticancer Res, 1998; 18:1703-1708.

[73] *The Natural and Synthetic Forms of Vitamin E Deliver Equal Health Benefits to Human Beings.* J Am Diet Assoc, 1998; 98(5):522.

[74] Devaraj, S., Adams-Huet, B., Fuller, C. J. and Jialal, I. *Dose-Response Comparison of RRR-Alpha-Tocopherol and All-Racemic Alpha Tocopherol on LDL Oxidation.* Arterioscler Thromb Vasc Biol, 1997; 17:2273-2279.

[75] Traber, M. G. *Vitamin E.* In Modern Nutrition in Health and Disease, 9th ed. William & Wilkins, Balt.,1999:347-362.

[76] *Transport of Alpha-Tocopherol During Pregnancy.* J Am Diet Assoc, 1998; 98(8):918.

[77] Traber, M. G., et al. *Discrimination Between Forms of Vitamin E by Humans With and Without Genetic Abnormalities of Lipoprotein Metabolism.* J Lipid Res, 1992; 33:1171-1182

[78] *An Overview of Vitamin E Efficacy.* VERIS Research Information Service, November 1998.

[79] Dakshinamurti, K. *Biotin.* In Modern Nutrition in Health and Disease, 8th ed. Lea & Febiger, Phil. 1994:426-431.

[80] Booth, S. L., Pennington, J. A. and Sadowski, J. A. *Food Sources and Dietary Intakes of Vitamin K-1 (Phylloquinone) in the American Diet: Data from the FDA Total Diet Study.* J Am Diet Assoc, 1996; 96(2):149-154.

[81] Booth, S. L., Pennington, J. A. and Sadowski, J. A. *Dihydro-vitamin K1: Primary Food Sources and Estimated Dietary Intakes in the American Diet.* Lipids, 1996; 31:715-720.

[82] Aschero, A. and Willett, W. C. *Health Affects of Trans Fatty Acids.* Am J Clin Nutr, 1997; 66:1006S-1010S.

[83] Turnland, J. R. *Bioavailability of Dietary Minerals to Humans: The Stable Isotope Approach.* Crit Rev Food Sci Nutr,1991; 30(4);387-396.

[84] Bollet, A. J. *Politics and Pellagra: The Epidemic of Pellagra in the U.S. in the Early Twentieth Century.* Yale J Biol Med, 1992; 65(3):211-221.

[85] *Organic Tomatoes, Vitamin C, and Calcium.* Nutr Week, 1998; 28(24):7.

[86] Erdman, J. W. and Poneros-Schneir, A. G. *Factors Affecting the Nutritive Value in Processed Foods.* In Modern Nutrition in Health and Disease, 8th ed. Lea & Febiger, Phil.,1994:1569-1578.

[87] Schroeder, H. A. *The Trace Elements and Man.* Devin-Adair, New Greenwich (CT), 1973.

[88] Leek, R. *Olestra? Just say no!* J ANMA AANC, 1996; 1(1):21.

[89] Daher, G. C., Cooper, D. A. and Peters, J. C. *Physical or Temporal Separation of Olestra and Vitamins A, E, and D Intake Decreases the Effect of Olestra on the Status of the Vitamins in the Pig.* J Nutr, 1997; 127(8):1566S-1572S.

[90] Schlagheck, T. G., et al. *Olestra's Effect on Vitamins D and E in Humans can be Offset by Increasing Dietary Levels of These Vitamins.* J Nutr, 1997; 127(8):1666S-1685S.

[91] Andrews, J. S., et al. *Food Preservation Using Ionizing Radiation.* Rev Environ Contam Toxicol, 1998; 154(1):1-53.

[92] Ghebremeskel, K. and Crawford, M. A. *Nutrition and Health in Relation to Food Production and Processing.* Nutr Health, 1994; 9(4):237-253.

[93] DeCava, J. A. *The Real Truth about Vitamins & Antioxidants.* A Printery, Centerfield (MA), 1997.

[94] Cronquist, A. *Plantae.* In Synopsis and Classification of Living Organisms, Vol 1. McGraw-Hill, NY, 1982:57.

[95] Thiel R. *Folic Acid is Hazardous to Your Health. What About Food Folate? The Original Internist,* 17(2) June 2010, 88-90

[96] Mursu J., Robien K., Harnack L.J., Park K., Jacobs D.R. Jr. *Dietary Supplements and Mortality Rate in Older Women: The Iowa Women's Health Study.* Arch Intern Med. 2011 Oct 10;171(18):1625-33

[97] Chen F, et al. Association Among Dietary Supplement Use, Nutrient Intake, and Mortality Among U.S. Adults: A Cohort Study. Annals of Internal Medicine: Apr 2019:e

[98] Thiel R., Fowkes S.W. *Can Cognitive Deterioration Associated with Down Syndrome be Reduced?* Medical Hypotheses, 2005; 64(3):524-532

[99] Kennedy, E. *The 1995 USDA/HHS Dietary Guidelines - An Overview.* USDA, Washington, D.C.,1995.

23

Mineral Salts are Food for Plants, Not Humans

When it comes to nutrition, plants and humans differ: "a typical plant makes its own food from raw materials... A typical animal eats its food" [1]. For plants, these "raw materials" include soil-based mineral salts [2]. For humans, the food is the plant.

Plants, with the aid of enzymes and soil-based microorganisms (which sometimes are depleted in the soil through synthetic fertilizers, herbicides, and pesticides [3,4]), can take in mineral salts (from soil) which they have an affinity for through their roots or hyphae [4]. After various metabolic processes, when these minerals no longer exist as mineral salts, they become complexed with various carbohydrates, lipids, and proteins present in the plant, as part of the living organism [5]. Thus for nutrition, humans eat plants (and/or animals which eat plants), whereas plants can obtain their nutrients from the soil [4]. This process is commonly referred to as the "food chain" [5].

Minerals are found as positively-charged ions in the body [6-8] often with some peptide [8,9]. When humans eat plants (or animals) they are consuming minerals in or near their ionic form (with some peptides). With the exception of sodium chloride (common table salt), humans do not normally consume minerals in the chemical forms known

as mineral salts (when they do, it is considered to be a disorder called 'geophagia' or 'pica' [10,11]). Unfortunately most mineral supplements contain minerals in the form referred to as 'mineral salts'. Even though mineral salts are often called "natural", they are rocks (e.g. calcium carbonate exists as the rock commonly known as limestone) or they are chemically produced in accordance with the *United States Pharmacopoeia* (USP). Mineral salts are natural food for plants, they are not a natural food for humans—humans do not have roots or hyphae!

Bioavailability is Not the Same

It is well known among nutrition researchers that most essential minerals are not well absorbed (some are less than 1%) [12]. "Bioavailability of orally administered vitamins, minerals, and trace elements is subject to a complex set of influences...In nutrition science the term 'bioavailability' encompasses the sum of impacts that may reduce or foster the metabolic utilization of a nutrient" [13]. University studies (which may or may not conform to peer-review standards) show that the bioavailability of food complex minerals are greater than that of isolated inorganic mineral salts or mineral

Food Complex Mineral	Compared to Mineral Salt?
Calcium	8.79 times more absorbed into blood [16]
Chromium	10-25 times more bioavailable [26]
Copper	1.85 times more retained in the liver [22]
Germanium	5.30 times more retained in the liver [14]
Iron	1.77 times more absorbed into blood [22]
Magnesium	2.20 times more absorbed into blood [23]
Manganese	1.63 times more retained in the liver [15,22]
Molybdenum	1.63 times more retained in the liver [15,22]
Selenium	17.60 times greater anti-oxidant effect [25]
Zinc	6.46 times more absorbed into blood [22]

chelates [e.g. 14-25]. These studies have concluded that natural food complex nutrients may be <u>better</u> absorbed, utilized, and/or retained than mineral salts.

It should be noted that humans can, and do, utilize minerals from USP mineral salts, but not as effectively as from foods [14-26]. However, Dr. Bernard Jensen, one of the earliest modern activists of food-based nutrition, has stated, "When we take out from foods some certain salt, we are likely to alter the chemicals in those foods. When extracted from food, that certain chemical salt is extracted, may even become a poison. Potash by itself is a poison, whether it comes from a food or from the drugstore. This is also the case with phosphorus. You thereby overtax your system, and your functions must work harder, in order to throw off those inorganic salts or poisons introduced... The chemical elements that build our body must be in biochemical, life-producing form. They must come to us as food, magnetically, electrically alive, grown from the dust of the earth... When we are lacking any element at all, we are lacking more than one element. There is no one who ever lacked just one element. We don't have a food that contains only one element, such as a carrot entirely of calcium or sprouts totally made of silicon" [27].

Isolated mineral salts are not normally found in foods. To determine what type of mineral is in a supplement, try to read the label. Most mineral salts are listed on the label with a two word description, while most food complex minerals list the mineral name and the source. For example, if next to the word 'calcium' the label says citrate or carbonate (such as calcium citrate or calcium carbonate), it is clear that this is a mineral salt. If on the other hand, next to the word 'calcium' it says it is in a food complex (or otherwise states the food source) then it is usually from a food (it is of interest to note that calcium citrate is actually the rock known as limestone processed with lactic and citric acids—it is not a product of citrus fruits).

Information by Individual Mineral

Some differences between food complexed minerals and mineral salts have been documented by published research and are shown by individual mineral:

Boron "Boron complexes with organic compounds containing hydroxyl groups" [8], which is how it is found in foods. Boron affects macromineral and steriodal hormone metabolism; without sufficient boron bone composition, strength, and structure weaken [8].

Calcium "The amount of calcium absorbed depends on its interaction with other dietary constituents...The absorbability of calcium is mainly determined by the presence of other food constituents" [28]. This is one of the reasons why isolated calcium mineral salts (such as calcium carbonate) are not absorbed as well as calcium found in natural food complexes [28,29]. "Calcium carbonate, an antacid, counteracts not only the absorption of calcium, but also the absorption of iron" [10] (though its calcium absorption appears to be better with food [29]). At least one researcher has concluded that commonly used mineral salts such as calcium lactate and calcium gluconate primarily succeed in creating high blood calcium levels (hypercalcemia) instead of alleviating symptoms of low tissue calcium [30]. "Calcium has a structural role in bones and teeth" as well as in some enzymes involved with blood clotting [28]. Calcium can affect mood and blood pressure [7,16,28]. A human study found that food complex calcium was 8.79 times more bioavailable than calcium carbonate (which is the most common form found in supplements) and 2.97 times more than calcium gluconate (which is calcium carbonate processed with gluconic acid) [16]. This same study found that the placebo group and calcium gluconate group had no significant change in diastolic blood pressure, but those who took food complex calcium had a 8.2% drop by the end of the seven-week study [16]. Some researchers have concluded that natural food complex calcium "produced no undesirable side effects and was the most suitable form of calcium for long-term supplementation" [16].

Chromium, GTF "The biologically active form of chromium, sometimes called glucose tolerance factor or GTF, has been proposed to be a complex of chromium, nicotinic acid, and possibly the amino acids glycine, cysteine, and glutamic acid. Many attempts have been made to isolate or synthesize the glucose tolerance factor; none have been successful" [31]. Chromium is not naturally found in the body in the commonly supplemented forms such as chromium picolinate or chromium chelate.

"Chromium is generally accepted as an essential nutrient that potentiates insulin action, and thus influences carbohydrate, lipid, and protein metabolism" [31]. Research suggests that there is much less likelihood of toxicity from natural food complex chromium than from inorganic chromium [32]. Only 1% or less of inorganic chromium is absorbed vs.10-25% of chromium GTF [26]. One small study found that natural food complex chromium GTF reduced blood glucose levels by 16.8% versus 6.0% for inorganic chromium [17], thus it was 2.80 times more effective. One study found that food complex chromium benefited certain diabetics by improving blood glucose control, lowering serum lipids, and decreasing the risk of coronary heart disease [18].

Copper In the human body, in addition to various plasma-bound coppers, "at least one copper peptide complex" has been isolated [9]. Copper is not naturally found in the body in the form of copper gluconate or copper sulfate. "Anemia, neutropenia, and osteoporosis are observed with copper deficiency"; copper is involved in connective tissue, iron metabolism, the central nervous system, melanin pigment, thermal regulation, cholesterol metabolism, immune function, and cardiac function [9]. A human study found that food complex copper was 1.44 times more absorbed into the blood than copper sulfate and 1.43 times more than copper gluconate [22]. Animal studies showed similar results, plus concluded that food complex copper was retained in the liver 1.85 times more than copper gluconate and 1.42 times more than copper sulfate [22].

Germanium Germanium is an ultra trace mineral which affects mineral composition of bone and the liver [33]. Organic germanium complexes have been shown to inhibit tumor formation in animals, yet inorganic germanium mineral salts can be toxic [33]. Food complex germanium was found to be retained 5.30 times more in the liver than germanium sesquioxide and 2.88 times more than germanium oxide [14]. High intakes of inorganic germanium mineral salts can cause kidney damage [33].

Iodine Most of the iodine in the body exists in the form of iodine-containing amino acids [34]. Iodine is needed by the thyroid gland to produce thyroid hormones which influence most of the body's metabolic processes [34]. Kelp is an excellent food source of iodine [34].

Iron Most researchers acknowledge that organic iron is better absorbed than inorganic iron [35]. The body has different mechanisms for the absorption of iron depending upon its form [36]. Iron in foods is found in an organic form. Iron is required for growth and hemoglobin formation; inadequate amounts can lead to "weakness, fatigue, pallor, dyspnea on exertion, palpitation, and a sense of being overly tired" [36]. An animal study found that food complex iron was absorbed into the blood 1.01 times more than ferrous sulfate and 1.77 times more than amino acid chelated iron and was retained in the liver 1.21 times more than ferrous sulfate and 1.68 times more than amino acid chelated iron [15,22].

Magnesium "The percentage of absorption of ingested magnesium is influenced by its dietary concentration and by the presence of inhibiting or promoting dietary components [6]. There are no promoting dietary components in inorganic isolated magnesium salts. "Magnesium is involved in many enzymatic steps in which components of food are metabolized and new products are formed"; it is involved in over 300 such reactions [6]. Clinical deficiency of magnesium can result in "depressed tendon reflexes, muscle fasciculations, tremor, muscle spasm, personality changes, anorexia, nausea, and vomiting" [6]. A human study found that food complex magnesium was 2.20 times more absorbed into blood than magnesium oxide and 1.60 times more than amino acid chelated magnesium [23].

Manganese In the body, absorbed manganese complexes with various peptides [8]. Manganese is predominantly found in foods in a manganese peptide complex (such as Mn superoxide-dismutase). It is not found in the body in forms like manganese sulfate. Manganese deficiency can cause "impaired growth, skeletal abnormalities, disturbed or depressed reproductive function, ataxia of the newborn, and defects in lipid and carbohydrate metabolism" [8]. It can also affect skin, hair, nails, and problems with calcium metabolism [8]. An animal study found that natural food complex manganese was absorbed 1.56 times more into the blood and was retained 1.63 times more in the liver than manganese sulfate [15,22].

Molybdenum Molybdenum...in foods...is readily absorbed" [8]. "Molybdenum functions as an enzyme cofactor," thus "detoxifies various pyrimidines, purines, pteridines, and related compounds"

[8]; it may also affect growth and reproduction [8]. An animal study found that food complex molybdenum was absorbed 6.28 times more into the blood and was retained 16.49 times more in the liver than ammonium molybdate and 10.27 times more than molybdenum amino acid chelate [22].

Potassium Potassium is found in plants [10]. Potassium is the leading intracellular electrolyte and is necessary for electrolyte balance, stimulating aldersterone for the adrenal glands, and blood pressure regulation [10]. Dr. Bernard Jensen seems to believe potassium is only safe in its natural food complex form [27].

Selenium "The predominant form of selenium in animal tissues is selenocysteine" [37]. That is how it is predominantly found in certain foods. One study found that diets naturally high in selenium (daily consumption as high as 724mcg) produced no signs or symptoms of selenium overexposure while another found that exceedingly high consumption of selenium salts could induce selenium poisoning [37]. Interestingly, an animal study concluded that food complex selenium was 3 times less toxic than sodium selenite [38]. Selenium seems to support thyroid hormone production, function as part of many enzymes, and have antioxidant effects [37]. Larry Clark, Ph.D. and others have found that selenium in yeast appears to reduce risk of certain cancers [39]. Julian Whitaker, M.D. reports, "The best absorbed form of selenium, and the one used by Dr. Clark's research, is high-selenium yeast" [39]. Research suggests that food complex selenium is 2.26 times more retained in the liver and 1.22 times more absorbed in the blood than sodium selenite [15,24]. An *in vitro* study found that natural food complex selenium had 17.6 times the antioxidant effect than did selenomethionine [25]. One study found that natural food complex selenium was 123.01 times more effective than sodium selenite in preventing nonenzymatic glycation in diabetics [19].

Silicon "In animals, silicon is found both free and bound" [33]. Silicon absorption is quite dependent upon the form [33]. Silicon is involved in bone calcification and connective tissue formation [33]. It is also needed for healthy hair and skin [7]. Silicon is found in foods in an organic form.

Trace Minerals Trace minerals, including "ultra trace minerals" are necessary for the proper functioning of human health [2,8,33]. There are many in the human body, some of which are known to be essential and others of which their "essentialness" is under investigation [2,8]. Sea vegetables and certain yeasts are a good source of trace minerals [10,15,34,40]. It is also of interest to note that some researchers have concluded that, "yeast trace elements and natural vitamins are more slowly absorbed in animals and man; are more bioavailable; and therefore are the preferred form for supplementation" [15,40].

Vanadium "Vanadate forms compounds with other biological substances" [8]. "Vanadium has been postulated to play a role in the regulation of (NaK)-ATPase, phosphoryl transferase enzymes, adenylate cyclase, and protein kinases; as an enzyme cofactor in the form of vandyl. and in hormone, glucose, lipid, and tooth metabolism" [8]. Vanadium in foods is found in an organic form.

Zinc Most researchers acknowledge that organic zinc is better absorbed than inorganic zinc [35]. Zinc itself is generally found in the human body in ionic form [11,35]; it is often bound with albumin [11,41] or alpha2-macroglobulin [41] or exists as part of one of the many zinc metalloenzymes [11,41]. Zinc is predominantly found in foods as zinc peptide complex (such as that complexed with superoxide dismutase). Zinc is not naturally found in the body as zinc gluconate, zinc orotate, zinc sulfate, nor zinc picolinate. In humans "zinc deficiency does not exist without deficiency of other nutrients" [11]. Zinc deficiency in humans can cause alopecia, impotence, skin problems, immune deficiencies, night blindness, impaired taste, delayed wound healing, impaired appetite, photophobia, difficulty in dark adaptation, growth retardation, and male infertility [41]. Studies indicate that natural food complex zinc appears to be 1.72-1.75 times more absorbed in the blood than zinc sulfate (1.71 times more than zinc chelate; 6.46 times more than zinc gluconate; 3.11 times more than zinc orotate) and 1.75-1.87 times more retained in the liver than zinc sulfate (1.45 times more than zinc amino acid chelate; 3.68 times more than zinc gluconate; 1.50 times more than zinc orotate) [15,20,22].

Food and Food Processing

"In the historic struggle for food, humans ate primarily whole foods or so-called natural foods, which underwent little processing...The nutrient content of food usually decreases when it is processed" [42]. "Intensive animal rearing, manipulation of crop production and food processing have altered the qualitative and quantitative balance of nutrients of food consumed by Western society. This change, to which the physiology and biochemistry of man may not be presently adapted to, is thought to be responsible for the chronic diseases that are rampant in the Industrialized Western Countries" [43]. Some reports suggest that simply taking a synthetic multi-vitamin/mineral formula does not change this [44,45].

Dr. Burr-Madsen has written:

Nutrition—in its most basic sense the process by which the organism finds, consumes, liberates, absorbs, and utilizes the nutrients it must have to live. Although food and therefore nutrients are seemingly plentiful, because of modern use of chemical herbicides and pesticides as well as poor air quality and bad water, the nutrients we buy in the market are very inferior. Human bodies require nutrition found in the form of plants, meat, milk, eggs and water, but all animals get their food directly or indirectly from plants, and all plants get their food from the soil. Therefore mineral deficient soil may be one of the greatest original sources of disease in the world today.

Real soil—We cannot appreciate enough the importance of our relationship with the land, with soil. This is particularly so in this era of artificial chemicals, artificial foods, and the abundance of artificial materials on which we have come to depend. This system cannot replace real soil and the living food crops it produces. Our dependence on artificial, man-made products interferes with our relationship with the soil and the natural world in general. Because of this, nutritional supplementation is necessary.

Soil Condition

After genetics and weather, the condition of the soil is the most important factor in the nutrient content of any plant food and, indirectly, of animal foods. The soils of the world have suffered, and continue to suffer, at the hands of farming. The present food production system, while correcting some abuses of the past, inflicts on the soil a variety of new and old insults that diminish its nutrient value. Because of intensive farming, poor crop management, erosion, commercial fertilization, the use of pesticides, and other problematic factors, much of the soil in which our crops are now raised has been depleted, particularly of essential minerals.

The Human Food Chain

The human food chain includes animals, animal products and plants, which depend directly or indirectly on the soil. Plants draw their nutrients and general health from a complex of inorganic and organic factors. Inorganic substances include oxygen and carbon, nitrogen, phosphorus, and potassium, along with iron, calcium, and an array of other minerals. The chief organic factors range from decaying plant material and animal wastes to earthworms and an amazing variety of microscopic organisms including bacteria, fungi, algae, and protozoa (Hall 1976: 134). All of these elements are important to the health and nutrient value of the crop—and of the animals that feed on it.

Healthy Soil

Healthy soil is America's greatest natural resource. But few realize that the current state of wide spread soil erosion in North America threatens our way of life. It may be hard to believe, but only a few inches of topsoil stand between you, me, and starvation. We cannot appreciate enough the importance of our relationship with the land, with soil. What is popularly called topsoil is the rich, nutrient-laden cover of the Earth's crust from which food crops draw their sustenance. Underneath the topsoil there may be clay, shale, or rock —substances that do not support food crops. It is only in the precious shallow topsoil that plants are seeded, germinated, sprouted, nurtured, and grown. These plants serve as food for animals on the lowest ends of the food chain. Animals that eat these plants supply food to animals on the highest ends of the food chain. Attention is important because topsoil is easily exhausted from lack of care. The best farmers replenish the soil as it is farmed. Unfortunately, this practice has become an exception to the rule, this is particularly so today.

Depleted Soil

When the soil becomes depleted, the plants often show symptoms of poor nutrition, much like human deficiency diseases. For example, a general yellow or pale green color (chlorosis) indicates a lack of sulfur and nitrogen and a white or pale-yellow color iron deficiency. Some of these deficiencies are apparent enough to hurt the marketability of the crop. Most, however, are not visible to the shopper's or even the farmer's eye, and the crop is shipped to market deficient as it is. The toll that fertilization and pesticides take on the soil is wide-reaching, ultimately including the kind of soil erosion that is now plaguing the Midwest. The most direct and immediate loss are the mineral and vitamin deficiencies in the soil that are passed up the food chain to humans (it is a domino effect). [46]

(Dr. Burr-Matson cites the Kelly report as the source of this information.)

Commercial Food Processing

Commercial food processing definitely reduces the nutrient content of food [47] and can be dangerous to human health [48]. The refining of whole grains (including wheat, rice, and corn) has resulted in a dramatic reduction of their natural food complex nutrition [10,47]; specifically the milling of wheat to white flour reduces the natural food complex vitamin and mineral content by 40-60% [47]. Food refining appears to reduce trace minerals such as manganese, zinc, and chromium [2] and various macrominerals (such as magnesium) as well [10,47]. The treatment of canned or frozen vegetables with ethylenediaminetetraacetic acid (EDTA) can strip much of the zinc from foods [11]. The high incidences of disorders of calcium metabolism [28] suggest that the forms of calcium many are consuming simply do not agree with the body (and sometimes result in calcium loss [10]).

Organically-grown produce appears to contain higher levels of some essential minerals than does conventionally (non-organically) grown produce [49,50] and appears to contain lower levels of toxic heavy metals [51]. Even if modern food practices did not affect nutrition (which they do), all minerals that humans need for optimal health do not exist uniformly in soils. "Soils in many areas of the world are deficient in certain minerals; this can result in low concentrations of major or trace minerals in drinking water, plant crops, and even tissues of farm animals, thus contributing to marginal or deficient dietary intakes of humans [42]. From a geological perspective, a few examples include iodine, molybdenum, cobalt, selenium, and boron [2,34,42]. Although humans need at least twenty minerals (over sixty have been found in the body), most plants can be grown with only the addition of nitrogen, phosphorus, and potassium compounds [2,26]. If other minerals necessary for human health are reduced in the soil, the plant can (and will) grow without them. This means, though, that constantly farming the same ground can result in the reduction of some of the essential minerals we as humans require for optimal health [43].

Conclusion

Food complexed minerals are better for humans than isolated USP mineral salts [14-26]. Humans should not be eating rocks or mineral-chemical compounds as a source of nutrition [10,11] (there are roles for clays in naturopathic detoxification, however). One of the naturopathic standards adopted in 1947 included the statement, "Naturopathy does not make use of synthetic or inorganic vitamins or minerals" [46]. Why? Mineral salts are not natural food for humans. Mineral salts are essentially rocks and should primarily be consumed by plants [1,2].

Isolated industrially-processed rock minerals are dangerous. Isolated "Calcium supplements are associated with an increased risk of myocardial infarction" (heart attacks), while calcium in food did not have this terrible risk [52]. A major study in the USA involving 37,882 women concluded that those that took multi-vitamin-mineral formulas died sooner than those that did not take them [53]; iron, copper, zinc, and magnesium were the most dangerous minerals in that study [53]. The reality is that it is safe for humans to get their minerals from real food or nutritional supplements that are only composed of 100% real foods.

And speaking of real foods, a paper that I co-wrote reported how food minerals were much more effective in preventing the accumulation of advanced protein glycation end-products [54]. These glycation end-products are believed to be a major source of problems for those with Alzheimer's, Down syndrome, and diabetes. Two of these disorders are increasingly becoming problems in Western societies and the right food, not rock, minerals can help.

Most people can increase their consumption of food complexed minerals by eating more whole grains and whole grain products [10,55] as well as by eating sea vegetables. Whole grains contain more natural food complexed minerals than refined ones [10]. Sea vegetables naturally contain food complexed minerals, though (with the exception of iodine) in small amounts [10,34]. For additional support, many, who understand natural health choose to consume food supplements which contain minerals in a natural food complex, as opposed to consuming isolated mineral salts. Mineral nutrition should come from foods or supplements which are as close to food as possible. Why 'break the food chain' by eating rocks known as mineral salts? It is a fact of science that "humans rely totally on plants and animals for life" [56]. It therefore seems logical to conclude that mineral salts are for plants and that food complexed minerals are for humans.

References

[1] Cronquist, A. *Plantae.* In Synopsis and Classification of Living Organisms, Vol 1. McGraw-Hill, NY, 1982:57.

[2] Schroeder, H. A. *The Trace Elements and Man.* Devin-Adair, New Greenwich (CT), 1973.

[3] Howell, E. *Enzyme Nutrition.* Avery Publishing, Wayne (NJ), 1985.

[4] Milne, L. and Milne, M. *The Arena of Life: The Dynamics of Ecology.* Natural History Press, Garden City (NJ), 1972.

[5] Wallace, R. A. *Biology: The World of Life,* 6th ed. Harper Collins, New York, 1992.

[6] Shils, M. *Magnesium.* In Modern Nutrition in Health and Disease, 8th ed. Lea & Febiger, Phil., 1994:164-184.

[7] Burger, S. *Vitamins and Minerals for Health.* Wild Rose College of Natural Healing, Calgary, 1988.

[8] Nielsen, F. *Ultratrace Minerals.* In Modern Nutrition in Health and Disease, 8th ed. Lea & Febiger, Phil., 1994:269-286.

[9] Turnland, J. R. *Copper.* In Modern Nutrition in Health and Disease, 8th ed. Lea & Febiger, Phil.,1994:231-241.

[10] Whitney, E. N. and Hamilton, E. M. N. *Understanding Nutrition,* 4ed. West Publishing, New York, 1987.

[11] Cunnane, S. C. *Zinc: Clinical and Biochemical Significance.* CRC Press, Boca Raton (FL), 1988.

[12] Turnland, J. R. *Bioavailability of Dietary Minerals to Humans: The Stable Isotope Approach.* Crit Rev Food Sci Nutr, 1991; 30(4);387-396.

[13] Schumann, K., et al. *Bioavailability of Oral Vitamins, Minerals, and Trace Minerals in Perspective.* Arzneimittelforshcung, 1997; 47(4):369-380.

[14] Vinson, J. A. *Comparative Bioavailability of Different Forms of Germanium.* University of Scranton, Scranton (PA), 1988.

[15] Vinson, J. A. and Bose, P. *Comparison of Bio-Availability of Trace Elements in Inorganic Salts, Amino Acid Chelates, and Yeast.* Mineral Elements 80, Proceedings II, Helsinki, Dec 9-11, 1981.

[16] Vinson, J., Mazur, T. and Bose, P. *Comparisons of Different Forms of Calcium on Blood Pressure of Normotensive Males.* Nutr Reports Intl, 1987; 36(3):497-505.

[17] Vinson, J. A. and Hsiao, K. H. *Comparative Effect of Various Forms of Chromium on Serum Glucose: An Assay for Biologically Active Chromium.* Nutr Reports Intl,1985; 32(1):1-7.

[18] Vinson, J. A. and Bose, P. *The Effect of High Chromium Yeast on the Blood Glucose Control and Blood Lipids of Normal and Diabetic Human Subjects.* Nutr Reports Intl, 1984; 30(4):911-918.

[19] Vinson, J. A. and Howard, T. B. *Inhibition of Protein Glycation and Advanced Glycation End Products by Ascorbic Acid and Other Vitamins and Nutrients.* Nutr Biochemistry, 1996; 7:659-663.

[20] Vinson, J. *Rat zinc Bioavailability Study.* University of Scranton, Scranton (PA).

[21] Jenkins, D. J. A., Wolever, T. M. S. and Jenkins, A. L. *Diet Factors Affecting Nutrient Absorption and Metabolism. In Modern Nutrition in Health and Disease,* 8th ed. Lea and Febiger, Phil.:583-602, 1994.

[22] Vinson, J., Bose, P., Lemoine, L. and Hsiao, K. H. *Bioavailability Studies.* In Nutrient Availability: Chemical and Biological Aspects. Royal Society of Chemistry, Cambridge (UK) 1989:125-127.

[23] Vinson, J. *Bioavailability of Magnesium.* University of Scranton, Scranton (PA) 1991.

[24] Vinson, J. In Selenium in Biology and Medicine. Van Nostrand Rheinhold, New York,1987:445.

[25] Vinson, J., Stella, J. and Flanagan, T. *Selenium Yeast is an Effective In Vitro and In Vivo Antioxidant and Hypolipemic Agent in Hamsters.* Nutr Res, 1998; 18:735-742.

[26] Ensminger, A. H., Ensminger, M. E., Konlade, J. E. and Robson, J. R. K. *Food & Nutrition Encyclopedia,* 2nd ed. CRC Press, New York, 1993.

[27] Jensen, B. *The Chemistry of Man.* Bernard Jensen, Escondido (CA), 1983.

[28] Allen, L. H. and Wood, R. J. *Calcium and Phosphorus.* In Modern Nutrition in Health and Disease, 8th ed. Lea & Febiger, Phil., 1994:144-163.

[29] Heaney, R. P., Dowell, M. S. and Barger-Lux, M. J. *Absorption of Calcium as the Carbonate and Citrate Salts, with Some Observations on Method.* Osteoporosis Int, 1999; 9:19-23.

[30] Timon, S. *Mineral Logic: Understanding the Mineral Transport System.* Advanced Nutrition Research: Ellicottville (NY), 1985.

[31] Nielson, F. *Chromium.* In Modern Nutrition in Health and Disease, 8th ed. Lea & Febiger, Phil.,1994:264-268.

[32] Vinson, J. *Chromium Toxicity Study.* University of Scranton, Scranton (PA).

[33] Nielson, F. *Ultratrace Minerals.* In Modern Nutrition in Health and Disease, 9th ed. Lea & Febiger, Phil., 1999:283-303.

[34] Hetzel, B. S. and Clugston, G. A. *Iodine.* In Modern Nutrition in Health and Disease, 9th ed. Lea & Febiger, Phil., 1999:253-264.

[35] Greene, H. L. and Moran, J. R. *The Gastrointestinal Tract: Regulation of Nutrient Absorption.* In Modern Nutrition in Health and Disease, 8th ed. Lea and Febiger, Phil., 1994:549-568.

[36] Fairbanks, V. F. *Iron in Medicine and Nutrition.* In Modern Nutrition in Health and Disease, 8th ed. Lea & Febiger, Phil., 1994:185-213.

[37] Levander, O. A. and Burk, R. F. *Selenium.* In Modern Nutrition in Health and Disease, 8th ed. Lea & Febiger, Phil., 1994:242-263.

[38] Vinson, J. *Selenium Toxicity Study.* Third International Symposium in Biology and Medicine. Van Nostrand Rheinhold, New York, 1987.

[39] Whitaker, J. *Minerals, Part 1: Cut your cancer Risk with Selenium.* Health & Healing, 1999; 9(4):6-8.

[40] Ha, S. W. *Rabbit Study Comparing Yeast and Isolated B Vitamins* (as described in Murray RP. Natural vs. Synthetic. Mark R. Anderson, 1995:A3). Ann Rev Physiol, 1941; 3:259-282.

[41] King, J. C. and Keen, C. L. *Zinc.* In Modern Nutrition in Health and Disease, 8th ed. Lea & Febiger, Phil. 1994:214-230.

[42] Bauernfeind, J. C. *Nutrification of Foods.* In Modern Nutrition in Health and Disease, 8th ed. Lea & Febiger, Phil., 1994:1579-1592.

[43] Ghebremeskel, K. and Crawford, M. A. *Nutrition and Health in Relation to Food Production and Processing.* Nutr Health, 1994; 9(4):237-253.

[44] Bazzarre, T. L., Hopkins, R. G., Wu, S. M. and Murdoch, S. D. *Chronic Disease Risk Factors in Vitamin/Mineral Supplement Users and Nonusers in a Farm Population.* J Am Coll Nutr, 1991; 10(3):247-257.

[45] Sax, N. I. and Lewis, R. J. *Hawley's Condensed Chemical Dictionary,* 11th ed. Van Nostrand Rheinhold, New York, 1987.

[46] Burr-Madsen, A. *Gateways College of Natural Therapies, Module 1.* Gateway College, Shingle Springs (CA), 1996.

[47] Erdman, J. W. and Poneros-Schneir, A. G. *Factors Affecting the Nutritive Value in Processed Foods.* In Modern Nutrition in Health and Disease, 8th ed. Lea & Febiger, Phil., 1994:1569-1578.

[48] Ascherio, A. and Willett, W. C. *Health Effects of trans Fatty Acids.* Am J Clin Nutr, 1997; 66:1006S-1010S.

[49] Hornick, S. B. *Factors Affecting the Nutritional Quality of Crops.* AM J Alternative Ag, 1992; 7(1-2).

[50] *Organic Tomatoes, Vitamin C, and Calcium.* Nutr Week, 1998; 28(24):7.

[51] Smith, B. L. *Organic Foods vs. Supermarket Foods:* J Applied Nutr, 1993; 45(1):35-39.

[52] Bolland M.J., Avenell A., Baron J.A., Grey A., MacLennan G.S., Gamble G.D., Reid I.R. *Effect of Calcium Supplements on Risk of Myocardial Infarction and Cardiovascular Events: Meta-analysis.* BMJ. 2010 Jul 29;341

[53] Mursu J., Robien K., Harnack L.J., Park K., Jacobs D.R. Jr. *Dietary Supplements and Mortality Rate in Older Women: The Iowa Women's Health Study.* Arch Intern Med. 2011 Oct 10;171(18):1625-33

[54] Thiel R., Fowkes S.W. *Can Cognitive Deterioration Associated with Down Syndrome be Reduced?* Medical Hypotheses, 2005; 64(3):524-532

[55] Kennedy, E. *The 1995 USDA/HHS Dietary Guidelines - An Overview.* USDA, Washington, D.C., 1995.

[56] Perry, N. *Symbiosis.* Sterling Publishers, New York, 1983.

24

Why are Synthetics Sold as Imitations of Natural Foods and Drugs?

If you have read this far, you probably have already asked yourself that question. This question was raised a half-century ago. To answer it, Dr. Royal Lee, in 1948, wrote the following paper which he titled, *How and Why are Synthetic Poisons Sold as Imitations of Natural Foods and Drugs?:*

> An honestly enforced food and drug law is just as essential to the proper operation of commerce in foods and drugs as the rules and an umpire to administer them in a ball game.
>
> It is obvious to all that such a law should stop the sale of poisonous imitations of common foods and drugs, except where proper labeling warns the buyer of just what he is getting, New synthetic products are constantly appearing, and are sold without proper tests or proper investigation of what their real properties are.
>
> In fact, the Food & Drug laws seem to be suspended where synthetic imitations of good foods are concerned, and often actually perverted to persecute makers

and sellers of real products, as we shall later show.

Let us first get to the bottom of this question of how synthetic products differ from natural. There are two ways in which a difference may exist:

a. The synthetic product may not be the same thing, but something that resembles the natural product.

b. The synthetic product is always a simple chemical substance, while the natural is a complex mixture of related and similar materials.

The first situation, where the synthetic material is not the same thing, is common. Take lactic acid, originally made from sour milk, now made synthetically in large quantities. The sour milk lactic-acid consisted entirely of molecules that were of a right-handed character. The synthetic is a mixture of equal parts of right-handed molecules (dextro-lactic acid) and left-handed molecules (laevo-lactic acid). Such mixtures are known as racemic compounds. (In catalogs, etc., the prefixes l-, d-, or r-, are used before the name of the substance.)

About thirty years ago, Dr. Crofton, an English endocrinologist, explained how digestive enzymes could only act **upon part of the food** available. Here are his words:

"It will not be unprofitable now to inquire into the raison d'etre of this curious adaptor mechanism. How is it that the ferments of the tissue-cells themselves cannot deal with the comparatively simple food material presented to them without the aid of adapters?

Pasteur first discovered that there are certain compounds of carbon which, while identical in every other respect having the same chemical formulae and the same chemical reactions, differ only in their behavior to polarized light, that is one compound rotated the light to the right, the other to the left. Such compounds have the same specific gravity, molecular volume melting point, solubility, heat of solution, of combustion and of neutralization. They have the same amount of chemical affinity and index of refraction.

Their absorption spectra are the same, and they have the same chemical action, yet one body rotates the light to the right as much as the other to the left. Pasteur's discovery was made with ammonium tartrates, and he found that if the common mould penicillium glaucum was made to grow in a solution of both (ammonium racemate) it lived on the dextro-isomer but left the levo-salt, as he thought, quite untouched, But it now appears it is broken up to a small extent."[1]

This requirement of the living cell for a minute amount of the laevo-salt, and the reason for their requirement for the major amount to be the dextro- form is explained by Lee and Hanson in their discussion of cell reactions in their book, "Protomorphology", 1947, Lee Foundation. [2]

Few people know that dextro-lactic acid is a food and laevo-lactic acid is a poison. (One is converted into sugar in digestion, the other is a waste product.) Lactic acid once was found useful as a source of carbohydrate as a milk modifier for babies, and began to get into use in special cases where sugars were not well tolerated. In Halifax, some time ago, a number of babies died from the administration of lactic acid in milk, and here was a case where the synthetic product was inadvertently used in place of the natural, because of inadequate labeling precautions. [3] The doctors who recommended its use probably did not even know that there was a difference between the synthetic and natural lactic acid, although the drug catalog of Eli Lilly and Company of 1938, page 195, offers some information on the subject. The basic trouble is that the makers of synthetic products do not want a stigma of inferiority to be put on their imitation products, and will not label their imitations as different unless forced by conscientious food and drug inspectors to do so. And it is a notorious fact that the law is being ignored in many ways.

Where a food product must be composed of, say right-handed molecules, the left-hand may be as useless as in the case of left and right hand bolts and nuts in machinery. If you needed right hand cap screws to put the head of your auto engine back on, left hand screws would only serve to cause confusion and probably a failure to get the machine back into operation, unless you could find among them enough of the right screws to

finish the job. To feed racemic or wrong "handed" food products is just as foolish. In the case of the babies in Halifax it caused death to feed the racemic product.

In 1895, Paul Walden, of the University of Rostock, (Germany), announced his discovery of the "Walden Effect," the phenomena of the alteration of the optical inversion of natural organic substances that had been isolated M- crystal purity, over a period of time, apparently a result of removal from their normal environment and association with other protective and colloidal factors.

Walden, in a series of lectures at Cornell University, (1927-28), stated:

The phenomenon of autoracemization is of interest in connection with the question of permanency of optically active substances. Let us consider a pure organic substance such as the dextrorotatory bromo-succinic ester. When it is kept for some time in a closed flask at ordinary temperatures, it undergoes spontaneous intramolecular rearrangement and a gradual decrease of the optical rotation results; in other words, it racemizes. Several examples may be cited to illustrate this remarkable fact...Might we not speak of 'dying molecules' much as we speak of 'dead catalysts'?... The effect of these reactions is, as we may express it, a complete turning 'inside out' of the molecule.

Dr. Emil Fischer, in 1906, said: "This discovery is the most surprising observation in the field of optically active substances since the fundamental investigations of Pasteur."

Amino acids are also useless if not toxic when present in synthetic forms. only left handed (laevo-) amino acids can be assimilated. All synthetic aminos are racemic.

Adrenalin is an outstanding example of a synthetic product that is being commercialized in disregard of the difference in physiological action. The natural adrenalin is fifteen times as 35 active as the synthetic dextro form [4] in its effect on blood vessels, while the dextroadrenalin is eighteen times as effective in promoting glycosuria.

Now, since the commonest use of adrenalin is to promote the vascular changes that relieve the asthmatic patient, the glycosuria (diabetes promoting) effect is definitely not wanted. But to get the same vascular effect, 15 x 18 or 270 times as much of the synthetic stuff must be used, in terms of its unwanted effect of putting sugar into the urine.[5]

The cost of calling a doctor and of getting a shot of adrenalin by the asthmatic patient when he is struggling for a breath of air is far too much to offset the two-cent saving made by the pharmaceutical manufacturer who puts synthetic adrenalin in the ampule used by that doctor. But, if neither the doctor or the patient knows the difference, the synthetic stuff certainly would be the one he gets. Although natural adrenalin can be made as a by-product in the processing of glands in making adreno-cortin, makers of this material tell us there is no market for natural adrenalin because of the low price of the synthetic product.

Pantothenic acid is a vitamin now commercially available only in the synthetic form. Probably this is the reason for its effect of causing a loss of sex function, particularly in females. This castrating action has been found both in test animals and in human patients receiving the "vitamin", according to unpublished reports to us.

Pure natural Vitamin E was found three times as potent as pure synthetic Vitamin E.[6]

Of course, the poisonous nature of the synthetic Vitamin D sold as "Viosterol" and "Vigantol" is well established. It causes blood in the urine very quickly in children, by its destructive action to the kidneys. Deaths have been reported from the ordinary dosages used to "protect" from rickets. [7]

WHY DO THE PEOPLE AND MEDICAL MEN NOT KNOW THESE FACTS? Is it because the commercial promoters of cheap imitation food and drug products spend enough money to stop the leaking out of information?

Here is a good example of how hard it is to get the facts. In "Good Housekeeping" for September, 1943, in the "Question Box'" department, the question was asked, "Are synthetic vitamins as beneficial as those from food sources?" The answer was made "Manufactured vitamins are identical with those found in foods. They are just as beneficial."

When asked what references they could offer to substantiate that statement, "Good Housekeeping" quoted the journal of the American Medical Association, December . 21, 1940, page 2185: "There is no detectable difference between the synthetic chemical vitamin and the natural ones.

Ascorbic acid is just as good Vitamin C as one gets from an orange."

When pressed for actual experimental evidence instead of swivel chair opinions, the Editor of "Good Housekeeping" referred the question to a group of "experts." Here are their opinions:

Dr. E. V. McCollum of Johns Hopkins: "… each and every one of these synthetic vitamins is identical with the natural product."

Dr. Henry C. Sherman, Columbia University: "In some cases the natural and synthetic forms seem to be identical while in other cases there may be more than one natural or more than one synthetic form." When asked for factual evidence from experimental work to prove that the synthetic vitamins in "enriched" flour, were equal to the natural, he replied, "…any answers that a scientific worker would give you would be based upon facts and that nothing would be gained by spending time on library researches in order to attach specific references to our answers."

Dr. George R. Cowgill, Yale University School of Medicine: "In answering the question raised in your letter about relative values of synthetic as compared with 'natural' vitamins one should keep clearly in mind the meaning of the terms involved. There is no difference between these two sources of the vitamins as such. However, in many nutritional experiments one works with highly artificial diets containing the synthetic vitamins and there is no supply of various unknown factors that are needed for nutrition. If these unknown factors are missing, obviously some malnutrition will result, but it seems clear in this situation that one is not thereby justified in concluding that the synthetic vitamins are inferior to the 'natural' vitamins."

This is the position taken by most of the authorities in the vitamin field. Thiamine as thiamine will meet the body's needs for this vitamin whether it is the synthetic variety or if it comes as a part of a food like a whole-grain breakfast food. The natural food, of course, may contain the unknown factors that are missing from a specific mixture of vitamins, and therefore, be superior to this extent."

(Dr. Cowgill was not aware of the fact that natural thiamine can not be separated from B4, the vitamin that prevents some kinds of heart disease [8]. Therefore, it is impossible to compare natural thiamine with synthetic thiamine. He is comparing the synthetic B1 to a product purely hypothetical that is not known to science, not available for tests.)

We also obtained the opinion of Dr. S. Ansbacher, U. S. Vitamin Corporation, New York: "There is no difference whatsoever in the physiological activity of vitamins from natural sources and the ones made synthetically."

(Dr. Ansbacher here differs from a book his own firm published, "Vitamin and Mineral Therapy," by H. E. Dubin and Casimir Funk, 1936, (Dr. Funk was the discoverer of Vitamin B and the man who invented the word "vitamin."), in which is the comment: "Synthetic Vitamins: These are highly inferior to vitamins from natural sources, also, the synthetic product is well known to be far more toxic." Page 65)

Dr. Funk's opinion is significantly different from that of Dr. Ansbacher, present Research Director of the company. Why is it that none of these men seem able to refer to any concrete reason for their present opinions? Could it be that the profits involved in the sale of synthetic foods and drugs are so great that there is a constant campaign on to cover up the facts?

In the September 1948 issue of "Reader's Digest" is an article by Paul de Kruff, "Harry Steenbock Trapped the Sun," that appears to be for the express purpose of reviving the reputation of Steenbock and Viosterol the synthetic and poisonous form of Vitamin D. Aside from the dangerous nature of Steenbock's vitamin, its promotion by the Wisconsin Alumni Research Foundation was an unconscionable racket. Its nature is well exposed in the appended reprint from "This Month," June 1945…

Viosterol is still on the market. It will still poison your child if YOU do not watch out. Your doctor has not yet been informed by his medical society, (if he is a member of the A. M. A.), that they made a mistake in approving it as real Vitamin D, although all vitamin authorities, including Steenbock himself, who first published the fact, knows that Viosterol is NOT Vitamin D. [9]

The same issue of "Reader's Digest" carries an article on the nickel-cadmium storage battery, a common article in Europe for the last 40 years. It is relatively unknown in this country.

WHY? Simply because the American makers of lead storage batteries have succeeded in keeping out any knowledge of this battery from all American territories, and have limited production in this country by hook or crook, (as the article tells it, by acquiring control of the European concerns), all to protect their racket of selling a short-lived battery to their customers while ignoring the cadmium battery.

In Canada the adulteration of white flour with synthetic vitamins is a criminal offense. In this country it is an approved practice, and the makers of synthetic vitamins reap a fat harvest for their contribution to the advertising propaganda of the flour millers. The real vitamins are removed to keep insects and molds out of the flour. Synthetic vitamins are added to fool the public, which knows that white flour without vitamins is unfit to eat. The fact that insects and molds still cannot live in the flour any better than before the synthetic vitamins were added is not mentioned. Neither is the fact mentioned that test animals fed "enriched" diets, ("enriched" with synthetic imitations of natural vitamins), DIE SOONER than control animals fed the deficient diets. Proof that synthetic vitamins are worse than none as food fortifiers, [10], proof that they are put into foods to defraud the buyers, cheat him out of his health and life, as well as his money.

This situation cannot be an accident. It must be a carefully planned conspiracy, with varying degrees of guilt for all the pseudo-scientists who have varying degrees of knowledge of the real situation, and who do not dare to expose the truth.

Food & Drug Inspectors and Officials are as helpless to combat this overwhelming influence as they would be to stop the sale of bootleg whiskey during prohibition days. To keep their jobs they have to keep one eye shut.

Dr. Harvey W. Wiley, the first head of the Federal Food & Drug Department, tried to stop the use of synthetic sugar, known as glucose of corn sugar, in preserved fruits and canned goods. He felt that it was a fraudulent practice to load up such foods with synthetic materials of an unknown effect on the human body. Further, people eat sugar as a sweetener, and the synthetic sugar was far less sweet than cane sugar, and would have to eat much more to get the same taste when added to preserves, etc. Dr. Wiley lost out in his desire to even get the label warning on containers that the product carried synthetic sugar, in fact, lost his job because he tried to protect the public.

Only this year have supporting tests confirmed Dr. Wiley's fears. On May 10, 1948, the University of Pennsylvania released the news to the Associated Press that they had found that the feeding of glucose to test animals caused diabetes. (Dr. Francis D. W. Lukens and Dr. F. Curtis Dohan.)

204

Dr. Wiley thought that glucose was a possible cause of diabetes, but had no way to prove it. He felt that the makers of glucose should not be permitted to experiment on the whole population of the United States to find out.

It is the use of glucose in candy, soft drinks, bakery goods, ice cream, canned fruit etc., the low price of which enables their users to undersell all competitors who may try to use better sugars, and put them out of business. It is a clear case of where the public SHOULD be protected by a law, but, as Dr. Wiley said when he was forced to leave his job,

Thus, the very law which the Supreme Court has said was enacted chiefly to protect the public health has been turned into a measure to threaten public health and to defraud the purchaser of flour.

When you add up the industries that depend upon their foisting of synthetics as foods alone, (not considering drugs), you will find you have a list of the biggest in the country. Naturally, they are watching all loopholes where their rackets might start to crack. It is probably impossible for any research worker operating under the auspices of a university or in a government laboratory to be free from their indirect influence. Such items as have been quoted here are leaks that have commonly been quickly suppressed. No further work is done on these important questions. If a book like Dr. Daniel W. Quigley's, "The National Malnutrition" which exposes these food racketeers, gets into public libraries, these influences get it off the shelves. This happened at Rochester, New York, where twelve of the Quigley books were donated by request, for the library and its branches. Later, when it was found that the books had been taken off the circulating list, the librarian admitted that no book inimical to local industries could remain on the library shelves. Later, that same librarian was written up in the local paper as a "Champion of FREE libraries" where no outside influence could alter the nature of the "free speech" of the library. (Rochester Democrat & Chronicle, November 21,

1944.) Was this a deliberate attempt to nullify a truth by circulating a lie, or maybe just a coincidence?

The Food & Drug Administration, and the Federal Trade Commission, instead of getting the facts in this situation and protecting the public against these dangerous imitations of natural foods, are bending their energies it seems to cover up for the racketeers.

We cannot find a single instance of where a maker of synthetic imitation vitamins has been prosecuted by the Food & Drug Administration for improper claims on his labels or advertising. But many makers of NATURAL products have been prosecuted for making claims IDENTICAL to what the makers of synthetic products are constantly and continually promoting. WHY THE SELECTION OF THE MAKERS OF NATURAL PRODUCTS FOR PERSECUTION? In one case in which we have the transcript at hand, the prosecuting attorney was successful in getting the testimony of a key witness REVERSED in the process of printing the record, which the Court of Appeals was able to use to support their argument to uphold the original judgment. Without this help, it is hard to see where the original verdict could have been sustained, obtained as it was by obvious fraud, where Government "experts" declared no vitamin deficiency could create either a degenerative, infectious, or a functional disease.

The Federal Trade Commission has issued orders and interpretations to makers of natural vitamins to "cease and desist" stating that a synthetic vitamin is in any way inferior to a natural.

Pages could be filled with examples of misuse of authority of this kind, where special business interests are being protected by police activity. If one asks the question, "Why do they prosecute one concern for a violation, and then let far bigger ones continue to use the prohibited advertising—if it is wrong for one to make a statement why is it not wrong for another? The answer you get is "action can only be taken where a complaint is made, no one has filed a complaint against these concerns."

If a police authority can stop a murderer only after someone files a complaint, lets get busy and start filing complaints. A lot of people are being murdered, slowly maybe in most cases, but none the less surely, by food racketeers, who are constantly finding ways to make a poor product worse, and sell it for less, thereby driving better ones off the market. On top of this, they are using the police power to stop the maker of better products from telling the truth on his label as to the difference.

Just WHY should the TRUTH be subservient to the OPINIONS of hired crooks who sell their reputations as EXPERT WITNESSES?

Can you imagine a better way to protect racketeers under the Federal laws? Or a better way for them to discredit their competitors? [12]

References

[1] Crofton, W. M. *An Outline of Endocrinology.* Wm. Wood and Company, New York, Second Edition, 1929.

]2] Lee, R. and Hanson, W. A. *Protomorphology.* Lee Foundation for Nutritional Research,, Milwaukee, Wisconsin, 1947.

[3] Young, E. G. and Smith, R. P. *Lactic Acid: A Corroxive Poison.* Journal of American Medical Association 125:1179-1181) 1944.

[4] Harrow and Sherman. *The Chemistry of the Horomones.* Williams & Wilkins, Baltimore, Maryland, page 122, 1934.

[5] Dyson. *The Chemistry of Chemotherapy.* The Chemical Publishing Company, Brooklyn, New York, page 66.

[6] *The Relative Activity of Natural and Synthetic Vitamin E.* Nutrition Reviews 5:251-253,1947.

[7] Bauer, J. M. and Freyberg, R. H. *Vitamin D Inoxication with Metastatic Calcification.* Journal of American Medical Association 130:1208-1215,1946.

[8] Stepp, W., Kuhnau, J. and Schroeder,H. *The Vitamins and their Clinical Applications.* English translation published by The Vitamin Products Company, Milwaukee, Wisconsin, page 24, 1938.

[9] Steenbock, H., Kletzein, S. N. F. and Halpin, J. G. *The Reaction of the Chicken to Irradiated Ergosterol and Irradiated Yeast as Contrasted with the Natural Vitamin D of Fish Liver Oil.* Journal of Biological Chemistry 97:249,1932 and DeSanctis, A. and Craig,J. D. *A Five-Year Clinical Study of the Prophylactic Value of Antirachitic Agents.* New York journal of Medicine 34:712-714,1934.

[10] Morgan, Agnes Fay. *The Effect of Imbalance in the "Filtrate Fraction" of the Vitamin B Complex in Dogs.* Science page 261, March 14,1941.

[11] Wiley, H. W. *The History of a Crime Against the Pure Food Law.* Published by himself, page 391, 1929.

[12] Lee, R. *How and Why Synthetic Poisons are Sold as Imitations of Natural Foods and Drugs.* Lee Foundation for Nutritional Research, Milwaukee, 1948.

25

Glandulars and Enzymes

You have probably noticed that some naturopathic products contain glandular ingredients. The author and many other doctors have used glandulars for years with great success. However, it is unclear precisely how these substances may affect energy levels and/or mental function. When the author first started using them, there was little idea how they might work, but it was quickly learned that they did. This chapter should give some ideas why glandulars may have a use in your office based on current and historical explanations.

It should first be noted that it is unlikely that all the essential nutrients have been discovered, for ill, or even healthy people [1] and that many biochemical substances are contained within glandulars. Glandulars contain peptides, hormone precursors, and (if not heated) enzymes, all of which may be beneficial and contribute to their reported efficacy.

Although it is believed by some that oral consumption of dried glandulars is no different than consuming any other protein containing food, this is not completely true. This incomplete belief appears to be based on the fact that since the stomach breaks down proteins into their constituent amino acids, there is no benefit from consuming foods containing specific peptides; however, this belief ignores the fact that not all ingested protein is broken down into its constituent amino acids.

Evidence suggests that with oral consumption of glandular extracts, a small percentage (5-10%) of their peptides are not broken down into their constituent amino acids but are available for intact absorption in the small intestine [2-5]. A small amount of these absorbed peptides then circulate and some of them appear to assist the human body (especially for ill persons) in performing various anabolic and catabolic processes [2-5]. Since some loss does occur, this affects the quantity of glandular supplements that is normally taken. Howell and others have reported that the amount of enzymes that pass through the stomach is even higher (nearly 50% [6]). Howell has also reported that individuals with significant health problems have been found to have lower levels of enzymes than healthy individuals and that oral enzyme supplementation has been helpful for many such people [6]; although this position is not universally accepted [7], a recent study in the Journal of Surgery showed that oral pancreatic supplementation resulted in improved enzyme and growth levels for children who had a pancreaticoduodenectomy [8].

Some glandular extracts also contain small, safe amounts of hormones which may at least contribute to their possible effectiveness. The thymus gland contains thymic hormones which Schulof found may enhance immune response for people with HIV [9]. It should be noted that many substances contained within animal tissues are similar (or identical) to their human counterparts [1,10,11], including certain enzymes [10] and even T cell gene regions [11]. Oral supplementation with bovine thymus has been shown to be capable of enhancing T-lymphocyte activity, probably due to a thymosin-like activity [12].

It is of interest to note that some research has indicated that protein contained within cow's milk appears to slow the growth of certain human toxic cells [13] (also cows do not appear to get breast cancer [13]), thus it may be reasonable to conclude that it is possible that other substances contained within or derived from bovine/ovine sources may be helpful for other human diseases.

Harrower (a pioneering researcher of oral glandulars) believed glandulars were effective because endocrine glands experienced something he referred to as "hormone hunger" [14]. Harrower wrote:

> The practical application of this idea concerns the administration of combinations of glands in presumed pluriglandular disturbances. If, for instance, in the conditions mentioned above there is a noticeable deficiency in several of the glands of internal secretion, the thyroid, ovaries and pituitary gland for instance, there may be varying degrees of hormone hunger on the part of the organs involved, and this will influence very definitely the amount of hormones that may be missing or needed by the glands to be stimulated. [14]

It should be pointed out that when Harrower used the term "hormone" this probably should be interpreted to also include nutrients, both known and unknown (including enzymes, peptides, and hormone precursors). This is based upon the fact that Harrower referred to vitamins (then newly discovered) as "plant hormones" and that he called hormones the "active principles obtained from certain glands" [14].

Glandulars can be made many ways. The cheapest way is through desiccation, which essentially dries the glandular at high temperatures. The biggest problem with desiccation is that it destroys all the enzymes that are in the tissue. Desiccation may also destroy other active substances contained within the gland. One of the most expensive ways to produce glandulars is through the air drying process known as lypholization. This freeze-drying, fat-removing, process helps preserve many of the naturally-present enzymes. Lypholization is strongly preferred to desiccation, even though that does increase the cost of the product (neonatal glandulars which are used by some are also more expensive). Regarding specific glandular materials, most U.S. firms only use glandular materials which are certified to be free of detectable amounts of drugs, growth hormones, bacteria, etc. Although some questions have been raised concerning the substances used to reduce possible glandular rancidity, it has been the author's experience that these do not adversely affect efficacy and that the concentration is too small to have negative effects in most people.

Animal glands have been consumed since the beginning of history [15]. "Glandular products have been produced and used in the U.S. for over 60 years with absolutely no reports of microbial contamination or resultant illness" [16]. They are consumed in many countries, including the U.S. as food [15,16]; they may even contain substances to reverse diseases associated with Western diets [15]. "Since hormones are not part of the substance, overdosing is not a concern. Even when excess amounts have been ingested, the body can easily deaminize them" [16]. A search of the literature found one report (in a letter to the editor) outside the U.S. of a single, temporary complaint (it raised thyroid hormone levels which normalized when consumption was discontinued), from using a thyroid glandular product combined with lithium, but the daily consumption (45 tablets) was in excess of any reasonable consumption (daily quantity of thyroid hormones present: 0.5 T4 and .09mg of T3) [17]. Glandular suppliers provide products which are not contaminated with Bovine Spongiform Encephalopathy (BSE) and have been collected under USDA inspection [i.e.18]. The USDA has announced that no BSE has ever been detected in cattle in the U.S. [19]. No long-term, negative, side effects from taking glandular supplements is known [16].

Colostrum is similar to glandulars as it is an animal product. Colostrum is life's first food. It is the "pre-milk" that mothers produce (and babies eat) for a couple of days. It is full of a variety of immune stimulating substances [20]. Various immunoglobins have been found in it [21]. Although bovine colostrum is often recommended (from New Zealand), it is not the panacea some promoters suggest it is (nothing is). For some though, it is quite helpful.

Like many of the pioneering glandular researchers [22], Bovine or ovine source glandulars are preferable to glandulars from other animals for many reasons: 1) Doctors using them (including the author) have a history of receiving positive results from people with a wide variety of disorders, 2) Bovine/ovine tissues are commercially available, 3) Bovine/ovine glandulars have a long history of being safe to consume (and are governed by the U.S.D.A.), 4) Bovine/ovine tissues are dietary supplements under the Dietary Supplement Health and Education Act of 1994 (DSHEA) [23] and as such are not considered to be food additives, 5) Earlier research has demonstrated that heterologous tissues (such as bovine/ovine for humans) do not produce the adverse and possibly toxic side effects that more homologous tissues can (such as simian for humans) [22], and 6) Some earlier research suggested that immune response in humans was improved at a much greater rate with the use of substances from ruminant sources (bovine and ovine) as opposed to non-ruminant sources (simian and feline) [24]. At least one researcher reported long ago that rat tissue extracts also appear to cause a variety of problems when forced into some animals [22].

Bovine and ovine glandulars have been used with great success. Even though this section cannot conclusively state how glandulars work, it is hoped the theories and explanations will be helpful to those of you who now use (or plan to use) glandulars.

Enzymes

Related to the subject of glandulars is the subject of enzymes. Many non-vegetarian enzymes are actually a form of glandulars. Plants and animals both contain enzymes (when they have not been cooked [6]). "Enzymes increase the action of antibodies against circulation immune complexes, which can otherwise build up and be cancerous" [25]. A little known truth about nutrition, is that almost no metabolic (which includes nutrition) reaction will occur without enzymes [6]. Enzymes are biological catalysts that can help the body rebuild. They are needed everywhere in the body. "Unless enzymes function properly, vitamins and minerals cannot do their job" [23].

However, it needs to be understood that most enzymes that are sold in supplements (as enzymes) are actually digestive enzymes. Protease, amylase, and lipase are enzymes which help digest proteins, carbohydrates, and fats (lipids), respectively [6]. Although these certainly do help digestion (and may have other benefits), they are not all the enzymes that are in the body (there actually are thousands [6]). Some enzymes have more than one function, though, "pancreatic enzymes can stimulate anticancer factors in the blood, i.e., natural killer cells, T cells, and tumor necrosis factor" [23].

One of the reasons to use freeze-dried glandulars is that they help the body rebuild tissues, such as endocrine glands. Enzymes are quite specific [6] and it is believable (for example) that liver enzymes can help rebuild the liver. One of the reasons that it sometimes takes longer for some vegetarians to improve is that they need to wait until enzyme levels can rebuild before they improve, whereas one who consumes (when appropriate) enzymes in glandulars has that happen nearly immediately begin after ingestion, thus the healing time for the non-vegetarian is reduced.

Of the other kind, from a dietary standpoint, many vegetarians ingest more dietary enzymes than non-vegetarians. Raw foods, almost exclusively plants, contain natural enzymes (the cooking of food destroys enzymes) thus, on a maintenance program many vegetarians will consume more enzymes than non-vegetarians—which normally is better for health [6].

References

[1] Hulsey, M. G. and Martin, R. J. *The Role of Animals in Nutritional Research.* Nutr Today, 1993; 28 (5):1993.

[2] Gardner, M. *Intestinal Assimilation of Intact Peptides and Protein from the Diet — A Neglected Field?* Cambridge Philosophical Society, Biological Reviews, 1984;59: 289-331.

[3] Popov, I. M., et al. *Cell Therapy.* J International Academy of Preventive Medicine, 1977; 3:74-82.

[4] Burns, D. *Accumulating Scientific Evidence Supports Glandular Therapy.* The Digest of Chiropractic Economics, Nov/Dec 1987: 74-79.

[5] Schwartz, E. F. *Glandular Therapy.* The American Chiropractor, January/February 1983:14-18.

[6] Howell, E. *Enzyme Nutrition.* Avery Publishing Group: Wayne (New Jersey): 11-29, 1985.

[7] Green, S. *A Critique of the Rationale for Cancer Treatment with Coffee Enemas and Diet.* JAMA, 1992; 268 (22): 3224-3227.

[8] Shamberger, R. C. and Hendron W. H. and Leictner, A. M. *Long-term Nutritional and Metabolic Consequences of Pancreaticoduodenectomy in Children.* Surgery, 1994; 115(3): 382-388.

[9] Schulof, R. S., et al. *Phase I/II Trial of Thymosin Fraction 5 and Thymosin Alpha One on HTLV-III Seropositive Subjects.* J of Biologic Response Modifiers, 1986; 5: 429-443.

[10] McCarren, M. *Animals in Research: Researchers Use Animals to Learn More About Human Diabetes.* Diabetes Forecast,1993; 46 (8): 26.

[11] California Institute of Technology. *Large Genome Comparison Reveals Details of Genomic Evolution.* Cancer Weekly Feb 10, 1992;6: 3

[12] Bland, J. *Glandular Therapy.* Circa 1989.

[13] *Protein in Cow's Milk Slows Growth of Cancer Cells in Lab Tests: Mammary Derived Growth Inhibitor (Cornell University).* Cancer Weekly April 20, 1992; 12:2.

[14] Harrower, H. *Practical Organotherapy.* 3rd ed. W.B. Conkey Co.: Hammond (Indiana): 31-36, 1921.

[15] Dunbar, R. *Foraging for Nature's Balanced Diet.* New Scientist. August 31, 1991:25-28.

[16] DeCava, J. A. *Glandular Supplements.* Nutrition News and Views. 1997; 1(3):1-10.

[17] Cooper, N. and Palmer, B. *Thyroid Hormone in a Health Food Capsule.* New Zealand Medical Journal. 1994: 231.

[18] Jackson, J. *Glandular Products* (letter). American Laboratories, Inc., Omaha. April 4, 1996.

[19] *Release No. 139.95 BSE Announcement in UK.* U.S. Department of Agriculture. Washington (DC). March 20, 1996.

[20] Clark, D. G. and Wyatt, K. *Colostrum, Life's First Food.* CNR Publicatons, Salt Lake City, 1998

[21] Brandtzaeg, P. *The Secretory Immune System of Lactating Human Mammary Glands Compared with Other Endocrine Organs.* Ann NY Acad Sci, 1983; 409:353-378.

[22] Lee, R. and Hanson, W. *Protomorphology: The Principles of Cell Auto-Regulation.* Lee Foundation for Nutritional Research, Milwaukee, 1947.

[23] Schauss, A. and Winters, C. *Citizens for Health.* Tacoma, October 25, 1994.

[24] Nuttall. *Blood Immunity and Blood Relationships.* Cambridge University Press, London, 1904.

[25] Null, G. *The Complete Encyclopedia of Natural Healing.* Kensington Books, New York, 1998.

26
Herbology

After "Herbal Terms", much of the first portion of this chapter is written by William von Peters, N.M.D., H.M.D., Ph.D. and was largely taken from <u>Naturae Medicina and Naturopathic Dispensatory</u> (portions in this chapter, by permission, were edited by Dr. Thiel). Much of the middle of portion of this chapter was written by Angela Burr-Madsen, N.D and taken from her writings.

Herbal Terms

Most guides and references to herbs use terms to describe some of their properties which are not always in common usage. This list is placed at the beginning of this chapter so that the reader will have one place to look any unfamiliar terms up. Here is a brief list of some herbal terms (with some terms defined in more detail later in this chapter):

Adaptogen: Believed to improve the body's ability to adapt, normally to changes (including stress), generally through support of the adrenal and/or pituitary glands.

Alterative: Sometimes these are called blood cleansers. They are believed to gradually restore health and vitality to the body.

Anodyne: These are believed to soothe tissues or reduce pain.

Anthelmintic: These are believed to kill or expel worms.

Anti-angiogenic: These are believed to reduce the formation of blood vessels, thus they are usually contraindicated for pregnant women or people who recently have had major surgery or a heart attack.

Antibilious: These are believed to help the body remove bile.

Anticatarrhal: These are believed to remove excess catarrhal build-ups, normally from the sinuses.

Antidepressive: These are believed to reduce symptoms of depression.

Anti-emetic: These are believed to reduce feelings of nausea and to reduce/prevent vomiting generally through carminative or stomachic properties.

Anti-inflammatory: These are believed to help the body eliminate fluids present in various inflammations. They generally are not believed to prevent inflammation.

Antilithic: These are believed to help prevent the formation of urinary stones, either through dissolving properties or through the stimulation of their elimination.

Antimicrobial: These are believed to fight or help the body fight microbial infections; some appear to kill invading microbes.

Antiparasitic: These are believed to help kill or expel worms.

Antipsoric: These are believed to reduce itching.

Antipyretic: These are believed to help reduce fever.

Antiscorbutic: These are believed to fight scurvy.

Antispasmodic: These are believed to relieve tension and thus reduce spasms or other cramps, generally due to the presence of tannins.

Antitussive: These are believed to reduce coughing.

Aperient: These are believed to be mild bulk laxatives by promoting natural intestinal action.

Astringent: These are believed to tighten tissue, normally due to the presence of tannins.

Bitter: These are bitter tasting and are believed to trigger a sensory system response in the mouth, and thus indirectly stimulate the central nervous system or digestive system.

Blood Cleanser: They are believed to gradually restore health and vitality to the body.

Carminative: These are believed to stimulate the digestive system, basically by soothing or settling the stomach wall.

Cholagogue: These are believed to stimulate the flow of bile or to increase the production of bile.

Demulcent: These are believed to be high in mucilage which can soothe and protect irritated/inflamed internal tissue(s).

Depurative: They are believed to gradually restore health and vitality to the body (also called alterative or blood cleanser).

Diaphoretic: These are believed to promote sweating, most often through dialating surface capillaries.

Diuretic: These are believed to increase circulation and/or fluid elimination.

Emetic: These are believed to induce vomiting, generally through irritating the stomach or nervous system.

Emmenagogue: These are believed to stimulate menstrual flow and related activities.

Emollient: These are believed to soften/smooth the skin, generally through mucilage or oils.

Expectorant: These are believed to remove excess mucus from the lungs through bronchial irritation or stimulation of internal reflex mechanisms.

Galactagogue: These are believed to increase the flow of milk in lactating women, probably through stimulation of the anterior pituitary.

Hepatic: These are believed to aid the liver; some are believed to increase bile flow.

Lactogenic: These are believed to induce milk secretion.

Laxative: These are believed to stimulate contractions in the intestines, thus directly promoting bowel movements.

Nervine: These are believed to have beneficial effects on the nervous system by providing direct nutritional support.

Nutritive: These are believed to have general nutritional properties.

Pectoral: These are believed to have strengthening effects on the lungs and other tissues, probably due to nutrients they possess.

"Qi" (pronounced chee): The life-force or air principle behind "yin" and "yang."

Rubifacient: These are believed to promote vasodilation, generally through mild inflammation.

Sedative: These are believed to calm the nervous system or otherwise reduce stress on the body.

Spasmolytic: These are believed to relieve tension and thus reduce spasms or other cramps, generally due to the presence of tannins.

Stimulant: These are believed to increase physiological actions generally due to the presence of alkaloids.

Tonic: These are believed to strengthen or stimulate one or more organs, probably through supplying nutrients or enzyme precursors.

Vulnerary: These are believed to promote wound healing or reduce inflammation. Their actions are probably caused by tannin or mucilage components.

"Yin" and "Yang": In Chinese herbal medicine these are the two opposites. Yin is like water and yang is like fire. Yin tonics are supposed to be good for the parasympathetic type person, whereas yang tonics are supposed to be good for the sympathetic type person. [1]

History

Dr. von Peters has written:

In the beginning God created the heavens and the earth. . . Then God said "Let the earth bring forth vegetation: seed-bearing plants and all kinds of trees that bear fruit containing their seed." And so it was. The earth brought forth vegetation, every kind of seed-bearing plant and all kinds of trees that bear fruit containing their seed. God saw that it was good." . . . God also said, "See, I give you every seed-bearing plant on the earth and every tree which has seed-bearing fruit to be your food. To every bird of the air, and to every creature that crawls on the earth and has the breath of life, I give the green plants for food." And so it was. Genesis 1:1, 11-13, 29-30. "He causes the grass to grow for cattle, and herbs for the service of man" (Psalms 104:14).

Such is the origin of herbs and the beginning of the use of herbs both for food and for cure. All peoples on the face of the earth, regardless of their race or religion have traditionally used herbs as the natural medicine of humankind. Herbal medicine was developed to high degrees among the Chinese (Traditional Chinese Medicine), Aryans of India (Ayurveda), among others.

Hippocrates (460–377B.C.) who is known as the "Father of Modern Medicine," was a naturopath. He is undoubtedly the most celebrated physician of antiquity by Western history. It was he who developed and formulated the Hippocratic oath still taken by naturopaths and medical doctors. His writings stressed the effect of the body to heal itself; and we know that during his time the use of homeopathic, spagyric and allopathic compilations of herbals was used by the healers.

"The symptoms of disease are partly symptoms of defense and partly symptoms of failure," he said. In his book on "Epidemic Diseases," *Hippocrates* says: "Nature is the healer of all disease," and "Let your foods be your medicine and your medicine be your foods." Much as he recognized the success of Nature's own healing effort he did not hesitate to call attention to the many instances where it succeeded only partly or failed entirely. "The physician is only the servant of Nature," he said.

The earliest Chinese book dealing with medicinal herbs was written by the emperor Chan–nung – 3000 B.C.; it mentions a thousand valuable herbs, placing ginseng first as the most potent remedy for all disease. This plant was worshipped by the ancient Greeks as the plant of the sorcerers. Ginseng was in general use when *Marco Polo,* in 1274 A.D. traveled through China. Also in Asia, the *Atharva Veda,* the most ancient medical book of India, mentions many medicinal herbs.

The native Indians of America have been practicing certain branches of natural therapeutics since times immemorial, ages before the advent of naturopathy in Europe. It is said that the ancient Mayas and Incas had developed the science and art of healing by natural methods to the highest degree at the time when Europe was inhabited by cave dwellers. It is well known that the first white settlers of America found the native Indians practicing herbalism and other methods of natural healing. The

American Indian, a close observer and worshipper of nature, was expert in herbalism and up to this day, still is. The writer observed that some animals, when sick or wounded, will select and eat only certain herbs, berries, barks, etc., (herbalism) or go into a swamp or mud hole (mud or clay pack) or in a creek (hydrotherapy) and will stay there a considerable length of time (rest cure) without taking any food (fasting) or, if they do eat, then only a certain type and a limited amount of certain foods (dietetics), or they will clean their wounds by licking with the tongue or bathing (antisepsis) or they will stretch, stroke, rub or scratch the sore portion of their bodies (massage) to relieve stagnation and promote circulation of the blood—a complete system of Naturopathy.

It was from the Indians that the white settlers in pioneer days learned the curative value of many herbs and plants, and other methods of natural healing. The mother's ingenuity in American pioneer days had to meet pioneer medical deficiencies, and she did well enough with her knowledge of the healing powers and medicinal properties of wild plants, berries, roots, leaves, flowers, and bark which she collected throughout the seasons, dried and labeled, and kept them to be used upon short notice.

During the medieval times the Catholic Church fostered the various healing arts among which the methods of natural healing were outstanding. Faith cures were encouraged which gradually replaced the superstitious practices of the primitive folk. Herbals played a great part of these natural healing arts as the church recognized the scriptural premise: "He causes the grass to grow for cattle, and herbs for the service of man" (Psalms 104:14).

In the post-Reformation period England became the first country in Europe to actually provide government regulation and recognition of the practice of Herbalism and Hydrotherapy in opposition to the Physicians with their poisons and chemicals. This use of herbals in the treatment of human ailments was first legalized by

Royal Charter in the Reign of *Henry VIII* of England. This statute, known as the "Herbalist Charter", is quoted in full in Chapter 1.

The practitioner under this old statute was therefore fully qualified to treat ailments by the use of application of natural therapeutics, backed by law and ancient usages in addition to a professional training of high order. The naturopath is the successor to the herbalist of old. The importance of this Herbalist Charter to Americans today comes from the fact that it became a part of the law of the Thirteen Original States and continues in force as a part of U.S. common law.

The most famous herbal treatise in English is undoubtedly Nicholas Culpeper's (1616-1654) *Herbal*, originally titled *The English Physician*. One author states of Culpeper: "He apprenticed with a master apothecary in London and cultivated an interest in medical botany and subsequently a very busy medical practice. A humble Puritan iconoclast, Culpeper lambasted the physicians of his day for their greed, their dedication to the health of the rich, their use of toxic 'remedies' and bloodletting, and for their resistance to incorporating advances in knowledge into medical practice. Culpeper combined an empirical common sense with a Christian conviction that God provided, in English fauna, cures for every English ill, and therefore Englishmen needed 'no American or Indian drugges.'" (Kline, M. Culpeper Biography. Indiana School of Medicine, December 19, 1997.)

Naturopathic Botanicals

Naturopathy is a complete system of therapeutics, embracing the use of Nature's agencies, forces, processes and products. The use of plant and animal substances, whether for alimentation or for therapy, belongs in the realm of Nature's products. In the choice of such material the naturopath is guided by the philosophy behind naturopathic practice. This philosophy dictates that one should use such agencies, processes and products as are Nature's own. Furthermore, the philosophy teaches that Nature is a sensitive agent and that she possesses the faculty of making its own cures; but when this is flagging she welcomes assistance, but only by her own forces. Naturopathic philosophy also dictates that one should use only such preparations and in such doses as will act with gentleness — altering perverse functions — cleansing the body of its catabolic wastes — and promoting the anabolic processes of the body by the use of those agencies and products as are found in Nature, or are components of the body.

It is not the intention to convey the impression that the recommendations of the agents contained herein is the sole function of naturopathic therapy. These agents are used only in a small but important measure. The use of botanical or biological products naturopathically is to correct any deficiency or hygienic problem within the body and to give Nature's agencies therein the necessary material to correct such deficiencies or anomalous physiological behaviors. It cannot be too strongly emphasized that the use of herbs of almost any variety, from a naturopathic point of view, should not be meant as a permanent indulgence, but as a helping hand until the physical, hygienic and psychic anomalies of the patient (which are frequently the essential causes) are corrected.

While the terms Medicine and Drug are used at times interchangeably, there is, however, a distinction between the two. Medicines are remedial substances of any nature used in the treatment and prophylaxis of disease. The word "drug" was borrowed from the Dutch word "Droog," meaning dried. It was adopted from them during that era when the Dutch were considered the foremost collectors and traders in common and rare botanicals which their trading fleets gathered from the four corners of the world.

A systematic approach to the study of naturopathic botanicals and biologicals is to consider the material pharmacologically. Pharmacology is the study of the behavior of medicines, their nature, identification, administration, preparation, dosage, and their effects upon the body.

Pharmacology is divided in to the following specific divisions:

1. *Pharmacognosy,* which deals with the identification or recognition of these substances microscopically, macroscopically, physically and chemically.
2. *Pharmacodynamics* or physiological action considers the behavior of these agents upon the body.
3. *Naturae Medicina,* which means Natural Medicines, considers the study of all substances of natural origin used in the prevention or treatment of diseases.
4. *Therapeutics* is the science of choosing and applying these materials to the treatment of diseases or the rebuilding of health.
5. *Pharmacy* is the knowledge of the art of compounding these materials into effective interventions.
6. *Posology* considers the proper dosage as related to age, sex, pathological entities and methods of administration.
7. *Toxicology* is the science and art of detecting and treating the effects of poisons.

PHARMACOGNOSY

The Source and Origin of Botanical Agents

The use of botanical and organic substances in therapeutics is of ancient origin. In the beginning it was based upon empiricism, their therapeutic rationale later evolving as the sciences of biology, physics and chemistry advanced. Many botanicals are still used empirically, and with efficiency, without so-called adequate scientific reasons insofar as their chemistry justifies. This is due more to our lack of comprehensive knowledge of their true cellular chemistry as well as to alterations the agent is inadvertently subjected to by the various processes of manipulation. In humbleness it may be said that there is much to science which is still beyond the comprehension of mortal minds.

The ancient Greeks recommended the use of Alyson or Biscutella didyma for hydrophobia. Hippocrates suggested that overdoses of Coriander seeds produced mental derangements and that an ointment of Saffron applied to the head cured dementia. The Hippocratic school of medicine taught that the Male Fern had anthelminthic properties and shrewdly observed that overdoses of this botanical produced sterility. They recommended Kankamon for obesity, Iris Root and the Great Century Plant as an antiphlogistic in abscesses. The botanical Asclepias or Lungwort was named after the great Greek physician Asclepiades, and the plant Wild Yam or Cramp Root was named Dioscorea after Dioscorides.

From the Arabic physicians we received the efficient laxative Senna as well as such valuable plant remedies as Aconite; Nutmeg; Cassia; Cloves; Camphor; Cubeb; Cannabis; Sandalweed; Myrrh; the Syrups; Spirits and Aromatic Waters.

The ancient Hebrews taught us the anthelminthic virtues of the onion, wines and peppers for gastric upsets, that goat's milk had curative merits in dyspepsia, and that in metrorrhagias, gum and alum had antihemorrhagic properties.

Much of our Naturae Medicina has felt the influence of the American Indian's herbal lore. The early pioneers received their knowledge of these agents from the Indians, establishing a common domestic practice in these herbal remedies. Subsequently these herbals were accepted into our professional armamentaria as useful and reliable therapeutic agents, notwithstanding the fact that many have defied accurate analysis and their use is purely empirical. Among these Indian remedies we have Hydrastis or Golden Seal, a very useful alterative, stomachic bitter and carminative. At one time it was used as a yellow staining war-paint. Lobelia was recommended by them for dyspepsia, pectoral affections and coughs. Sassafras was adopted from them for its tonic and alterative values. Pennyroyal as a diaphoretic in colds, influenza, and as a tonic and antispasmodic in dysmenorrhea, amenorrhea and pertussis. The rubefacient properties of pennyroyal was applied in rheumatic pains and for insect bites. The scope of the Indian's herbal lore seems boundless and many interesting volumes have been written about these useful agents.

However, since people are individuals, no herb in this book is being recommended for any specific person or ailment. At this time several governmental agencies are at work re-analyzing their merits and re-admitting them into official use.

Our agents of botanical origin are derived from one or more parts of the plant (or in some cases from the entire plant) and frequently from excrescences or exudates of the plant. The underground portions are the root, rhizome, corm, tuber and bulb. The above ground portions are made up of the bark, wood, twigs, leaves, herb, flower (with their style, stigma, ovary and calyx), the fruit and seed.

The Root or Radix is the descending axial subterranean portions the plant which are devoid of leaves or their modifications. Being a storage house for plant food roots are abundant in many phytochemicals for which these parts are used therapeutically. Some roots are enveloped in a well defined bark or cortex. Tubers or Tuberous Roots are the underground stems, resembling rootstocks, and having knotty enlargements or swellings referred to as eyes or buds. As other underground portions, Tubers are rich in the therapeutic biochemicals. Rhizome or Rootstock is the underground modifications of stems, growing horizontally, obliquely and on occasions traveling on the surface of the ground. They are marked by indentations or annual scars. Corms or Solid Bulbs are the solid bulb-like subterranean expansions resembling to some extent tubers.

Bulbs are fleshy enlargements marked by leafy bases and are of two varieties. The scaly bulb resembling the Lilacea; and the Tunicated as the Onion.

The Bark or Cortex is the outer layer of a stem or root, beneath which is found the cambium. Woods are the thin chips, shavings or granulated (sawdust) portions of medicinal bearing plants. Twigs are usually the small woody branches of medicinal plants. When they are of the outer small stems of the plant and contain the flowers, tender end leaves and their stems, they are referred to as Herbs.

Leaves are the foliole portions of the plant. Their variations in size, contour, surface markings, the character of their veins (whether parallel or reticulated), and if they are singular or multiple, are often used to identify their species. Leaves are the elaborators of intricate biochemical substances used therapeutically. The Flowers or Flores are the florescent, showy portions of the plant. They are composed of the Calyx, Corolla, the Stamen with their Anthers, the Pistil and their Styles, and the Ovary containing the Ovules. Fruits are the fleshy outer portions of the mature ovary within which are the seeds or semen. Some fruits are desiccated. Seeds are the tunicated fertilized ovules. They have an external coating referred to as an integument. When this coating is hard or crustaceous it is called a shell. The inner part of the seed is known as the kernel.

Methods Employed in Pharmacognosy

There are several methods employed in the proper identification and evaluation of botanicals from a pharmaceutical standpoint. These differential characteristics must be learned with the nomenclature, dosage and therapeutics of each agent. Some mention of the principal constituents of the botanicals is included herein. While the active principles within a botanical may be an alkaloid, glucoside or some volatile oil; there are other complex substances as resins, fixed oils, oleoresins, tannins, and a multiplicity of phyto-sterols and acids which give to each botanical a distinct therapeutic action. When one is acquainted with the physiological action of such substances as amodin, tannin, oxalic and gallic acid, a reasonable knowledge may be had of the properties of plants containing these substances.

The organoleptic evaluation of plants considers the impression these agents leave on the organs of special sense. The impressions made on vision as to color, size, contour both macroscopically and microscopically, on the tactile organs the feel, the character of the snap when it is broken and the type of fracture it leaves, assist, in a measure, in its identification, on the taste organs if it is sour, salty, saccharine, bitter or alkaline. Often the sense of taste is a compound one, in which several sensations are experienced; such as aromatic, spicy, terebinthinate, camphoraceous or balsamic. At times the taste is referred to as mucilaginous it slimy; nauseous it tending to produce vomiting; pungent if it leaves a warm, burning after-sensation; if the after-sensation is irritating or tingling it is called acrid; an astringent leaves a puckered or contracted feeling.

The microscope, both the wide field and narrow field, gives much information of value in identifying botanicals. They reveal the amount and nature of adulterants in the specimen. Under the microscope and by the aid of microchemistry the variations of allied species may be studied. In this procedure, thin sections are made of the specimen and when subjected to suitable specific staining or reagent processes, reveal differentiating characteristics.

Biological evaluations or bioassays have yielded much information on the physiological behavior of many agents. They are still resorted to in determining and standardizing the potencies of our agents. The goldfish, frog and cat have contributed much in the standardization of foxglove or digitalis. Rats, mice, rabbits, guinea-pigs and hamsters have helped us in evaluating our knowledge of nutrition, cause of endocrinology as a medium for hormone potency evaluations. Botanicals are also evaluated by certain physical characteristics of their constituents. Their liquid components are viewed as to their degree of solubility in water, alcohol, ether, chloroform or other solvents. Their specific gravity under varying conditions; their melting point and congealing points; also such optical characteristics as dextro or levorotation, refractive index and fluorescent characteristics under ultraviolet illumination yield information of value.

Chemical analysis of botanicals, while revealing much information as to the plant's chemical composition, is not relied upon by our school of practice as the sole criterion of an agent's therapeutic nature. We realize that the various chemical and physical manipulations that the plant is subjected to will often alter the chemical results so as to mislead us in evaluating their true nature and therapeutic value.

In the past the dogmatic statements of many so-called scientists on the merits of such simple botanicals as sassafras, sarsaparilla, etc., claiming them valueless and therapeutically inert, has in the light of recent investigations and clinical studies been proved erroneous. How many more valuable agents have been condemned to oblivion by such unqualified statements remains to be seen. In the past, the tendency has been to regard the spectacular in medicine and ignore those slow acting relatively innocuous agents which are of particular value in naturopathic medicine. The long ranged ill-effects of such "Wonder Drugs" as the sulfa group cannot be denied. The naturopathic physician should give more credence to the clinical value of an agent than to the so-called frigid "scientific facts," for Naturopathy is, strictly speaking, a clinical art based upon the natural sciences.

The foregoing remarks are not meant to discredit the chemical values of our plants, but to assist in viewing them in the light of qualified judgment. Let us realize that while certain alkaloids, glucosides, volatile and fixed oils are present, there are still certain unknown factors at play to explain variations in behavior.

Principle Constituents of Certain Known Agents

All plants contain substances which are regarded as producing certain physiological behaviors when applied to animals or their tissues. These substances, often complex in nature, are regarded as the principle, chief or active constituents of the agent. Their application to living animals will produce alterations in tissue composition and modifications in systemic behavior characteristics due to the principle constituents. Such behaviors are spoken of as the Physiological Effect, or Action; or Pharmacological Action.

Principle constituents are classified according to certain chemical natures: as alkaloids, glucosides, carbohydrates, tannins, chlorophyll, proteins, volatile oils, fixed oils, fats, waxes, saponins, resins, oleoresins, gums and gum-resins, balsam and balsamic resins, vitamins, enzymes, etc. ...

ALKALOIDS are crystalline or oily compounds of basic reaction, obtained from plant(a few from animal) tissues. They are found more abundantly in roots and seeds, although some are obtained from the leaves of plants. Their actions are energetic, often bordering on toxic, and their chemical nature is complex. They may be classified chemically as to their derivatives into five groups:

1. Pyridin Group— is antiseptic, antispasmodic and cardiac stimulant; and is obtained from tobacco and hemlock.
2. Pyrrolidin Group—is found in tobacco, cocaine and atropine.
3. Quinoline or Chinoline Group—is a tertiary amine found in coal tar, quinine,
4. Cinchonine—it exhibits antipyretic, antiseptic and antiperiodic properties.

5. Isoquinoline Group—is found in berberine, hydrastine, cotarnine, papaverine and narcotine.
6. Phenanthrine Group—possesses analgesic and narcotic effects and is found in codeine, thebaine and morphine.

Alkaloids are bitter to the taste, usually insoluble in water but soluble in ether, chloroform and organic solvents. To render them water soluble they are converted into a salt (hydrochloride, nitrate, phosphate or sulphate).

GLUCOSIDES are substances found in plants which upon hydrolysis or enzyme action yield a variety of sugars leaving a non-sugar residue referred to as an aglycon. In classifying glucosides, the aglycon grouping, while not entirely satisfactory, is considered the most inclusive and least complex.

1. The Phenolic Group—contains in it such glucosides as baptism found in wild indigo, iridin from blue flag, and arbutin found in pippsissewa and bearberry.
2. Oxy-coumarin Group — contains such glucosides as fraxetin found in the cortex of the ash, horsechestnut; scopolin found in belladonna and jasmine.
3. Alcohol Group—the chief among which hydrolysis of the salicin yields saligenin (salicylic alcohol), populin (benzosalicin), and coniferin which hydrolyzes into coniferyl alcohol.
4. Aldehyde Group—among which is amygdalin found in apricots, peaches, almonds, plums and cherries, particularly the seeds. Amygdalin yields benzaldehyde. Salinigrin is found in the black willow.
5. Acid Glucoside Group—yield upon hydrolysis a phyto-acid. The principal representatives of this group are found in gaultherin which yields salicylic acid; and

convolvulin which hydrolyzes into convolvulic acid.

6. Anthraquinone Group—are usually considered as pigment glucosides and exhibit laxative or cathartic actions. The chief plants yielding this group are the cascara segrada, senna, aloes, frangula, rhubarb, rumex, etc. This compound is complex and either di-, tn-, or tetra hydroxy-methylanthraquinones.

7. Thiocyanate Group—which hydrolyzes by the enzyme, myrosin, into thiocyanates. They are represented by the Sinapis nigra (black mustard), Sinapis alba (white mustard) and gluconapin from rape seed.

8. Cynophore Group—are glucosides which yield, upon hydrolysis, hydrocyanic acid. They are found among the rosaceae family of plants of which the cherry, plum, peach, apricot are representative.

9. Saponin Group—contain a wide variety of glucosides, of which sarsaparilla, senega, and quallaja are representatives. They are hemolytic to erythrocytes and are quite toxic. They emulsify oils, and when shaken with water, produce a foam. Their aglycon, sapogenin, will upon acetylization crystallize to produce characteristic identifying patterns.

10. Cardiac Group—of glucosides are found in digitalis (digitalin and digitoxin), scilla (scillaren), apocynum (cymarin), strophanthus (oubain), and convallaria (convallotoxin). Their action is upon the cardiac and vascular muscles.

CARBOHYDRATES or starches are found extensively in plants and are one of the most important creations of plant life. They are found in the chloroblast cells of the plant and vary in chemical structure as their carbon atoms increase. The simple carbohydrates are hexoses or monosaccharides with six carbon atoms to the molecule. The disaccharides possess twelve carbon atoms to the molecule. The trisaccharides have eighteen carbons, and the polysaccharides posses increasing numbers. Only the simple saccharides exhibit the saccharine taste. They are chiefly nutrients for plants and animals.

TANNINS are widely distributed in plants, and are our principal therapeutic astringents. They precipitate proteins, alkaloids and gelatin. In combining with proteins they retard the action of proteolytic enzymes; a factor to be considered in digestion and dietetics. Tannins are non-crystalline complex substances forming colloids in aqueous solution and possess a bitter taste and puckering feel. In plants they are often associated in sugar and phenolic groups. Tannins are classified into:

1. Phlobatannins—which yield catechol (pyrocatechol) when subjected to heat. Upon boiling with hydrochloric acid, a red insoluble substance is produced, called phlobaphcnc. Phiobatannins produce a greenish discoloration upon the addition of ferric chloride and are precipitated by the addition of bromine water.

2. Pyrogallotannins—form pyrogallol when heated and yield a blue color with ferric chloride. They are not precipitated by the addition of bromine water.

The different tannins can only be separated with difficulty when found together. When subjected to hydrolysis they form polyhydnic phenols which ultimately decompose into catechol, pyrogallol, ellagic and protocatechuic acids.

CHLOROPHYLL is a greenish pigment obtained from all plants having a very close structural formula to hemoglobin, except for the absence of iron. It is water insoluble but soluble in alcohol, ether and fatty acids. It is alterative and nutrient, improving cellular metabolism and facilitating repair.

PROTEINS are complex nitrogenous substances found in both plant and animal tissues. They are essential to the economy of living tissues and are present in the simple (amino acid), conjugate and derived proteins form. Their complexity is created by the condensation of several amino acids, possessing a high molecular weight and colloidal dimension. Proteins are, therefore, mixtures of amino acids which are organic acids in which one or more residual hydrogen atoms have been replaced by amino group. Amino acids are classified physiologically as "essential amino acids" and "non-essential amino acids." Proteins, and their precursors the amino acids, occupy an important role in nutrition and natural therapeutics.

VOLATILE OILS are the essential oils of plants which are at times elaborated from special parts or glandular cells. They are volatilized readily by heat or steam and are obtained from plants by distillation. They do not leave a residual stain, as fixed oils do, but evaporate readily emitting their characteristic odor. In chemical structure they are hydrocarbons, yielding terpenes, alcohols, ketones, aldehydes and ethers. The terpenes are the most common of the volatile oils. Volatile oils are used as condiments, antiseptics, carminatives, and some possess distinct rubefacient properties.

FIXED OILS, fats and waxes are hydrocarbon compounds of fatty acids and glycerol. They are obtained from the plant by expression or extraction as esters of aliphatic compounds. They are elaborated by the plant from carbohydrates where they are stored for food. Seeds contain a high percentage of fixed oils.

SAPONINS are bitter, acrid, irritating, non-nitrogenous drug elements which emulsify oils and form colloidal substanc-

es in water. Saponins foam when shaken in water and many are toxic, producing hemolysis of the erythrocytes.

RESINS are solid or semisolid amorphous substances, the result of oxidation of terpenes as an end product of plant metabolism. They are water insoluble but alcohol soluble. Chemically they are complex, yielding resinotannins, resin acids and resin alcohols. They enter into combination with gums, balsams, fixed and volatile oils, forming gum resins, balsamic resins and oleoresins.

GUMS are translucent colloidal amorphous substances produced by plants as a protection to injury. They are allied to mucilage, pectin and cellulose being condensation products of pentose. They are water soluble and alcohol insoluble. Some gums contain salts of magnesium, potassium or calcium. Among the therapeutic gums are kino, tragacanth and acacia.

BALSAMS are mixtures of resins, cinnamic and benzoic acids, or their esters. The common balsams are styrax, peru, benzoin and tolu.

VITAMINS are essential, micro-chemical organic substances found in food; in themselves they are non-productive of energy but behave as nutritional catalysts promoting cellular metabolism and influencing normal growth and physiological activity. Their acceptance as nutritional essentials and therapeutic agents is based upon clinical recognition in deficiencies, experimental proof, and therapeutic success when applied in deficiency diseases. Vitamins are discussed in more detail in Chapter 22.

ENZYMES are complex, organic, colloidal substances elaborated by living cells and behaving as biological catalysts. They are colloidal in nature, exhibiting specificity in action and a high sensitivity to hydrogen ion concentration variations, temperature changes, electrolytic action and the action of activators, co-enzymes and toxins. They are classified according to the substrate or compound they act upon as amylase (starch), lipase (fats) and pepsin (proteins). Co-enzymes are inorganic and organic substances which accelerate or control enzyme activity. Among such co-enzymes are vitamin B_1, nicotinic acid, riboflavin, etc. Enzymes are found in both plants and animals.

HORMONES are specific biochemic activators elaborated by specialized cells of the organs of internal secretion, exhibiting their influence either upon the same cell or tissue as intracellular autocoids, or as circulating hormones exerting their influence quite remote to their source. Chemically they are diverse: thyroxine is an iodine derivative of an amino acid, tyrosine; estrogen, androgen and suprarenal cortex are sterols; insulin is a polypeptide. Recent investigations have shown that many of our animal hormones have related substances in the plant kingdom. This may account for the apparent glandular stimulation obtained by such botanicals as phytolacca, sarsaparilla, senecio, etc.

PHARMACODYNAMICS

Pharmacodynamics, frequently referred to as physiological action, considers the behavior modes of therapeutic materials upon the organism. While much of our knowledge of the action of these agents has been obtained through animal experimentation, there are frequently unexplainable voids between the experienced action of these substances upon animals and their clinical behavior in humans.

The physio-chemical theory of drug action considers that these agents produce an alteration in the physical and chemical nature of cellular and extracellular substances. This theory has a wide application whether the agencies are physical, chemical or biological. It is, further,

an explanation of what is accomplished whether by use of herb or by diet.

When we remember that cells are the basic units of organic structure, and that a tissue is made up of groups of similar cells aggregated for a common purpose; further, that an organ is composed of groups of dissimilar tissues banded together for a definite function; we can readily see that whatever change in organic activity is to be obtained must be instituted within the cells themselves.

The metabolism and physiological expressions of these cells are influenced by the nature of their nutritive material and extracellular environment. Thus, if we desire a stimulation in these cells, we must employ agents which will accelerate their activity through a change in the physio–chemical nature of their environment and their protoplasm. When a depression in activity is desired such agents are employed as will alter the physio–chemical nature of the cells' environment and protoplasm resulting in decreased activity.

Agents, further, manifest their action upon cells and tissues either as irritants, stimulants or depressants. An irritant's behavior on cells depends upon the degree and character of the agent. Mild irritants have a stimulating effect upon cells increasing their metabolism and at times producing a transitory but reparable damage to the cell. Harsh irritants yield a short phase of stimulation followed by a longer phase of depressed activity. They very frequently do permanent damage and mass cell destruction by precipitation and dehydration of the cellular protoplasm.

In contradistinction to the irritant stimulants, we have agents classed as pure stimulants. These pure stimulants behave as cellular excitants, increasing the cell's metabolism. The converse of these pure stimulants are known as pure depressants which decrease cellular activity and metabolism. However, it should be remembered that an agent can be a stimulant to one system and behave as a depressant to another system.

Certain agents exhibit a selective action on tissues and systems. This selectivity may be more marked for one system than another. It is through this selectivity that we are able, at times, to treat a system directly without influencing some other system.

Physical agents are those which, by their action, produce no chemical alterations in cellular or environmental conditions but affect tissues in the physical realm of science. Among these physical agents are certain ointments, oleoginous substances and inert powders which exert a protective physical influence upon the skin and mucous surfaces without chemical action on these tissues. Agents may further act in a physical manner by altering the ionic composition of the intracellular and/or extracellular substances; alterations in cell membrane potential; changes in colloidal structure; or alterations in osmotic pressure.

Chemically, the most common reactions of physiological processes are: hydrolysis, whereby complex compounds are split into smaller components; and oxidation-reduction reactions, which are creators of energy. In a naturopathic sense, this may be considered the chief object of our therapeutics. The encouragement of these processes is the basis of our treatment. Such substances as carbon monoxide, cyanide, certain endogenic and exogenic toxins produce an oxygen deficit, of varying stability, by combining with the hemoglobin, retarding oxygenation.

Factors Influencing Pharmacological Action

There are many factors which influence pharmacological behavior and require an exercise of judgment. However, such exercise is not without set reasons or rules.

The influence of an agent on the body depends upon its diffusibility and solubility. A substance chemically inert produces no effect other than that of a physical agent.

Dosage must be regulated so as to produce the desired therapeutic effect;
and the method of administration must be appropriate to yield prompt results. The dosages included herein represents the average adult dose for a male of approximately 150 pounds. Variations in dosage should be calculated for children, women and in the aged.

In calculating the Child's Dose, [Dr. von Peters] feels one of the following rules can often be employed:

Young's Rule:

$$\frac{\text{Child's Age}}{\text{Child's Age plus 12}} = \text{fraction of adult dose to be used}$$

Cowling's Rule:

$$\frac{\text{Child's Age on Next Birthday}}{24} = \text{fraction of adult dose to be used}$$

Clark's Rule:

$$\frac{\text{Weight of Child in Pounds}}{150 \text{ (average adult weight)}} = \text{fraction of adult dose to be used}$$

While Young's Rule is most frequently used, Clark's Rule is the more scientific for it takes cognizance of the application of the therapeutic agent to the surface area of the patient. This consideration of regulating the dose to the surface area of the subject is particularly applicable to women.

Women, as a rule, require smaller doses than men. Certain physiological epochs, menstruation, pregnancy and lactation, must be taken into account in the use of various agents.

Physiological temperaments have a bearing on the pharmacological action of some agents. Patients with a highly organized nervous system require smaller doses of a stimulant than a phlegmatic or depressed patient. Certain depressants may initiate a depressive psychosis in susceptible subjects.

The state of freshness of an agent, particularly botanicals having highly volatile active principles, is affected by its age. Frequently, botanicals are subjected to deterioration by bacterial and mold action, rendering them valueless. Some aqueous solutions of botanicals (ergot, arisaema, digitalis, etc.) will deteriorate in time, losing much of their therapeutic efficiency.

A cumulative effect is exhibited by some botanicals after repeated doses. This is due to the slow, or at times retarded, elimination of this particular agent from the body. Often cumulative effects are displayed more quickly than is usual for the agent as the result of impairment of the eliminative organs.

The pharmacologic action of some botanical compounds may be influenced in a positive or synergistic, or in a negative or antagonistic manner. Synergistic action is the ability of one substance to enhance the therapeutic or physiological action of another. Synergistic action is often relied upon to enhance the effect of an active, and at times toxic, agent permitting it to be used in smaller dosage effectively. Antagonistic action is obtained when two or more elements in a compound exercise opposing or neutralizing effects. This antagonistic action of drugs is employed in toxicology in treating poisoned patients.

Tolerance is a state of relative resistance possessed by some persons to the normal action of an agent. This may be produced by faulty assimilation, too rapid excretion, or destruction of the agent in the intestines by bacterial action. It may be congenital in some, or acquired in others. Some forms of habituation are considered as acquired tolerance. Many persons who become addicted to the "Cathartic Habit" become tolerant to that particular cathartic and are required to increase the dosage to obtain the desired results, or change to some other type of cathartic.

Factors Influencing Absorption and Elimination of Agents

The destiny of an agent is variable. It undergoes many devious changes from the time that it is administered to its elimination. The rate of absorption of agents varies with:

1. The type and nature of the agent; its diffusibility and its solubility.
2. The state of permeability of the skin or membrane to which the agent is applied. This is influenced greatly by deviations in the health of these structures. In skins with thick cornified layers the absorption rate is diminished. Dermas which have excessive sebaceous secretions will retard the absorption of certain substances. Mucous membranes with excessive catarrhal or mucus secretion will appreciably retard the absorption of many agents, a factor influencing the assimilation of foods, minerals and vitamins. The capillary circulation of skin and mucosa must be adequate.

Within the body these agents may be subjected to various chemical alterations by oxidation-reduction, hydrolysis and chemical combination or synthesis. These changes may occur in the stomach, intestines, liver or kidneys. During the process of cellular nutrition these agents are, further, altered by the cellular enzymes into chemical substances quite different than the original agent. Biochemic compatibilities vary as the biochemic deviations of individuals do, which accounts for occasional atypical and erratic reactions, ranging at times from simple allergic manifestations to distinct anaphylactic shock.

Such defensive detoxifying organs as the liver and kidneys will alter the chemical structure of agents rendering them, not only less toxic, but, at times facilitating their therapeutic properties. The selective affinity of certain cells for special chemical substances accounts for individual cellular or tissue responses to certain agents.

In the main, the endeavor of therapeutics is to accomplish changes in cellular physiology from one of perverted expression to a state of normal. Our efforts in this respect are to alter perverted physio-chemical behaviors either by changes in the cellular chemistry or alterations in the electric arrangement of the cells' chemistry.

Agents are eliminated from the body through the usual channels of elimination, e.g., the feces, bile, kidneys, lungs, saliva, sudoriferous and at times the lacrymal secretions. Their rate of elimination depends upon the solubility, diffusibility, and molecular complexity of the agent, as well as upon factors influencing the functional activity of the eliminating organs.

Some agents are eliminated unchanged and are readily recoverable in the urine, feces, perspiration, etc. Other substances, as benzoic acid and glycocoll, are converted into hippuric acid by the kidneys and excreted in the urine.

Classification of Physiological Actions

Physiological or Pharmacological Action refers to the behavior or influence an agent exhibits upon certain organs or systems. Many terms employed in nomenclature are superficially descriptive and often several terms are synonymous. Further, there are many terms, inherited from the past, used to describe physiological behavior which are not specific nor descriptive of the manner in which these agents produce their effects. These terms are still regrettably adhered to by not only the older writers on herbal therapy but have been adopted and carried on by many of our newer writers on botanical agents.

Among the most abused terms describing the pharmacological properties of agents is the word *Tonic.* This word expresses no adequate pharmacological attributes of the agent other than that it is presumed to give tone to some particular organ or system. Often the term Tonic is modified by descriptive adjectives, e.g. Blood Tonic, Nerve Tonic, Kidney Tonic, denoting specific organic or systemic actions, but these terms of themselves are non-descriptive as regards to stimulative, depressive or alterative effects.

In an endeavor to overcome this confused terminology we have within the recent twenty years adopted such specific terms as, cardiant, sympathomimetic, neuro-stimulant, neuro-depressant, etc., in an effort to become more precise in describing our agents. While the term *Tonic* is still used in this text, it is used to describe a stimulative or accelerative influence.

EMOLLIENTS, DEMULCENTS AND PROTECTIVES are materials which act as Physical Agents. They are chemically inert and are used for their protective influence upon the skin or mucous surfaces.

Emollients are chemically inactive oily, fatty or glycerinic in nature acting as bland softening agents, applied to the derma or mucosa as a protective agent. Emollients are frequently used as vehicles for active medicinal agents. The chief emollients are lard, wool fat (lanolin), almond oil, paraffin, olive oil, glycerine.

Demulcents are gummy or gluey colloidal substances used in inflammatory conditions to hold highly active ingredients in suspension for slow action or absorption, and oils in emulsified suspension. They act as protective coatings to irritated surfaces to prevent further absorption of irritants. The demulcents most frequently used are Acacia (Acacia senegal, Tragacanth (Astragalus gummifer), and Starch (Zea mays).

Protectives are chemically inert physical agents applied to abraded, broken or wounded surfaces to protect them from external infection or irritation. Among the most commonly used protectives are Flexible Collodion, Talcum, Calamine and Subnitrate or Subcarbonate of Bismuth.

IRRITANTS are agents which produce a varied local reaction depending on their degree of activity. They are classified as to their action as, (a) Rubefacient, when they produce a redness of the surface with a sense of heat; (b) Vesicant, when in addition to reddening and a sense of heat they produce blisters or vesicles; (c)

Pustulants, when their action is harsh and they produce pustules.

Aside from the slightly raised local temperature, irritants frequently produce a slight but definite systemic effect. Due to its vasodilator influence it stimulates metabolism and creates a mild leucocytosis.

COUNTER–IRRITANTS are irritants employed with a different therapeutic object in view. They are used to overcome irritation in some distant or deep seated locale. The most reasonable explanation for counterirritant action is based upon Head's Law. Head quoted his law as follows: "When a painful stimulus is applied to a part of low sensibility in close central connection with a part of much higher sensibility, the pain produced is felt in the area of higher sensibility rather than in the part of lower sensibility to which the stimulus is applied." Thus, if the primary and secondary areas are supplied by the same segmental arrangement, (as the epigastric surface pain in gastric ulcers) the application of a counterirritant to the accessible skin of the epigastrium would also produce stimulative effects upon the stomach. As outlined under irritants, there are positive effects produced, and counterirritants are essentially irritants applied to secondary areas of homologous segmental innervation and will have similar effects upon the primary area. By its vasodilator effect it tends to relieve visceral congestion.

The common uses of counterirritants are best illustrated by the application of mustard poultices for correcting vascular engorgement in pneumonia and peptic ulcers; or the use of turpentine stupes in acute gallbladder attacks.

ASTRINGENTS are agents which when applied locally to a surface produces contraction of the tissues. They moderately precipitate the tissue proteins of the top layers, creating a puckering of the surface. Astringents are vasoconstrictors, diminishing transudates, leucocytic action and pyogenic formation. They are frequently used to control capillary bleeding and catarrhal exudates as in vaginitis and diarrhea. In swellings, astringents are used as embrocations. The most frequently used astringents are Krameria (Rhatany), Kino (Gum Kino), Achillea (Yarrow), and Tannic Acid.

BITTERS or STOMACHICS are drugs which promote nutrition by stimulating the appetite and digestion. Some bitters are mild irritants stimulating vascular and motor activity of the stomach. They should be given about twenty minutes before eating to allow sufficient time for their stimulative action upon the secretion of digestive juices. The most frequently used bitters are Nux Vomica (Quaker Buttons), Tincture of Gentian Compound (Gentian 10%, Bitter Orange Peel and Cardamon), Calumba (Calumbo).

DIGESTANTS are agents used to promote or stimulate digestion. They are either stimulants, irritants encouraging the digestive secretions or are used as replacement or substitutional therapy. In deficiencies of the digestive elements, such as hydrochloric acid, pepsin, pancreatic substance and bile, the prescribing of these agents as supplements, stimulates nature to supply its own and overcome these deficiencies.

CARMINATIVES are substances which stimulate the expulsion of flatus from the gastro-intestinal tract. They increase the tone of the gastro-enteric musculature and stimulate peristalsis. Carminatives should be given for some time to accomplish their purpose particularly when the flatus is in the intestines. The most popular naturopathic carminatives are ginger, capsicum, cloves and rectified turpentines. In intestinal or colonic flatus, 8 to 10cc of Rectified Spirits of turpentine to two quarts of soap suds water given as an enema is helpful. For gastric flatus the Oil of Peppermint, 5 drops on sugar, has received endorsement.

ABSORBENTS and ADSORBENTS may be considered as Carminatives for they tend to eliminate intestinal flatus by absorbing or adsorbing the gas and relieving the distention. The most frequently used Adsorbent is animal charcoal.

EMETICS are agents which produce evacuation of the stomach's contents by vomiting. Care must be used in employing emetics, bearing in mind the contraindications to their use in hernias, possible perforating ulcers of the stomach or bowel, pregnancy, debilitating conditions of advanced tuberculosis, cardiac diseases, corrosive poisoning, narcotic poisoning and convulsive diseases. The most frequently used emetics are mustard (Sinapis) 1 to 2 teaspoonful in hot water; salt 2 tablespoonful in hot water, or Ipecac which is a slow acting and debilitating emetic.

ANTHELMINTICS are substances which are used to expel worms from the gastro-intestinal tract. It must be remembered that in the choice of anthelmintics the toxicity of these agents require adequate care; furthermore, certain anthelmintics have a specific action for different species of worms, hence, a careful diagnosis is required by fecal analysis to insure prompt and effective results. Vermifuges tend to paralyze worms and expel them, often alive but debilitated. Vermicides tend to kill the parasites in vivo before expelling them.

CATHARTICS are agents which stimulate the evacuation of the bowels. They may be classified according to their degree of action as:
1. Aperients which are quite mild in their physic action, as rhubarb, agar, and olive oil.
2. Laxatives which have a moderate evacuative effect, as aloes, senna and mineral oil.
3. Purgatives and drastic purgatives which have a varied degree of harsh, energetic evacuative effect upon the bowels.

Cathartics may be further classified according to their method of action.
1. Emollient cathartics which act as a lubricant to the intestinal walls and soften the feces, as mineral oil and olive oil.
2. Bulk cathartics, which produce evacuation by increasing the intestinal bulk and stimulate peristalsis by pressure. Bulk cathartics are psyllium, agar and bran.
3. Irritant cathartics, which through their irritating action on the intestinal mucosa and nerve endings produce increased peristaltic action, as croton oil.
4. Saline cathartics, which withdraw water through the intestinal mucosa by osmosis and act partly as bulk and partly as irritating cathartics, such as epsom salts and sodium sulphate.
5. Cholagogues which produce evacuation by stimulating the secretion and discharge of bile into the intestines and produce their action in this manner, such as ox-gall, chionanthus, chelidonium and bile salts.
6. Neural stimulants, which increase the peristaltic action of the bowel and promote evacuation, the most common drug of this type is pituitrin.

While on the subject of cathartics, it will be proper to view the subject of constipation from a naturopathic viewpoint. It is the contention of our school of healing, as well as the more sincere elements of the regulars, that the indiscriminate use of cathartics is one of the major health vices indulged in by the American people. It can be said, without fear of contradiction, that in no country has the 'Cathartic Habit' a more vicious hold.

Most cases of constipation are due to violations of some of the laws of personal hygiene. The average American takes little time or effort about the less conspicuous but more important problem of personal hygiene. The average lunch of the busy American is a ham on rye and a coke; some a cigarette, a cup of coffee and a candy bar.

Most cases of constipation begin by dietary violations, either by off balanced desires for certain classes of foods with a marked aversion for other essential nutriments. Irregular feeding habits, the indulgence in soft bland bulkiness diets and what is more serious the self instituted restricted diet, whether due to fancied overweight or personal cravings. The total neglect, willfully or because of ignorance, of the "Habit Time."

The next common factors causing constipation are the excessive psychic and nervous strain. We are always in a hurry, whether at work or at play, trying to crowd two life-times into one. The sedentary businessman hurries and worries himself into a good state of psychic and neural tension through his active years, only to find himself in his forties a neurotic with spastic colitis and addiction to the cathartic habit.

Constipation is not a pathologic entity, but a symptom of some physiological inadequacy, for which the prescribing of a laxative alone is poor therapeutics. The use of colonic irrigations while excellent in certain cases during preliminary treatment have never, in themselves, cured constipation, but, to the contrary have often aggravated the condition by further diminishing intestinal tone and reducing the natural intestinal protective agents which maintain the normal intestinal flora.

TOXICOLOGY is that branch of science which undertakes the study of poisons; investigating their source, composition, detection, action, diagnostic appearance and treatment.

The subject of poisons is indeed an ancient one, its origin lost in antiquity, and interesting mentions of their diverse use have been made by historians. Although poisons have been by and large employed with criminal intent, certain toxins have been and are put to the good service of man.

A poison or toxin is any substance which, when applied to or introduced within the body, produces a disturbed physiological equilibrium or even death. This definition does not take cognizance of the popular saying that "one man's meat is another man's poison," as exemplified by the many allergic manifestations certain civilized individuals show for simple innocuous substances.

The classifications of poisons are varied, some consider the chemical nature of the agent, but for our purposes the physiological classification is best suited. This classification considers poisons as Irritants, Neurotoxins and Hematotoxins.

Irritant Poisons are substances which produce irritation and inflammation of the tissue. They may be corrosive in action, producing precipitation and coagulation of cellular protoplasm; or they may be stimulant irritants, accelerating cellular activity and, at times, producing hyperactivity to the point of convulsions.

Neurotoxins or Cerebral Poisons are substances which produce disturbances of the neuromuscular mechanism. They may be depressant in action, exhibiting varied degrees of diminished sensory-motor activity, at times to the point of paralysis, as curare, phenobarbital, etc.; or they may be stimulant or convulsant, producing exaggerated involuntary movements, as strychnine.

Hematotoxins are substances which produce disturbed physiological equilibrium by alterations in the blood constituents. They may be stabile compounds affecting oxygenation, as carbon monoxide or cyanide. Hemolysis may be produced by saponins, insect and reptile bites. Endogenic toxins are often concentrated within the body fluids, being the product of accumulated catabolic wastes, faulty metabolism or leukomaines; or the exogenic products of bacterial action of fermentation, putrifaction or ptomaines.

Leukomaines are alkaloidal metabolic substances of excrementitious origin, their toxicity depending upon their degree of accumulation in the tissue fluids. Leukomaines are of three classes: the uric acid group, the creatine group, and the aromine group. Leukomaines are by far the most common of our systemic toxins.

Ptomaines are the product of bacterial putrefaction. They are alkaloidal in nature the result of the splitting off of carbon dioxide from an amino acid group. Botulin is the most characteristic ptomaine and is produced by protein putrefaction by the Clostridium botulinum. Botulin exerts a depressing effect on the neuromuscular mechanism, circulation and hemogenic functions of the body.

SENSORY DEPRESSANTS are agents which diminish the transmission of sensory impulses, or impede their reception by the brain. Sensory Depressants are usually named according to specific qualifications they may possess: Analgesic, Calmative or Sedative, Hypnotic, Narcotic and Anesthetic.

An Analgesic is any agent which will diminish sensation to pain. Analgesics will promote sleep only to the extent that they diminish pain and make sleep possible.

A Calmative is any agent which allays excitement. It is frequently used as synonymous with Sedative.

Hypnotics are agents which induce sleep. They frequently control pain.

Narcotics are agents which produce a stuporous sleep.

A Soporific is an agent which produces profound sleep. The term is used at times synonymously with narcotic.

Anesthetics are agents which produce an abolition of sensation. A Local Anesthetic is one which diminishes sensation in a particular locale, without influencing consciousness. A General Anesthetic is an agent which renders the entire body insensible and influences consciousness by producing sleep.

Sleep has been theorized as a temporary and reversible reduction or complete suspension of consciousness; produced normally by fatigue toxins, CO_2, NO_2, lactic acid, an oxygen debit, etc.; or induced by agents called hypnotics, narcotics or soporifics.

The pharmacodynamics of narcotic agents considers the physicochemical effects of these agents on protoplasmic alterations. The theory of Myer and Overton is based upon the observation that the efficacy of narcotics are in relation to their fat solvency and lipoid affinity. This affinity of the depressing agent to the lipoid of the surface membrane of cell decreases its permeability, influencing its metabolism and response to stimuli. The theory of Moore and Roaf suggests that the narcotizing agent forms a labile compound in the protoplasm of the cerebral cells, diminishing their receptivity. Verworn's theory assumes that narcosis is produced by an anoxemia created when the narcotizing agent combines with the available oxygen. All of these theories have been well substantiated by research, their application depending upon the type of sensory depressant under consideration.

Botanical Pharmacy

Pharmacy is that branch of pharmacology which undertakes the study of the methods of gathering, preparing and compounding the various medicinal agents. Naturopathic Pharmacy entails an individualized knowledge (no longer adequately considered in the modern undergraduate pharmacy curriculum) of a broad understanding of the botanical and chemical characteristics of all medicinal plants as well as the differentiations of related species. The modern herb gatherer must now, in addition to the knowledge of ancient herbal lore, be an expert botanist and analytical chemist, if he expects his collections to be saleable, for the accepted standards of the Department of Agriculture and the Food and Drug Administration are strict in regulating the purity or adulterant content and the principle constituents content of a large portion of our common botanicals.

As with all living and growing life, the health and chemical corn-position of our botanicals are influenced by the composition of the soil. In recent years the cultivation of many medicinal plants has received a renewed impetus. This has been brought about by such factors as the gradual disappearance of many effective indigenous plants, by the encroachment of civilization on their natural habitat and by vandalism. Furthermore, many botanicals indigenous to other countries have been satisfactorily naturalized by controlled cultivation. Economic stresses, brought on by a curtailed foreign supply, has resulted in the effective cultivation of many plants heretofore imported. Many of our agricultural colleges as well as certain drug manufacturers have contributed to the scientific cultivation and controlled propagation studies with the result that the plants produced are healthier and possess a more equitable principle constituent content.

Naturopathically these botanicals may be employed, either as the crude herb (compounded or used singly) prepared as a decoction, infusion or pulverized and filled into capsules or compressed into tablets. They are frequently prescribed as a fluid-extract, extract or tincture. As to the most effective way of administering these botanicals (whether the crude herb or fluidextract, extract and tincture) is controversial as far as our particular profession is concerned. In justice to the two schools of thought, the salient theories of each should receive a brief review.

The crude herb proponents believe, and rightly so, that only the true, whole herb possesses the desired full therapeutic properties; and that in extraction certain undetermined synergistic and antagonistic substances are left behind and not carried over into the extract or tincture. These naturopaths and herbalists feel that only in the use of the entire botanical can effective results be obtained. This is in some instances apparently true, for we do know that certain crude herbs often show properties not demonstrable in the fluid extract, extract or tincture.

The proponents for extracts, fluid extractions and tinctures also possess impressive and true reasons to prove their stand. They feel, and rightly so, that under the improved new methods of extraction the former objections have been largely removed, and that the newer extractions represent more closely the full components of the crude herb. Also, that in a properly prepared fluid extract, extract or tincture, the principle constituents have been accurately determined and hence the dosage is more accurate. They also point out that adulteration and contamination is under better control in such preparations. Another factor to be considered from an economical standpoint is that deterioration, contamination and spoilage is more easily controlled in these preparations. Furthermore, and an important factor from patient resistance standpoint, is the feature that in prescriptions of fluid extract, extracts possible where they have to brew their own medication cautiously. Some physicians find that the advising of fluid extracts, extracts and tinctures are better suited to their practice from a storage point of view.

In the choice and compounding of botanical agents there is one rule which requires observation, whether dealing with the crude herb or their fluid extract, extract or tincture, and that is the rule of simplicity. By following these dicta one can reasonably escape the errors of incompatibilities.

As the result of a most careful assessment, determine the exact nature of the perverted physiology, then choose that botanical whose pharmacological behavior is indicated for the case under consideration. Should, after the use of this prescription, there remain some residual factors then prescribe as a second remedial agent that other botanical which will further correct the remaining perverted physiological picture.

Factors Influencing Botanical Efficacy

In the choice of a botanical there are many things to be considered in obtaining a satisfactory therapeutic result. The agents listed herein each have a specific peculiarity in physiological conduct which causes them to perform definite duties. While one agent's cathartic action is due to its cholagogue properties another may produce its action as an irritant to the intestinal mucosa and musculature. Furthermore, some alternatives are better suited for a given condition than another would be. In the choice of ingredients it is more important to understand the actual pathological physiology present, than it is to be able to classify the disease in high sounding euphonious terms. To exemplify the importance of understanding the nature of the perverted physiology in the choice of the proper therapeutic botanical, one may cite the following example. In a case of nervous exhaustion due to extreme mental application, overwork and worry, the choice of Quaker Buttons with its strychnine alkaloid would be less suited to this case than pulsatilla, passiflora and viburnum, because with Quaker Buttons, one would be whipping an already tired horse when rest and regeneration is required. Therefore, the naturopathic physician must be well informed on the (a) physiological aberrations of each case, (b) the physiological properties possessed by each botanical, (c) and the manner in which these therapeutic agents will influence the given case.

The supply of each botanical must be from a healthy reliable source and should meet with the appropriate standards of purity and principle constituents content. No substandard botanical should be considered for therapeutic use. The physician should be on his guard against the evils of adulteration, sophistication, admixture and substitution.

Even though the highest quality of a botanical has been supplied by the dealer; properly prepared, freed of all adulterants and contaminants and approvedly packaged to prevent spoilage and deterioration; it remains the duty of the physician and compounding pharmacist to keep their botanicals protected from the many causes of their deterioration and spoilage. This is,

in itself, no small task, particularly in certain hot and humid climates, for molding and other parasitic destruction will often begin under the most scrupulous conditions.

In recording the compounding of, or in writing a prescription (or recommendation) for, two or more botanical ingredients, the physician should employ the accepted botanical name of each ingredient and use the accepted apothecaries or metric weights and measures. The use of common or lay terms should be avoided, for they are descriptively inaccurate, leaving the way open for substitutions and are the chief cause for unsatisfactory therapeutic results.

It is regrettable to note that many of our recent writers on herbal preparations and their compounding still adhere to such descriptive inaccuracies as "a handful of this and a pinch of that" method of weights and measures.

Therefore, in summary, the accuracy of botanical therapeutics lies

1. A thorough understanding of the pathological physiology that exists.
2. Complete information on the physiological properties of the botanicals under consideration with a knowledge of their specific peculiarities.
3. Employing botanicals of the highest purity and potency obtainable.
4. Treat the patient as an entity, not symptomatically.

Medical Prescribing

The prescription is an order or instruction from the physician to the patient or the druggist outlining the kind, amount and method of administration of any remedial agent. Originally written in Latin, prescriptions in the early days were essentially for the use and administration of strictly pharmaceutical preparations. Of late, many other forms of prescriptions have come into vogue. Thus, we have refractive prescriptions for glasses, orthopedic prescriptions for braces and trusses, audiometric prescriptions for hearing aids and physiotherapy prescriptions issued by the physician to the physiotherapist for the treatment of the patient.

A pharmaceutical prescription consists of the following parts:

(A) Patient's name and address
(B) Date
(C) Age
(D) Superscription or Heading which is made up of the symbolic "Rx" meaning "take thou" or "take."
(E) The Inscription which gives the ingredients and their amounts consists of:
  (a) Principle or Active Ingredients
  (b) Adjuvant or Synergistic Ingredient
  (c) Corrigent which modifies any undesired effects of the other ingredients
  (d) Vehicle, which is the medium or carrier of all the ingredients
(F) The Subscription which is the direction to the pharmacist
(G) The Signature which is the direction to the patient or his nurse
(H) Finally, the Physician's Full Signature and his Registry Number

Illustration:

Mrs. Martha M. Jones
2745 E. 5th St.
Elmwood
Date: March 6, 1948
Age: 19

Rx

Wild Valerian Root	Drahms X
Rue Herb	Drahms II
Watermint Herb	Drahms II
European Wurmuth Herb	Drahms II
Blue Skullcap Herb	Drahms IV
St. Johnswort Herb	Drahms II
Cassia Bark	Drahms II
Sweetwood	Drahms V

Mix well and divide equally into twenty packaged doses.

Sig. Prepare as decoction; add one dose to one cupful of boiling water, let boil for three minutes, let steep and cool for ten minutes, strain and give one cupful three times daily.

(signed) H. P. Meadows, N.D.

Illustration:

Mr. William Barnes
1154 Wilson Drive
Centerville
Date: April 5, 1947
Age: 32

Fluidextract of Drosera	Fl drm VI
Syrup Squill Comp.	Fl drm II
F.E. Senna and Spigelia Comp.	Fl drm IV
Mist. Rhubarb and Sodae	q.s. Fl oz. IV

Misce Fiat Sol.
Sig. Drahms II, q.4.h. (every four hours)

(signed) J. H. WINTERS, N.D.

In the past, universal use required that prescriptions be written in Latin. However, in recent years the American medical and pharmaceutical profession have encouraged the adoption of English nomenclature in the writing of the entire prescription. This has measurably reduced errors in interpretation, particularly in illegible prescriptions. There are still, however, some who adhere to the Latin, often to the incongruity of writing the inscription in English and the subscription and signature in Latin.

The following is a list of the few common terms still employed.

aa, or ana	"of each"
a.c.	"ante cibum," before meals
ad	"up to," or "to"
Agit	"Agita," shake
Aq. destil.	"Aqua destillata," distilled water.
b.i.d.	"bis in die," twice daily
c.c.	cubic centimeter
Cap.	"Capsula," capsule
Comp.	"Compositus," compound
Cort	"Cortex," bark
da	Give
Decoct.	"Decoction"

Dil..................."Dilut," or "Dilutum," dilute
Div.................."Dividendus," to be divided
et....................and
Ext. ...."Extractum," or extract
x.....................Fluidrahm
x.....................Fluidounce
F. of ft. or ft....."Make, or Let there be made"
Ft. emul........."Make an emulsion"
Ft. garg. ...."Make a gargle"
Ft. mist.........."Make a mixture"
Ft. pulv. ...."Make a powder"
Ft. sol or Ft. solut."Make a solution"
Ft. ung..........."Make an ointment"
Gm. ....Gramme, gram (use capital G
                   to avoid confusion with grain)
gr...................Granum, grain
gtt. or gutt. ....Gutta or guttae, drop or drops
H.s ....Hora somnis, at bedtime
Infus. ....Infusio, infusion
In dies. ....Every day or daily
M.F.Mist. ....Misce et fiat mistura, mix to
                   form a liquid mixture
M.F.P. ....Misce et flat pulvis, mix to
                   form a powder
ne rep. or ......Ne, or Non repetatur, do
  non rep.   not repeat
o.d. ....Omni die, daily
P.Ae...............Partes equales, equal parts
p.c. ....Post cibum, after meals
p.r.n. ....Pro re nata, when required
                   or as needed
Pulv. ....Pulvis, powder
q.h. ....Quaque hora, every hour
q.3.h. ....Every three hours
Q.l. ....Quantum libet, as much as
                   is desired
Q.s ....Quantum sufficiat, as much
                   as is required
Rx. ....Recipe, "take or take thou"
Rad. ....Radix, root
S., or Sig. ....Signa or Signetur, "write thou
                   directions to patient
Spt. ....Spiritus, spirit
Syr..................Syrupus, syrup
ss. ....Semis, a half
t.i.d. ....Ter in die, three times a day
Tab. ....Tabellae, or tabulae, tablet
Tinct..............Tinctura, tincture
Tnt. ....Tnitura, trituration
Ut.dict............Ut dictum, as directed

Weights and Measures

Apothecaries' Weight:
1 scruple	=	20 grains
3 scruples	=	60 grains or 1 drahm
8 drahms	=	480 grains or 1 ounce
12 ounces	=	5,760 grains or 1 pound

Apothecaries' Fluid Measure:
1 fluid drahm	=	60 minims
8 fluid drahms	=	1 fluidounce
16 fluidounces	=	1 pint
2 pints	=	1 quart
4 quarts	=	1 gallon

Metric Weight:
1 Milligram (mg. 0.001 gram) = grain 5/64
1 Centigram (cg. 0.01 gram) = grain 1/6
1 Decigram (dg.0.1 gram) = grain 1 1/2
1 Gram (Gm. 1.0 gram) = grain 15 1/2
1 Kilogram (Kg 1000 gram) = 2.7 apoth.
                              pounds, or
                              2.2 avoirdu-
                              pois

Metric Fluid Measure:
15 minims	=	1 cubic centimeter (cc)
60 minims	=	1 fluidrahm (4 cc)
450 minims	=	1 fluidounce (30 cc)
7,500 minims	=	1 pint (500 cc)
15,000 minims	=	1 liter (1,000 cc)

This ends the comments from Dr. von Peters. [2]

Recommendations

Although some naturopaths prescribe, most simply make recommendations. This is because naturopathy recognizes that the individual and not the doctor is responsible to decide what to do for their own health (it is also an issue of legality in many states). Of course, it is helpful for the naturopath to understand prescriptions and how they are written as many people who seek naturopathic assistance take one or more prescribed medications. Also, it is quite helpful knowledge if the naturopath needs to get a formula compounded in some special way.

Naturopaths base their recommendations on the overall health of the individual and preferences (i.e. some vegetarians do not wish to swallow dairy-containing products and some others have objections to herbs tinctured in alcohol, thus changes in recommendations should be made to accommodate personal preferences when possible). A naturopath's job is not to make impossible orders, but to recommend the combination of dietary changes, lifestyle improvements, herbs, homeopathics, nutrients, and other interventions that the individual is likely to at least try to follow. Naturopaths also explain their recommendations to their clients (and try to answer their clients' questions). One of the reasons that naturopathy is so successful is that it appears that naturopathic "compliance rates" are often higher than that of some of our medical colleagues. It seems logical that people would generally follow recommendations they understand, better than prescriptions that they do not.

Of course, naturopathy being eclectic, there are various subtle (and not so subtle) differences in what they recommend as well as how they view herbs.

Dr. Burr-Madsen has written the following about herbs:

Bio-Chemistry

The major way in which plants help cure and prevent diseases can be explained on a biochemical level, but more importantly they help us on an energetic level which is not explained as easily. There are many individual's compiling information and explaining there findings in biochemical terms. The Chinese have abundant information on the function of herbs, i.e., is the herb cooling, or heating, is the action rising or falling, is it drying or moistening and so on. Herbal medicines are not used to cure disease as such. Herbalists try to choose a remedy that will, from their experience, return the body's balance to normal; however, many herbs relieve symptoms rapidly which the patient sees as a cure. The remedies stimulate the body's own defenses to produce the desired effects. Most herbalists, however, won't simply give the patient a bottle of the remedy and expect them to go away and carry on living as before. The modern herbalist also concerns themselves with food. An integral part of the treatment is lifestyle, diet, exercise, breathing, etc., and also looking for the cause of the problem

Herbs as Foods

In naturopathy as well as all ancient healing arts, foods have been used in a medicinal way to help prevent and overcome illness. An example of that in modern day society would be "chicken soup" for colds and flus and "cranberry juice" for bladder infections. Herbs are special foods and there unique qualities such as strong flavors - peculiar textures - colors - energetic qualities - and very special biochemistry. Long before nutritional supplementation and homeopathy, common plants and herbs were used to maintain health. Hippocrates stated; "The body heals itself" and "Let your foods be your medicine and let your medicine be your foods." The special value of herbs used medicinally is according to their heating or cooling energies and their flavors.

Anatomy of Plants

Roots: Roots anchor a plant to the oil, from which they absorb water and dissolve mineral nutrients. The root then transports these substances from the point of absorption (root tip) to stem. In many species roots are food-storage organs. Some have nutritional and medicinal value while others are poisonous. There are four types of root systems. 1) The primary root system. A taproot is a dominant root with many smaller secondary roots and rootlets branching from it. The dividing line between the root and the stem is called the collar, the other end is a called the root cap. 2) Food storage tap roots have long been important in the human diet such as carrots, radishes and parsnips. 3) Primary roots may also develop into a cluster of fibrous roots, cereals, grains and grasses are examples of plants with fibrous roots. 4) Adventitious root systems are ground-hugging stems that send down fibrous adventitious root clusters at intervals marked by nodes.

Stems: The stem supports the leaves that catch the sunlight needed for photosynthesis. Stem tissues conduct water, minerals, and organic nutrients throughout the plant. There are Aerial stems which grow above ground, and underground stems called Rhizomes. Branches and branchlets, spreading from an aerial stem, form a plant's distinctive above ground shape, or crown. Strawberries and certain other plants produce aerial stems called stolons, or runners, that creep over the ground then root adventitiously to produce a plant like the parent plant. Rhizomes, which are also known as rootstocks, are stems that burrow beneath the soil, producing at intervals both adventitious roots and aerial stems and leaves. Thick fleshy rhizomes can be rich sources of potentially useful chemical compounds. Common white potatoes are tubers, thick-ended ends of rhizomes. A lily bulb is an underground bud that stores food in fleshy bulb scales. Onions are bulbs whose food-storage leaves form overlapping rings.

Leaves: Appendages of the stem, leaves are the main organs of photosynthesis, the process by which a leaf's green chlorophyll pigments absorb solar energy and use it to make organic molecules from carbon dioxide in the air and water in the soil. The simplest of these organic substances are carbohydrates and sugars such as glucose; but with the mineral elements from the soil added, more complex organic compounds, such as amino acids and fatty acids, are manufactured. As by-products of this manufacturing process arise the medicinal compounds found in plants. Most leaves consist of a blade and a stalk, or petiole. A blade's waxy upper surface helps retard the evaporation of water, the petiole connects blade and stem; on its base may be found outgrowths called stipules, which protect the budding leaf. Axillary buds form in the angle between petiole and stem. Sessile leaves have no petiole; the blades attach directly to the stem. The sessile leaves of the plants in the grass family form a sheath around the stem as they grow from the node.

Veins: Extensions of the leafstalk, veins serve as the leaf's supporting skeleton and its network for the inflow and outflow of water, minerals, dissolved gases, and organic compounds. There are many different patterns of veins.

Flowers: The flower is an organ for sexual reproduction. What is called a perfect flower contains its own bisexual reproductive system; it has both male (stamens) and female (pistils) sex organs. Imperfect (unisexual) flowers, such as those of willows and corn, have one or the other kind of sex organs, not both. A flower is called complete when it has sepals, which are usually green and collectively form the calyx; petals, which usually give the species its characteristic flower color and collectively form the corolla; a set of stamens (pollen producing male organs); and one or more pistils, the pollen- receiving, seed-producing female organs. Almost invariably the arrangement of these floral parts follows the same order, from the outside to the inside – sepals – petals – stamens – pistil.

Fruits: A fruit is the mature product of a fertilized ovary or ovaries. The ovules within the ovary have matured into seeds, which are ready to germinate and give rise to other plants of the same species. There are many types of fruits; fleshy fruits, dried fruits and aggregate fruits. There are three types of fleshy fruits; drupes or stone fruit (one single seed is protected within a hard-walled stone; pomes, their mature ovary wall is less distinct than that of drupes and forms only the inner core, a papery layer around the seeds; and berries which include grapes and tomatoes but not strawberries are fleshy fruits with many seeds embedded right in the juicy pulp. Dry fruits have no juicy pulp that surround the seeds. There are several types of dandelion seeds that are an example of dried fruits as well as legumes, such as peas are dry fruits with woody or papery protective pods. Poppy fruits, called capsules, open when dry to release seeds, capsules develop from a compound ovary—that is one capable of producing multiple seeds. Aggregate fruits form from a single flower that has many separate pistils. The fleshy part of a strawberry develops from the receptacle, the tip of the stalk where the flower was attached. Each "seed" is an achene from a separate ovary.

About Plant Names

The common names of many plants such as angelica, eyebright, queen anne's lace and church steeple have a charm and poetry of their own. Some describe outstanding features of a plant. Butterfly weed, for example, does seem to be irresistible to butterflies, which are drawn to the nectar in its orange blooms. Other plants got their names from the use people have made of them, such as snakeroots to treat snake bite. This can create some confusion as often the same plant has many names. For example, butterfly weed is also known as pleurisy root as it was used to treat pleurisy. Just as confusing as having plants with more than one common name is having the same name applied to two or more different species. Across North America there are a number of completely unrelated plants called snakeroots. Squawroot refers to different species in different areas.

Two-Part Names

To avoid such confusion, scientists use a standardized two-part naming system called binomial nomenclature for both plants and animals. Carolus Linnaeus was a Swedish naturalist who pioneered this nomenclature in the 18th century. His system grew into the rules now set down in the *International Code of Botanical Nomenclature,* a book on international botanical naming conventions. The first part of a plant's name gives its genus, the group to which it belongs and with which it

shares many features. Violets, for example, belong to the genus Viola, roses to the genus Rosa. The second part of a plant's name tells its species - the particular kind of plant in a genus. Thus *Rosa multiflora is* the scientific name for the multiflora (many-flowered) rose, and *Rosa canina is* the internationally recognized botanical name of the dog (canine) rose. A botanical name is often followed by an abbreviation of the name of the person who classified the plant scientifically. Thousands of plant names, for example, are followed by the initial "L." for Linnaeus.

Scientific Names

Plants scientific names are based on Latin and Greek. Many Latin and Greek genus names, in fact have become the familiar, everyday names of plants such as; iris, geranium and nasturtium. Some genus names, such as *Achillea, Artemisia,* and *Asclepias,* come from the names of mythological figures. Linnaeus simply borrowed from the Latin or Greek common name, making *Alnus* the generic (genus) name for alders, Populus for poplars, and so on. Other genus names were coined to honor somebody. The genus *Kalmia,* which includes the North American mountain laurel *(Kalmia latifolia),* was named for Peter Kalm, a student of Linnaeus's who traveled in North America to collect plants for him. The second (species) part of a botanical name, more often then not, describes something specific about the plant. Sometimes it tells about the color of a plant's flowers: *alba* for white, *rubrus* for red, *purpureum* for purple. It may describe foliage: *grandifolia* for large leaves, *rotundifolia* for round leaves, *millefolium* for thousand or many leafed. It may describe some other salient characteristic: *erectus* for upright, *hirsutum* for hairy, *odorata* for fragrant, *mvrtilloides* for myrtlelike. Some specific (species) names describe where a plant is typically found: *montana,* on the mountain; *maritima,* by the sea; *aquatrilis,* in the water. Others tell how people have used the plants: *edulis,* edible; *cathartica,* cathartic.

Types of Herbal Preparations

Because of their considerable advantages, liquid preparations are widely used. Their main advantage is that, properly prepared, the minimal of processing is involved, and the result can truly reflect the chemical characteristics of the original herb. Liquids are also ideal for the preparation of individual formulations for each client (extemporaneous dispensing), a method still used by many herbalists.

The main disadvantage of liquids is taste. However, in the case of bitters, taste is an essential part of the treatment in stimulating the reflex secretion of gastric juices. Many clients get used to the taste of their medicine and some even grow to like it.

There are many different types of herbal preparations available. It is important to clarify certain terms and concepts:

Comminution Before herbs are processed they need to be cut and broken into suitable sizes. This is primarily for easier handling and to increase the amount of surface area of the herb exposed. This process is called comminution.

Extraction Comminution used to be the hardest work of all the processes of preparation, entailing hours of labor with pestle and mortar. Now modem cutting, slicing or grinding machines do the work more rapidly and more efficiently. If the preparation is required to be powdered, special mills and sieves are used.

This is the procedure by which the soluble and active constituents of crude drugs are extracted or separated out. The aim is to obtain a preparation that is reasonably concentrated, optimally active and whose qualities can be predicted and reproduced. A liquid is chosen which is most advantageous for dissolving out the required ingredients of a particular plant and is called the menstruum. The solid material left after extraction is completed is referred to as the marc.

The main procedures used in the extraction processes are *Infusion* and *Decoction* (in which the menstruum is usually water) and *Maceration* and *Percolation* (in which the menstruum is usually in alcohol/water mixture).

Maceration This is the process in which the herb is steeped at room temperature. The menstruum used needs to prevent fermentation and deterioration during the procedure, which can take up to two weeks. In most cases an alcohol/water mixture is used, although vinegar is sometimes the preferred choice for certain herbs. The plant material is cut or powdered, soaked in the alcohol/water mixture and kept in a closed vessel for a prescribed length of time, in a cool dark place. At the end of the period, the liquid is drained off and the wet marc pressed to extract as much of the remaining fluid as possible. The liquid is then strained, filtered and bottled.

Percolation Percolation is an efficient way of extraction, It is commonly used in the domestic kitchen with coffee percolators. Percolation involves letting the menstruum trickle down through a mass of herbs that has been finely ground, and placed in a columnar percolator. Sufficient menstruum is added to cover the powder completely. The vessel is covered and maceration allowed for around 24 hours. The liquid is then drained off slowly at a rate of 10 to 30 drops per minute, with more fluid being added at the top as required. The marc is then pressed and any extra fluid added to the percolate. The extract obtained from percolation can be used to make tablets and capsules or other herbal end-products. Percolations are now rarely used to extract herbs because of the necessity for special equipment.

Infusions Infusions are used when the active principles of the crude herbs are readily soluble in water and easily obtained from the plant tissue. It is appropriate for leaves, flowers and non-woody stems. The method is to grind or bruise the plant material, pour boiling water over it and allow it to stand for half an hour or so with occasional stirring. Then strain so that you are left with a clear liquid. Herb teas commonly consumed, are infusions.

Decoction This process is used when the constituents are water soluble, but the crude material is slow to yield its constituents e.g., roots, barks, and woody stems. Decoctions are prepared by pouring cold water upon the cut, bruised or ground herb and boiling the mixture for some time (up to 4 hours in some cases). The mixture is then cooled and strained.

Infusions and Decoctions involve heat and may thus offer some of the more sensitive active constituents of the plants. These processes extract only the water soluble components, tending to leave the fat soluble constituents behind.

Decoctions are inconvenient, but is sometimes the only way of extraction from a hard herb such as a bark or stem like chaparral. It is an established way of preparing many Chinese herbs, and this is often done in the clients own kitchen.

Tinctures The active constituents of many herbal preparations are destroyed by heat and/or are unsatisfactorily extracted by water alone. For these plants, the process of maceration (most commonly using an alcohol/water mixture) is widely used and the resulting product is called a tincture.

Alcoholic tinctures have been used by medical herbalists for over 150 years and are now considered to be one of the best methods for extracting and preserving a medicinal herb. A number of studies have shown that the alcohol concentration can significantly affect the quality of the final tincture.

It has been shown that an alcohol concentration of between 40 to 60% has the advantage of achieving a good balance of both the water soluble and fat soluble constituents of each plant. This balance is important in reflecting the proportions of each constituents in the plant, in its fresh or original state. This alcohol water ratio is very important, and is usually calculated for individual plants to give the most efficacious extraction process. Higher percentages of alcohol do not necessarily improve the process and indeed can have an adverse effect on the strength and efficacy of the final product. So too, if there is not enough alcohol the herb will not completely extract all of its constituents into the menstruum, and the tincture will not be as strong or effective.

The best range of alcohol concentration of 40 to 60% (depending on the herb) also give the best anti-bacterial and anti-fungal action. Surprisingly, concentrations higher than 70% are not as effective in maintaining sterility. One of the major advantages of tinctures is that alcohol acts as a natural preservative and avoids the problems of deterioration of the herbs during storage. The active constituents of the herbal preparation are found to be more stable in a tincture. The alcohol content also prevents bacterial and fungal contamination. The absorption of the herbal preparation is also enhanced by the alcohol. A tincture can be absorbed via the mouth and the esophagus as well as through the lining of the stomach.

Liquid Extracts Liquid extracts are made in a variety of ways. The best method of preparation is to evaporate, under vacuum, the alcohol extract of the herb. The liquid will be evaporated until the extract is of the correct volume. Extracts may also be prepared by the method of cold percolation, or by preparation in a pressure vessel. In all cases, special equipment is necessary.

Juices The principle of juices is exemplified by the example of freshly squeezed oranges. Fruit juices are commonly found, but juices from roots are much more rare. Certain authorities support the use of juices on the premise that they are the pure way of taking herbs. However, juices suffer from the disadvantage of stabilization and are active for only a short time after preparation. They also have the disadvantage of securing only the water soluble components, leaving behind the lipid soluble constituents, and thus, do not always give an extract of the complete herb.

There are many advantages to the absorption of medicines through the mucous membranes of the mouth and gullet:

- The active ingredients enter the blood quickly.

- The active ingredients are not affected by the digestive enzymes in the stomach.

- The medicine by-passes the liver.

It is a familiar concept that, to get the best out of a homeopathic medicine, it should be allowed to dissolve under the tongue and in the mouth. There are many reasons for this. Homeopathic medicines are very delicate and many external influences can destroy the "energy" and upset the constitution of the medicine. The enzymes present in the gastric secretions of the stomach can for example, destroy homeopathic medicines. Absorption through the mucous membranes of the mouth also allows the medicine to enter the blood much more speedily. As well as this, the medicine is distributed to all the tissues of the body before it reaches the liver. This route of absorption by-passes the liver, and has a number of unique advantages.

The liver is a complex organ which is vital for the body's health. Among its many functions is the responsibility for detoxifying the blood. Any toxins or chemicals (both beneficial and harmful) are broken down by the liver. This obviously has protective and beneficial properties, where unwanted toxic chemicals such as lead and mercury are ingested. However, it can also work to deactivate medicines which are taken into the digestive tract. Any substance of food which is absorbed by the stomach and small intestines enters the blood-stream via the blood vessels surrounding these organs. These vessels then transport the blood into the hepatic vein, carrying it to the liver. This mechanism which brings all the matter absorbed from the gut first, to the liver to be detoxified is called "Hepatic First-pass Metabolism."

If a homeopathic herbal tincture were to be absorbed in the stomach, for instance, it will be carried via the hepatic vein to the liver, where the enzymes present would de-activate the medicine. There are certain other circumstances where it is important to avoid the Hepatic First-pass Metabolism. The pharmaceutical preparation, Glyceryl Trinitrate (GTN), commonly used for angina, both as a sub-lingual spray or as tablets, is the most commonly found example in the pharmaceutical world.

Solid Preparations

There are many different preparations of herbs which are in solid form and these have the advantage of being convenient and easily portable.

Solid Extracts This method of preparation reduces an infusion of the fresh juice to the consistency of treacle. The material is simmered gently for a long period with constant stirring until most of the water is boiled off. It should then be stored in a refrigerator and used quickly. Solid extracts are commercially made for the preparation of tablets, pills and ointments.

Pills This is the oldest method of administering solid medication in predetermined doses, being commonly used in China over 4,000 years ago. It is still used in Chinese herbal medicine. The constituents are herbal extracts in crude form, mixed with damp excipients such as glucose and edible gums, then rolled in grooves on a board with a smooth piece of wood until they are firm and uniform in size. They are now usually coated but can also be rolled in dry icing sugar or powdered licorice to conceal any noxious taste.

Tablets Pills, contrary to popular usage and reference should not be confused with tablets, which are by far the commonest method of presenting modem medicines. Pills, although still available, are losing their popularity as they have a shorter shelf life than tablets and their clinical purity is more difficult to achieve.

Herbal tablets are a convenient dosage form and avoid the problems with taste or alcohol. However, one of the major difficulties with tablets is the degree of processing required. As well as the active ingredients, tablets have to contain inert substances called excipients. These substances include Calcium salts, Lactose, Stearates and Starch. The purpose of the excipients is to provide bulk for the tablets, as well as to ensure even mixing and binding of the tablets during the manufacturing process. Ironically, tablets are usually made from liquid extracts of herbs. The herb is extracted with an appropriate solvent and the resultant liquid is dried into either a soft or powdered concentrate using processes like vacuum concentration or spray drying. This concentrate is then mixed with the excipients before tablets are formed by "pressing" (the use of pressure with a die, to shape the tablet).

Heat may sometimes be used in the tablet making process, for example, where the mixture is wetted and then oven dried before the final pressing. However, heat sensitive or volatile components can be damaged or lost by this process, thus risking further damage to the components. There are, however, tabletting processes which do not require heat and these are the most effective in the manufacture of herbal tablets. Tablets keep better than pills. They are usually and accurately formulated, and dissolve faster in the stomach when compared to pills.

Capsules Capsules are a convenient way to deliver powdered herbs because they conceal unpleasant tastes or textures. They are uniform sized gelatin containers which are filled with the active material, then sealed, either by mechanical means or by the application of heat. Because they mask unpleasant odors or tastes, they are popular with children who are old enough to swallow capsules, but have the disadvantage that even large capsules may only hold 300-600 milligrams of powdered herb. This means that a few capsules need to be taken to achieve adequate dosage.

Capsules can contain many forms of active ingredients, including liquids, oils, powdered herbs, dried herbs or fresh herb extracts.

Powders Occasionally the best way to prescribe herbal medicines is in the form of a powder. This particularly applies to herbs which contain mucilage such as slippery elm, as when these herbs are mixed with water, the mucilage reacts to form a gel and swells to many times original volume making it difficult to handle. Linseed is a good example of a mucilaginous herb. It is usually used as whole seed and sometimes as a powder. The bulking property of mucilage is at its best when the herb is taken with a copious amount of water. Powdered linseed will absorb water easily, but when taking whole linseed, it is best to chew the seeds, so that the total outer casing of the seeds is broken. This allows water to be absorbed into the seed causing the mucilage to swell and giving the bulk which is so effective.

Where the fat soluble components are an important part of the activity of an herb, the dose of an herb mixed in water should be followed by a dose of vegetable oils/soy milk to assist in absorption. The big advantage of powders is that the total constituents of an herb are presented to the user's digestive tract rather than those constituents which only dissolve in water.

Suppositories and pessaries These are shaped vehicles made from quickly melting material such cocoa butter and are used for the introduction of medicine via the rectum or the vaginal tract.

They can be a particularly useful remedial method as it brings the drug in direct contact with the mucous membrane. Hamamelis suppositories, used for hemorrhoids, uses this principle to good effect. Suppositories are useful where oral remedies cannot be taken. In certain countries such as France, it appears to be the preferred route of administration of many herbals and homeopathics. [3]

Essential Oils and Aromatherapy

Essential oils (also referred to as volatile oils) are herbal extracts that many believe contain the most active components of an herb. In many cases they are. Unlike other herbal preparations, essential oils are not generally ingested. They are applied to the skin and then they either are absorbed transdermally or breathed in. They are often used in massage. Essential oils are believed to have a pharmacological effect (or nutritional effect by supplying substances in the body), physiological effect (whether stimulatory or sedative), and a psychological effect (how one responds to the aroma, which may be part physiological) [4,5].

An essential oil is usually extracted from the plant through simple pressure or in the case of citrus oils, through distillation [4]. "Aromatherapy is the application of an essential oil for healing purposes" [6]. Aromatherapy (under various names) has been used for thousands of years [4-6].

The term aromatherapy is credited to a French chemist named Rene'-Maurice Gattesfoose'. He accidently discovered that lavender oil could promote rapid healing of a severe burn on his hand without scarring [4]; he also found that the oil was better than the synthetics that were available to him [4]. Aromatherapy is getting very popular these days—it is also fairly noticeable if someone who uses it goes in the public. It is usually wise to use essential oils sparingly [6]. My clinical experience suggests that unless the oil has been excessively altered, many people who are otherwise chemically sensitive (but not all) seem to tolerate the smell of pure essential oils better than they do many synthetic perfumes.

Just like with diet and nutrition, one herb (whether ingested or breathed) is not necessarily the answer for everyone with seemingly the same health condition. However, herbs and/or herbal combinations can be recommended to people most everyday with excellent results.

Food or Drug?

As a naturopathic practitioner and nutritionist, the author uses herbs as foods. It is believed that the body uses their many constituents to build and promote good health. It is a concern that many wish to use herbs as drugs. The tendency towards "standardized extracts" is a major concern. If substances within herbs become extracted and isolated, they are no longer being used as foods. The herbal foods have protective effects which can be removed through certain types of extraction.

Others have similar concerns. Andrew Gaeddert wrote, "The problem with obtaining a specified amount of a standard constituent is that a plant can contain hundreds of active constituents. By concentrating on one component, we may lose synergistic compounds which may improve effectiveness and lessen adverse reactions. Often scientists do not fully understand which constituents are beneficial for the clinical results of an herb" [7]. This is true for other forms of nutrition, which is one of the reasons why synthetic vitamins and rocks (known as mineral salts) are used in supplements.

"Advocates of standardized herbs are usually academics with little clinical experience with herbs, or researchers whose work is funded by companies that manufacture standardize products. Traditional herbalists seldom use standardized products" [7]. Neither should traditional naturopaths. Foods are not standardized! It is also true that "traditional herbalists will continue to recommend herbs in their more natural state which may include water and alcohol extracts, teas and pills that have not been standardized" [7].

References

[1] Thiel, R. J. *Serious Nutrition for Health Care Professionals.* California Health Group, Ayyoro Grande (CA), 1995.

[2] von Peters, W. *Naturae Medicina and Naturopathic Dispensatory.* American Association of Naturopathic Physicians and Surgeons. Chattanooga, 1998.

[3] Burr-Madsen, A. *Natural Therapies, Module 1.* Gateways College, Shingle Springs (CA), 1996.

[4] Lawless, J. *The Illustrated Encyclopedia of Essential Oils.* Barnes & Noble Books, New York, 1995.

[5] Williams, D. G. *New Uses for an Age-Old Remedy.* Alternatives, 1999; 8(4):25-27.

[6] Null, G. *The Complete Encyclopedia of Natural Healing.* Kensington Books, New York, 1998.

[7] Gaeddert, A. *Are Standardized Herbs Better?* Townsend Letter for Doctors, 1999; 190:20.

27

Homeopathy, Cell Salts and Isopathy

Many people turn to homeopathy to deal with their health concerns. It is not necessary to use homeopathy to help people through naturopathy, but most practitioners may find information on it helpful in this day and age. Homeopathic remedies are intended to stimulate the body to heal itself. It is not the goal of this chapter to make you any type of professional homeopath (much more training is needed), but to give you background in its use.

Homeopathy was developed nearly 200 years ago in Germany. Homeopathy is popular in Europe and parts of Asia (especially India); it is also gaining popularity in the United States. Homeopathic philosophy is based on the 'Law of Similars', a concept which was expanded by Samuel Hahnemann, the recognized founder of homeopathic therapy [1]. This 'law of similars' was originally recognized by Hippocrates (the 'father of medicine') when he wrote, "By similar things a disease is produced and through the application of the like it is cured" [2]. Also, the Greek physician Galien (130-200A.D.) wrote of the natural cure of likes [2]. The Swiss physician Dr. Theophastus Von Bombast (1493-1541) stated that "sames must

be cured by sames" [2]. According to Dr. Madsen, "The first precise enunciation of the fundamental homeopathic principle was given in the early 17th century by a Danish physician, Dr. George Stahl. He wrote, 'To treat with opposite acting remedies is the reverse of what ought to be. [Stahl is] convinced that disease will yield to, and be cured by, remedies that produce similar affections'" [2].

Homeopathy basically holds that a substance which can produce specific toxicity symptoms in large quantities can raise 'vital force' to correct metabolic imbalances as indicated by similar symptoms in extremely minute quantities [organon]. The oriental concept of 'chi' is similar to Hahnemann's concept of 'vital force' (as is 'prana', the Indian Sanskrit word meaning life force [2]).

Any substance might be used homeopathically, but most are natural substances made from vegetable, animal, and mineral sources. Homeopathic manufacturers take the substance and then dilute it and shake it up. This occurs as many times as necessary to attain the desired potency. The homeopathic dilutive process is called succussion. Interestingly, the higher the potency, the more diluted the substance is.

The Initial work of Hahnemann (which was revised several times) was called the *Organon of Medicine*. Homeopaths still study it today. In this book he lists various principles, which he referred to as aphorisms. Here is some of what Dr. Hahnemann wrote in it:

Aphorism 1

The physician's high and only mission is to restore the sick to health, to cure, as it is termed.

Aphorism 2

The highest ideal of cure is rapid, gentle and permanent restoration of the health, or removal and annihilation of the disease in its whole extent, in the shortest, most reliable, and most harmless way, on easily comprehensible principles.

Aphorism 3

If the physician clearly perceives what is to be cured in diseases, that is to say, in every individual case of disease (knowledge of disease, indication), if he clearly perceives what is curative in medicines, that is to say, in each individual medicine (knowledge of medicinal powers), and if he knows how to adapt, according to clearly defined principles, what is curative in medicines to what he has discovered to be undoubtedly morbid in the patient, so that the recovery must ensue—to adapt it, as well in respect to the suitability of the medicine most appropriate according to its mode of action to the case before him (choice of the remedy, the medicine indicated), as also in respect to the exact mode of preparation and quantity of it required (proper dose), and the proper period for repeating the dose—if, finally, he knows the obstacles to recovery in each case and is aware how to remove them, so that the restoration may be permanent: then he understands how to treat judiciously and rationally, and he is a true practitioner of the healing art.

Aphorism 4

He is likewise a preserver of health if he knows the things that derange health and cause disease, and how to remove them from a person's health.

Aphorism 5

Useful to the physician in assisting him to cure are the particulars of the most probable exciting cause of the acute disease, as also the most significant points in the whole history of the chronic disease, to enable him to discover its fundamental cause, which is generally due to a chronic miasm. In these investigations, the ascertainable physical constitution of the patient (especially when the disease is chronic), his moral and intellectual character, his occupation, mode of living and habits, his social and domestic relations, his age, sexual function, etc. are to be taken into consideration...

Aphorism 32

But it is quite otherwise with the artificial morbific agents which we term medicines. Every read medicine, namely, acts at all times, under all circumstances, on every living human being, and produces in him its peculiar symptoms (distinctly perceptible, if the dose be large enough), so that

evidently every living human organism is liable to be affected, and, as it were, inoculated with the medicinal disease at all times, and absolutely (unconditionally), which, as before said, is by no means the case with the natural diseases.

Aphorism 33

In accordance with this fact, it is undeniably shown by all experience that the living human organism is much more disposed and has a greater liability to be acted on, and to have its health deranged by medicinal powers, than by morbific noxious agents and infectious miasms, or, in other words, that the morbific noxious agents possess a power of morbidly deranging man's health that is subordinate and conditional, often very conditional; whilst medicinal agents have an absolute unconditional power, greatly superior to the former.

Aphorism 34

The greater strength of the artificial diseases producible by medicines is, however, not the sole cause of their power to cure natural diseases. In order that they may effect a cure, it is before all things requisite that they should be capable of producing in the human body an artificial disease as similar as possible to the disease to be cured, ['which, with somewhat increased power, transforms to a very similar morbid state the instinctive life principle, which in itself is incapable of any reflection or act of memory. It not only obscures, but extinguishes and thereby annihilates the derangement caused by the natural disease.' In the Sixth Edition] in order, by means of this similarity, conjoined with its somewhat greater strength, to substitute themselves for the natural morbid affection, and thereby deprive the latter of all influence upon the vital force. This is so true, that no previously existing disease can be cured, even by Nature herself, by the accession of a new dissimilar disease, be it ever so strange, and just as little can it be cured by medical treatment with drugs which are incapable of producing a similar morbid condition in the healthy body. [1]

When first starting consulting as a naturopath, the author would suggest that certain people make dietary changes (including avoiding sensitive foods). To others, nutritional supplements were suggested. To still others, homeopathic remedies were recommended. The results were mixed—some were successful and some were not. Later the three began to be combined. The results improved dramatically. This is significant because most people do not see a naturopath until after they have tried many doctors as well as tried other approaches on their own (thus it was unlikely that their problems would simply go away on their own). The results we achieved have included persons with various health conditions. Samuel Hahnemann, though a medical doctor (who rejected much of his medical training) employed various aspects of naturopathy as well. As Dr. Madsen wrote, "Hahnemann urged the need for public hygiene, for fresh air, adequate sleep and regular exercise and a sensible diet. He proposed that houses should be spaced apart from one another, that they should be light and admit plenty of fresh air and sewage should be properly treated" [2].

Nutri-homeopathy is a term the author has personally coined to describe the combining of nutritional and lifestyle improvements, with the utilization of a homeopathic remedy which plays a role in the nutritional deficiency of a particular individual. By combining the subtle dynamism of the selected homeopathic remedy with the appropriate synergistically important vitamin, mineral, enzyme, or other supplement(s), and/or diet changes, this combination works better than either of them separately. (Of course, this approach falls clearly within the bounds of naturopathy.)

In an experiment conducted involving nutri-homeopathy, all people who followed it reported improvement (it was the study involving seasonal allergic rhinitis [3], please also see Exhibit A). The author's clinical experience has shown that homeopathic remedies can be helpful for people with a variety of health concerns.

Chronic problems normally are best dealt with using higher potency remedies, whereas acute problems are best dealt with lower potency remedies. Many companies produce combination homeopathic remedies that usually contain lower potencies (though some have higher potency combinations as well). The number signifies the number of times the substance was diluted and the X signifies that each dilution was done at a ratio of 10:1. Some remedies are diluted to C potencies which signifies that each dilution was done at a ratio of 100:1.

To employ homeopathy, the homeopath studies the person in great detail. The aim is to know and understand the whole person and not just a single part of the person. It is not easy to do correctly.

Research has shown benefits

Several published studies concerning homeopathy involve hay fever or some environmental illness. The research suggests that improvements from homeopathy are statistically greater than a placebo response [4,5]. Researchers from the University of Glasgow did a study involving 150 hay fever patients using homeopathic supplements and placebos. The study concluded that homeopathic potencies were superior to the placebos [4].

A German study using homeopathy on 201 patients concluded that it was more effective than placebos in improving nasal and eye symptoms for patients with pollenosis [5].

A double-blind study was performed by this researcher in the San Joaquin Valley involving homeopathics and placebos. This study concluded that, overall, single homeopathic remedies were more effective on reducing the symptoms associated with seasonal allergic rhinitis than were placebos or combination isopathic pollen dilutions, but that the results varied considerably by individual [3]. It also improved energy levels of the participants (a copy of the shortened version of that study is found in Exhibit A). Additionally, most participants who were taking medication for their rhinitis reduced or eliminated it [3]. This is consistent with the results of another double-blind placebo controlled study involving asthmatics which found that inhaler use was decreased without a worsening in symptoms for those who took a homeopathic remedy [6].

A randomized placebo-controlled study found improved immune response and an improved sense of well being from homeopathy [7]. An interesting study which compared medical and homeopathic interventions for people with otitis media found that 70.7% using homeopathy had no recurrence in one year vs. only 29.3% using conventional medicine [8]. Another randomized placebo-controlled trial involving vertigo in Germany found that homeopathic remedies were just as effective as medical ones [9] (which to me means more effective, since there are no serious side-effects from the homeopathic). Another study, however, found no benefit for migraine headaches using homeopathy [10] (in the author's opinion this result occurred because dietary restrictions and nutritional support were not included, a study by his office performed on migraines is shown in Appendix A).

A homeopathic remedy must be tailored to the person. "Self-determination" of the appropriate remedy is usually faulty, as are recommendations made by employees of many health food stores (most simply do not have the time or the training to do a complete and proper homeopathic assessment). To increase the chances of getting the right homeopathic remedy, many people purchase what is known as a "combination" remedy which often contains four or more different homeopathic substances. Although combination remedies have helped some people, classic homeopaths do not consider them to be ideal because the affects of the unneeded remedies can make an optimal selection less likely [1]. However, some combination homeopathic remedies are not often recommended (as well as isopathic remedies, both of which are discussed later in this chapter).

It is best to consult an exhaustive homeopathic materia medica to learn more complete information on each homeopathic remedy. The homeopathic materia medicas contain the results of thousands of homeopathic tests called "provings." In a proving, a healthy person is given a homeopathic substance over a period of time and writes down all the symptoms that the person temporarily develops; this includes personality traits and changes as well as physiological ones [2]. The writers of the various materia medicas have condensed the provings by homeopathic remedy and usually add their own commentary as well as other useful information on the remedy. The professional homeopath attempts to match the personalities and symptoms of their clients to those shown in the materia medicas. The closer the match the better the expected results. The materia medicas also suggest which remedies should follow one another as well as various precautions.

Space does not permit including a complete homeopathic materia medica within this book. A good materia medica to use is "The Dictionary of Practical Materia Medica" by J.H. Clarke [11] which contains over 2,500 pages. Although ho-

meopathics are considered to be somewhat safe and without permanent side effects, In the author's experience, 1 out of every 5 people who take a homeopathic remedy reports that they get temporarily worse for between two days and two weeks. This is probably caused by having a less than optimal potency, although many homeopaths consider this to be "normal" and a good sign that the remedy selected is the right one and is starting to work. It is not essential to have negative side effects.

The founder of homeopathy, Dr. Samuel Hahnemann, suggested that people who took homeopathic remedies would do better if they improved their diet and avoided certain behavioral practices. Most homeopaths agree with this position. However, little evidence (other than case histories and other anecdotal evidence) can be found which validates this belief. This was one of the reasons that our experiment on seasonal allergic rhinitis included involving diet, nutrition supplements, and homeopathics.

For optimal results, homeopathy should be used in conjunction with dietary restrictions and/or nutritional supplements [12]. Dr. Hahnemann referred to these as "diet and regimen" factors. Although some modern homeopaths only recommend homeopathic remedies while minimizing diet and nutrition, this is not consistent with Dr. Hahnemann. In the "Organon of Medicine" as translated by R.E. Dudgeon, he wrote:

Aphorism 259

Considering the minuteness of doses necessary and proper in homeopathic treatment, we can easily understand that during treatment everything must be removed from the diet and regimen which can have any medicinal action in order that the small dose may not be overwhelmed and extinguished or disturbed by any foreign medicinal irritant.

Aphorism 260

Hence the careful investigation into such obstacles to cure is so much more necessary in the cases of patients affected by chronic diseases, as their diseases are usually aggravated by such noxious influences and other disease-causing errors in diet and regimen, which often are passed unnoticed.

Thus, Dr. Hahnemann felt that diet and regimen factors could be major obstacles towards improvement for those who took a properly determined homeopathic remedy. In his footnote to aphorism 260, Dr. Hahnemann wrote that persons taking homeopathic remedies "should avoid all excesses in food, and in the use of sugar and salt, as also spirituous drinks, ... the frequent indulgence in mere passive exercise, ... sitting up long at night, ... over-exertion of mind or body, dwelling in marshy districts, damp rooms, penurious living, &c. All these things must be as far as possible avoided or removed, in order that the cure not be obstructed or rendered impossible [1].

There is another, more compelling reason, that nutri-homeopathy is recommended instead of simply homeopathy itself—modern air pollution. Air pollution, as mentioned previously, is a serious problem. The nearly constant effects of air pollution (since we are always breathing) often can overpower the homeopathic remedy and thus render it almost useless. Although obviously not familiar with modern air pollution, Hahnemann recognized that noxious influences could negate the effects of homeopathy. These noxious influences included residing in unhealthy localities, those deprived of exercise in open air, and living in a constant state of worry [1]. Since more and more people now live in "unhealthy localities", greater attention to diet, nutrition, and lifestyle factors is now critical when using homeopathic remedies for chronically ill persons.

Even during Hahnemann's day there were various forms of homeopathy. He did not approve of brands other than his own [1]—his form is usually referred to as "classical homeopathy." There are still many debates today about the different forms [13]. Many like to combination remedies [13,14], while others like isopathic remedies—both existed during Hahnemann's time but he disapproved of them [1].

Quantic Homeopathy

One current understanding of the "Law of Similars" is that it is really an energy relationship [13]. One branch of homeopathy has a "Belief that disturbances in the individual's 'energy field' is the underlying cause of conditions of imbalance and illness" [13]. This is consistent with the concept that

enervation causes illness in chapter 3. It is also believed that by using "energetic testing methods for each individual case" (such as muscle testing, please see chapter 8) the proper recommendation can be made [13].

The following was written by Dr. Theresa Dale (who also uses a muscle testing technique) regarding a form of combination homeopathy she refers to as *Quantic Homeopathy:*

Every plant or mineral that is consumed produces not only a physical symptom, but also a mental and emotional symptom. Thus, homeopathic remedies have the ability to affect the entire picture of the person's physical and emotional make-up. When you release the identity and the belief that is stored as an electromagnetic charge in the cells' DNA using homeopathy, a rebalancing occurs in the cellular blueprint. The application of homeopathy is unlimited and there are no side effects.

Homeopathy is commonly called "the energy medicine." Homeopathy is legal, inexpensive and safe. It is globally acclaimed as a profoundly effective medicine historically dating back to the eighteenth century. Homeopathy is a natural form of medicine, comprised of botanical and mineral sources, including some poisonous substances as well. Realize, however, that even organic and botanical substances may have a poisonous effect. This is precisely the reason why homeopathic remedies are diluted and succussed (shaken) to such a degree, and for this reason, there are absolutely no residual poisonous effects that remain in a homeopathic remedy. It is truly fascinating to learn that when diluted and succussed Into higher and higher potencies, there is eventually no physical substance left at all, just pure energy, The once poisonous substance has been rendered completely safe, even for children, and can be instrumental in curing many physical and emotional conditions.

The basis for homeopathy stems from the theory, "like cures like", more commonly called the Law of Similars. it was researched and developed by a German doctor, Samuel Hahneman, who wrote:

Disease in man is destroyed in a permanent manner by another more powerful force that bears a strong resemblance in its mode of manifestation, Those substances in a gross material form that product symptoms will cure those same manifestations in a diluted and dynamized form. He discerned far ahead of his time that each homeopathic remedy has a mental symptom that corresponds to it. For example, the remedy Calendula Officinalis, otherwise known as Marigold, creates the following mental symptoms when eaten, and also cures the same mental symptoms when diluted and made into a *homeopathic* remedy. These include, great irritability, being easily frightened, acute hearing, and intense depression. Another remedy, Arsenicum Album, white oxide of metallic arsenic, is used for many physical ailments, such as acne, abscess, alcoholism, anemia, and so on. The mental component of Arsenicurn Album cures melancholy, anguish, anger anxiety, restlessness and the sensations of coldness and madness. What actually occurs when a homeopathic remedy is administered? The remedy itself emits an electromagnetic signal which locates and then adheres to a "similar signal" within the body, thus neutralizing the "similar signal." The "similar signal" that has been located and adhered to is the energy pattern containing the disease. Thus the disease, the identity and the entire energy pattern is dissolved

An important development leading to Dr. Hahneman's remarkable discovery occurred when he first tried to dilute the substances without succussion. This procedure succeeded in reducing the toxicity of the substance, but it also *proportionately* reduced the therapeutic effect, Then Hahneman experimented with adding kinetic energy into the dilution through shaking or "Succussion." The results of this research led to "potentization," which is a combination of, succussion and serial dilution. The importance here is that the more the substance is succussed and diluted, the higher the potency, while nullifying any, toxic effect the original substance may have had.

The procedure is as follows. The substance is dissolved in an alcohol/water isolution called a tincture. Then one drop of the tincture is diluted into from 9 to 99 drops of 40% alcohol/water solution. This dilution is then firmly succussed or, shaken 100 times. One drop of this dilution is then added to from 9 to 99 drops of fresh alcohol/water, which is again succussed 100 more times. This process can be continued again and again, with each dilution increasing the therapeutic effect.

The examples given in this chapter on homeopathic remedies and the emotions they address are only a minuscule part of the entire library of information available on the uses of homeopathy.

The hierarchy of treatment to employ with regard to suggesting homeopathic use is as follows, (1) mental; (2) emotional; (3) physical. The mind stimulates the emotion which is then resisted, creating the physical illness. The emotional and physical levels are symptomatic levels. The physiology of homeopathy, according to the late Dr. Hans Reckweg, MD, indicates that when you take a remedy, it works from the present time backward to conception, and addresses all traumatic incidents connected to the health or emotional issue.

Quantic Remedies

Recent research in psycho-neuro- immunology indicates a direct correlation between stress, emotions and disease and has shown that stress has a profound effect on the immune system. As incredible as it may seem, it has also been found that the immune system responds directly and immediately to creative intent and to positive change. This fact inspired the author's development of certain neuro-emotional quantic homeopathic remedies. The emergence of this new system of healing, integrates the ancient theory of acupuncture with its emotional correlation to meridians, and homeopathy with its corresponding mental symptoms. The precise combination of homeopathic remedies in each actually resurfaces and then dissolves the identity along with the subconscious cellular memory of traumatic events.

These remedies have properties to drain and detoxify the entire energy pattern from the body through the lymphatic system, the urine, bowels and perspiration. Through researching the formula for them, it was discovered that homeopathy works along acupuncture meridian pathways and in conjunction with the *immune system.* Each ingredient was evaluated and chosen for its precise emotional and mental correlation to the "Five Element Theory." What evolved was the development of high potency homeopathic remedies with added drainage properties that virtually eliminate homeopathic aggravation. Homeopathic aggravation is a normal aspect of homeopathic treatment and it means that symptoms may get worse before they get better. However, with the addition of a drainage remedy, homeopathic aggravation can be lessened or virtually eliminated. [14]

Isopathy, Airborne Allergies, and Environmental Illness

Isopathic allergens are also referred to as homeopathic antigens. Is there a role for isopathy for people with allergies or environmental illness? Are these remedies a waste of time? What if someone has multiple allergies (such as the environmentally sensitive)? [15]

Like many homeopaths, this researcher learned classical homeopathy. Countless hours were spent trying to understand and internalize Hahnemann's writings in the *Organon of Medicine*. Primarily based on Aphorisms 48, 56, 66, 272, and 273, the traditional "one remedy at a time" approach and avoided isopathic ("same heals same") remedies was believed to be accurate [1]. Therefore, the combination remedies which are widespread in France and in many American health food stores were rarely recommended. However, combination homeopathic antigens (isopathics) are another matter. The first time the use of isopathics was considered by this author was in a clinical trial for people suffering from seasonal allergic

rhinitis. In this trial, which involved nutrition and homeopathy(the homeopathic portion was double-blind), 80% of participants who consumed a specially prepared homeopathic pollen combination reported improvement [16]. This preparation included six of the most commonly expected pollens for the season in which the trial was conducted. The nature of the trial was such that all participants who received the combination pollen homeopathic remedy (and it was not a substantial percentage), received the same pollen combination. If the remedy had been properly individualized that the percent of participants which improved may have been possibly 100%. A few years back, a French study also concluded that isopathic pollen remedies were effective for reducing symptoms associated with pollinosis [17]. The Chinese have long used isopathy. Recent research has shown that the use of isopathic glandular proteins may increase oral tolerization for people with overactive immune system disorders, such as autoimmune diseases. German research appears to confirm the Chinese results. The same principle appears to work for the atopic and environmentally sensitive individuals. Now the author personally takes one or more isopathic remedies each Spring.

It is astounding to note that one of America's most common chronic diseases, pollinosis (which affects between 10-15% of Westerners and is medically considered to be due to an inherited predisposition [18]), was not even listed as a medical condition before the Industrial Age [19]. Since fewer people spend a great deal of time outside, more develop pollen allergies. It appears that the body starts to identify the natural proteins in "pollen" as unnatural allergens (probably because to some degree the body gets accustomed to the unnatural environment). Perhaps as frequently as pollinosis, are people who are ill due to "unnatural" environmental sensitivities. In modern America, everyone lives in areas affected by "noxious influences" (please read Aphorisms 77 & 260 [1]). We see painters bothered by paint, wood workers bothered by varnish, homemakers bothered by cleaners, and others that are bothered by nearly everything else (for this reason we have a sign posted in our office asking people to not wear perfumes or colognes). These environmentally sensitive people (sometimes referred to as universally reactive) do not always seem to respond well to "one remedy at a time." Many appear to be bothered by paint, perfumes, smoke, household cleaners, petroleum products, and cosmetics. Unlike pollinosis, the cause is near constant exposure to completely unnatural chemicals and chemical combinations— a toxic overload.

Total Toxic Threshold

According to toxicologists, toxins can be handled until a "total toxic threshold" is reached, then one will start to react [20]. Thus, if one can detoxify by reducing exposure, duration of exposure, eliminating other toxins, or reducing reaction (like through an appropriate isopathic remedy at optimal potency), then symptoms should tend to reduce (or eliminated). This is one reason why people who are chemically sensitive need to be more careful than some others about consuming foods they may be intolerant to—those intolerant foods may be increasing toxic load and bringing them to the point of "total toxic threshhold" earlier than might otherwise occur (if it would even occur at all!). Ideally, one homeopathic remedy would be preferred, but often the noxious environmental influences appear to overpower the homeopathic [1]. My solution has been to recommend isopathic allergens (as well as nutritional improvements and other methods of detoxification). The results have been overwhelmingly positive. People who have food allergies should not take isopathic remedies in order to immediately challenge those food allergies (challenging a peanut allergy can be fatal). However, people with food intolerances (which are not allergic and are not related to some type of undiagnosed infection) can (in some cases) reduce their sensitivities through a program which includes consumption of isopathic remedies.

This researcher has a tendency toward skepticism. It took years to accept that isopathic allergens could be effective, but research and clinical experience continues to demonstrate that they are. Further examination is encouraged into the use of isopathic allergens by other homeopaths to see if they will reach similar conclusions.

The Use of Cell Salts

Cell salts (also called tissue salts) are considered to be a form of homeopathic remedies by some. They are different from classical homeopathic remedies in several respects. They are intended to provide certain inorganic salts to the cells in the blood system (as opposed to raising "vital force" in classical homeopathy). The salts recommended are less individually specific than homeopathic remedies and are often combined. Actually, it is fairly easy to take all of them together (many products that contain them contain all of them).

The twelve are: calcarea fluorica, calcarea phosphorica, calcarea sulphurica, ferrum phosphoricum, kali (potassium) muriaticum (chloride), kali phosphoricum, kali sulphuricum, magnesia phosphorica, natrum (sodium) muriaticum, natrum phosphoricum, natrum sulphuricum, silicea (silicon). Although they are believed to have many benefits, one benefit for each is listed in the following chart.

Cell Salt	Also Called	Possible Benefits [21, 22]
Calcarea Fluoricum	Lime/Calcium Fluoride	Heart support
Calcarea Phosphoricum	Lime/Calcium Phosphate	Nutrient assimilation
Calcarea Sulphurica	Lime/Calcium Sulfate	Eliminating old red blood cells
Ferrum Phosphoricum	Iron Phosphate	Blood support/ oxygen carrying
Kali Muriaticum	Potassium Chloride	Certain infections
Kali Phosphoricum	Potassium Phosphate	Oxygen carrying support
Kali Sulphuricum	Potassium Sulfate	Blood and muscle support
Magnesia Phosphorica	Magnesium Phosphate	Blood and muscle support
Natrum Muriaticum	Sodium Chloride or Salt	Circulatory support
Natrum Phosphoricum	Sodium Phosphate	Respiratory support
Natrum Sulphuricum	Sodium Sulfate	Digestive stimulation
Silicea	Silicic Acid	Mental support

This researcher almost never recommends cell salts alone; thus, he is not certain if they provide the possible benefits listed above. When recommending the herbal products which contain them, results are achieved and it is believed that the cell salts may help speed the healing process.

References

[1] Hahnemann, Samuel. *Organon of Medicine.* Reprint by B. Jain Publishers, New Delhi, written 1833.

[2] Burr-Madsen, A. *Natural Therapies, Module 1.* Gateways College, Shingle Springs (CA), 1996.

[3] Thiel, R. J. *Effects of Naturopathic Interventions on Symptoms Associated with Seasonal Allegic Rhinitis.* ANMA Monitor, 1997; 1(2):4-9.

[4] Reilly D. et al. Is homeopathy a placebo response?: Controlled trial of homeopathic potency, with pollen in hay fever as model. The Lancet 11, 1986: 881-885.

[5] Weisenaur, M., et al. *Treatment of Pollenosis with Homeopathic Preparation Galphimia Glauca.* Allergologie, 10, 1990: 359-363.

[6] Matusiewicz, R. *The Homeopathic Treatment of Corticosteriod-Dependent Asthma.* Biomed Ther, 1997;15(4):117-122.

[7] Kuzeff, R. M. *Homeopathy, Sensation of Well Being and CD4 Levels.* Compl Ther Med, 1998; 6:4-9.

[8] Friese, K. H., et al. *Acute Otis media in Children: A Comparison of Conventional and Homeopathic Treatment.* Biomed Ther, 1997; 15(4):113-116.

[9] Weiser, M., et al. *Homeopathic vs. Conventional Treatment of Vertigo.* Arch Otolaryngol Head Neck Surg, 1998; 124:879-885.

[10] Whitmarsh, T. E., et al. *Double-Blind Randomized Placebo Controlled Study of Homeopathic Prophylaxis of Migraines.* Cephalgia, 1997; 17:600-604.

[11] Clarke, J.. H. *Dictionary of Practical Materia Medica.* Vol.2. B. Jain Publishers: New Delhi, Reprint 1990, written circa 1870.

[12] Thiel, R. J. Diet, *Regimen, and Homeopathy: Hahnemann was Right.* Resonance in Homeopathy, 1995; 17(4):17.

[13] Farr, R. *Which Homeopathy.* Townsend Letter for Doctors, 1999; 191:74-76.

[14] Dale, T. *Transform Your Emotional DNA.* Wellness Center for Research and Education, Los Angeles, 1997.

[15] Rea, W. and Pan, Y. *Fat and Blood Levels of Toxic Chemicals in Chemically Sensitive Patients.* J Nutr Environ Med,1995; 5:387-390.

[16] Thiel RJ. Clinical trial on the effects of dietary restriction, homeopathy, and combination nutritional supplementation on symptoms associated with seasonal allergic rhinitis. Dissertation. Union Institute, Cincinnati, 1993.

[17] Ruff, D. P., et al. *Effects of Dilution of Pollen as an Antihistamine and Releasing Histamine In Vitro on Subjects with Allergies.* Cahlers de Biotherapie, 1988;98:63-89

[18] Patterson, R. *Allergic Diseases: Diagnosis and Management.* Lipponcott, Phil., 1980.

[19] Edelson, E. *Allergies.* Chelsea House, New York, 1980.

[20] Klassen, C., et al. *Toxicology, the Basic Science of Poisons.* McMillan, New York, 1986

[21] Chapman, J. B. Dr. *Schuessler's Biochemistry.* New Era Laboratories, London, 1975.

[22] Chapman, E. *How to Use the Twelve Tissue Salts.* Pyramid Publications, New York, 1971.

28 Concluding Comments

Throughout this book, it is hoped that a sense about what true naturopathy is all about was conveyed. It is hoped that by showing you scientific validation of many of the old naturopathic interventions, you can better appreciate that naturopathy is truly scientific and truly the system of choice for the 21st century.

While naturopaths do recommend natural interventions, just because something is natural does not mean it is something a naturopath should recommend. As mentioned in chapter 23, limestone is natural and a natural food for plants. Since it is not a natural food for humans, it is not something that naturopaths should recommend (unless the body cannot handle calcium as found in food). Sometimes, though, this cannot be avoided as many special nutritional supplements include mineral salts. In time it is hoped that more supplements will be available that do not include mineral salts or isolated USP vitamins.

Hormones are also natural, but they do not help to actually rebuild the body. They have pharmacological as opposed to nutritional effect, they can lead to dependence, and they can lead to endo-crine gland atrophy, thus they are not appropriate to recommended by naturopaths. Glandulars (as mentioned in chapter 25) on the other hand can help rebuild endocrine glands nutritionally so that they can produce hormones (vegetarian approaches can work too).

It is not possible for anyone to know everything there is to know about health. Light exposure, magnet therapy, acupressure, and even nutrition (AND ESPECIALLY NUTRITION) are controversial subjects. No one, no matter their education, can learn everything about medicine and naturopathy in a four-year school (the author has eleven years of college and does not know everything about naturopathy and continues to research it extensively). If naturopaths embrace allopathic medications as part of their modalities, not only will they betray their naturopathic foundation, they will cease to become naturopaths. Naturopaths who prescribe medications are telling their clients that they do not feel they can be helped through naturopathic methods. Naturopaths who routinely prescribe medicines are not, in my opinion, being true to this profession.

If a naturopath knows he/she is limited to naturopathic interventions, even in difficult cases, then the naturopath will either improve his/her education, perform research, or will refer out to other practitioners. This can only help the naturopathic profession. Eventually, it is suspected with these types of referral, there will be a bit more specialization in naturopathy (though hopefully nowhere near that which has happened in medicine)—which should be a good thing. As time goes on it is believed that our modalities will continue to gain additional acceptance through clinical results.

Naturopathic interventions are successful. They do help people get better. As a naturopath, while valuing anecdotal evidence, when a supplement company wants their product carried, real proof is required. Everyone these days seems to have a lot of anecdotal stories, but few statistics. Keep statistics. This demonstrates, to those willing to look, that naturopathic interventions are not some placebo-effect, but are a serious attempt to rebuild health. The study papers in Appendix A show that 98.4% of people who suffered from a variety of disorders who followed the author's naturopathic interventions (which included nutrition, herbology, homeopathy, diet, food avoidance, counseling, and electrical modalities) reported improvement. A lot of different naturopathic modalities are used (though clinical nutrition happens to be the author's main specialty), but some more than others (based upon training and the needs of clientele). If not able to adequately help someone, the problem is not naturopathy, but it is the lack of detailed knowledge of some aspect of naturopathy (which is one of the reasons to always keep studying and researching).

It is felt that natural vitamins (minerals, etc.) are better for humans than synthetic ones. Synthetics do have some value, but they are not food and thus it is believed that they do not lead to optimal health (for more details please refer to chapters 22-24).

Synthetic isolates are unnatural and dangerous. They are so dangerous that various researchers believe that they can cause people to die prematurely and/or suffer from preventable health problems. While isolates perform some of the known functions of natural vitamins, they have not been proven to have all the positive effects that natural vitamins can provide. As no one (nor one group) can possibly know everything about human health (even Dr. Lust said that), it is dangerous to synthesize and isolate vitamins, herbs, etc. By allowing our food supply to be altered (processed, fortified, and/or genetically-altered), we humans are asking for increases in health problems.

It is the author's opinion that those who believe synthetics are as good as natural nutrients are doing a disservice to the entire food supply. If synthetics are as good, then it is okay to process food, remove natural nutrients, and fortify the foods with synthetics. If synthetics are not as good, then we all need to realize this and change our food supply back to a more natural, sustainable production system. Because it is believed that natural nutrients are superior to synthetic ones, it is a high concern that there are genetic altered "foods", synthetic "foods" (including sweeteners and various fats), and new food processes such as irradiation.

Natural foods and interventions have stood the test of time. Whether one believes God created everything a long time ago or believes we evolved from randomness, it does not change the fact that humans have been around a long-time. Humans survived on natural foods and natural interventions. Be extremely hesitant to accept unnatural substitutes developed by Ph.D.s (and I have a Ph.D. in nutrition science) as equivalent or superior to real food. It is not the type of experiment many would trust their bodies to. Would you?

Naturopathy will stand the test of time into the 21st century and beyond!

Appendix A1

Effects of Naturopathic Interventions on Symptoms Associated with Seasonal Allergic Rhinitis

Published as: Thiel, R.J. *Effects of Naturopathic Interventions on Symptoms Associated with Seasonal Allergic Rhinitis.* ANMA Monitor 1 (2): 4-9, 1997; Townsend Letter 201, 2000:93-95.

Abstract: The purpose of this trial was to determine if naturopathic inerventions such as homeopathy, isopathy, nutrition, herbology and dietary changes could reduce symptoms associated with seasonal allergic rhinitis. 94.7% of those that followed the recommendations reported improvement.

Introduction

An eighty-day clinical trial was conducted during the spring season involving forty-nine adults who suffered from seasonal allergic rhinitis. The objective of the trial was to determine if various naturopathic interventions could reduce the severity of symptoms associated with the disease.

The trial site was the San Joaquin Valley of central California. The area produces vine, tree, and field crops and has high pollen counts [1]. The air quality is considered below state and federal guidelines for ozone, carbon monoxide, and PM 10 (particulate matter ten microns or smaller in diameter) [2].

Methodology

Subjects

The clinical trial included 40 participants and 9 non-participants. Thirty-one of the forty participants were female. The average (mean) age was 46 years.

Participants were non-institutionalized volunteers with a history of seasonal allergic rhinitis. Additional inclusion criteria included age of at least 20 years, report of symptoms which were most pronounced during the period of the trial, residence in the central San Joaquin Valley, and the ability to provide informed consent. Participants completed a symptom-severity questionnaire before and after the period of the clinical trial. The non-participant group consisted of those who originally inquired about participation, completed the initial symptom severity questionnaire, suffered from the disease during the time period, but chose to not actively participate.

Protocols

Protocol selection was based upon the investigator's research into previous studies and examination of case histories. The trial was an attempt to test these approaches under "real world" conditions and intentionally did not control the use and frequency of medications (medications are further discussed in the results section).

Avoidance of certain refined carbohydrates (dietary restrictions) was recommended for all participants in both protocols. Specifically, participants were instructed to avoid all foods containing white sugar (sucrose or dextrose) and white wheat flour. Some health advocates have suggested that white sugar consumption can predispose one to hay fever [3] or worsen symptoms associated with it [4]. In order to not adversely affect caloric intake, as well as to encourage greater compliance, subjects were allowed to consume foods containing other sweeteners such as honey, fructose, aspartame, etc. It was also suggested that participants substitute products containing whole wheat for products containing white flour (whole wheat products have a lower glycemic effect than white flour products [5] and greater amounts of trace minerals [6]).

Protocol 1 included the preceding dietary restrictions plus the consumption of a real or placebo homeopathic remedy. Twenty-two people were assigned to protocol 1. The homeopathic remedies used in this trial were: Aconite, Nux Vomica, Sabadilla, Allium Cepa, and Diluted Pollen (containing seven local pollens). For this experiment, homeopathics and diluted pollens were provided in the 12x potency. The homeopathic portion of the trial was double-blind.

Protocol 2 was the combination of diet restrictions and homeopathic remedies in protocol 1, plus combination nutritional supplements. Participants were automatically assigned to protocol 2 unless they were taking vitamin/mineral supplements or medications containing retinoid derivatives. The separation into protocols one and two was to reduce the possibility of developing hypervitaminosis A [7]. Eighteen participants were assigned to protocol 2. The combination nutritional supplements they were given contained various vitamins, minerals, bovine materials, and herbs. The vitamins and minerals contained in them (daily quantities shown in parentheses) was as follows: vitamin A (5,000 i.u.), vitamin B-1 (7 mg.), vitamin B-12 (57 mcg.), niacin (20 mg.), vitamin B-5 (200 mg.), vitamin C (800 mg.), vitamin E (20 i.u.), calcium (719 mg.), magnesium (100 mg.), manganese (50 mg.), and montmorillonite (400 mg.). The bovine materials included adrenal (80 mg.), liver (45 mg.), lung (20 mg.), pancreas (90 mg.), parathyroid (2.5 mg.), spleen (9 mg.), and thymus (10 mg.). The supplements also contained the herb fenugreek (50 mg.) and other materials. The combination nutritional supplementation of this trial was single-blind.

Statistical significance was determined at P < 0.05 using multiple regression analysis. Regression analysis is a technique which calculates correlation of independent variables to a dependent variable.

Results

90.0% of participants reported improvement, 2.5% reported no change, and 7.5% reported a worsening of symptoms. 11.1% of the non-par-

ticipants reported improvement, 44.4% reported no change, and 44.4% reported a worsening of symptoms. Actually, 94.7% of those participants who could have been expected to improve (based on diet changes made and whether or not they received placebos or real supplements) reported improvement. Table 1 shows the regression output.

Table 1: Regression Output

Constant	0.012
Std Err of Y Est	0.292
R Squared	0.381
No. of Observations	49
Degrees of Freedom	45
Correlation Coefficient	0.617
Sign	5.489

P Value < 0.03
X Coefficients: Diet Alone 36.8%;
Homeopathics 6.1%; Supplements 23.5%
Std Err of Coefficients: Diet Alone 0.112;
Homeopathics 0.10; Supplements 0.094

The x coefficients in Table 1 suggest that avoidance of refined carbohydrates contributed an approximate 36.8% improvement, consuming real single remedy homeopathics an additional 6.1%, and consumption of the nutritional supplements an additional 23.5%. These results also suggest that combination of dietary restrictions, real single-remedy homeopathics, and nutritional supplements were more helpful for improving the symptoms associated with seasonal allergic rhinitis, than either individually. For example, if a someone in the trial reduced refined carbohydrates 100%, took a real single remedy homeopathic, and took the nutritional supplements, this individual could have been expected to improve by approximately 66.4% (+/- 14.6%). For an opposite example, if someone did not reduce refined carbohydrate consumption, did not take a real single-remedy homeopathic, and did not take the nutritional supplements, this individual could have been expected to improve (negative indicates a worsening of symptoms) by approximately -1.2% (+/- 14.6%).

The results demonstrate that the nutrition-based approaches used were a significant factor for improvement in this trial (P < 0.03).

Other variables may have played a role in improvement. For example, since most of the participants had been taking medication in prior years, the use of medication may also have had a role on the results. 85% of participants (34/40) had been taking medications for their seasonal allergic rhinitis. 88.2% of those who normally took medication (30/34) reduced or eliminated (10 totally eliminated taking medication) their consumption of medications during the period of this clinical trial compared to the same period last year, and yet improved.

Age appeared to have a small negative effect on improvement, but was not statistically shown to have been a major factor. None of the participants reported improvement unless they were taking real homeopathics and/or the combination nutritional supplements and/or reduced their consumption of the restricted items.

As stated earlier, each participant ranked the severity of their symptoms at the beginning and end of the clinical trial. As can be seen in Table 2, participants reported improvement for all monitored symptoms.

Table 2: Average (Mean) Improvement By Symptom

% Improvement

Sneezing	48.28%
Watery Eyes	46.43%
Running Nasal Mucus	50.00%
Post Nasal Drip	46.88%
Pain in Sinus Cavity	50.00%
Nose Congested	48.39%
Dry Nasal Mucus	52.38%
Itching Eyes or Sinuses	41.94%
Tired Eyes	57.14%
Itching Throat or Mouth	38.46%
Exhaustion/Tiredness	41.38%
Other	66.67%
Overall Average	47.65%

Discussion

Although it is doubtful that the subjects in this experiment were clinically allergic to sucrose or dextrose or refined wheat flour (none of the participants listed allergies to any of those items), it is likely that they may have been somewhat sensitive to those foods. Food sensitivities (or intolerance) are defined to include nonimmunologic mediated defects such as enzyme defects, food toxins, microbiotic contamination, and idiosyncratic reactions [8]. Since food allergies often trigger asthmatic attacks [9], it could be speculated that consumption of foods that one is sensitive to may increase symptoms associated with seasonal allergic rhinitis.

It is interesting to note that all persons who took real single-remedy homeopathics reported improvement. The mixed pollen dilution was not shown to have been effective, however. This could have been because the dilution only contained seven different pollens, whereas there are normally substantial quantities of at least twenty-one different pollens/mold spores in the air during the spring months [10].

The results of taking the nutritional supplements in this clinical trial, which contained vitamins A, C, E, and other substances appeared to enhance the reduction of severity of symptoms associated with seasonal rhinitis; they may also help reducing toxicity of airborne pollutants. Previous research has indicated that the combined effects of vitamins C and E and beta-carotene seemed to have had beneficial effects on persons living in areas with airborne environmental toxins [11,12].

Thirty of the participants reported that they reduced the amount of medications that they normally took for their hay fever. Side effects associated with commonly used rhinitis medications (such as antihistamines and nasal corticosteroids) include drowsiness, headache, insomnia, nausea, nasal irritation, nervousness, and wheezing [13,14]. The reduction of consumption of medications would suggest an additional benefit from employing nutrition-based approaches as an adjunct to medical treatment, that of decreasing the likelihood of side effects from the medications.

Avoidance of certain refined carbohydrates, consuming single-remedy homeopathics, and taking combination nutritional supplements did reduce reported symptom severity of seasonal allergic rhinitis adults residing in the San Joaquin Valley (P <0.03). These approaches may also be helpful for dealing with the effects of air pollution [15]. Further research into the area of naturopathy and airborne particulates is encouraged to see if researchers in other geographic locations would reach similar conclusions.

References

[1] Ipps, D. T. *Nature and Causes of the PM 10 Problem in California.* Technical Support Division of the State of California Air Resources Board, Sacramento. pp. 3-4, May 1987.

[2] Sweet, J. *Fresno County 1990 Air Quality Data Summary.* San Joaquin Valley Unified Air Pollution Control District, Fresno, p.1, 1991.

[3] Lee, R. *Therapeutic Food Manual.* National Academy of Research Biochemists, Biloxi (Miss.), p. 28, Circa 1957.

[4] Tilden, J. H. *Toxemia Explained.* Life Science Institute, Manchaca (Tex.), pp. 37-39, Circa 1926.

[5] Holm, J. and Bjorck, I. *Bioavailability of Starch in Various Wheat-Based Bread Products: Evaluation of Metabolic Responses in Healthy Subjects and Rate and Extent of In Vitro Starch Digestion.* Am J Clin Nutr 55: 420-429, 1992.

[6] Whitney, E. N. and Nunnelley, E. M. *Understanding Nutrition.* West Publishing, St. Paul, Table H-1: H22-H32, 1987.

[7] Geubel, A. P., de Galocsy, C., Alves, N., Rahier, J. and Dive, C. *Liver Damage Caused by Therapeutic Vitamin A Administration: Estimate of Dose-Related tToxicity in 41 Cases.* Gastroenterology 100: 1701-1709, 1991.

[8] Chandra, R. *Food Allergy: Diagnosis and Strategies for Prevention.* Nutr and the M.D., 17 (4): 1-3, 1991.

[9] Spector, S. *Common Triggers of Asthma.* Postgraduate Med 90 (3): 50-58, 1991.

[10] Ziering, W. H. *California, Fresno.* In: Statistical Report of the Pollen and Mold Committee of the American Academy of Allergy, Ross Laboratories, Columbus (OH), pp. 3-4, 1982.

[11] Crystal, R. G. *Oxidants and Respiratory Tract epithelial Injury: Pathogenesis and Strategies for Therapeutic Intervention.* J Med 91 (Suppl. 3C): 3C - 44S, 1991.

[12] Menzel, D. E. *The Effects of the Exposure of Air Pollution on the Need for Antioxidant Vitamins.* In: Beyond deficiency: new views on the function and health effects of vitamins. Academy of Sciences Abstract 13, February 9-12, 1992.

[13] *Histamines and Antihistamines.* In: Remington's Pharmaceutical Sciences. Mack Publishing, Easton (PA), pp. 1123-1131, 1991.

[14] *Antihistamines/Antipruitics/Other Allergy Agents.* In: Compendium of Drug Therapy. McGraw-Hill, NY, pp. 16-18, 1988.

[15] Scarbeck, K. *Indoor City Life May Increase Asthma Mortality.* Family Practice News: 39, January 15, 1996.

Appendix A2

Nutrition-Based Interventions for Attention-Deficit Disorder and Attention-Deficit Hyperactive Disorder

Published as Thiel, R.J. Nutrition-Based Interventions for Attention-Deficit Disorder and Attention-Deficit Hyperactive Disorder. ANMA Monitor 1 (3):5-8 1997

Abstract: The purpose of this preliminary study was to determine how often nutrition-based interventions could result in behavioral improvement for children and adults with attention-deficit disorder and/or attention-deficit hyperactive disorder. 100.0% who followed the recommendations reported behavioral improvement within 40 days. The 33 participants were given nutritional supplementation, the significance of the results were P < .0001. Food intolerances were found in 90.9% of participants.

Introduction

Millions of children and adults have attention deficit disorder (ADD) and/or attention deficit hyperactive disorder (ADHD) (sometimes known as hyperkinesis) [1]. ADD is characterized by difficult concentration, a tendency towards distraction, and impaired visual/spacial coordination [2]. ADHD is characterized by inattentiveness, impulsiveness, and hyperactivity: it is the most common neurobehavioral disorder found in children [3]. Males are affected more often than females, and it is estimated that between 1-15% of children suffer from them [4]. Although the causes are not clear, genetics, food additives, nutrition, infections, and abnormalities related to neurotransmitters and the central nervous system are suspected [3,5]. ADD and ADHD are often difficult to differentiate from other disruptive behaviors [6]. Though in some ways similar to major depression, bipolar disorder, and generalized anxiety disorder [7], ADD and ADHD to some degree have become the diagnoses of choice. ADD and ADHD are often incorrectly diagnosed by school teachers (based on their perception of behavior) [5] and sometimes even pediatricians who occasionally improperly use Ritalin as a diagnostic tool [8].

Most standard interventions rely on stimulant drugs and psychological counseling [9]. The heavy reliance on drugs has resulted in a near drug epidemic: the number of prescriptions for the main stimulants used for people with ADD/ADHD (Ritalin, Dexedrine, and Cylert) tripled from 1990-1994 [1]. Ritalin is a form of speed which many experts feel should be used less frequently [1,5,8]. It should be noted that even many people without ADD/ADHD show greater focus when taking Ritalin [8] and around 20-25% of people with ADHD show no response to it [9].

This report includes the results of a pretest-posttest trial involving 33 people who suffered from ADD, ADHD, or related disorders. The purpose of this trial was to measure how often nutrition-based recommendations could help improve behavior associated with these conditions and to identify dietary factors that may be involved. It did not attempt to address counseling, medical, or other non-nutritional interventions.

Selection Criteria

Participants were eligible for inclusion in this trial if they resided in California, came to our office, agreed to provide (and did provide) feedback, signed a consent agreement, and indicated that they suffered from ADD, ADHD, or related disorders. This report includes every client who met these criteria during the time period of this study. 36 people were eligible, but three failed to follow the recommendations and/or provide the required feedback. Of the 33 actual participants, the ages of the participants ranged from 2-58; the mean age was 13.1 years. 19 of the participants were male and 14 were female.

Method

After completing the selection documentation, all subjects were interviewed for approximately 45 minutes. All subjects were then assessed using Reflex Nutrition Assessment (RNA). RNA is a non-invasive technique used to assess nutrition status by observing the response of muscles under externally provided human-force (it is similar to other forms of muscle testing [10]). Performing RNA for people with ADD/ADHD normally consists of performing three assessments. The first assessment is to determine if a reflex indicates a nutritional need (by observing a reduction in muscular strength); the second is to determine which nutritional intervention can help fit that need (by observing an increase in muscular strength). The third is to assess for possible food intolerances—a weakness when exposed to the food is considered an indication of a possible intolerance. Many have reported success in using RNA or similar techniques [10-12].

Participants who appeared to have (through the interview process combined with reflex assessment) a sensitivity to one or more foods were advised to discontinue consumption of them. Participants were also advised to consume an average of three tablets per day of one or more nutritional supplements for each related reflex concern (younger children generally took less supplements). Although the supplements varied, bovine thyroid or fortified flaxseeds for thyroid reflex concerns (located above the thyroid); soluble calcium, magnesium, potassium, phosphorus, and alfalfa for calcium reflex concerns (located above the parathyroid glands); fortified glandulars, GABA-S (gamma-amino butyric acid), L-Tyrosine (amino acid), or fortified flaxseeds for mental fatigue reflex concerns (located approximately 3 inches over the right eye); chromium GTF with B vitamins for pancreatic reflex concerns (located above the pancreas; and fortified herbs or fortified glandulars various infectious concerns (located above the lower colon, naval, and collar-bone respectively. Other products were used instead if the reflex checked as better.

Subjects were interviewed at approximately 20 day intervals to determine any change in behavior.

Results

51.5% of participants appeared to need calcium support, 48.4% nutritional mental fatigue support (other than calcium or thyroid), 45.2% nutritional thyroid support, 29.0% nutritional infection support, 9.7% nutritional pancreatic support and 16.1% other (mainly b-vitamins or iron). Approximately 20% of participants had been taking Ritalin or some prescription for their ADD/ADHD; all either reduced or eliminated taking these medications, yet reported improvement. Including the food sensitivity assessment, the average participant had 2.9 reflex concerns.

100.0% of participants (or their parents) reported behavioral improvement within 40 days; the P value of this result was < 0.0001. Age and gender did not appear to play any role in determining improvement.

Possible food intolerances were found in 28 (90.3%) of the participants; many had multiple intolerances. Those foods by occurrence were bovine dairy products 41.9%, food colors/preservatives 22.6%, refined carbohydrates (sucrose, white sugar, white rice, white flour) 19.4%, wheat (whole and white) 19.4%, and caffeine containing products 9.7%. One participant each was bothered by apricots, black pepper, brown rice, chocolate, citrus, millet, and oats.

Discussion

The fact that 51.5% of participants appeared to need calcium is consistent with the findings of a panel convened by the National Institutes of Health which found 1/2 of American diets were deficient in calcium [13]. Dr. Sheldon Hendlor has written that calcium can function as a natural tranquilizer, calm nerves, and relieve cramps in legs [14]. This researcher's experience is that children who do not consume dairy products or who are unknowingly sensitive (or allergic) to bovine dairy products are at risk for developing at least mild

ADD (non-bovine dairy sources of calcium include goats' milk, bok choy cabbage, turnip greens, spinach, sardines, and broccoli [15]). Since calcium is needed for the neuromuscular system [16], it is no wonder that children with deficiencies demonstrate so-called behavioral problems. Regarding supplementation, typical multi-formulas do not appear to be adequate of themselves (not enough calcium is available for absorption).

Nutritional mental fatigue support has been found to be helpful by others. Dr. Steve Nugent has found that substances contained within herbs, as well as gamma-amino butyric acid (GABA) and vitamin B-6 are effective for people with ADD and ADHD [5]. Interestingly, males with primary unipolar depressive disorders have been reported to have significantly less plasma GABA than others [17]; this researcher considers low plasma GABA levels to be a predisposing factor for mood disorders such as ADHD. Dr. Nugent reported that the highly touted proanthocyandins, often marketed as "pycnogenols", do not on their own appear to be effective for ADD/ADHD [5]. However, when combined with flaxseeds and vitamin B-6, this researcher has found this combination to be helpful for ADD/ADHD. Flaxseeds contain essential unsaturated fatty acids omega 3 and omega 6 [18]. It has been observed that hyperactive children (especially males) may have deficiencies in essential fatty acids (EFAs) due to problems metabolizing linoleic acid or because they may have a greater than normal need for it [19]. An experimental study with supplemental EFAs confirmed this [19]. A study involving 96 boys with behavior and learning problems found that they had below normal plasma levels of omega-3 and omega-6 fatty acids [20]; there were greater behaviorial problems in the boys with the lowest omega-3 concentrations and a greater use of antibiotics in boys with the lowest omega-6 concentrations [20]. Flaxseeds also supply substances essential for the enzyme activity of the brain [5]. Julian Whitaker (MD) who once advocated consumption of flaxseed oil, now instead recommends consumption of whole flaxseeds for general well being [21]. Another useful nutrient, vitamin B-6, is involved in gluconeogenesis, niacin formation, erythrocyte metabolism, hormone modulation, and nervous system function [22]. One researcher found that overactive children with low serotonin levels did better on oral vitamin B6 than they did on Ritalin [23]. Low serotonin levels

are often found in children with hyperkinesis [23].

The relatively high incidence of thyroid involvement in this preliminary study was not a surprise. It is consistent with some of this researcher's other work [24] as well as that of headache researcher Dr. Cass Igram. Dr. Igram's clinical experience suggests that, due to dietary habits and food processing techniques, every American will suffer from low thyroid function at some time [25]. He (as well as this researcher and others [26]) has found this will not often be correlated with a medical blood test for hypothyroidism; he and this researcher have found that bovine glandular supplementation is helpful when this problem is encountered [25]. This researcher's clinical experience suggests that flaxseeds can also be helpful for people with thyroid nutritional concerns. This can especially be helpful when dealing with vegetarians. It should be noted that certain medically-oriented researchers tend to feel that thyroid involvement in ADD/ADHD is rare and that it occurs as the result of the body being resistant to thyroxin as opposed to an inability to produce it [27]. While this resistance to thyroxin is correct for a small portion of the population, the results of this study seem to suggest (at least from a nutritional point of view) that thyroid involvement is not rare for people with ADD/ADHD.

Participants with pancreatic reflex concerns were the ones most frequently bothered by sugar. Chromium supplementation has been used by others when hypoglycemia was suspected [28] (which it was for 9.7% of the participants); in this study chromium GTF was combined with B vitamins and other synergists. Lower glycemic diets consisting of more whole grains, certain fruits, vegetables, proteins, and fats and less sugar and refined carbohydrates [29] were recommended to this group along with supplementation. Dr. Carlton Fredericks found that low blood sugar and food sensitivities were often involved with hyperactive children [30].

Sensitivities to foods were commonly found in this study at a rate (90.3%) which greatly exceeds that found by most medically-oriented researchers [4]. This may be because most people with ADD/ADHD probably do not have class I food allergies (were IgE is raised). Dr. Nugent's work appears to correlate with mine in this area: he has found the incidence of dietary involvement in people with ADD/ADHD greatly exceeds that which is stated by the American Pyschiatric Association [5].

Notice this study found twelve different foods/food groups which were involved and that none of the items appeared to universally affect people with ADD/ADHD. It is this individualization which is hard for many to accept. Since virtually no one needs food colors/preservatives, excess refined carbohydrates, and caffeine-containing items, it is not unreasonable for people with ADD/ADHD to avoid them when possible; beyond that, they should seek professional assistance from practitioners properly trained to look for specific food intolerances. While this researcher will acknowledge that critics will disapprove of the use of individualization techniques such as RNA [31], it appears that the critics have not attained the high success rates that RNA has accomplished for people with ADD/ADHD or even other common problems (i.e., 99.01% for chronic fatigue [24]; 98.8% for musculoskeletal pain relief [32]). This preliminary study demonstrates that individualized nutritional interventions, including selected food avoidance, can be effective in improving behavior for people with ADD, ADHD, or similar disorders. It is hoped that practitioners of all types will look more towards individualized interventions to help those who suffer with these concerns.

References

[1] Batoosingh, K. *Ritalin Prescriptions Triple Over Last Four Years.* Family Practice News, June 1,1995.

[2] Pedley, T. Brain, *Nerve, and Muscle Disorders.* In: The Columbia University College of Physicians & Surgeons Complete Home Medical Guide, 2nd ed., Columbia University, New York, 1989.

[3] Leung, A.., et al. *Attention-Deficit Hyperactive Disorder.* Postgraduate Med, 1995 95 (2): 153-160.

[4] *Facts About Childhood Hyperactivity.* National Institute of Child Health and Human Development, Nov. 1990.

[5] Nugent, S. D. *Natural Therapies for ADD and ADHD.* Presentation at the 13th Annual Meeting of the American Naturopathic Medical Association, Las Vegas, Sept. 6-8 1996.

[6] Searight H., et al. *Attention-Deficit/Hyperactive Disorder: Assessment, Diagnosis, and Management.* J Family Practice,1995; 40 (3): 270-279.

[7] Milberger, S., et al. *Attention Deficit Hyper-Activity Disorder and Comorbid Disorders: Issues of Overlapping Symptoms.* Am J Psychiatry, 1996; 152 (12): 1793-1799.

[8] Goldman, E. *Ritalin Wrongly Used to Diagnose ADD.* Family Practive News, Nov 1995.

[9] Pliszkra, S. *Attention-Deficit HyperActivity Disorder: A Clinical Review.* Am Family Physician, 1995; 43 (4): 1267-1275.

[10] Thiel, R. J. *Serious Nutrition for Health Care Professionals.* Arroyo Grande (CA): California Health Group, 1995.

[11] Burr-Madsen, A. *Body Polarity Reflex Analysis and the Nutritional Connection.* Carson City: Thoth, Inc., 1992.

[12] Rosen, M. S. and Williams, L. *The Research Status of Applied Kinesiology, Part II: An Annotated Bibliography of Applied Kinesiological Research.* In: A.K. Review, 1991; 1(2): 34-47.

[13] *Many American Diets Deficient in Calcium.* NIH Committee. Nutr Week, 1994 22:7.

[14] Hendlor, S. *The Doctor's Vitamin and Mineral Encyclopedia.* Simon and Schuster, New York, 1990.

[15] Whitney, E. N. and Nunnelley, E. M. *Understanding Nutrition.* 4th ed. West Publishing, New York, 1987.

[16] Allen, L. and Wood, R. *Calcium and Phosphorus.* In Modern Nutrition in Health and Disease, 8th ed.: 144-163, Lea & Febinger, Philadelphia, 1994.

[17] Petty, F., et al. *Low Plasma Gamma-aminobutyric Acid Levels in Male Patients with Depression.* Biological Psychiatry, 1992; 32:354-363.

[18] Bagely, J., et al. *Cellular Nutrition in Support of Early Multiple Organ Failure.* Chest, 1991; 100 (3): 182S-188S.

[19] Colquhoun, I. and Bunday, S. *A Lack of Essential Fatty Acids as a Possible Cause of Hyperactivity in Children.* Med Hypotheses,1981; 7: 673-679.

[20] Stevens, L., et al. *Omega-3 Fatty Acids in Boys with Behavior, Learning, and Health Problems.* Physiology and Behavior, 1996; 59:4-5.

[21] Whitaker, J. *Add Flax to Your Diet for Health.* Health & Healing 6 (7): 6-7, July 1996.

[22] Leklem, J. E. *Vitamin B-6.* In: Modern Nutrition in Health and Disease, 8th ed. Lea & Febiger, Phil.: 383-393, 1994.

[23] Coleman, M., et al. *A Preliminary Study of Pyridoxine Administration in a Subgroup of Hyperkinetic Children: A Double-Blind Crossover Comparison with Methylphenidate.* J Biological Pyschology, 1979; 14 (5): 741-751.

[24] Thiel, R . J. *Chronic Fatigue Assessment and Intervention: the Result of 101 Cases.* ANMA & AANC Journal, 1996; 1(3):17-19.

[25] Igram, C. *Who Needs Headaches?* Literary Visions: Hiawatha (Iowa), 1991.

[26] Haggerty, J. *Subclinical Hypothyroidism: A Modifiable Risk Factor for Depression?* Am J Pyschiatry, 1995; 150: 508-510.

{27] Greco, R. *ADD, A Rare Thyroid Disorder, and the Media.* Pediatric Report's Child Health Newsletter, 1993 (2): 43.

[28] Anderson, R. *Chromium Metabolism and Its Role in Disease Processes in Man.* Clin Physiology Biochem, 1986; 4:31-41.

[29] Jenkins, D. J., et al. *Glycemic index of foods: A Physiological Basis for Carbohydrate Exchange.* Am J Clin Nutr, 1981;34: 362-366

[30] Fredericks, C. *Nutrition Guide for the Prevention & Cure of Common Ailments & Diseases.* Simon and Simon: New York, 1982.

[31] Kenny, J. J., Clemens, R. and Forsythe, K. D. *Applied Kinesiology Unreliable for Assessing Nutrient Status.* J Am Diet Assoc, 1988; 88(6).

[32] Thiel, R. .J. *Musculoskeletal Pain Relief for People with Arthritis, Lupus, and Fibromyalgia.* ANMA Monitor, 1997; (1): 8-10.

NOTE: Dr. Thiel is not a medical doctor. None of this research is medical advice, nor should it be construed as medical advice; nor is any of this information specific for any individual.

Appendix A3

Bioelectrical Stimulation for People with Patterns Consistent with Certain Chronic Infections

Published as: Thiel R. Bioelectrical Stimulation for People with Patterns Consistent with Certain Chronic Infections. ANMA Monitor 2(4):5-9,1998; Townsend Letter 203:65-67, 2000.

Abstract: The purpose of this pilot trial was to determine whether there may be any efficacy to combining the use of bioelectrical stimulating units with nutritional interventions for people with patterns consistent with chronic fungal, bacterial, viral, or parasitic infections. This trial was a pretest-posttest, natural control-group design where subjects were assessed before and after bioelectrical stimulation was introduced by the use of a device, most commonly referred to as a "zapper." 140 of 143 (97.9%) participants reported improvement within 45 days, P<.01; 48.2% improved substantially and 49.7% improved minimally. Thus, it appears that combining bioelectrical stimulation with nutritional interventions may have efficacy and deserves further study.

Introduction

Reports of infections are on the increase [1-4]. Within the past two decades, at least twenty new infectious diseases (or new presentations of old infectious diseases) have become universally recognized as problems for humans [3,4]. Increases of infections are believed to be caused by changes in lifestyle, diet, agricultural practices, travel, and medical interventions [2-4]. Regarding medical interventions, the excessive use of antibiotics has led to an increase of bacteria which are resistant to antibiotics [5]. This, in turn, has led to the development of stronger antibiotics, which then has led to an increase of the amounts of strains of bacteria which are resistant to antibiotics [5,6]. There is even a strain of staphylococcus aureus that was initially described as "a deadly bacterium that can resist every drug in science's infection-treatment arsenal" [7].

Approaches other than antibiotics are needed to deal with these and other infections [2,5]. One approach, as advocated by Hulda Clark (Ph.D., N.D.), involves the use of bioelectrical stimulation (which she terms "zapping") combined with herbal interventions [2]. Dr. Clark believes that all invading organisms are parasitic and can be destroyed by zapping or by being exposed to an electronic field at a frequency taken from its own bioradiation band width, and that devices exist which can generate the proper frequencies. Similar to my hypothesis that all matter appears to emit some type of electro-magnetic energy [8], Dr. Clark has hypothesized that all living matter emits some type of high frequency energy (which she terms as "bioradiation"). Dr. Clark believes that a particular frequency range for each form of living matter can be identified and that a lethal effect can be obtained through a device she refers to as a "zapper" [2]. Others have made units which predate her comments, even back in the 19th Century [9,10]. Actually, instructions on how to make such devices are now nearly universally available from a variety of copyrighted sources (and these devices are often made and used by the lay public without any type of supervision) [2,9,11,12]. Dr. Clark has stated that a zapper can selectively electrocute parasitic organisms without adversely affecting humans because humans are not harmed by such a low voltage (9v) and that the frequencies that affect parasites are sufficiently far removed from those that could bother humans [2]. A clinical trial was performed to determine if such interventions may have any efficacy when combined with nutritional interventions.

Materials and Method

Non-HIV infected adults were eligible for inclusion in this pretest-posttest trial if they resided in California, came to our office, agreed to provide (and did provide) feedback, signed a consent agreement, had evidence of a pattern of chronic infection consistent within the scope of this trial, had not completely responded to previous nutritional interventions, were not pregnant, did not wear a pacemaker, underwent at least one zapping session, and followed the nutritional recommendations. The natural control group met the same criteria, except that they did not undergo a zapping session. This report includes every subject who met these criteria during the twelve month time period of this trial.

158 people were eligible, but 15 failed to provide the required feedback. Of the 143 actual participants, 41 of the participants were male and 102 were female. Ages ranged from 5 to 84 years. 34 were in the natural control group, but 3 failed to provide the required feedback. Of the 31 actually in the natural control group 9 of them were male and 22 of them were female; ages ranged from 4-82.

All were interviewed for approximately 30 minutes. Signs and symptoms associated with their possible infections were noted. Five categories of infection were considered without regard to specific species, strains, or varieties. All continued with their nutritional recommendations (taking commercially available vitamin, herbal, and glandular combinations), including dietary restrictions when involved. As the nutritional interventions, have been written about extensively elsewhere by this investigator [8,13-15] and are not the independent variable being tested in this trial, they are not detailed in this paper. Subjects then underwent one or more zapping sessions. Subjects were re-interviewed approximately three weeks later to determine any change. As the State of California does not allow naturopaths to order medical tests, changes in health in this pilot trial was based upon subject reports of improvement.

A zapping session consisted of having the participant hold a zapping unit (two different ones were used in this study) three times for between 7 to 15 minutes each time, with a break of between 10-20 minutes (time varied depending upon the zapper used). Two different zappers were used: A commercial model and a specially engineered model. The commercial model used was a SyncroZap Pulse Generator Model B3 from Self Health Resource Center, Imperial Beach, California; it is operated by a 9 volt battery and produces a 32KHz output. The engineered model was based upon the same design as the commercial model (was also operated by a 9 volt battery), but due to an extra integrated circuit, its output sweeps the frequency in steps of 2 KHz from 20 - 40 KHz (this sweeping is believed by the developer to generate an output at 10 times as many frequencies than the commercial model). The commercial model was normally held for 7 minutes with 15-20 minute breaks, while the engineered model was normally held for 15 minutes with 10 minute breaks.

Results

Reflex assessment, combined with the interview process, suggested that the average participant had 1.1 chronic infections (note that reflex assessment is not diagnostic [8]). 48.2% reported substantial symptomatic improvement (between 75% improvement to complete remission), whereas 49.7% reported minimal improvement (less than 75% improvement); total with any improvement was 97.9%. In the control group, the average control also had 1.1 chronic infections; 12.9% reported significant improvement, whereas 48.4% reported minimal improvement; total with any improvement was 61.3%. Improvement (from both groups) was reported for symptoms including bloating, diarrhea, constipation, flatulence, fecal incontinence, congestion, fatigue, lethargy, skin rashes, itching, abdominal pain, indigestion, and coughing. Analyzing the results utilizing Chi-square, comparing the two groups for total improvement and any improvement revealed P<.01 and P<.01 respectively.

The improvement by possible infection type for the participants is shown in the following table:

Type		% Substantially Improved	% Minimally Improved
Strep	2.8%	75.0%	25.0%
Staph	10.5%	60.0%	33.3%
Viral	21.7%	35.5%	61.3%
Fungal	33.6%	39.6%	60.4%
Parasitic	42.7%	59.0%	37.7%

The commercial zapping model seemed to require more repeated sessions than the engineered model to get similar results: this could be because the engineered model was designed differently (with an extra circuit) and/or because it was held by the participants longer. When long-term staphylococcus infections were present that did not clear-up with conventional antibiotic treatments, the engineered model seemed to be substantially more effective than the commercial model.

97.9% of participants reported symptomatic improvement; with 97.4% zapped with the commercial model and 98.4% with the engineered model (both combined with supplementation) reporting improvement. Neither age nor gender were found to have any significant impact on improvement.

Temporary (lasting less then one hour) adverse reactions to zapping, specifically dizziness or a near intoxicating feeling, were noted from three (2.1%) of the participants; all of which stated that benefits associated with the zapper exceeded the temporal adverse reactions. (A recent monograph by Dr. Robert Beck regarding the use of a similar device states "if subjects ever feel sleepy, sluggish, listless, bloated or headachy, or have flu-like reactions, they may be neglecting sufficient water intake" [16]. Dr. Clark advises that those who are pregnant or wearing a pacemaker should not use a zapping unit [2]) A more commonly heard comment was that some participants (5.1%) felt refreshed or relaxed after undergoing the zapping sessions. Temporary adverse reactions to supplementation included increased itching (in subjects who had previously complained of itching), increase of various reported symptoms, and mild intestinal discomfort: these complaints were only temporary when they occurred (generally less than one week).

Discussion

This trial did not include anyone who completely responded to previous nutrition-only interventions. My previous research has clearly shown that nutritional interventions can, on their own, result in symptomatic improvement when chronic infections are present [14,15]. This trial attempted to see if adding the intervention of bioelectrical stimulation could result in symptomatic improvement to greater degrees for people with chronic infections. Many of the participants were greatly impressed by the effectiveness of the zapper; some who improved, however, felt the zapper had no effect and improvement was entirely due to the continued use of supplementation.

Although most understand that bacterial and viral infections are common [1-4], many health practitioners do not seem to understand that yeast/fungal infections and parasites are often found in humans [17,18]. Although one major study found parasites in 20.1% of stool samples [18], many of these parasites appear to not always cause detectable symptoms [1]. In humans, most parasites are believed to live within the digestive tract [1,18] (though Dr. Clark has implied that this may not be the case [2]). Parasites, by nature, must be able to live in an organism for a long-time without killing the host organism or getting killed by it [19]. Thus, it is not surprising that the highest percentage of the participants had this type of infection.

How does zapping work? Dr. Clark has written, "Any positively offset frequency kills all bacteria, viruses and parasites simultaneously given sufficient voltage (5 to 10 volts), duration (seven minutes), and frequency (anything from 10 Hz to 500,000 Hz)" [2]. A positive offset frequency is one which alternates between positive and zero voltage. I am not at all certain that zapping actually kills any invading microorganism. This trial suggests that since only 48.3% improved substantially, zapping probably did not kill "all bacteria, viruses and parasites" (according to Dr. Clark's book, the reason could be that possibly the current did not access all body regions, specifically the bowel contents [2]).

There are several reasons to believe that there may be scientific justification for the use of zappers. First, it needs to be understood that precisely how the body combats parasitic infections is not fully known [20]; this may be because many of the disease causing parasites have the ability to turn off immune responses [20]. (Both immune and non-immune responses are involved in the body's defenses against pathogens of all types [20].) It is possible that the body produces additional acid, has an IgG response [1,21], or has other actions to deal with intestinal parasites [20]. Second, it needs to be understood that both the colon and the small intestine produce electrical spike bursts [22]. Third, animal studies support the hypothesis that electrical stimulation has various effects on the body, including the inactivation of muscle acetyl CoA carboxylase and increasing AMP-activated protein kinase [23]. The inactivation of muscle acetyl CoA carboxylase may temporarily increase pyruvic acid [24] or decrease the effectiveness of normal portions of the immune system [25]. It has been reported that researchers from the Albert Einstein College of Medicine found that passing a current of only 50 microamps can prevent certain viruses (including HIV) from replicating [26]. It is of interest to note that a technique recently developed at the Royal London Hospital uses gracilis muscle augmentation combined with electrical stimulation to improve sphincter control in individuals with fecal incontinence [27] (some of the subjects in this trial had this symptom).

It may be possible that some of the body's defense mechanisms against pathogens include electrical activity or that electrical activity may improve nutrient absorption. This last hypothesis is consistent with work performed by Dr. J.C. Weaver. Dr. Weaver performed a study in which he found that electrical stimulation appeared to make the body's cell walls more permeable so that its response to infection after ingesting supplemental nutrients was enhanced [28]. It is also consistent with a similar hypothesis written in 1924 by Dr. E.W. Cordingley that "electrotherapy" increases "local nutrition" [29].

Why does a subject undergo three zappings? Dr. Clark and this investigator have different opinions. Dr. Clark has written that the first zapping "kills viruses, bacteria, and parasites. But a few minutes later, bacteria and viruses (different ones) often recur. I conclude they had been infecting the parasites, and killing the parasites released them. The second zapping kills the released viruses and bacteria, but soon a few viruses appear again. They must have been infecting some of the last bacteria. After a third zapping, I never find any viruses, bacteria, or parasite, even hours later"[2]. This investigator does not agree, however, because often the same infection remains. It appears that repeated zappings are needed because it takes that long for the proper portion of the immune system to be properly stimulated into action. And I should add, for some people it only seems to be needed one or two times (some many more).

There are at least 130 different parasites [2,17], many different bacteria and viruses [4-7], and at least 150 medically significant yeast/fungi (Candida albicans is only 1 of them) [17,30]. Is the solution to the multiple infectious agents, as has been proposed by some [6], new antibiotics? With deadly infections that do not respond to "drug-based" treatments [4-7], should not other avenues be explored?

The results of this study suggest that zapping combined with nutritional interventions may have helped most of the participants improve. Nutritional interventions give the body substances which it can use to improve immune responses [18]. Although this is not certain, it appears that either nutrient absorption is somehow improved [28,29] or IgG (immunoglobin G) [1,19], some T cell (T-lymphocyte), biochemical acid, or some other defense mechanism is somehow stimulated through zapping and thus some segment of the immune system, but not the zapper, destroys the invader. Regardless of which (or whose) hypothesis is correct, it can be concluded that zapping and nutritional interventions can be helpful adjuncts for people with various forms of chronic infection and does deserve additional study.

References

[1] Targan, S. and Shanahan, F. *Immunology and Immunopathology of the Liver and Gastrointestinal Tract.* Igaku-Shoin Medical Publishers, New York 1990.

[2] Clark, H. *The Cure for All Diseases.* New Century Press, San Diego, 1995.

[3] Lorbor, B. *Changing Patterns of Infectious Disease Revisited.* Am J Phar 1991; 1163:5-17.

[4] Nugent, S. *New Viruses in the Jungle.* ANMA Update 1995; 1 (2): 1.

[5] Norby, S. R. *Antibiotic Resistance: A Self-Inflicted Problem.* J Int Med 1996; 239:373-375.

[6] Bradley, J. and Scheld, W. *The Challenge of Penicillin-Resistant Streptococcus Pneumoniae Meningitis: Current Antibiotic Therapy in the 1990s.* Clin Inf Dis 1997; 24 (Sup.2):S213-S221.

[7] *Supergerm Resists Antibiotics.* The Good News 1997; 2 (5):13.

[8] Thiel, R. J. *Serious Nutrition for Health Care Professionals.* California Health Group, Arroyo Grande (CA), 1995.

[9] Circa, D. *The Scalartronix: Rife Generator Operations Manual and Training Program.* San Diego, 1987.

[10] Card #36 *Shock Machine at Ripleys Odditorium,* Hollywood, California (Specifically Identified as *Electric Magneto Machine*).

[11] Beck, R. *Experimental In Vivo Blood Clearing Device for Eliminating Viruses Pathogens, Microbes, Bacteria, Fungi, and Parasites.* Robert Beck, Santa Ana, March 16, 1996.

[12] Miller, T. *Building the Bioelectrifier: Can You Heal Yourself and Take a Poke at the Medical Establishment at the Same Time?* Amateur Radio Today, May 1997:13-19.

[13] Thiel, R. Natural Interventions for Systemic Mycoses. JANA, in review 1998.

[14] Thiel, R. J. *Nutrition to Improve the CD4 Count of Persons with AIDS.* National Institutes of Health, Bethesda. April 1997:Submittal NTN B1.

[15] Thiel, R. J. *Chronic Fatigue Assessment and Intervention.* ANMA & AANC J 1996; 1 (3):17-19.

[16] Beck, R *Expanded Instructions for experiMental/Theoretical Blood Electrification.* Robert Beck, Santa Ana, March 20, 1997.

[17] Chandler, F. W. and Watts, J. C. *Mycotic, Actinomycotic, and Algal Infections.* In Anderson's Pathology, 9th ed., Mosby, St. Louis, 1990:391-432.

[18] *Results of Testing for Intestinal Parasites by State Diagnostic Laboratories, United States, 1987.* Morbidity and Mortality Weekly 1992; 40 (SS4):25-30.

[19] Frank, S. A. *Models of Parasite Virulence.* Qtr Rev Bio 1996; 71 (1):37-78.

[20] Keusch, G. *Nutrition and Infection.* In Modern Nutrition in Health and Disease, 8th ed.. Lea & Febiger, Philadelphia, 1994:1241-1258.

[21] Akue, J. P., et al. *High Levels of Parasite-Specific IgG1 Correlate with the Amicrofilaremic State in Loa loa Infection.* J Inf Dis 1997; 175 (1):158-163.

[22] Medeiros, J. A., Pontes, F. A. and Mesquita, O. A. *Is Colonic Electrical Activity a Similar Phenomena to Small-Bowel Electrical Activity?* Dis. Colon Rectum 1997; 40 (1):93-99.

[23] Hutber, C. A., Hardie, D. G. and Winder, W.W. *Electrical Stimulation Inactivates Muscle Acetyl-CoA Carboxylase and Increases AMP-Activated Protein Kinase.* Am J Phys 1997; (2pt1):E262-E266.

[24] Sidransky, H. *Malnutrition and Deficiency Diseases.* In Anderson's Pathology, 9th ed. Mosby, St. Louis, 1990:546-565.

[25] Dakshinamurti, K. *Biotin.* In Modern Nutrition in Health and Disease, 8th ed. Lea & Febiger, Philadelphia, 1994:426-448.

[26] *Shocking Treatment Proposed for AIDS.* Science News, March 30, 1991:207.

[27] Stuchfield, B. *The Electrically Stimulated Neoanal Sphincter and Colonic Conduit.* Brit J Nurs 1997; 6 (4):219-224.

[28] Weaver, J. C. *Electroporation: A General Phenomenon for Manipulation of Cells and Tissue.* J Cell Bio 1993; 51:426-435.

[29] Cordingley, E. W. *Principles and Practices of Naturopathy.* Health Research, Mokelume Hill (CA), 1924 (Reprint 1971):12-14.

[30] Larone, D. H. *Medically Important Fungi,* 2nd ed. American Society of Microbiology, Washington, 1993.

NOTE: Dr. Thiel is not a medical doctor. None of this research is medical advice nor should it be construed as medical advice; none of this information is specific for a particular individual.

Appendix A4

Chronic Fatigue Assessment and Intervention: The Result of 101 Cases

Published as: Thiel, R.J. Chronic Fatigue Assessment and Intervention: The Result of 101 Cases. ANMA & AANC Journal, 1996; 1(3):17-19 and Thiel, R.J. Chronic Fatigue Assessment and Intervention: The Result of 101 Cases. Townsend Letter 174, 1998:70-71.

Abstract: The purpose of this trial was to measure how often individualized nutrition-based interventions could benefit people with complaints of chronic fatigue within 60 days. Of the 101 participants, 88.12% of participants reported improvement within 30 days and 99.01% reported improvement within 60 days; P< 0.0001.

Introduction

Most natural health professionals see people with chronic fatigue on a regular basis. Additionally, fatigue appears to be the number one complaint that even medical doctors hear [1]. Chronic fatigue has been defined as persistent or relapsing debilitating fatigue for at least 6 months with symptoms of abrupt onset, low grade fevers, arthralgias, myalgias, post-exertional fatigue, neurophyscological complaints, and sleep disturbances [2]. Glandular malfunction, hypotension, infections, allergies, and various nutritional deficiencies have been speculated as potential causes of chronic fatigue [2-8]. Some researchers have speculated that chronic fatigue syndrome is not a discrete disease with a specific cause but is instead a clinical condition involving multiple factors [2,8].

This report includes the results of a clinical trial involving 101 people with long-term (chronic) fatigue. The intention of this trial was to measure how often individualized recommendations could benefit people with complaints of chronic fatigue within 60 days as well as to measure some of the types of factors that were present in the chronically fatigued population.

Selection Criteria

Adults were eligible for inclusion in this trial if they resided in California, agreed to follow the recommended intervention, agreed to provide (and did provide) feedback, signed a consent agreement, and indicated they suffered from fatigue, CFS, fibromyalgia, tiredness, low energy, or similar problems for a period of at least 3 months. 108 people met these criteria, but seven later failed to provide the necessary feedback (nor did they participate for the length of the trial), thus this trial only includes the results of the 101 actual participants. Of the 101 participants, 90 of them had complaints of fatigue for 6 months or more. The ages of participants ranged from 18 to 82; the mean age of the participants was 47.8 years. 27 of the participants were males and 74 of the participants were females.

Method

After completing the selection documentation, all subjects were interviewed for approximately 45 minutes. All subjects were then assessed using Reflex Nutrition Assessment (RNA). RNA is a non-invasive technique used to assess nutrition status by observing the response of muscles under externally provided human-force (it is similar to other forms of muscle testing [9]). Performing RNA normally consists of performing two assessments. The first assessment is to determine if a reflex indicates a nutritional need (by observing a reduction in muscular strength) and the second is to determine which nutritional intervention can help fit that need (by observing an increase in muscular strength). Many have reported success in using it and similar techniques [9-11].

The reflex points assessed for this trial included adrenal, blood, heart, hemoglobin, hypoglycemia/other (checked at the pancreas or other digestive reflexes), parasite, staph, strep, thyroid, viral, and yeast (checked at the umbilicus) [9]. It should be noted that having a problem indicated by any of these reflexes does not necessarily mean that they would be confirmed by any type of allopathic diagnosis.

Participants who appeared to have (through the interview process combined with reflex assessment) hypoglycemia were given a dietary plan to follow which essentially recommended increasing consumption of lower glycemic food while decreasing consumption of high glycemic foods: high glycemic foods include sucrose, alcohol, and other refined carbohydrates; lower glycemic foods include fruits, whole grains, nuts, animal products, and vegetables [12]. Participants who had reflex problems were advised to consume an average of three tablets (per day) of one nutritional supplement for each fatigue-related reflex concern. Although the actual supplements varied, generally what was used was a bovine glandular for adrenal reflex; fortified glandular with l-carnitine for heart reflex, iron with synergists for the blood reflex; herbs and b vitamins for hemoglobin reflex; chromium GTF with synergists for hypoglycemia for (the pancreatic reflex; fortified herbs for parasite; bovine glandular for staph reflex; fortified herbal-glandular for strep reflex; bovine glandular for thyroid reflex; fortified herbs for viral reflex; and fortified herbs for yeast (other products were used instead if they reflex-checked as better).

Subjects were interviewed at approximately 30 day intervals to determine any change in energy level or fatigue.

Results

The interview process suggested that nearly all participants could remember some stress, trauma, illness, or event (or combination of factors) that proceeded their bout with fatigue. Reflex assessment revealed that some participants had problems with as many as five fatigue-related reflexes. This trial found that the average participant had problems with 2.0 fatigue-related reflexes. The following table demonstrates the frequency:

Table 1: Frequency by Reflex

Thyroid	57.4%
Adrenal	33.7%
Hypoglycemia	29.7%
Hemoglobin	24.8%
Heart	15.8%
Blood	10.9%
Yeast	8.9%
Strep	5.9%
Staph	5.0%
Parasite	5.0%
Viral	2.0%

88.12% of participants reported improvement within 30 days. 99.01% reported improvement within 60 days; the P value of this result was less than .0001. This trial did not attempt to quantify the degree of improvement.

Every participant who reported having fibromyalgia (all of whom were female) had problems with adrenal and heart reflexes; some had other reflex concerns as well. In this trial, gender did not appear to play any significant role in determining improvement.

Discussion

This trial confirms that a variety of factors can contribute to fatigue. Low thyroid function [5], nutritionally related heart concerns [7], adrenal issues [2], parasites [4], infections [2], diet [6,13], and nutrient deficiencies [6,8] have all been shown to play some role in chronic fatigue.

The high incidence of thyroid reflex involvement (57.4%) may be consistent with a medical study which found that 61% of people with chronic fatigue syndrome ate little, if any, salt or highly salted foods [7]. Consumption of iodized salt is the main way that most Americans receive iodine [14] (the other way is eat foods which naturally contain organic iodine such as sea vegetables [15]). The only known need for iodine in the human body is to support the thyroid gland for the production of its hormones [14].

The relatively low incidence of viral reflex involvement is not surprising. It is consistent with the findings of other researchers who have found that viruses appear to be present in only a very small percentage of people who are chronically fatigued [8,16].

Dr. Demitrack (M.D.) has hypothesized that acute infection, stress, physchiatric illness, and other factors which existed before chronic fatigue is manifested, appear to ultimately converge into a final common biological pathway that is then known as chronic fatigue [2]. This hypothesis is consistent with the findings of this report. It is believed that it is the combination of seemingly unrelated factors which has frustrated many people with energy complaints.

Although this trial was restricted to California residents, it is believed that similar results could be obtained by properly trained researchers in other areas.

References

[1] Kroenke, K. *Interviewing the Patient with Chronic Fatigue Syndrome.* Infectious Disease News, Oct 1991:2.

[2] Demitrack, M. *Chronic Fatigue Syndrome: A Disease of the Hypothalamic-Pituitary-Adrenal Axis?* Ann Med, 1994;26:1-3.

[3] Defreitas, E.. et al. *Evidence of Retrovirus in Patients with Chronic Fatigue Immunity Deficiency Syndrome.* CFIDS Chronicle, Sep 1990:1.

[4] Galland, L. *Giardia Lamblia Infection as a cause of Chronic Fatigue.* J Nutr Med, 1990:1:27-30

[5] Lathan, R. *Chronic fatigue? Consider Hypothyroidism.* Physician and Sports Med,1991; 19 (10):67-70

[6] Lapp, C. and Cheney, R. *Chronic Fatigue Syndrome: Self Care Manual, February 1991.* CFIDS Chronicle Physician's Forum, 1991;1(1):14-17.

[7] Bou-Holaigah, I. *The Relationship Between Neurally Mediated Hypotension and the Chronic Fatigue Syndrome.* JAMA, 1995;274 (12):961-967.

[8] Williams, D. *Chronic Fatigue Syndrome: The Search for a Cookbook Solution Instead of Eliminating a True Problem?* Alternatives for the Health Conscious Individual, 1995; 6 (6):41-46.

[9] Thiel, R. J. *Serious Nutrition for Health Care Professionals.* Arroyo Grande (CA): California Health Group, 1995.

[10] Burr-Madsen, A. *Body Polarity Reflex Analysis and the Nutritional Connection.* Carson City: Thoth, Inc., 1992.

[11] Rosen, M. S. and Williams, L. *The Research Status of Applied Kinesiology, Part II: An Annotated Bibliography of Applied Kinesiological Research.* A.K. Review, 1991; 1(2):34-47.

[12] Jenkins, D. J., et al. *Glycemic Index of Foods: A Physiological Basis for Carbohydrate Exchange.* Am J Clin Nutr, 1981;34:362-366.

[13] Bondy, P. and Felig, P. *Disorders of Carbohydrate Metabolism,* 1974;221-340. In Duncan's Diseases of Metabolism. Phil.: W.B. Saunders, 1974.

[14] Clugston, G. A. and Hetzel, B. S. *Iodine.* In Modern Nutrition in Health and Disease, 8th ed. Phil.: Lea & Febinger, 1993:252-263.

[15] Jensen, B. *The Chemistry of Man,* Vol II. Escondido: Bernard Jensen, 1983.

[16] Buchwald, D. *Chronic Fatigue and the Chronic Fatigue Syndrome: Prevalence in the Pacific Northwest Health Care System.* Ann Int Med,1995;123(2):81-88.

NOTE: Dr. Thiel is not a medical doctor. None of this research is medical advice nor should it be construed as medical advice; none of this information is specific for a particular individual.

Appendix A5

Natural Interventions for People with Fibromyalgia

Published as: Thiel R. Natural Interventions for People with Fibromyalgia. ANMA Monitor 2(2):6-8, 1998.

Abstract: The purpose of this preliminary trial was to determine how often natural interventions could result in symptomatic improvement for people with fibromyalgia. Interventions included dietary restrictions, nutritional supplementation, and bio-electrical stimulation. All forty participants reported improvement (P <0.0001); improvement was noted in 95.3% of symptoms monitored. Possible food intolerances were found in 92.5% of the participants.

Introduction

Fibromyalgia is an underdiagnosed syndrome that affects between 2-4% of the population [1]. Although its cause is uncertain, genetic factors, stress, insomnia, dietary factors, immune dysfunction, a virus, hypometabolism, and calcium disorders have all been speculated as possibly having a role [1-3]. It has been described by this researcher and others as chronic fatigue combined with a nearly overwhelming pain [1,4]. Symptoms vary, but common symptoms include widespread pain (97.6%), tenderness in multiple points (90.1%), fatigue (81.4%), morning stiffness (77.0%), sleep disturbances (74.6%), paresthesias (abnormal burning/prickly sensations 62.8%), headaches (52.8%), anxiety (47.8%), prior depression (31.5%), and irritable bowel syndrome (29.6%) [5]. Although fibromyalgia is a multi-symptomatic syndrome, this researcher has found that most people with it will complain most about the one symptom that affects them the most: common are overwhelming fatigue, overwhelming pain, insomnia, or stomach/digestive distress.

According to Julian Whitaker (M.D.) [2] and others [1], conventional medicine often knowingly treats fibromyalgia with ineffective drugs. So it is not surprising that research has shown that most people with fibromyalgia seek help from non-medical sources [6-7].

Selection Criteria

Adults were eligible for inclusion in this trial if they came to our office, agreed to provide (and did provide) feedback, signed a consent agreement, and indicated that they suffered from fibromyalgia or symptoms of fibromyalgia. Forty people were eligible and participated: 35 were female and 5 were male.

Method

After completing the selection documentation, all subjects were interviewed for approximately 45 minutes. All subjects were then assessed using Reflex Nutrition Assessment (RNA). RNA is a non-invasive technique used to assess nutrition status by observing the responses of muscles under externally provided human force (it is similar to other forms of muscle testing [8]). Performing RNA for people with fibromyalgia normally consists of three assessments. The first assessment is to determine if a reflex indicates a nutritional need (by observing a reduction in muscular strength); the second is to determine which nutritional intervention may help fit that need (by observing an increase in muscular strength); the third is to assess for possible food intolerances (observable muscular weakness when exposed to the food is considered to indicate a possible intolerance). Reflexes associated with fibromyalgia include heart (when major fatigue and circulation are issues), adrenal (when stress and fatigue are issues), sleeping/headache (when insufficient sleep is involved), calcium (when pain is a major factor), thyroid (when mood and circulation are issues), and parasite (when digestive issues are involved).

Participants who appeared to be intolerant to one or more foods were advised to avoid them. Participants were advised to consume an average of three tablets per day of one or more nutritional supplements. Monitored symptoms included muscle pain, hip/joint pain, headaches, fatigue, gastro-intestinal upset, insomnia, and depression/anxiety. Subjects were interviewed at approximately 20 day intervals to determine changes.

Results

All participants (100.0%) orally reported improvement within 60 days; the P value of improvement was < 0.0001. Ages ranged from 24 - 83; the mean participant age was 52.3 years. The average participant had problems with 4.3 symptoms; improvement was noted in 95.3% of symptoms monitored. By symptoms, improvement was noted in 93.8% with muscular pain, 89.3% with hip/joint pain, 92.9% with headaches, 100.0% with fatigue, 100.0% with gastro-intestinal upset, 92.9% with insomnia, and 96.2% with depression/anxiety. The data showed that 97.4% with muscular pain and/or hip/joint pain noted some pain reduction in either or both. It should be added, that although paresthesia was not a monitored symptom, the majority of those who complained of it noted improvement. Age and gender did not appear to play any significant role in improvement. This preliminary trial did not attempt to differentiate degrees of improvement.

Possible food intolerances were found in 92.5% of the participants with bovine dairy the most prevalent (45.0%), followed by caffeine (35.0%), whole wheat (12.5%), oats (10.0%), chocolate (5.0%), and canola oil (2.5%).

Discussion

Until relatively recently, fibromyalgia was considered a psychiatric disorder (or secondary to a psychiatric disorder) even though it is now considered to be a rheumatic disorder [1,8]. It is believed by many that some metabolic disorder is probably involved [1-3]. This investigator would concur. Calcium metabolic disorders are primary in many. Since calcium can impair magnesium absorption [9], this investigator suspects that the opposite is probably true: this could explain why some show some pain relief from taking magnesium combined with malic acid [2,10]. Thyroid issues, though often underdiagnosed [11], are frequently seen [3].

This investigator's other research on chronic fatigue [12] and pain relief [13] has demonstrated that people with fibromyalgia can positively respond to nutrition-based interventions as well as to bio-electrical stimulation when gastro-intestinal upset is involved [14]. Since many with inflammatory bowels suffer from pains in joints which can be due to reactive arthritis caused by bacteria [15], it is possible that those who underwent bioelectrical stimulation may have had benefits in joint pain relief due to immune system stimulation [14]. This investigator wonders if this is why bioelectrical stimulation of a different sort, electroacupuncture, has been helpful for pain relief for people with fibromyalgia [16].

It is medically felt that fibromyalgia acts like an infection, though a medically diagnosable infection is rarely found [1]. This may be because of the relatively high incidence of food intolerance in people with it or because the infections associated with gastro-intestinal upset are not always found [17]. This investigator believes that certain food intolerances (such as bovine dairy and oats) can give the appearance of being infectious agents to the body (though this is usually not the case with caffeine). Exercise has been reported to be of value to people with fibromyalgia [1], including even aerobic exercise [18] (though caution is strongly advised before engaging in any strenuous exercise). In addition to the obvious benefits of exercise, this researcher wonders if some of the benefits may be due to heavy perspiration reducing the toxicities associated with food intolerances.

Dealing with people with fibromyalgia is both difficult and professionally rewarding. It is difficult, because many of them are desperate having been either ignored (prior to their diagnosis) or not properly treated [1,2]: this leads to frequent follow-up phone calls and some of them questioning your recommendations while they are improving (not all improve dramatically, especially at first). It is professionally rewarding, because major improvement is often seen in their symptoms while their outlook changes from being suffering semi-pessimists to improving optimists. (One of the youngest participants was somewhat this way. The good news was, although she had minimal improvement within 60 days, long-term interventions finally resulted in substantial improvement.) This researcher encourages doctors and health researchers to be willing to challenge long-standing misconceptions regarding fibromyalgia and to work toward cooperative interventions to help these people improve and lead as normal lives as possible.

References

[1] Nye, D. *Fibromyalgia—A Physician's Guide.* Internet: www.alternatives.com/cfs-news/fm-md.htm Dec. 14, 1996.

[2] Whitaker, J. *Four Things to do for Fibromyalgia.* Health & Healing 6 (9):3-4, 1996.

[3] Lowe, J. *A New Explanation of Fibromyalgia: The Hypo-Metabolism Hypothesis.* In: Clinical Pearls in Nutrition and Preventative Medicine, ITServices: Sacramento, 1997.

[4] Clauw, D. *The Pathogenesis of Chronic Pain and Fatigue Syndromes with Special Reference to Fibromyalgia.* Medical Hypothesis 44 (5):369-378, 1995.

[5] Wolfe, F., et al. The American College of Rheumatology 1990 criteria for the classification of fibromyalgia: Report of the multicenter criteria. Arthritis & Rheumatology 33:160, 1990.

[6] Dimmock, S., et al. *Factors Predisposing to the Resort of Complementary Therapies in Patients with Fibromyalgia.* Clinical Rheumatology 15(5):478-482, 1996.

[7] Pioro-Boisset, M. *Alternative Medicine Use in Fibromyalgia.* Arthritis Care Reviews 9 (1):13-17, 1996.

[8] Dunne, F. and Dunne, C. *Fibromyalgia Syndrome and Psychiatric Disorder.* British Journal of Hospital Medicine 54 (5):194-197, 1995.

[9] Shils, M. *Magnesium,* In: Modern Nutrition in Health and Disease, 8th ed.: 164-184 Lea & Febiger, Philadelphia: 1994.

[10] Russell, I., et al. *Treatment of Fibromyalgia with Super Malic: A Randomized, Double-Blind, Placebo Controlled, Crossover Pilot Study.* Journal of Rheumatology 22(5):953-958, 1995.

[11] Sawin, C. *Subclinical Hypothyroidism in Older Persons.* Clinics in Geriatric Medicine 11 (2):231-238, 1995.

[12] Thiel, R. *Chronic Fatigue Assessment and Intervention: The Result of 101 Cases.* ANMA & AANC Journal 1 (3):17-19, 1996.

[13] Thiel, R. *Musculoskeletal Pain Relief for People with Arthritis, Lupus, and Fibromyalgia.* ANMA Monitor 1 (1):8-10, 1997.

[14] Thiel, R. *Efficacy of Bioelectrical Stimulation for People with Chronic Infections.* Journal of Alternative and Complementary Medicine, In Review, 1998.

[15] Hazenberg, M. *Intestinal Flora, Bacteria, and Arthritis: Why the Joint?* Scandinavian Journal of Rheumatology 24 (Supp. 104):207-211, 1995.

[16] Deluze, C. *Electroacupuncture in Fibromyalgia: Results of a Controlled Trial.* British Med. Journal 305:1249-1251, 1992.

[17] Clark, H. *The Cure for All Diseases.* New Century Press, San Diego: 1995.

[18] Wigers, S., et al. *Effects of Aerobic Exercise Versus Stress Management Treatment in Fibromyalgia.* Scandinavian Journal of Rheumatology 23:77-86, 1997.

NOTE: Dr. Thiel is not a medical doctor. None of this research is medical advice nor should it be construed as medical advice; none of this information is specific for a particular individual.

Appendix A6

Natural Interventions for Migraine Sufferers

Published as: Thiel, R. Natural Interventions for Migraine Sufferers. ANMA Monitor 2(3):5-9, 1998.

Abstract: The purpose of this preliminary trial was to determine how often individualized natural interventions, used prophylactically, could result in symptomatic improvement for people with migraine headaches. Interventions included dietary restrictions and nutritional supplementation. 44 of the 45 participants (97.7%) reported improvement within 90 days (P <0.01). Possible food intolerances were found in 84.4% of the participants, with caffeine being the substance most frequently implicated.

Introduction

Migraine headaches cause severe pain. This pain seriously affects the quality of life of migraine sufferers. Migraines seem to occur as the result of functional disturbances of cranial circulation [1-3]. The head pain seems to be due to dilation of the scalp arteries, whereas prodromal (preceding) symptoms such as flashes of light and paresthesias are probably due to intracerebral vasoconstriction [2]. Women are more likely than men to suffer from them [2].

Migraines may be preceded by a short period of depression, irritability, and/or restlessness. The preceding symptoms may be gone before the migraine occurs or may merge with it. Pain can be unilateral or generalized. Some have attacks daily while others only have attacks once a month. With untreated attacks, nausea, vomiting, and photophobia are common. Extremities tend to be cold. Sufferers tend to be irritable and seek seclusion when an attack is present. Scalp arteries tend to be prominent during an attack. Diagnosis is usually based upon symptom pattern if there is no evidence of intracranial pathological changes [2,4].

Migraines can cause problems other than just pain. Migraines often result in the loss of productivity [4]. They often affect family relationships. Studies have shown that those who get migraine headaches (with and without auras) are at increased risk of ischemic stroke [5,6]; this risk is increased substantially for migrainous women if oral contraceptives or heavy cigarette smoking are involved [6].

Natural health practitioners have long worked with migraine sufferers [7-10]. Nutrition, including diet, has been found to affect migraine headaches [4,7-12]. A clinical trial was performed to determine how often individualized natural interventions, used prophylactically, would result in symptomatic improvement for people with headaches.

Selection Criteria

Adults were eligible for inclusion in this trial if they came to our office, agreed to provide (and did provide) feedback, signed a consent agreement, and indicated that they suffered from migraine headaches. 45 people were eligible and participated: 39 were female and 6 were male. Ages ranged from 23-73; the mean participant age was 43.3 years.

Method

After completing the selection documentation, all subjects were interviewed for approximately 45 minutes. All subjects were then assessed using Reflex Nutrition Assessment (RNA). RNA is a non-invasive technique used to assess nutrition status and possible food intolerances by observing the responses of muscles under externally provided human force [10]. Participants who appeared to be intolerant to one or more foods were advised to avoid them. Participants were advised to consume an average of three tablets per day of one or more nutritional supplements. Although the actual supplements varied by individual, they tended to include various herbs (such as dong quai, feverfew, kelp), vitamins (such as riboflavin), minerals (such as magnesium), fatty acids (from seeds), and/or bovine glandulars (primarily thyroid and adrenal).

Subjects were interviewed at approximately three week intervals to determine changes.

Results

44 participants (97.7%) orally reported improvement within 90 days; the P value of improvement (using a binomial Fisher's extract test) was < 0.01. Improvement was noted for reduced pain, duration, and/or frequency. The degrees of improvement ranged from 40% to 100%; the mean improvement was 83.3%. Age and gender were not found to be significant factors affecting improvement.

Possible food intolerances were found in 84.4% of the participants with caffeine the most prevalent (57.8%), followed by bovine dairy (28.9%), whole wheat (6.7%), oats (6.7%), chocolate (4.4%), eggs (4.4%), white sugar (2.2%), spices (2.2%), and soy products (2.2%). 6.7% of participants also seemed to be bothered by various household chemicals.

Reflex assessment revealed that the overwhelming majority of participants in this study (73.3%) had some need for nutritional thyroid support. It also revealed that yeast (15.5%) and parasitic infections (22.2%) were suspected in 37.2% of the participants (these participants were also provided with additional herbs, digestive enzymes, and other nutrients to help the body deal with them [10]).

Discussion

Low thyroid function appears to play a role in migraine headaches [9]. Interestingly, both migraine headaches and thyroid problems are much more common in women than in men [2,13]. The thyroid produces hormones which speed metabolism (such as thyroxine) and affect concentrations of calcium (calcitonin) [13,14]. Thyroid problems, clinical and/or subclinical, are exceptionally common [9,15-18]. The fact that between 10-48% of senior citizens are suspected of having subclinical hypothyroidism [16,17] and 11% of the population appears to have a clinical thyroid condition [15], suggests to this investigator that thyroid problems in migraine sufferers are often missed, even when they have been medically tested for. In other words, since thyroid blood tests do not always reveal that thyroid may be involved actual symptoms can be much more significant factors in determining whether a nutritional intervention may be effective; other doctors have reached similar conclusions [9,18].

Cold extremities, depression, and menstrual disturbances which can be a symptom of low thyroid function [13] are also associated with migraines [2,4]. Oral contraceptives (birth control pills) can trigger and even be the cause of migraine headaches [9,19]. This investigator believes this is because they raise estrogen levels to the point they negatively affect estrogen-thyroid hormone balance (these hormones seem to work together in a manner which affects behavior [20]) and that this subsequent imbalance ultimately results in migraine headaches.

Headache expert, Dr. Cass Ingram (D.O.), has written that synthetic approaches to thyroid problems (such as *Synthyroid*), have little, if any, effect on headaches; he prefers natural glandulars [9]. Herbs, such as dong quai and kelp, have been found to help low thyroid function [21]; when used in this study, they appeared to play a role in reducing the suffering associated with migraine headaches (one popular book specifically states that dong quai is helpful for "male migraines" [22]). Another herb, feverfew, though not directly involved with thyroid function, appears to improve vasodilatation and has historically been used to help migraine sufferers [7,9].

Caffeine was suspected to play more of a role in this study than any other single food substance. Dr. Alex Duarte places caffeine first in his list of foods which can cause migraine headaches [8]. Just like thyroxine [13,14], caffeine increases the metabolic rate [23]. A military study concluded that caffeine intoxication usually occurs with consumption in excess of 250mg [24]; this investigator believes it takes much less caffeine to affect women. This investigator also speculates that people who need nutritional thyroid support will often tend to use caffeine in an attempt to compensate for the positive feeling increased metabolism often gives. Perhaps not surprisingly, caffeine is the most widely consumed pyschotrophic drug [25].

In the U.S., most (around 75%) caffeine is consumed through coffee, followed by tea and sodas [26]. Caffeine is in many commonly consumed "foods" as follows [27]:

5 ounces of ground roasted coffee	85mg
5 ounces of instant coffee	60mg
5 ounces of decaffeinated coffee	3mg
5 ounces of tea (1 leaf bag)	30mg
5 ounces of instant tea	20mg
5 ounces of hot chocolate/cocoa	4mg
6 ounces of cola	18mg
6 ounces of chocolate milk	4mg
1 ounce of chocolate candy	1.5-6mg

Interestingly, caffeine seems to have an antioxidant effect [28]. This is probably one of the reasons that caffeine seems to relieve headaches in many [4] (another could be that caffeine may irritate the nervous system which results in temporary dilation). This investigator, though, suspects that the consumption of caffeine becomes a vicious cycle—it probably temporarily relieves, but ultimately contributes to additional migraine headaches. Its consumption also probably delays sufferers from seeking nutritional help for thyroid issues, since this investigator believes that caffeine may mask certain hypothyroid conditions.

Withdrawal reactions occur in 25-100% of coffee consumers and includes severe headaches, depressed mood, anxiety, and fatigue [24]. Caffeine withdrawal headache symptoms usually occur between 13 to 23 hours of discontinuing caffeine and it occurs most frequently with heavy consumers of caffeine [29]. More money is spent promoting caffeine and performing research in support of caffeine than is spent to warn consumers about caffeine [30].

Since 28.9% of subjects were advised to avoid bovine dairy, most of them were advised to take supplements containing calcium. This investigator suspects that many individuals who are sensitive to these substances often have difficulty absorbing calcium from dairy products. Calcium has been shown to help some women with migraine headaches [31]. Dr. Sheldon Hendlor has written that calcium can function as a natural tranquilizer, can calm nerves, and relieve leg cramps [32]. As calcium tends to be lost during periods of stress [33] (and since migraines increase stress [4]), it appears logical that many migraine sufferers should have at least nutritional benefits from taking supplemental calcium.

Although it has been reported that reducing fat consumption while increasing consumption of carbohydrates resulted in the reduction and intensity of headaches [34], it seems to this investigator that the types of fats consumed is more important than the quantity of fats. It has been found that prophylactic use of foods high in gamma-linolenic and alpha-linolenic acid can, **after several months**, reduce the severity and frequency of migraine headaches [35]. This may be because gamma-linolenic acid competes with arachidonic acid for the active site of cyclooxygenase and it appears to reduce the production of inflammatory leukotrines [36]. Various seeds are high in these oils [36].

Reduced brain concentrations of magnesium can result in migraine headaches [12]. Reduced amounts of magnesium in mononuclear blood cells has been found in patients while experiencing migraines or auras associated with their occurrence [12]. It has been speculated that migraines may respond to magnesium because decreases in serum ionized magnesium appear to 1) increase the affinity for serotonin cerebral muscle receptors, 2) potentate cerebral vasoconstriction induced by serotonin, and 3) facilitate tryptophan release from neuronal storage sites [37].

Many others have found that magnesium can reduce the frequency and duration of migraine headaches [38,39]. Magnesium has been found to be helpful for headaches associated with PMS [40]. Interestingly, one study found that one of the leading symptoms in certain hypomagnesemic children was recurring headaches [41].

In a study headed by Dr. Jean Schoenen at the University of Liege it was found that daily, high dose (400mg per day), consumption of riboflavin (vitamin B2) improved average headache scores for migraine sufferers by about two-thirds, which was the same as aspirin [42]. When riboflavin was involved in this study lower dosages were used (1mg-300mg). This investigator believes that riboflavin tends to be indicated for certain people who wake up with headaches. Dr. Schoenen concluded that it took **at least three months** for the riboflavin to have its full effect [42].

The total incidence of possible yeast and parasitic agents suspected (37.7%) was somewhat of a surprise, even though it was known that giardia lamblia (a parasite) and Candida albicans (a yeast) can cause these types of headaches [43,44]. Medical and natural interventions for Candida albicans have been found to reduce the frequency and severity of migraine headaches when patients also had elevated titers of Candida antigen [44]. Candida antigens can stimulate macrophages to produce prostaglandin E, which induce headaches; Candida may affect platelet glycoproteins and may result in platelet aggregation and headaches [44]. Interestingly, caffeine consumption may increase the risk of Candida overgrowth [45].

Migraine headaches can be induced in those who are exposed to cigarette smoke, air pollution, hair sprays, perfumes, and other pollutants [3,46]. This was the case for three of this study's participants.

Although monthly hormonal changes can influence the tendency towards migraines in female migraine sufferers, this is not universal [47]. In our small sample, this pattern seemed to affect less than 1/3 of menstruating participants. Low thyroid function has been speculated to play a role in such cases [9]. Supplemental calcium, vitamin D, and magnesium have sometimes been found to be helpful in menstrual-cycle related migraines [31,40].

Since migraine attacks are often frequent, some traditional health professionals believe that they require management with prophylactic agents to reduce their occurrence [1,4]. While this investigator concurs with this belief in many cases, is it necessary that these agents be synthetic? Although there is no doubt that some medical intervention can be helpful, there is no medical cur[33] (and since migraines increase stress [4]), it appears logical that many migraine sufferers should have at least nutritional benefits from taking supplemental calcium.

Prophylactic use of natural substances such as magnesium [38-40], riboflavin [42], fatty acids [35], glandulars [9], and herbs [7,21,22], has been shown to be effective to reduce the severity of and frequency of migraine headaches (although it takes several months for some of them to work, even when they are appropriate [35,42]. Natural interventions administered by properly trained professionals tend to have fewer negative consequences(pregnancy and other cautions, do apply) than the synthetic counterparts offered by some practitioners.

Food and nutritional problems do contribute to causing migraine headaches [4,7,9,35,38-40,42]. Migraines have negative effects on those that suffer from them [4-6] and on those associated with migraine sufferers (such as loved ones and employers) [4]. This researcher encourages doctors and health researchers to be willing to challenge long-standing misconceptions regarding migraines and to work towards cooperative interventions to help these people improve and lead as normal lives as possible.

References

[1] Goadsby, P.J. *How Do Currently Used Prophylactic Agents Work Inmigraines?* Cephalgia, 1997; 17 (2):85-92.

[2] *The Merck Manual of Diagnosis and Therapy,* 14th ed. Merck & Co: Rahway (NJ), 1982.

[3] Meggs, W.J. *Neurogenic Inflammation and Sensitivity to Environmental Chemicals.* Environmental Health Prospectives 1993; 101 (3):234-238.

[4] Mishkin, B. *Standards of Care for Headache Diagnosis and Treatment.* National Headache Foundation: Chicago, 1996.

[5] Buring, J., et al. *Migraine and Subsequent Risk of Stroke in Physicians' Health Study.* Archives of Neurology 1995; 52:129-134.

[6] Tzourio, C., et al. *Case-Controlled Study of Migraine and Risk of Ischemic Stroke in Young Women.* British Medical Journal 1995; 310:830-833.

[7] Murray, M. and Pzzorno, J. *Migraine.* In Encyclopedia of Natural Medicine. Prima Publishing, Rocklin (CA):410-421, 1991.

[8] Duarte, A. *Health Alternatives.* Mega Systems, Morton Grove (IL), 1995.

[9] Ingram, C. *Who Needs Headaches?* Literary Visions: Hiawatha (IA), 1991.

[10] Thiel, R. *Serious Nutrition for Health Care Professionals.* California Health Group: Arroyo Grande (CA), 1994.

[11] Borok, G. and Guldenpfennig, W.M. *Migraine: Treatment by Personalized Elimination Programme.* Neurological Congress, Abstract, March 1994.

[12] Gallai, V., et al. *Magnesium Content of Mononuclear Blood Cells in Migraine Patients.* Headache 1994; 34:160-165.

[13] Robinson, J., Rall, J.E. and Gordon, P. *The Thyroid and Iodine Metabolism.* In: Duncan's Diseases of Metabolism, 7th ed. WB Saunders, Phil.:1009-1104, 1974.

[14] Luciano, D.S., Vander, A.J. and Sherman, J.H. *Human Anatomy and Physiology.* McGraw-Hill, New York, 1983.

[15] *Many Thyroid Conditions are Underdiagnosed.* Medical Tribune, Jan 25, 1996; 2.

[16] Sawin, C.T. *Subclinical Hypothyroidism in Older Persons.* Clinics in Geriatric Medicine 1995; 11 (2):231-238.

[17] Woeber, K.A. *Subclinical Hypothyroid Disfunction.* Archives of Internal Medicine 1997; 157:1065-1068.

[18] Bakke, J. *Rethinking Thyroid Guidelines.* Cortlandt Forum 1991; 46-20:79.

[19] *Physician's Desk Reference,* 48th ed. Medical Economics, Montvale (NJ), 1994.

[20] Dellovade, T.L., Zhu, Y.S., Krey, L. and Pfaff, D.W. *Thyroid Hormone and Estrogen Interact to Regulate Behavior.* Proceedings of the National Academy of Science 1996; 93:12581-12586.

[21] Scalzo, R. *Naturopathic Handbook of Herbal Formulas.* Kivaki Press, Durango (CO), 1994.

[22] Tenney, L. *Herb Handbook.* Woodland Books, Provo, 1987.

[23] Spiller, G.A. *Metabolism and Physiological Effects of Methylxanthines.* In: Caffeine. CRC Press: New York: 225-231, 1997.

[24] Iancu, I. and Dolberg, O.T. *Is Caffeine Involved in the Pathogenesis of Combat-Stress Reaction?* Military Medicine 1996; 161 (4):230-232.

[25] Smith, B.D. and Tola, K. *Caffeine: Effects on Psychological Functioning and Performance* In: Caffeine. CRC Press: New York: 251-299, 1997.

[26] Lundsberg, L.S. *Caffeine Consumption.* In: Caffeine. CRC Press: New York: 199-224, 1997.

[27] Roberts, H.R., et al. *Caffeine Consumption.* Food and Chemical Toxicology, 1996; 34 (1):119-129.

[28] Shi, X. and Dalal, N.S. *Antioxidant Behavior of Caffeine: Efficient Scavenging of Hydroxyl Radicals.* Food & Chemical Toxicology 1991; 29 (1):1-6.

[29] *Caffeine-Withdrawal Headache in Post-Operative Patients.* Family Practice Recertification, 1992;14(8):47.

[30] James JE. *Caffeine, Health and Commercial Interests: Responding to Golding.* Addiction 1995; 90:985-990.

[31] Thys-Jacob, S. *Vitamin D and Calcium in Menstrual Migraine.* Headache, 1994; 34 (9):544-546.

[32] Hendlor, S. *The Doctors Vitamin and Mineral Encyclopedia.* Simon and Schuster, New York, 1990.

[33] Whitney, E.N, and Nunnelley, E.M. *Understanding Nutrition,* 4th ed. West Publishing, New York, 1987.

[34] Bates, B. *Low-Fat, High-Carbohydrate Diet Averts Migraines.* Family Practice News August 1, 1996:16.

[35] Wagner, W. and Nootbaar-Wagner, U. *Prophylactic Treatment of Migraine with Gamma-Linolenic and Alpha-linolenic Acids.* Cephalgia 1997; 17 (2):127-130.

[36] Bollet, A.J. *Nutrition and Diet in Rheumatic Diseases.* In Modern Nutrition in Health and Disease, 8th ed. 1994, Lea and Febiger, Philadelphia: 1362-1373.

[37] Kahn, J. *Low Ionized Magnesium Linked to Migraine Headaches.* Medical Tribune May 18, 1995:7.

[38] Peikert, A., et al. *Prophylaxis of Migraine with Oral Magnesium: Results from a Prospective, Multi-Center, Placebo-Controlled and Double-Blind Randomized Study.* Cephalgia 1996; 16:257-263.

[39] Mauskop, A.., et al. *Intravenous Magnesium Sulfate Relieves Migraine Attacks in Patients with Low Serum Ionized Magnesium Levels: A Pilot Study.* Clinical Science 1995; 89:633-636.

[40] Boschert, S. *Magnesium Can Curb Premenstrual Migraine.* Family Practice News, March 1, 1996:33.

[41] Schimatschek, H.F. and Classen, H.G. *Epidemiologic Studies on the Frequency of Hypomagnesemia and Hypocalcemic Children with Functional Disorders and Neurasthenia.* Magnesium-Bulletin 1993; 15 (3):85-104.

[42] Schoenen, J., et al. *High-Dose Riboflavin as a Prophylactic Treatment of Migraine: Results of an Open Pilot Study.* Cephalgia 1994; 14:328-329.

[43] Galland, L., et al. *Giardia Lamblia Infection as a Cause of Chronic Fatigue.* Journal of Nutritional Medicine 1990; 1:27-29.

[44] Heuser, G. *Candida Albicans and Migraine Headaches: A Possible Link.* Journal for the Advance of Medicine, 1992; 5 (3):177-187.

[45] *Vaginal Yeast Infections: Patient Guide.* The Female Patient 1991; 16:67-68.

[46] Anthony, M. *Platelet Superoxide Dismutase in Migraine and Tension-Type Headaches.* Cephalgia 1994; 14:181-183.

[47] Lokken, C., Holm, J.E. and Myers, T.C. *The Menstrual Cycle and Migraine: a Time-Series Analysis of 20 Women Migraineurs.* Headache 1997; 37 (4):235-239.

NOTE: Dr. Thiel is not a medical doctor. None of this research is medical advice nor should it be construed as medical advice; none of this information is specific for a particular individual. Although this paper has been reviewed by several doctors, none of these statements have been approved by the USFDA or similar agencies.

Appendix A7

Musculoskeletal Pain Relief for People with Arthritis, Lupus, and Fibromyalgia

Published as Thiel, R.J. Musculoskeletal Pain Relief for People with Arthritis, Lupus, and Fibromyalgia. ANMA Monitor 1 (1): 8-10, 1997 and Thiel, R.J. Musculoskeletal Pain Relief for People with Arthritis, Lupus, and Fibromyalgia. Townsend Letter 172:91-92, 1997.

Abstract: The purpose of this trial was to determine how often nutrition-based interventions could result in musculoskeletal pain relief for people with various forms of arthritis, lupus, and fibromyalgia. Of the 81 participants, all of whom were given nutritional supplementation, 85.2% reported pain reduction within 30 days and 98.8% reported pain reduction within 60 days (P < 0.001). 70.4% reported substantial reduction in pain, while 28.4% reported minimal reduction in pain. Possible food intolerances were found in 77.8% of the participants.

Introduction

Many people have musculoskeletal pain which is frequently caused by inflammation. Some of the most common types are from osteoarthritis, rheumatoid arthritis, gout, non-specific arthritis, lupus, and fibromyalgia [1]. Arthritis can afflict people of either sex or any age, although most with lupus or fibromyalgia are women [1].

This report includes the results of a pre-test–post-test trial involving 81 people who suffered from arthritic pain, lupus, and/or fibromyalgia. The purpose of this trial was to measure how often nutrition-based recommendations could help reduce the pain associated with these conditions and to identify dietary factors that may be involved.

Selection Criteria

Adults were eligible for inclusion in this trial if they resided in California, came to our office, agreed to provide (and did provide) feedback, signed a consent agreement, and indicated that they suffered from musculoskeletal pain of an arthritic nature or who had systemic lupus erythematosis or fibromyalgia.

This report includes everyone of our active clients who met these criteria. 88 people were eligible, but seven either failed to follow the recommendations or provide the required feedback. Of the 81 actual participants, four had systemic lupus erythematosis, twelve had fibromyalgia, and sixty-five had some form of arthritis. The ages of the participants ranged from 20-86; the mean age was 54.2 years. 21 of the participants were male and 60 were female.

Method

After completing the selection documentation, all subjects were interviewed for approximately 45 minutes. All subjects were then assessed using Reflex Nutrition Assessment (RNA). RNA is a non-invasive technique used to assess nutrition status by observing the response of muscles under externally provided human-force (it is similar to other forms of muscle testing [2]). Performing RNA for people with musculoskeletal pain normally consists of performing three assessments. The first assessment is to determine if a reflex directly over the area of pain indicates a nutritional need (by observing a reduction in muscular strength); the second is to determine which nutritional intervention can help fit that need (by observing an increase in muscular strength). The third is to assess for possible food sensitivities—a weakness when exposed to the food is considered an indication of a possible sensitivity. Many have reported success in using it and similar techniques [2-4].

Participants who appeared to have (through the interview process combined with reflex assessment) a sensitivity to one or more foods were advised to discontinue consumption of them. Participants were also advised to consume an average of three tablets (per day) of one or more nutritional supplement for each pain-related reflex concern. Although the supplements varied, substances used included tracheal concentrate (which contained chondroitin-sulfate-A with antioxidants), soluble calcium, glucosamine with synergists, fortified enzymes, fish oils, yucca and other herbs, and black cherry and other herbs. To assist with fatigue, participants with fibromyalgia (and some others) also consumed fortified glandular with l-carnitine, an herbal-adrenal formula, and lyophilized bovine thyroid). Other products were used instead if the reflex checked as better. Subjects were interviewed at approximately 30 day intervals to determine any change in pain levels.

Results

Possible food sensitivities were found in 63 (77.8%) of the participants; 33.3% had multiple sensitivities. Those foods by occurrence were bovine dairy products 42.0%, caffeine products 30.9%, refined carbohydrates (sucrose, white sugar, white rice) 14.8%, wheat 9.9%, oats 8.6%, high purine foods 2.5%, and others 4.8%.

85.2% of participants (69 of 81) reported pain reduction within 30 days. 98.8% (80 of 81) reported pain reduction within 60 days; the P value of this result was < 0.001. 70.4% reported significant or complete pain reduction, while 28.4% reported only minimal reductions in pain. All participants with systemic lupus erythematosis or fibromyalgia reported reductions in pain. The one participant that did not report pain reduction, did report increased energy within 60 days and within 30 additional days did report a reduction in pain. Gender did not appear to play any role in determining pain reduction.

Discussion

Osteoarthritis may be the most preventable form of arthritis. A panel convened by the National Institutes of Health stated that 1/2 of American diets are deficient in calcium [5]. My experience is that people who do not consume dairy products or who are unknowingly sensitive (or allergic) to bovine dairy products are the most likely to develop osteoarthritis. Non-bovine dairy sources of calcium include goats' milk, bok choy cabbage, turnip greens, spinach, sardines, and broccoli [6]. I am cautious about calcium supplementation since not all forms of calcium are absorbed well.

People with osteoarthritis appear to benefit greatly from nutritional approaches due to the physiology of the joints. The bony surfaces are covered by a thin layer of articular cartridge which is actually two layers of cartilage that slide past each other during motion [7]. In osteoarthritis this cartilage deteriorates. Polysulfated glycosaminoglycan has been reported to induce articular cartilage matrix synthesis and to decrease matrix degeneration [8].

Polysulfated glycosaminoglycan is a mixture of highly sulfated glycosaminoglycans, a major source being chondroitin sulfate extracted from bovine tracheal cartilage [8]. Since there is an increased turnover rate of articular cartilage matrix (joint tissues) in osteoarthritic joints [8], it appears logical that ingesting nutrients that the joints need would be helpful for people with this problem. Chondroitin sulfate compounds have been used in Europe for decades to decrease matrix degeneration in the joints of persons with osteoarthritis [8]. In a recent study involving 700 subjects with osteoporosis, 85% reported having good (26%) to excellent (59%) results in pain reduction [9]. Bovine tracheal cartilage has also been reported to reduce the need for anti-inflammatory medications for some people with arthritis [10].

Technically, rheumatoid arthritis is believed to be a T cell mediated reaction against an unknown antigen which causes joint inflammation [1]. Reducing arachidonic acid (such as going off of dairy) and increasing consumption of omega-3 fatty acids (as is found in fish or flax oils) has been reported to help people with rheumatoid arthritis [11]. This trial did not confirm the notion that people with rheumatoid arthritis uniformly benefit from avoiding plants in the nightshade family such as potatoes, tomatoes, eggplant, and red pepper (although some few will). It appears that many dietary factors are specific to the individual.

People with gouty arthritis have a problem which is almost always helped by natural methods. People with gout need to avoid foods high in purines. These purines cause painful uric acid crystals to form, many of which settle in the lower extremities [1]. Commonly consumed high purine foods appear to be whole wheat, organ meats, fowl, and shellfish.

In my opinion, non-specific arthritis is similar to rheumatoid arthritis in that avoiding certain foods can be helpful. My experience also suggests that the liver is involved in people with non-specific arthritis. It has been speculated that people with rheumatoid or non-specific arthritis sometimes have their problems worsened by free radical activity and can benefit from antioxidants [11]. Free radicals can damage joint tissues [12]. Free radical reactions continue to damage cell constituents until they are neutralized. They can be neutralized by antioxidant nutrients [13]. Proanthocyanidins are powerful antioxidants extracted from grape seeds, soybeans or pine bark; Passwater claims their ability to bond to collagen promotes renewed youthfulness, flexibility, and body integrity [14]. For best results, I personally like products which combine antioxidants (including proathocyanidins) and chondroitin sulfate.

Systemic lupus erythamatosis (SLE) is an autoimmune disorder with similarities to rheumatoid arthritis, though it has many additional symptoms [1]. Approximately 90% of people with SLE complain of intermittent arthralgias, polyarthritis, and similar articular problems [1]. Fibromyalgia is another autoimmune disorder. It is similar to rheumatoid arthritis combined with chronic fatigue [15]. I have found that most people with fibromyalgia or SLE are bothered by bovine dairy products. Nutrition-based interventions can be quite effective for people with either of these conditions. Thus far, I have helped every person who has come to my office with fibromyalgia who has followed my recommendations as well as most with SLE.

Be cautious about how you discuss pain and nutritional supplementation as the FDA has not yet accepted much of the scientific research as a basis of making claims (even though true). Having said that, it is my strong opinion (based on years of successful clinical experience) that people with musculoskeletal pain can be helped from nutrition-based interventions.

References

[1] Berkow, R. *The Merck Manual of Diagnosis and Treatment,* 14th ed. Merck & Co. Rahway (NJ), 1982.

[2] Thiel, R.J. *Serious Nutrition for Health Professionals.* Arroyo Grande (CA): California Health Group, 1995.

[3] Burr-Madsen, A. *Body Polarity Reflex Analysis and the Nutritional Connection.* Carson City: Thoth, Inc., 1992.

[4] Rosen, M.S. and Williams, L. *The Research Status of Applied Kinesiology, Part II: An Annotated Bibliography of Applied Kinesiological Research.* A.K. Review, 1991; 1 (2):34-47.

[5] *Many American Diets Deficient in Calcium:* NIH Committee. Nutr Week, 1994; 22: 7.

[6] Whitney, E.N. and Nunnelley, E.M. *Understanding Nutrition.* 4th ed. West Publishing, New York, 1987.

[7] Luciano, D., et al. *Articulations.* In: Human Anatomy and Physiology, 2nd ed. McGraw-Hill: New York: 170-182, 1978.

[8] Todhunter, R.J. and Lust, G. *Polysulfated Glycosaminoglycan in the Treatment of Osteoarthritis.* J Am Veterinary Med Assoc, 1994; 204 (8): 1245-1250.

[9] Kriegel, H. *Bovine Tracheal Cartilage.* Health Supplement Retailer, 1995; 1 (3):34-37.

[10] Nicolini, E. *Studies in Cartilage.* Presentation at the 12th Annual Convention of the American Naturopathic Medical Association, Las Vegas, September 8, 1995.

[11] Darlington, L.G. and Ramsey, S.W. *Clinical Reveiw of Dietary Therapy for Rheumatoid Arthritis.* Brit J Rheumatology, 1993; 32:507-514.

[12] Emerit, I. *Free Radicals and Ageing of the Skin.* Free Radicals and Ageing, 1992:328-340.

[13] Burger, S. *Vitamins and Minerals for Health.* Wild Rose College of Natural Healing, Calgary, Circa 1988.

[14] Passwater, R.A. *The New Superoxidant-Plus.* Keats Publishing: New Canaan (Conn.), 1992.

[15] Clauw, D.J. *The Pathogenesis of Chronic Pain and Fatigue Syndromes with Special Reference to Fibromyalgia.* Med Hypotheses, 1995; 44 (5):369-378.

NOTE: Dr. Thiel is not a medical doctor. None of this research is medical advice nor should it be construed as medical advice; none of this information is specific for a particular individual.

Index

A

B

R

S